"As we started with the development of the e-Platform at the Winterthur, we knew that there were still many questions to be answered. Today, we can look back at a process, which has created the corresponding architectural guidelines, pro̶ infrastructure components. In the meantime, we are reaping the ̶ strategy and are transferring, step by step, our traditi̶ loosely coupled SOA. This forms, as well, the basis of Business Process Management. This book clearly we painstakingly developed at that time and answers that are encountered on the way to an adaptable appli̶ enterprises. From my point of view, this is a book that who are considering remodeling their application lands

—*Daniele Lisetto, Head Technical and Application Platforms,*
Winterthur Group

"*Enterprise SOA* provides strategies that help large enterprises to increase the agility of their IT systems—one of the most pressing issues of contemporary IT. Covering both a business and architectural view, these strategies aim to promote the implementation of an IT infrastructure that can serve as a base for the development of truly flexible business processes. This book covers its subject with great profoundness based on real-world evidence. It is in the interest of everybody involved with software architecture—particularly for anybody who intends to establish a Service-Oriented Architecture—to read this book."

—*Dr. Helge Heß, Director Business Process Management, IDS Scheer AG*

"The SOA principles described in this book are the foundation on which enterprises can build an IT architecture that will satisfy today's most important IT requirements—agility and flexibility—at affordable costs."

—*Martin Frick, Head of IT, Winterthur Group*

"By delivering SAP's next-generation applications based on a Service-Oriented Architecture, SAP is at the forefront of making Web services work for the enterprise. The Enterprise Services Architecture enables unprecedented flexibility in business process deployment, allowing companies to execute and innovate end-to-end processes across departments and companies, with minimum disruption to other systems and existing IT investments. This strategy comes to life with SAP NetWeaver, which is the technological foundation of the Enterprise Services Architecture. It provides easy integration of people, information, and systems in heterogeneous IT environments and provides a future proof application platform. *Enterprise SOA* provides readers with the architectural blueprints and SOA-driven project management strategies that are required to successfully adopt SOA on an enterprise level."

—*Dr. Peter Graf, SVP Product Marketing, SAP*

The SOA principles outlined in this book enable enterprises to leverage robust and proven middleware platforms, including CORBA, to build flexible and business-oriented service architectures. The authors also clearly describe the right strategies for using Model Driven Architecture (MDA) to manage SOA Service Repositories in a platform-independent way, enabling enterprises to better address the problem of heterogeneity at many levels. The Object Management Group was created just to address this central problem of integration in the face of constantly changing heterogeneity and platform churn, so I strongly recommend this book for the bookshelf of every enterprise architect and developer.

—*Richard Mark Soley, Ph.D. Chairman and Chief Executive Officer,*
Object Management Group, Inc.

The Coad Series

Peter Coad, *Series Editor*

- David J. Anderson
  Agile Management for Software Engineering:
  Applying the Theory of Constraints for Business Results

- David Astels
  Test Driven Development: A Practical Guide

- David Astels, Granville Miller, Miroslav Novak
  A Practical Guide to eXtreme Programming

- Andy Carmichael, Dan Haywood
  Better Software Faster

- Donald Kranz, Ronald J. Norman
  A Practical Guide to Agile Unified Process

- James McGovern, Scott W. Ambler, Michael E. Stevens,
  James Linn, Vikas Sharan, Elias Jo
  A Practical Guide to Enterprise Architecture

- Jill Nicola, Mark Mayfield, Michael Abney
  Streamlined Object Modeling: Patterns, Rules, and Implementation

- Stephen R. Palmer, John M. Felsing
  A Practical Guide to Feature-Driven Development

Enterprise SOA

Service-Oriented Architecture
Best Practices

Dirk Krafzig
Karl Banke
Dirk Slama

PRENTICE
HALL
PTR

Prentice Hall Professional Technical Reference
Upper Saddle River, New Jersey 07458
www.phptr.com
Indianapolis, IN 46240

Publisher: *John Wait*
Editor in Chief: *Don O'Hagan*
Executive Editor: *Paul Petralia*
Editorial Assistant: *Michelle Vincenti*
Marketing Manager: *Chris Guzikowski*
Cover Designer: *Jerry Votta*
Managing Editor: *Gina Kanouse*
Project Editor: *Christy Hackerd*
Copy Editor: *Benjamin Lawson*
Indexer: *Lisa Stumpf*
Compositor: *Mary Sudul*
Manufacturing Buyer: *Dan Uhrig*

The publisher offers excellent discounts on this book when ordered in quantity for bulk purchases or special sales, which may include electronic versions and/or custom covers and content particular to your business, training goals, marketing focus, and branding interests. For more information, please contact:

U. S. Corporate and Government Sales
(800) 382-3419
corpsales@pearsontechgroup.com

For sales outside the U. S., please contact:

International Sales
international@pearsoned.com

Visit us on the Web: www.phptr.com

Library of Congress Cataloging-in-Publication Data:

200411032

ISBN 0-13-146575-9

Text printed in the United States on recycled paper at *Phoenix BookTech in Hagerstown, Maryland*
First printing, *November, 2004*

Contents

Acknowledgments

Many people have contributed to this book in many ways, both directly and indirectly over a period of two years. It is therefore impossible to list everybody who influenced, supported, or aided us on our journey from the initial idea to the final manuscript. Nevertheless, we owe our gratitude to at least the following people:

We would like to thank our publisher, Pearson Education, for the support that led to this book being completed. In particular, we would like to thank Paul Petralia, our editor, and Christy Hackerd.

The case studies in this book would not have been possible without extensive cooperation with SOA protagonists from different organizations. We would like to thank Uwe Bath (Deutsche Post), Fiorenzo Maletta (Winterthur), Claus Hagen (Credit Suisse), and Willie Nisbet and Allan Kelly (Halifax Bank of Scotland).

This book would also not have been possible without countless discussions and critical feedback of colleagues, friends, and reviewers. We extend our gratitude to Beat Aeschlimann, Arne Allee, Michael Aschenbrenner, Arnaud Blandin, Ndome Cacutalua, Frank Eversz, Dietmar Grubert, Stefan Havenstein, Georgia and Paul Hickey, Stefan Krahm, James McGovern, Dirk Marwinski, Manfred Mayer, Steve Morris, Ingrid Müller, Joanis Papanagnu, Arnold Pott, Kai Rannenberg, Kirsten Scharf, Uli Steck, Paul Stemmet, Michael Stevens, Harald Störrle, Peter Stracke, Josef Wagenhuber, and Frank Werres.

Sebastian-Svante Wellershoff contributed to the design of our artwork. Birgit Anders supported the author-team by proofreading, formatting, drawing figures, and many other activities that were necessary to produce a manuscript for this book. We all appreciated the accurate and swift manner in which she worked. Mark Roantree was our proofreader for linguistic and some of the technical aspects of this book.

Roland Tritsch and Joachim Quantz have both closely worked with the author team and developed many of the ideas that were presented in this book. They were like a virtual extension of the author team.

Last but not least, we owe our special gratitude to our partners, families, and friends for their patience, time, support, and encouragement. We know that we cannot make it up to you.

About the Authors

Dirk Krafzig

Dirk has been dealing with the challenges of enterprise IT and distributed software architectures throughout his entire working life. He devoted himself to SOA in 2001 when he joined Shinka Technologies, a start-up company and platform vendor in the early days of XML-based Web services. Since then, Dirk has acquired a rich set of real world experience with this upcoming new paradigm both from the view point of a platform vendor and from the perspective of software projects in different industry verticals.

Writing this book was an issue of personal concern to him as it provided the opportunity to share his experiences and many insights into the nature of enterprise IT with his readers.

Today, Dirk is designing enterprise applications and managing projects, applying the guiding principles outlined in this book. Dirk has a Ph.D. in Natural Science and an MSc in Computer Science. He lives in Düsseldorf, Germany, and is 39 years old, married, and the father of two children.

Karl Banke

Software architecture has been with Karl since he programmed his first TRON-like game on the then state-of-the art ZX81 in the early 1980s. After graduating as a Master of Physics, he gained his commercial experience in various consulting assignments, mostly in the financial and telecommunications sector.

He moved through stages of consultant, technical lead, software architect, and project manager using a variety of object-oriented technologies, programming languages, and distributed computing environments. Soon realizing that he was too constrained as an employee in doing what he thought necessary in software development, he co-founded the company iternum in 2000, where he currently acts as a principal consultant and general manager.

Karl permanently lives in Mainz, Germany when not temporarily relocated by a current project.

Dirk Slama

Having spent the last ten years at the forefront of distributed computing technology, Dirk has developed an in-depth understanding of enterprise software architectures and their application in a variety of industry verticals. Dirk was a senior consultant with IONA Technologies, working with Fortune 500 customers in Europe, America, and Asia on large-scale software integration projects. After this, Dirk set up his own company, Shinka Technologies, which successfully developed one of the first XML-based Web services middleware products, starting as early as 1999.

Dirk holds an MSc in computer sciences from TU-Berlin and an MBA from IMD in Lausanne. He is a co-author of *Enterprise CORBA* (Prentice Hall, 1999), the leading book on CORBA-based system architectures. Dirk is currently working as a solution architect for Computer Sciences Corporation in Zurich, Switzerland.

Contact: authors@enterprise-soa.com

Foreword

At the turn of the nineteenth century, a wave of new technologies such as the steam engine, electricity, the loom, the railway, and the telephone emerged. Urbanization and the mass production of goods in large factories fundamentally changed how mankind lived and worked together.

One hundred years later, the industrial revolution had not slowed down: At the turn of the twentieth century, automation, specialization, and a never-ending spiral of efficiency improvement have resulted in modern economies with unheard-of industrial productivity.

After a phase of consolidation during the transition from the twentieth to the twenty-first century, globalization and virtualization have now become the key drivers of our economic lives. Without a doubt, they will yet again change how we live and work together.

If we take a closer look at the past 20 years, we can observe that established business rules have been constantly redefined. New business models emerged; small companies quickly grew into billion-dollar multinationals, aggressively attacking other established companies. A wave of mergers, acquisitions, and buy-outs changed the overall industrial landscape.

IT has played a major role in all of this, be it through controlling production processes and supply chains or by creating real-time links between financial markets, thus virtually eliminating arbitrage opportunities by closing the time gaps of trading around the globe. The Internet boom and the "virtual enterprise" are cornerstones of this ongoing development. Entirely new products and services have been created, which would have been unthinkable without the support of modern IT.

Without a doubt, today's modern enterprises are completely dependent on their IT. Consequently, today's IT is driven by the same dynamics as the enterprise itself. Today, we expect an extremely high level of flexibility and agility from our enterprise IT. During the post Internet-boom years, cost efficiency quickly became another key requirement, if not the most important one.

Enterprise IT has changed as a result of the constantly increasing pressure. In the early days of enterprise computing, IT was merely responsible for providing storage and processing capacity, with more and more business logic being added throughout the decades. During the different boom phases in the 1980s and 1990s, a plethora of new applications emerged, often side by side with the information silos that had been developed in the previous 20 years.

Today, the increasing cost pressure is forcing us to efficiently reuse existing systems while also developing new functionality and constantly adapting to changing business requirements. The term "legacy system" is now often replaced with "heritage system" in order to emphasize the value that lies in the existing systems.

The increases in reuse and harmonization requirements have been fueled by the urgency of integrating the historically grown IT landscapes in order to improve IT efficiency and agility. As a result, we could observe at a technical level the emergence of middleware tools and Enterprise Application Integration (EAI) platforms in what can be seen as a post-RDBMS phase.

While a lot of trial-and-error projects were executed in the 1990s, with more or less high levels of success, the development of EAI and middleware concepts has now been culminated in the principles of Service-Oriented Architecture (SOA), which can be seen as an important evolutionary point in the development of integration technologies.

What is important about SOA is that it has taken away the focus from fine-grained, technology-oriented entities such as database rows or Java objects, focusing instead on business-centric services with business-level transaction granularity. Furthermore, SOA is not an enterprise technology standard, meaning it is not dependent on a single technical protocol such as IIOP or SOAP. Instead, it represents an architectural blueprint, which can incorporate many different technologies and does not require specific protocols or bridging technologies. The focus is on defining cleanly cut service contracts with a clear business orientation.

At the Winterthur, as in any other large company, we have been facing all of the preceding issues of historically grown systems and information silos. We had to find a solution to increase our IT efficiency and agility. The Winterthur, with approximately 20,000 employees worldwide and over 130 billion Swiss franks of assets being managed (as of December 31, 2003), is a leading Swiss insurance company. As is the case with any well-organized company, we rely on our IT infrastructure to manage assets, products, processes, customers, partners, employees, and any other aspect of business life.

Our core business systems are based on highly reliable mainframe computers that we invested in over the past decades. However, like most other enterprises relying on mainframes for their back-end systems, we saw the increasing need over the years to open up these back-end systems. The main reason for this was to enable reuse of the core business logic and data on these systems for new Internet and intranet front-end systems on nonmainframe platforms such as UNIX and Windows.

To facilitate this development, we built up an application and integration platform, which laid the technical basis for Winterthur's SOA. While the initial development started off at our core Swiss market unit, the platform is nowadays reused abroad, because of its success and the prevailing analogous technical requirements of other market units. Thus, we create the basis to realize synergies and enhance our international initiatives.

Building on our technical platform, combined with our in-house experience in the area of SOA and with the experience that our holding company Credit Suisse Group has gathered in similar re-architectural efforts, we have been extremely successful. The Winterthur SOA has achieved the goal of opening up our back-end systems in new application development areas on other platforms. A solid SOA-based architectural approach is at the heart of our IT strategy.

This book is important because it provides enterprise architects with a roadmap for the successful establishment of SOA at the enterprise level. While a lot of the underlying principles of the original Winterthur SOA have had to be derived from past experience and intuition due to lack of SOA literature at the time, this book provides a concrete guide, blueprints, and best practices for SOA architects. In addition to the Winterthur case study in chapter 15, you will find many more concrete examples of how large corporations have started to adopt the principles of SOA in their IT architectures.

It is also very important that this book not only focuses on the technical aspects of SOA, but also places strong emphasis on the delicate issues of establishing SOA at the enterprise level, truly deserving the title *Enterprise SOA*.

The SOA principles described in this book are the foundation on which enterprises can build an IT architecture that will satisfy today's most important IT requirements—agility and flexibility—at affordable costs.

Martin Frick, Head of IT at the Winterthur Group

Reader's Guide

The reader's guide provides an indication as to who should read this book and the benefits to be gained. A summary of each chapter provides an overview of the step-by-step approach required for the successful introduction of Service-Oriented Architectures (SOA).

Who Should Read This Book

This book is aimed at the various stakeholders of enterprise software architectures, including software architects and evangelists, designers, analysts, developers, members of IT strategy departments, project managers, representatives of product vendors, and those interested in software architecture and its relation to structures and processes within large-scale organizations. Furthermore, this book is an excellent introduction to the real world of commercial computing for students in a variety of disciplines.

If you are a **software architect,** this book provides you with hands-on guidelines for the design of SOAs. You will find the definition of an SOA together with its key terms as we distinguish the SOA from approaches such as component architectures and software buses. Furthermore, this book provides concrete guidance for the most important design decisions one will encounter in practice. These guidelines comprise identifying services, assigning the appropriate service type and allocating the ownership of data to services. You will also discover how to utilize expansion stages in order to enable stepwise SOA introduction. This book also provides valuable advice on the design of a functional infrastructure for business processes and on how to achieve process integrity, approach heterogeneity, and initiate the technical infrastructure. We discuss these guidelines with respect to different application types, including Web applications, fat clients, mobile applications, EAI, and multi-channel applications. For the purpose of software architects, Chapters 4 to 10 are most valuable. In addition, Chapter 13, which covers SOA project management, will be helpful in ensuring an efficient collaboration within an SOA project. Finally, the case studies in Part III give you practical examples of how architects in other organizations introduced an SOA.

Do you see yourself in the role of an SOA **evangelist**? If you intend to implement an SOA within your own organization, you must successfully promote your ideas. Most importantly, you must be able to communicate the benefits of the SOA to all stakeholders of the application landscape within your organization. Chapter 11 will be of special interest to you because it presents the key benefits of SOA for the organization and each individual stakeholder. In addition, Chapter 12 provides an in-depth description of the steps required to set up an SOA, with considerable practice-oriented advice as to the introduction of appropriate processes and boards. After reading this book, you should have a deeper understanding of SOAs, enabling you to effectively argue the benefits to different stakeholders and to establish the necessary processes and boards to make your SOA endeavor a success!

If you are a **software designer**, **analyst,** or **developer** working in an SOA project, although you are likely to work in a specific part of your application landscape, this book will help you obtain a better understanding of the entire process. Furthermore, there are key challenges you typically encounter in most SOA projects such as reuse or process integrity that directly impact your work. This book—in particular Chapters 7 to 10—helps to address these challenges in a coordinated manner within your SOA project.

If you work in the **IT strategy** department of an large organization, you should read this book in order to find out how SOAs can add to your IT strategy. Your work is likely to be driven by the demand for agility and cost effectiveness. Many enterprises have experienced projects that failed to deliver the required functionality and therefore lost business opportunities. Furthermore, many application landscapes suffer from high maintenance costs for their inherited assets and the integration of new applications. In Part II (Chapters 11–13) you will read about the various possibilities for overcoming these issues with an SOA. Finally, several strategies for introducing the SOA within the organization are presented. Part III (Chapters 14 to 17) contains several case studies with real-world evidence that validates the SOA approach. Those success stories provide "living proof" of SOA success and offer an impression of the different ways an SOA can be established.

If you are an experienced **project manager**, you should read this book in order to understand the specific benefits of SOAs for project management. The SOA approach implies a major simplification of the overall software development process, and this book makes these benefits accessible. However, SOAs will challenge you, and as a result, this book presents solutions to the most important problems one encounters in an SOA project, both from the technical and project management viewpoints. You will find Chapter 13, which focuses on project management, and Chapters 11 and 12, which depict the political environment, to be most beneficial. It should be noted that this book does not introduce a new software development methodology. You will require a sound knowledge of your organization's favorite methodology, accompanied with endurance, social competence, political cleverness, and management skills. This book will complement these skills so that they can be successfully applied in an SOA project.

For a **vendor of standard software packages**, this book presents valuable guidance for product management and sales. SOAs will soon gain tremendous importance in the enterprise software market. As a **salesperson** or a **product manager,** you need to understand the requirements of your enterprise customers in order to be able to offer solutions that fit your customer's needs. In particular, Chapter 11 will be very beneficial because it depicts the benefits of service-oriented software from the viewpoint of the various stakeholders. Being able to offer service-oriented software implies a significant competitive advantage. The inherent strength of SOAs will become the strength of your product. Thus, the SOA's value proposition enables you to sell sophisticated vertical solutions, generating product revenues for your company without the burden of high integration costs that inhibit the sales process.

A Roadmap for This Book

The successful adoption of an Enterprise SOA is based on three fundamental factors: architecture, organization, and lessons drawn from real-world experience. The IT architecture is the technical enabler for an SOA. A successful SOA adoption accelerates an enterprise by reducing the gap between strategy and process changes on one hand and supporting IT systems on the other. The IT architecture and the business organization are mutually dependent, although they both drive each other. Finally, real-world experience, in particular previous long-term IT infrastructure initiatives (both successful and unsuccessful) influence and validate many of the core concepts of SOA. Not surprisingly, this book is structured around these three factors. After we introduce the subject area in Chapters 1 to 3, Part I, Chapters 4 to 10, focuses on the **architecture**. Part II, Chapters 11 to 13, discusses the challenges of introducing an SOA at the level of the **organization,** depicting its benefits, processes, and project management. Part III, Chapters 14 to 17, provides **real-life examples** of successful SOA introductions.

    Chapter 1, "An Enterprise IT Renovation Roadmap," identifies the need for agility and cost savings as the main drivers for the introduction of SOAs.

    Chapter 2, "The Evolution of the Service Concept," describes how commercial information technology has moved toward the service concept over the last 40 years. Today's SOA is the preliminary endpoint of many years of painful "testing." Knowing and understanding previous pitfalls and mistakes help to avoid them in new projects.

    Chapter 3, "Inventory of Distributed Computing Concepts," introduces the fundamental concepts of distributed computing that are required for subsequent discussions in Part I (Chapters 4–10). Particular topics will be communication infrastructures, synchronous versus asynchronous communication, payload semantics, granularity, and loose versus tight coupling.

PART I: ARCHITECTURAL ROADMAP

Chapter 4, "Service-Oriented Architectures," describes the particular requirements of large organizations for building an architecture and defines the term "Service-Oriented Architecture" as it is used throughout this book.

Chapter 5, "Services as Building Blocks," is a direct continuation of Chapter 4. It introduces different service types—namely basic, intermediary, process-centric, and external services—and gives an in-depth discussion of their key characteristics.

Chapter 6, "The Architectural Roadmap," completes the discussion started in Chapter 5. Using the concept of building blocks, the high-level structure of SOAs is depicted. Chapter 6 introduces two key concepts: SOA layers and expansion stages. SOA layers aim to organize the aforementioned services at the enterprise level. Expansion stages are well-defined levels of maturity of an SOA that enable a stepwise implementation. In this book, three expansion stages are distinguished: fundamental SOA, networked SOA, and process-enabled SOA.

Chapter 7, "SOA and Business Process Management," shows how SOAs and BPM can complement each other in practice. This chapter draws a demarcation line between the responsibilities of a BPM infrastructure and the functional infrastructure provided by the SOA.

Chapter 8, "Process Integrity," delves into the challenges of distributed architectures with respect to consistency and how SOAs approach this major issue. This chapter provides numerous helpful, hands-on guidelines tackling real-world constraints such as heterogeneity, changing requirements, or budget.

Chapter 9, "Infrastructure of a Service Bus." By this point, the reader will know a lot about service types, the handling of business processes, and SOA layers. This chapter will address the issue of the type of runtime infrastructure that is required in order to put an SOA in place—an infrastructure that is commonly known as the "service bus." Chapter 9 highlights the fact that the service bus is often heterogeneous and provides technical services such as data transport, logging, and security.

Chapter 10, "SOA in Action," discusses how SOAs apply to specific application types such as Web applications, EAI, fat clients, mobile devices, and multi-channel applications.

PART II: ORGANIZATIONAL ROADMAP

Chapter 11, "Motivation and Benefits," provides a number of important reasons as to why an organization should implement an SOA. It depicts the benefits for the organization as well as for the individual stakeholders.

Chapter 12, "The Organizational SOA Roadmap," names four pillars for the success of an SOA introduction at the enterprise level—namely, budget, initial project, team, and buddies. This chapter deals with challenges such as conflicts of interests of different stakeholders or financing the overheads of the SOA infrastructure and gives practical advice on how to overcome these obstacles.

Chapter 13, "Project Management," provides best practices of SOA project management. Most importantly, this chapter depicts how service contracts can drive the entire development effort. It shows how different tasks can be decoupled and synchronized at the same time and how complexity and risk can be reduced. Furthermore, this chapter describes testing, configuration management, and risk assessment.

PART III: REAL-WORLD EXPERIENCE

Chapter 15, "Case Study: Deutsche Post AG." The Deutsche Post World Net is a multinational group comprising three main brands and more than 275,000 employees. The SOA was set up for the Mail Corporate division at Deutsche Post, a partner to three million business customers, providing services to 39 million households through 81,000 delivery staff, 13,000 retail outlets, 3,500 delivery bases, and 140,000 letterboxes. The SOA at Deutsche Post AG covers a mainly Java-based environment. This fact indicates that a SOA can also be beneficial in homogeneous environments.

Chapter 15, "Case Study: Winterthur." Winterthur Group, a leading Swiss insurance company, has approximately 23,000 employees worldwide achieving a premium volume of 33.5 billion Swiss Francs in 2003. In 1998, Winterthur's Market Unit Switzerland developed a concept for an Application Service Platform. Since then, this integration platform, called "e-Platform," has been implemented and used as the technological basis for the realization of an SOA. Today, the SOA includes most of the mission-critical business applications. Its technical focus is on mainframe-based CORBA services. Well-organized processes and a service repository have been recognized as key success factors at Winterthur.

Chapter 16, "Case Study: Credit Suisse." Credit Suisse Group is a leading global financial services company operating in more than 50 countries with about 60,000 staff. Credit Suisse reported assets under management of 1,199 billion Swiss Francs in December 2003. The SOA was initially implemented in order to create multi-channel banking applications and online trading portals. In addition, the SOA was utilized to consolidate the core business application portfolio. Credit Suisse has implemented three different service buses in order to approach the different requirements of synchronous communication, asynchronous communication, and bulk data transfer.

Chapter 17, "Case Study: Intelligent Finance." Halifax Bank of Scotland (HBoS) is a UK Financial Services provider with divisions in Retail Banking, Insurance & Investment, Business Banking, Corporate Banking, and Treasury. HBoS is the UK's largest mortgage and savings provider with a customer base of about 22 million. Intelligent Finance was launched as a division of Halifax plc with the aim of attracting new customers from outside Halifax and specifically to target the UK clearing banks. Intelligent Finance was launched as Project Green-field in 2000, starting an entire new banking operation from scratch, based on an SOA. Three years later, by the end of 2003, Intelligent Finance had 820,000 customer accounts, representing assets of £15.5 billion. The Intelligent Finance system was probably one of the largest and most advanced early SOA deployments in the financial services industry in Europe.

1

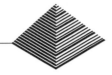

An Enterprise IT Renovation Roadmap

This book makes a big promise: It is offering an *IT renovation roadmap*, which will leverage the concepts of Service-Oriented Architectures (SOA) on both the technical and organizational levels in order to create sustainable improvements in IT efficiency and agility. The aim of this roadmap is to strike a good balance between immediate gains on one hand and long-lasting improvements to the enterprise IT landscape on the other. An SOA should increase the capability of an enterprise to address new business requirements on the short term by reusing existing business logic and data models, thus incurring only minimal cost, resource, and time overheads, while minimizing risks, especially when compared to rewriting entire application systems. In addition, an SOA should provide endurable benefits in terms of agility because it provides a long-term strategy for the increase of the flexibility of an IT infrastructure.

This chapter closely looks at the problems faced by enterprise software today, the resulting requirements for an enterprise IT architecture such as an SOA, and how such an architecture can be established on the organizational level.

1.1 Agony Versus Agility

In 2003, Nicolas G. Carr published the heatedly debated article "*IT doesn't matter*" in the *Harvard Business Review*, claiming that "*... like electrical grids or railroads, IT would become a ubiquitous commodity.*" Regardless of your position on this issue—whether or not you consider enterprise IT a commodity—enterprises heavily depend on the IT backbone, which is responsible for running almost all processes of modern enterprises, be they related to manufacturing, distribution, sales, customer management, accounting, or any other type of business process. Because of today's highly competitive global economy, these business processes underlie constant change: Enterprises must constantly sense changes in

1

market conditions and swiftly adapt their strategies to reflect these changes. Therefore, it is a key requirement for modern enterprise IT that changes in company strategy be reflected quickly and efficiently in the company's IT systems, which are the backbone for executing the strategy.

This is exactly where the enterprise software dilemma starts: Today's enterprise software development almost always suffers from *lack of agility* and from *inefficiency*. This means that enterprises are not able to match business requirements onto underlying IT infrastructure fast enough, effectively limiting the capability of the enterprise to react appropriately to market demands. In addition, the inefficiency of enterprise software development means that the development that is actually done costs too much when compared to the actual output.

If we look at a typical enterprise software system, we can normally observe an initial phase of high productivity and agility, as shown in Figure 1-1. During this Green field phase, the system is built with much new functionality, and initial change requests can be implemented relatively quickly and efficiently. However, after the initial system implementation has been put in place and the first couple of change requests have been executed, the ability to make more changes to the system deteriorates dramatically, and maintenance over time becomes harder and harder.

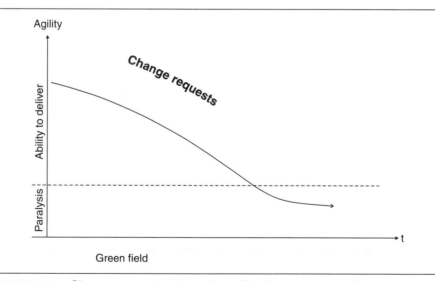

FIGURE 1-1   Change requests reduce the agility of a system over time.

This stagnation phase, which almost any enterprise software system experiences over time, cannot be explained by a single reason—a number of factors contribute to this phenomenon. Some of these reasons are related to software technology, such as the difficulty of making structural changes to an existing code base. However, most of the reasons are not of a technical nature but rather are related to reasons on the organizational level. For example, after the initial launch phase of a system, the project management and key domain experts are likely to move on to the next project, often leaving the maintenance of the system to less skilled maintenance workers, many times even without doing a proper hand-over. In addition, after the initial phase of euphoria about the new system, it might lose its internal lobby over time and thus the necessary political support within the organization. Tight project budgets often mean that fixes and changes cannot be done properly and are only done on an ad-hoc basis, without taking the existing order of the system into consideration. Typically, there is no time and budget for doing a proper refactoring of the system to ensure its long-term maintainability. Finally, critical structural decisions are often made on the side, without executing proper control—for example, an engineer might quickly write a small batch program to synchronize data between two systems, and 10 years later, a small army of developers is needed to deal with the consequences of this ad-hoc decision.

When looking at enterprise software, we are usually not looking at isolated systems, but at large numbers of systems with complex cross-dependencies that have grown over many years and with a high level of heterogeneity and redundancies. We rarely have sufficient in-house knowledge about the different systems, and we often need to cope with very different design and programming styles. Finally, people are getting used to this situation and are starting to think in terms of workarounds, not in terms of the "right" structures.

Some organizations might have found better ways of coping with these problems than others, but it's hard to find any organization today that can claim that it has completely sorted out these issues. For this reason, many organizations require an *enterprise IT renovation roadmap* to help providing a sustainable transformation into a more agile IT organization that is able to quickly and efficiently adapt to changing business requirements. This chapter lays out the cornerstones of this roadmap as it is presented in this book.

1.2 Enterprise Software Is a Different Animal

In order to better understand the problems of enterprise software, we need to look at the specific characteristics of it, which are different from those of other types of software, such as system software, desktop applications, embedded systems, scientific software, or video games.

As the name indicates, *enterprise software is tightly coupled with the internal organization, processes, and business model of the enterprise*. Enterprise software underlies both cross-departmental dependencies and external business relationships. Consequently, an architecture for enterprise software must deal with large numbers of different requirements. Many of these requirements are conflicting, while others are unclear. In almost every case, the requirements are a moving target due to the permanent change of markets, the organization of the enterprise, and its business objectives. It is this involvement in all aspects of the enterprise and the business that makes enterprise software highly complex.

Enterprise applications rarely contain a large amount of complicated algorithms. The code that describes a piece of business logic is usually very simple. The structure of a COBOL-based billing system is much simpler than, for example, an embedded system for a Mars robot with complex real-time and multithreading requirements. One also encounters comparatively simple data structures in enterprise applications which again are different from other systems such as geographic information systems (GIS).

Let's consider an example in order to illustrate the difference between enterprise applications and other software: An enterprise application such as a Customer Relationship Management System (CRM), a billing system, a shipping system, or an insurance claims processing system. The stakeholders in these systems include different business units and potentially even the CEO, as well as different IT projects, IT maintenance, and operations. In these scenarios, we will be facing highly heterogeneous teams and often very political environments. The technology landscape will be highly heterogeneous as well, including many different application and middleware platforms. The business data and content will have a very long lifetime, especially when compared with the much shorter cycles of technology innovation. We need to deal with constantly changing functional requirements that are usually not well-defined. In addition, we will be facing many cross-dependencies between functional requirements, as well as heterogeneous technology platforms. The number of end users will be potentially very large, and the applications will have to be rolled out to large numbers of PCs, often more than 10,000.

Take, on the other hand, a desktop application, such as a word processor or spreadsheet application. A smaller, more homogeneous technical team will develop this application. It will be used by office workers as well, but the problem space is more well-defined. The application logic is self-contained, with very few cross-dependencies. Finally, there is no roll-out problem because the end user is typically responsible for the installation himself.

As we can see from these examples, enterprise software is unique in many respects, and therefore, it requires unique measures to ensure the efficiency of its development and maintenance.

1.3 The Importance of Enterprise Software Architectures

According to the second law of thermodynamics, *any closed system cannot increase its internal order by itself*. In fact, any activity that is geared toward ordering the system will increase its overall disorder (called *entropy*). In many respects, this law is also applicable to enterprise software, which often has very similar characteristics. Consequently, *outside intervention* is continually required to help create a higher order and to ensure that development efforts are not lost.

In enterprise software, the architect takes on the role as an outside influencer and controller. It is his responsibility to oversee individual software projects from the strategic point of view of the overall organization, as well as from the tactical, goal-oriented viewpoint of the individual project. He has to balance different requirements while attempting to create an enduring order within the enterprise software landscape. The enterprise software architecture is the architect's most important tool at hand. Software architects are constantly confronted with changes to and expansion of functionality that increase system complexity and reduce efficiency. By refactoring current solutions, architects constantly strive to reduce complexity and thereby increase the agility of the system (see Figure 1-2).

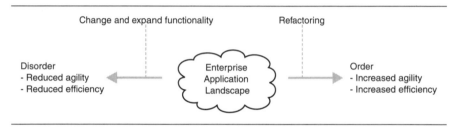

FIGURE 1-2   Software architects use refactoring to fight the constant increase in system complexity.

Apart from the events that increase complexity during normal usage of the architecture, single events can also have an important effect on enterprise IT. They might occur in major changes to existing jurisdiction, the end-of-life of a supported product, or the introduction of large chunks of computing infrastructure, such as in the course of a merger or acquisition. Such events require a major effort at very short notice to keep the architecture in a simple and maintainable state. Devastating consequences have been observed as a result of mergers and acquisitions: concise financial reporting being lost after a merger and raw system capacity being exhausted after an acquisition. Because it is unknown *a priori* when such effects will occur, it is vital to keep the enterprise architecture in a maintainable and changeable state all the time.

As we will see in the remainder of this book, Service-Oriented Architectures are particular well suited to cope with the needs of such an ongoing incremental process of optimization.

1.4   The Requirements for an Enterprise Software Architecture

As a result of the aforementioned tight coupling with the internal organization, processes, and business model of the enterprise, an enterprise software architecture must fulfill very different requirements than, for example, a software architecture for a system that is controlled by a small number of highly qualified domain experts, such as the Mars robot or a video game engine.

In order to improve agility and efficiency, an enterprise software architecture must provide particular characteristics:

Simplicity. The enterprise architecture must be simple in order to allow efficient communication between key personnel. As previously discussed, many people are involved in the specification and construction of enterprise software. All these people have different roles and consequently different viewpoints with regard to the software. It is also likely that several different skill sets exist among personnel. These might range from IT coordinators of functional departments to technical architects. Many IT coordinators will have detailed business domain knowledge but no technical expertise. On the other hand, technical architects will probably have an excellent technical education but have little understanding of the vertical business. Nevertheless, all the people involved must be able to understand and manage the architecture at their respective levels (e.g., specifying new functionality at the business level and implementing and maintaining it).

Flexibility and maintainability. Every enterprise system is subject to ongoing change. It must continuously be adapted to new requirements due to the need of evolving markets, legal changes, or business reorganizations. Therefore, the architecture must lead to a highly flexible and maintainable system. The architecture must define distinct components that can be rearranged and reconfigured in a flexible manner. Local changes cannot be permitted to have an impact on the global system. Providing that the external API of a component remains stable, an internal change should not affect operations outside the component. In this context, one needs to understand that external interfaces of components must be designed very carefully. To a great extent, interfaces must be generic and not specific to a single usage scenario. However, defining generic interfaces requires excellent domain knowledge, experience, and to some extent, luck. Finally, the internal implementation of a component must allow efficient maintenance, making it is easy to add or modify functionality.

Reusability. Reusability has been a major objective of software engineering for decades, with varying degrees of success. It is in the interest of an enterprise to gain as much benefit from its software assets as possible. This can be achieved by creating an inventory of useful building blocks and continually reusing them. One obvious reason for reuse is reduced development and

maintenance cost, which can be accomplished by sharing common functionality in code libraries that are used across different projects. However, perhaps a more important aspect of reusability is the ability to share data across
applications in real-time, thus reducing content redundancies. Having to
maintain the same dataset in multiple databases becomes a nightmare in the
long term. Unfortunately, it is not easy to achieve the goals of reuse. Large
organizations have learned that reuse is not always efficient because it is
particularly costly to administer, find, and understand the components that
should be reused, and sometimes this cost outweighs the benefits.

Decoupling of functionality and technology. The architecture must make
an enterprise organization independent of the technology. It must decouple
the long lifecycle of the business application landscape from the shorter
innovation cycles of the underlying technology. Moreover, an architecture
that is designed to last longer than one or two of these technology innovation cycles must cope not only with changing technologies but also with the
actual lifecycles of installed technologies, which can be much longer. It is
therefore a major requirement that the architecture tolerates both heterogeneity and change to its technical infrastructure. Furthermore, the development of business functionality must be decoupled from the underlying
technology. In particular, the architecture must avoid dependencies on specific products and vendors.

This book illustrates how a Service-Oriented Architecture can help achieve
the design goals for enterprise software systems as described previously.

1.5 The Relation of Enterprise Architecture and Enterprise Standards

For many decades, enterprise IT organizations have attempted to improve agility
and efficiency by homogenizing their systems through the introduction of enterprise-wide IT standards, but mostly with very limited success. Therefore, it is
important to understand that an enterprise architecture is not equal to an enterprise standard, as we discuss in this section.

In the 1980s, with relational database systems becoming mainstream, we
saw a wave of so-called *Enterprise Data Model* (EDM) projects. The idea of
these standardization projects was to define one global data model for all the
business entities in an enterprise, which was to be shared among all the different
organizations and systems in a company. Almost all of these EDM projects
failed, and today, there are usually as many different database schemas out there
as there are databases in an enterprise. There are a variety of different reasons for
the failure of these EDM projects, including political turf wars between different
departments, conflicting interests between the different stakeholders ranging

from business representatives over application specialists to DBMS administrators, the sheer technical complexity of the undertaking, and the fact that due to the dynamics and complexity of modern enterprises, it is usually impossible to capture a snapshot of the complete state of the enterprise at a given point in time.

In the 1990s, we saw the next attempt to homogenize the enterprise application landscape, this time through enterprise-wide middleware standards. The concept of the *Enterprise Software Bus* became popular. The idea was that by agreeing on a ubiquitous, technology-independent, enterprise-wide standard for communication between software modules, the problem of application integration would be solved once and for all. However, the reality in almost all enterprises today is that in addition to application heterogeneity, we now face the problem of middleware heterogeneity as well. In many cases, middleware such as CORBA was only used to solve point-to-point integration problems on a per-project basis, instead of being established as a global software bus; as a result, many enterprises now have nearly as many incompatible middleware systems as they have applications.

In general, it seems fair to say that enterprise standardization efforts in IT have failed to deliver on their promise of homogenization and easy application integration. Too many generations of middleware—ranging from DCE over CORBA to SOAP and WSDL—have been touted as silver bullets but have failed to become established as *the* ubiquitous Enterprise Software Bus, leaving behind a high level of cynicism among the people involved.

As a reader of a book on Service-Oriented Architectures, you might now be asking yourself, *"So what is different this time?"* Is SOA not yet another enterprise-wide standardization effort, this time under the label of the *Enterprise Software Bus*? How are SOAP and WSDL—while maybe technically superior and more flexible—going to address the organizational challenges of global standards that made the Enterprise Data Model, the Enterprise Software Bus, and many other enterprise standardization efforts fail to a large extent?

This book takes the position that SOA is neither a technology nor a technology standard, but instead it represents a technology-independent, high-level concept that provides architectural blueprints, such as the ones outlined in the first part of this book. These architectural blueprints are focusing on the slicing, dicing, and composition of the enterprise application layer in a way that the components that are created and exposed as services in the SOA are not only technically independent but also have a direct relationship to business functionality. They enable the structuring of application components on the local level while also catering for global integration of these components. As we will show in this book, an SOA does not rely on the support of particular runtime protocols, such as SOAP or IIOP. Therefore, an SOA does not impose adherence to technical standards on the global level and is not based on strict norms and specifications (see Figure 1-3).

Applications that are structured according to the guiding SOA principles laid out in this book will be able to fit into any integration scenario, regardless of the runtime protocols required. Having said this, work will still be required to bridge technology gaps, such as different communication protocols, but the efforts required to bridge these gaps will be marginal when compared to the complexity of integrating applications on the structural level.

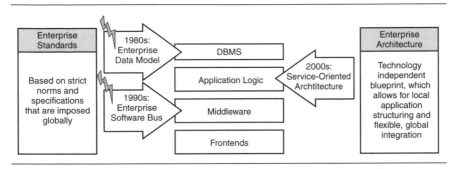

FIGURE 1-3 Enterprise Data Models and Software Buses were popular approaches to the challenges of enterprise computing in the 1980s and 1990s.

1.6 Organizational Aspects

When talking about enterprise IT, it is important to realize that many—if not most—of the problems associated with it are not of a technical nature but can be found on the organizational level instead. Quite naturally, we have already implicitly touched on many of these organizational aspects in our discussion so far (for example, when discussing the reasons for the failure of enterprise standards such as the *Enterprise Data Model* or the *Enterprise Software Bus*, which largely resulted from problems on the organizational and not the technical level).

The IT organization and the way projects are managed in a large enterprise are again very different from what one would find, for example, in a company that produced embedded systems or games. First and foremost, it is important to realize that most likely in no other part of the software industry will we find a development and maintenance process that is so closely aligned with the end customer. If an enterprise is developing a new financial reporting system, it will have to be done hand-in-hand with the finance department and any other stakeholders of the financial reporting system, possibly up to the CEO. A software team that is developing embedded control software for a dishwasher is unlikely to have daily meetings with a housewife about the exact functionality of the software.

An important consequence is that we are dealing with a much more complex and more ambiguously defined decision-making process, which is driven more often by business strategy and political agendas than by technical arguments. The organizational environment we are dealing with is extremely heterogeneous, and many different opinions will have to be incorporated into any decision that is made, be it a decision about budgets, functional requirements, project priorities, or the interesting question of what actually defines the success of an IT project.

For all these reasons, it is vital that our *enterprise IT renovation roadmap* provides not only a *technical roadmap* but also an *organizational roadmap*, which outlines how the technical architecture is to be established on the enterprise level from the political and organizational point of view. The second part of this book provides an overview of this organizational roadmap.

1.7 Lifelong Learning

Enterprise software has always suffered from the mismatch between technical and business-related concepts and the different languages spoken by the people on both sides of the fence. As a result, we have not only faced inefficiencies, but we also have often lost important knowledge and consequently had to reinvent many solutions.

Many attempts have been made in the past to find a common denominator between business and technical concepts. For example, SQL was invented in the 1970s with the vision that it would give non-technical business analysts a tool to access, analyze, and manipulate business data directly. Today, SQL is largely seen as a tool for technical experts, and it has turned out that most of the entities found in relational databases are too fine-grained and closely intertwined with technical concepts to have a meaning on the business level.

It is a *key goal of an SOA to provide services that have a concrete meaning on the business level*. Because of this one-to-one mapping between business and technology entities, *SOA provides a unique chance for the first time in IT history to create artifacts that have an enduring value for both the business as well as the technology side*. SOA provides a chance to make things that have been learned the hard way usable for the organization in the long run.

Similarly to human beings, organizations will never be able to stop learning if they want to be successful for long. SOA provides an excellent platform for this lifelong learning on the organizational level because an SOA enables us to constantly compare the nominal and the actual and to react accordingly to fill the gaps or adapt the architecture to reflect changes in business strategy.

Consequently, the third part of this book provides a number of real-world case studies, which can provide a good starting point for learning the lessons resulting from other organizations' adoption of SOAs and the impact they had.

1.8   The Enterprise IT Renovation Roadmap

As we have outlined in this introduction, we need strong enterprise architecture concepts to address the structural problems of the enterprise IT landscape, accompanied by a strategy for how to establish the architecture on the organizational level. SOA provides these concepts, but we have to be aware that implementing an architecture like an SOA is an ongoing process, requiring constant guidance and overseeing. The SOA architect needs to bridge many conflicting requirements, resulting from frequent changes of business requirements, the evolution of application and infrastructure technology, and last but not least, changes to the architecture itself. We need ways to introduce step-wise improvements, which will bring us slowly but steadily closer to our goal. We will have to accept that the path we are about to enter will not be a straight path, and there will be many influences outside of our control. Nevertheless, the authors believe that the introduction of an SOA will bring many long-term benefits to an enterprise. Figure 1-4 depicts the overall vision for how our roadmap can bring an enterprise that is suffering from development inefficiencies back to a level of high efficiency and agility.

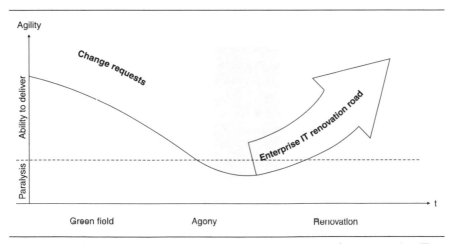

FIGURE 1-4   Service-Oriented Architecture is a key element of an enterprise IT renovation roadmap.

This book aims to flesh out an *enterprise IT renovation roadmap*. This roadmap is not only related to technology, but it also equally addresses organizational challenges. The roadmap anticipates constant changes in strategic directions and assumes that the underlying architecture will have to be constantly adapted to include the results of lessons learned as we go along. Consequently, the three parts of this book are structured to capture these different requirements.

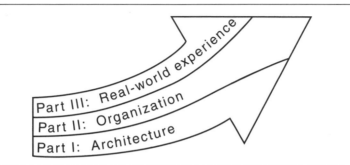

FIGURE 1-5   An Enterprise IT renovation roadmap needs to address three dimensions: architecture, organization, and real-world experience.

Part I of this book provides the *architectural roadmap*, mapping out the different *expansion stages* of an SOA, which will gradually help IT organizations to get back to a high level of agility and efficiency on the technical level.

Part II of this book looks at the *organizational roadmap*, providing an in-depth discussion of how the architecture can be established on the organizational level, the different stakeholders and how they must be involved, and how an SOA can be leveraged to drive project management more efficiently.

Finally, Part III of this book provides a number of case studies, which provide *real-world experiences* from large corporations that have already started their journey on the SOA-based enterprise renovation roadmap.

2

Evolution of the
Service Concept

Before looking at the road ahead, we want to take a step back and look at the evolution of the service concept by examining the milestones of enterprise computing and how they have shaped the concept of "services." We will look at three core development directions: programming languages, distribution technology, and business computing. Each has undergone a major evolution in the past 40 years, leading to a level of abstraction that supported the emergence of Service-Oriented Architectures.

2.1 Milestones of Enterprise Computing

The term "service" has been present in commercial computing for a long time and has been used in many different ways. Today, for example, we find large companies, such as IBM, promoting the concept of "services on demand." At the beginning of the new century, the term "Web services" became extremely popular, although it has often been used to refer to very different computing concepts. Some people use it to refer to application services delivered to human users over the Web, like in the popular salesforce.com application. Other people use the term "Web services" to refer to application modules made accessible to other applications over the Internet through XML-based protocols.

Because of the many different ways in which the term "service" has been used over the years in the IT industry, it is necessary to define more precisely how we use it in this book. However, before looking at a more formal, technology-oriented definition in Chapter 4, "Service-Oriented Architectures," we will look at a more generic definition that better suits the purpose of this chapter, which is examining the roots of "our" understanding of services.

The Merriam Webster's Dictionary gives various definitions for the term "service," including *"useful labor that does not produce a tangible commodity"* and *"a facility supplying some public demand."*[1] In this book, the term "service" takes its meaning from these definitions. It denotes some meaningful activity that a computer program performs on request of another computer program. Or, in more technical terms, a service is a remotely accessible, self-contained application module. Application frontends are making these services accessible to human users (see Figure 2-1). Often, the terms "client" and "server" are used synonymously for "service consumer" and "service provider," respectively.

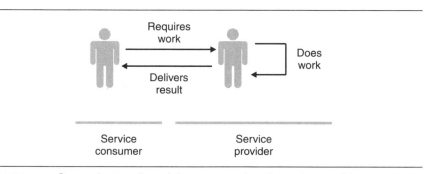

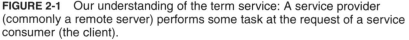

FIGURE 2-1   Our understanding of the term service: A service provider (commonly a remote server) performs some task at the request of a service consumer (the client).

The services covered in this book provide abstraction from a lot of their technical details, including location and discovery. Typically, our services provide business functionality, as opposed to technical functionality. Consistent with the definition from Merriam Webster's Dictionary, our services are not designed for one specific customer, but instead they are *"a facility supplying some public demand"*—they provide a functionality that is reusable in different applications. The cost effectiveness will depend strongly on the number of different customers a service has, that is, the level of reuse that can be achieved.

A concrete implementation of an SOA provides service consumers with seamless access to the different services available in it. Thus, after a service consumer is "wired" into the instance of the SOA—after the "ring tone" of the SOA is available—usage of the services is seamless and transparent. However, Chapter 1 said that an SOA is an architecture *per se* and not a service bus or any other specific middleware, and therefore, it describes structure, not concrete technology. Consequently, instances of SOAs might take very different technical shapes and forms in different enterprises.

A crucial factor in the development of services as we understand them in the context of this book is the quest for the right degree of abstraction. Ultimately, a service encapsulates some activity of a certain complexity. Using a

---

[1] http://www.m-w.com.

service makes the world more convenient for the service consumer. Consequently, an appropriate interaction pattern must exist between the service provider and service consumer. Given the analogy of the telephone network as the service infrastructure, services can be anything from hectic chatter to concise and focused conversation. They can also include some form of telephone conference, answering machine, or call redirection. In the remainder of this book, you will notice surprising similarities between the service concept and the telephone analogy.

It is interesting to notice that the service model, as it is defined in this book, has been preceded by many technologies and technical concepts in the last 30 years that shared many of the same underlying ideas and concepts. For example, look at the creation of reusable business functions on mainframe computers. Small computer networks created a fertile ground for service-related innovations, most notably the creation of remote procedure calls. Component-based development and object orientation promoted interface-driven design paradigms. Combinations of these concepts spawned platforms for distributed computing. At the same time, relational database development progressed rapidly, creating reliable data stores for enterprises. Business functionality left the mainframes and moved to one of several distributed paradigms. In the 1980s, packaged business solutions became available to a wide range of functional areas and industries. By 1995, the World Wide Web offered an extremely simple yet extremely successful service: the provision of content over a global network. The same network infrastructure is used today to enable interaction between remote computer systems through Internet protocols such as ebXML and SOAP.

The roots of service-orientation can be found in three different areas: programming paradigms, distribution technology, and business computing. The development of different programming language paradigms has not only contributed to the implementation platform for the different elements of an SOA but also has influenced the interfacing techniques used in an SOA, as well as the interaction patterns that are employed between service providers and service consumers. Many of the concepts originally found in programming languages have also made their way into the distribution technology that is presently used to offer remote access to services provided by different applications on different technical platforms. Finally, and maybe most importantly, the evolution of business computing has resulted in a large number of proprietary as well as packaged applications (see Figure 2-2) such as Enterprise Resource Planning (ERP), Customer Relationship Management (CRM), and Supply Chain Management (SCM), which today are providing the content—the data and the business logic—that brings an enterprise SOA to life. Because of the closeness of services to concrete business functionality, service-orientation has the potential to become the first paradigm that truly brings technology and business together on a level where people from both sides can equally understand and talk about the underlying concepts.

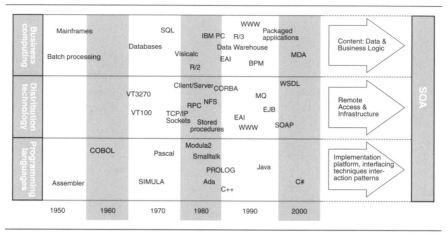

FIGURE 2-2   The long history of programming languages, distribution technology, and business computing has influenced the development of a new paradigm, called service-orientation.

2.2   Programming Paradigms

Functions/ Procedures

One of the first programming paradigms that enabled abstraction from the details of computer programs was functional decomposition and the related technology of functional analysis. Functional decomposition pioneered the formal introduction of flow charts, showing data that flows through a number of processes. One of the first people to formalize it was Myers in 1976 [Myers76]. However, the first language that was suited to functional decomposition was the COBOL (Common Business Oriented Language) programming language that was created as early as 1959 by a body called CODASYL (Conference on Data Systems Languages) and that was later adopted as an ANSI standard. Having undergone many improvements and additions since then, it is still a prevailing programming language in many major organizations. Apparently, more code is written in COBOL than any other language. In 1970, while working at the Polytechnic University of Zurich, Niklaus Wirth invented Pascal, a language that explicitly encouraged functional decomposition and that remains one of the most popular teaching languages for computer science.

Functional programming concepts remain popular because they are easy to understand by students, programmers, and customers. They provide a powerful tool to create reusable blocks of code—functions—that can even be sold in the form of software libraries.

Functional programming contributed to the service concept because functions essentially provide some form of abstraction. However, the amount of abstraction they can provide is limited.

It soon became apparent that the functional paradigm had its limits. Multi-purpose reusable functions are hard to create. Often, the caller must provide many parameters, and a lot of data must be passed into multiple functions in order to obtain the required result. The concepts of software modules and software components were created to cope with this growing complexity. These concepts came in many different flavors. The first time these concepts appeared was in the original implementation of the ADA programming language, modules in the Modula2 computing environment (also created by Niklaus Wirth in 1979), and the hugely commercially successful MS Visual Basic's VBX components. *COMPONENTS* Although very different, they share the common abstraction of <u>software components as a container for both data and the functions that operate on that data</u>. Even before the advent of software components, it was considered good programming practice to shield a function's user from its internal details. At this point, the concept was introduced as a language element known as encapsulation.

The significant increase of abstraction and encapsulation that components provide are an important step towards service orientation. However, their main purpose was in-situ development reuse, while service orientation focused on distribution and runtime reuse.

By the early 1980s, modularization and component programming were widely recognized as the next big trend in software development, and the MODULA language provided a stable and mature programming platform for this trend. However, the Japanese and U.S. governments poured massive amounts of money into the development and marketing of their own programming environments, PROLOG and ADA.

The uncertainty that emerged from this proliferation of platforms delayed the adoption of component-oriented programming long enough for it to be outrun *OBJECTS* in popularity by object-oriented programming,[2] which introduced the object as a programming and runtime concept. Originally, object-oriented programming was developed for simulation purposes. The first object-oriented language, SIMULA, was developed as early as 1967 at the Norwegian Computing Center in Oslo by Ole-Johan Dahl and Kristen Nygaard, and it has since been developed further [Kirk89]. Object orientation entered mainstream programming paradigms in the mid 1980s with the creation of Smalltalk [Gold83] and C++ [Stro85]. New versions of most other object-oriented languages, such as Java, were invented, while others, such as Pascal or even COBOL, were extended to embrace object orientation in one way or another.

Objects are much like components in that they support encapsulation and the bundling of data and functions and add the concept of individual entities (the objects) as instances of classes. The objects communicate through message exchange, but more importantly, object orientation adds the concept of inheritance, where types can be derived from other types. The derived type inherits all

---

[2] It took approximately 15 years until the concepts of component-orientation reemerged in the late 1990s, this time supported by concrete component platform implementations such as Enterprise Java Beans.

the internals and behavior of its ancestor. This spawned new concepts such as the programming by interface paradigm.

A common problem of object-oriented programming is that the level of abstraction and granularity that is exposed to the clients of a component is too fine to enable efficient reuse, let alone distribution (see Figure 2-3). Therefore, object-orientation—while being great for large, usually relatively isolated and monolithic applications—proved to be a dead-end from the point of view of distributed computing. Service-orientation aims to overcome a lot of the problems of distributed object computing, especially with respect to the right level of granularity and access patterns for remote services. Service-orientation also often goes a step backward when it comes to the question of how tightly data and functionality should be coupled—while OO imposes encapsulation of data and functionality, service-orientation often assumes that data and functionality are separated.

SERVICES

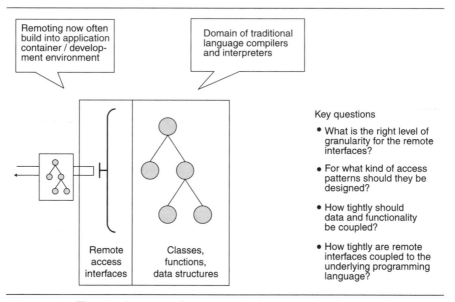

Remoting now often build into application container / development environment

Domain of traditional language compilers and interpreters

Key questions

• What is the right level of granularity for the remote interfaces?

• For what kind of access patterns should they be designed?

• How tightly should data and functionality be coupled?

• How tightly are remote interfaces coupled to the underlying programming language?

Remote access interfaces

Classes, functions, data structures

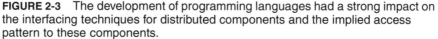

FIGURE 2-3   The development of programming languages had a strong impact on the interfacing techniques for distributed components and the implied access pattern to these components.

As we can see, the evolution of the different programming paradigms also had a huge impact on the concept of service-orientation. Modern programming languages and development environments are providing the technical foundation for enterprise-level services. However, not all programming concepts are directly applicable on the enterprise service level. With the ever tighter coupling of remoting and programming language technology, it becomes even more important to be aware of these mismatches between programming languages and enterprise services and to avoid falling into the trap of exposing too finely grained technical concepts to the enterprise level.[3]

2.3 Distributed Computing

Where the term service is used in this book, we usually assume that the service does not necessarily reside on the same physical machine as the calling application. The capability to call a remote computer program from another computer program in a seamless and controlled way is at the heart of our understanding of services.

An important challenge of distributed computing is to find abstractions for both remoteness and the actual service task at the same time. Although remoteness can be hidden from the service consumer, the service provider must still choose its invocation scenarios with the right granularity.

The distributed computing infrastructure was developed in the last 30 years. Business computing originally meant mainframe computing and involved large computers with costs in the multimillions of dollars, performing tasks mostly on their own. At some point, they morphed into more interactive multi-user systems. Rather than distributing the computing power, only data capture and display was distributed using terminal devices such as the DEC VT100 or the IBM3270. Some of the first things such systems had to share among themselves were data and output devices such as tape recorders or printing systems. In the early 1970s, computers became smaller and cheaper. The price/performance ratio made computer technology suitable for a broad range of applications. Research institutions quickly realized that they could operate both more economically and more independently when they were able to use various small computers rather than one mainframe system. At the universities of Stanford and Berkeley, two research programs eventually led to the creation of the Unix operating system. The Stanford University Network spun off the company Sun Microsystems in 1982, which is today one of the largest vendors of Unix computers. Unix is different from its predecessors—and many of its successors—in that its design quickly adopted the network as an essential part of the system environment. Two ideas fostered this design perspective: facilitating remote control of computers and programs and providing services to other computers in the network. The first train of thought created tools such as *telnet* and the Berkeley *r-tools* suite. The second one featured remote printing and the transparent provision of storage space—the NFS file system released by Sun Microsystems in 1984. In fact, the latter was the original raison d'etre for the SUN-RPC standard, one of the first Remote Procedure Call systems.

---

[3] See Sections 9.1.2.2 and 9.1.2.3 for detailed insight into this specific discussion.

Even though distributed computing was available as early as 1980, it was mainly confined to the academic world until well into the 1990s. Unix computers mainly acted as so-called workstations—powerful computational and visualizing engines—in research facilities and universities. In the business environment, a hub-and-spoke distribution model prevailed until well into the 1990s. A number of desktop computer systems would typically access a central system for storage and printing. Often, these file servers used an entirely different operating platform from its clients. As structured and relational databases became more mature, businesses adopted a client/server approach. A large chunk of the application resided with the client that remotely accessed a database server. Execution logic was split between client and server as databases, most notably Sybase, introduced the concept of functions that were executed within the database and that did not need to be shipped with the client application—so-called stored procedures. Another remarkable innovation was Novell's NetWare Loadable Modules (NLM), which were programs that ran on the server.

The next logical step was to blur the distinction between the client and the server. Combining concepts from distributed computing platforms such as the Distributed Computing Environment (DCE) with the newly emerging paradigm of object-oriented development, CORBA (Common Object Request Broker Architecture) was created. Instead of providing servers, which expose large numbers of remotely accessible functions, the functionality was now broken down into uniquely identifiable, remotely accessible objects that were able to manage their own state. Different objects could communicate with each other by means of an Object Request Broker (ORB). To connect to these objects, no knowledge of where they actually reside is necessary. Instead, an ORB provides abstraction mechanisms, such as naming services, which take care of the runtime discovery of the objects. Similarly to object-oriented programming, CORBA embraced the concept of programming by interface—in fact, all CORBA objects can be implemented in various programming languages, while their interfaces are described using the common Interface Definition Language (IDL).

Technically very elegant and sophisticated, CORBA promoted the actual reuse of live objects but lent itself to a design with rather small entities. CORBA's vision of distributed business objects never fully materialized because its fine-grained model often proved to be too complex to be suitable for the purposes of enterprise-level software reuse. In addition, CORBA programming is rather demanding for inexperienced developers because they must cope with many complex technical concepts, such as the non-trivial language mappings of the CORBA IDL. However, CORBA is still a widely used distribution technology, especially in telecommunications and financial services, although we rarely see the full feature-set of CORBA used in these applications (see Chapter 9, "Infrastructure of a Service Bus," for more details).

As a result, the evolution of distributed infrastructures changed its direction in the mid 1990s, taking the limitations of the early distributed object architectures into consideration. In a new attempt, the idea of clustering a set of objects into a single server was developed to provide a higher level of abstraction and to increase the richness of the service that such a server could offer. Driven by the high demand for more sophisticated platforms for Internet applications, Sun Microsystems introduced Enterprise Java Beans (EJB) in 1997. Similar to CORBA, EJB also relies on a distributed object model. However, the EJB model is based on a controlled—and therefore usually limited—number of servers that host the actual objects. EJB was inspired by CORBA but also by older application containers and transaction monitors, such as CICS or Tuxedo. EJB caters for different types of objects, including data-centric entity beans, as well as session-oriented objects. For example, stateless session beans do not need the concept of instance identity. Another strength of EJB is the container concept, which is responsible for the management of resources (objects, connections, transactions, etc.) in an EJB server. Although not a new concept (the core resource management concepts found in EJB can be traced back to CICS and other mainframe transaction monitors), EJB put a lot of effort into making resource management as transparent to the developer as possible. Finally, similar to other remote computing platforms, such as DCE and CORBA, EJB includes higher-level technical services, such as transaction management, naming services, and security.

In addition to core-application remoting technologies, such as RPC, CORBA, DCOM, and EJB, the 1990s saw the emergence of a large number of additional distributed computing middleware solutions, addressing distributed transaction management (e.g., the X/open-based CORBA Object Transaction Service, the Java Transaction Service, and the Microsoft Transaction Server), messaging (e.g., CORBA Notification and Java Messaging Service), EAI (Enterprise Application Integration, often including message routing and transformation, as well as application adapters), security (most notably the Secure Socket Layer), and many other problem areas.

Although they provided a great infrastructure for the development of individual systems, the sheer number of different distributed computing concepts, standards, and products also caused a problem: *middleware heterogeneity*. Given that most of the middleware was initially developed to address the problem of *application heterogeneity*, this is an ironic development, caused by the fact that it proved to be literally impossible to impose enterprise-wide standards for middleware in large enterprises (refer to Section 1.6 in Chapter 1, "An Enterprise IT Renovation Roadmap").

As a result of this development, XML became popular in the mid 1990s as a middleware-independent format for the exchange of data and documents between different applications. XML is basically the smallest common denominator upon which the IT industry could agree. Unlike CORBA IDL, Microsoft IDL, or Java interfaces, XML is not bound to a particular technology or middleware standard and is often used today as an ad-hoc format for processing data across different, largely incompatible middleware platforms. XML does not require a heavy-weight infrastructure, such as an ORB, and it comes with a large number of tools on many different platforms, which enables the processing and management of XML data, including different open-source parsing APIs, such as SAX and DOM. XML's inherent flexibility positions it as the most suitable standard for solving the application heterogeneity problem, as well as the middleware heterogeneity problem.

However, XML's great flexibility is potentially also its biggest problem because efficient application integration and data management requires higher-level data structures and messaging formats. As a result, a plethora of higher-level standards that attempt to address these issues has emerged in XML space. It took a long time for people to agree upon even the core standards for the specification of XML-based complex data types, such as XML DTDs and Schemas.

Recognizing the need for higher-level XML messaging standards on one hand, and attempting to leverage the ubiquity of the Internet on the other, engineers at Microsoft invented XML-based Web services with the creation of SOAP (Simple Object Access Protocol) in 1998. The initial SOAP version was specifically designed to work on the widely established HTTP Internet protocol, enabling server-to-server communication over the infrastructure that was already established for browser-to-server communication. Given that the established Internet infrastructure already addressed many pressing problems, such as security (SSL, firewalls, access control, etc.), load balancing, failover, and application management, this seemed like a logical next step.

Using standard HTTP POST and GET request, SOAP clients were able to call functions using the established Internet infrastructure. Microsoft later also developed an interface definition language for SOAP services called WSDL (Web Service Definition Language). WSDL describes the service interface, much as IDL describes the object interface when using CORBA. With the problem of *middleware heterogeneity* in mind, SOAP and WSDL are designed to enable the definition of various bindings to different lower-level communication protocols, for example, to enable SOAP communication over an existing messaging middleware. SOAP was carried forward by IBM and Microsoft and became a W3C recommendation in 2001.

As we see later in this book, XML-based Web services (e.g., based on SOAP and WSDL) can be a great platform for a Service-Oriented Architecture. However, it is important to keep in mind that Web services are not the only viable technology platform for an SOA because the SOA architectural concepts are not dependent on a single technology platform.

The development of distributed computing architectures, such as DCE, CORBA, DCOM, EJB, and XML Web services—and the real-world experience won with it in large-scale application developments—has provided the basis for the concepts of Service-Oriented Architectures. Similar to object orientation, which today seems to present the endpoint in the development of programming concepts, service orientation is the result of a long evolutionary process and has the potential to finally provide some stability in an environment that has been constantly evolving over the past 30 years.

2.4   Business Computing

Although the evolution of programming languages and distributed computing eventually provided the technical concepts that today are the first cornerstone of Service-Oriented Architectures, it is equally important to look at the developments in business computing that provided the content that represents the second cornerstone of Service-Oriented Architectures: business data and business logic.

The history of computing was always closely related to solving business problems, starting as early as 1940 with computers being used as large-scale calculators and as a replacement for large filing cabinets. Functions that nowadays are considered "technical" provided immediate business value in the advent of computing.

The following decades created further levels of abstraction, making it easier to think of a computer in terms of a provider for business services. However, business computing maintained its focus on mainframe computers. Most software was custom-built, originally written in machine language and later in functional languages such as COBOL or FORTRAN. Yet business computing proved a crucial success factor for enterprises. For example, logistics companies used computers to compute routes for shipments through their vast international transport networks. Retail giant Wal-Mart was among the first to create custom-made supply-chain management systems to optimize the purchase and distribution of goods.

In the 1970s, the original homegrown filing cabinet applications were gradually replaced using fully fledged database systems, including relational databases, which encapsulate the storage of complex interrelated data. Although today we regard the storage mechanism itself as a technical concept, it seemed fairly business-oriented when it was created. In fact, SQL was developed as a language that was intended to be used mainly by business analysts, not database programmers.

In 1972, four former IBM employees founded SAP in Germany, an event that marked a milestone for business computing. SAP introduced R/2 in 1981, the first business-computing platform that enabled enterprise-wide real time processing of financial data and resource planning information.

However, by the mid 1980s, corporate software development seemingly reached saturation level. Most companies were convinced that they had achieved most of what was possible with computing in their environment. College students were discouraged from majoring in software development because people assumed that only maintenance would be needed in the future, which probably would be performed in some remote offshore location.

Then computers began to reach employee desktops. Systems such as the Commodore PET and others introduced a new concept to computing. Data was obtained from remote storage, while computation and visualization were performed locally. This paradigm was boosted by the huge success of the IBM PC, which was launched in 1984. Through several stages of hardware and software development at both the client and server sides, the client/server paradigm held steady. The focus for advancement shifted back and forth between the two. On one hand, client computers became more powerful, sporting graphical user interfaces and raw computational power, and networks became faster. On the other hand, database vendors worked hard to add value to their systems by providing fault tolerance, scalability, and load balancing using cluster techniques and procedures that were executed within the database.

Driven by an increasing economical globalization and new manufacturing models such as Just-in-Time production, the supply and distribution chains of companies became increasingly sophisticated, relying more on complex IT systems to manage these processes. The software market reacted to this newly awakened demand in enterprise computing by developing complex enterprise applications, such as Enterprise Resources Planning (ERP) and Supply Chain Management (SCM). Over two decades, the market for enterprise solutions has become increasingly complex, offering applications ranging from Customer Relationship Management and Product Lifecycle Management to highly specialized applications, such as applications that manage complex transportation networks or billing systems for telecommunications companies. As a result, a plethora of new enterprise software companies emerged, and old ones grew even bigger, including SAP, Siebel, Oracle, PeopleSoft, J.D. Edwards, Baan, Manugistics, and others.

With the emergence of the Internet, many of these companies transformed their enterprise applications to make use of the new technology (e.g., mySAP) and to cater for new business models in the area of eCommerce and B2B. New companies, such as salesforce.com, emerged even after the heydays of the Internet were over, taking on established companies such as Siebel by delivering its applications entirely over the Internet.

However, the availability of new enterprise software often caused as many problems as it aimed to solve. Often, ERP, CRM, and Enterprise Portal solutions competed within a single organization to become the central repositories of business data and processes. Keeping in mind that as late as 1990, most enterprise IT systems served no more than a single department, it comes as no surprise that many challenges emerged on the organizational level along with a huge demand for Enterprise Application Integration (EAI). However, suffering from problems similar to the Enterprise Software Bus model, the EAI-typical hub-and-spoke model was often limited to solve the problems of individual application integration projects, failing to deliver a more holistic view to the problems of having to integrate across organizational boundaries.

An enterprise SOA aims to leverage the business logic and data that resides in the many applications, databases, and legacy systems of today's enterprises, offering them a sustainable strategy for flexibly adapting their IT systems to changes in functional requirements and business strategy without imposing onto them the use of a single middleware or EAI platform. The services exposed in an SOA are intended to be mapping directly to business entities, thus enabling enterprise integration on the business level, not the technical level.

2.5 Conclusion

This chapter looked at the historical developments of programming languages, distribution technology, and business computing and how each of these areas contributed to the development of service orientation.

The evolution of programming languages has not only provided us with more productive development platforms but has also significantly contributed to the understanding of interfacing techniques and access patterns for services in an SOA. A key lesson learned is that not all programming language concepts are suitable in distributed computing and that service orientation is a deliberate step back from object orientation, aiming to provide more coarse-grained components with simpler access patterns.

The evolution of distribution technology has given us a variety of remote access technologies from which we can choose today, together with an infrastructure for transaction management, security, load-balancing, failover, and other critical features.

Finally, the evolution of business computing has lead to the development of advanced enterprise applications, such as ERP and CRM, which are today providing the content that represents the second cornerstone of an SOA—the data and business logic that brings our services to life.

References

Myers, Glenford J. *Composite/Structured Design*. Van Nostrand Reinhold Co. 1976. [Myers76]

Goldberg, Adele and David Robson. *Smalltalk-80: The Language and its Implementation*. Addison-Wesley. 1983. [Gold83]

Kirkerud, Bjorn. *Object-Oriented Programming with Simula*. Addison-Wesley. 1989. [Kirk89]

Stroustrup, Bjarne. *The C++ Programming Language*. Addison-Wesley. 1991. [Ctro85]

URLs

http://www.m-w.com

3

Inventory of Distributed Computing Concepts

Before examining SOA elements in detail in the following chapters, we will review existing concepts of distributed computing. This is important because we are not planning to develop an SOA from scratch. Instead, an SOA will have to incorporate existing middleware technologies and distributed computing concepts. This is particularly important because earlier attempts to replace existing middleware with a new, ubiquitous software bus (e.g., CORBA) have failed, and a successful SOA will have to embrace existing and upcoming technologies instead of replacing or precluding them. Many authors cover the intrinsic details of communication networks and middleware, such as Tanenbaum [Tan2002, Tan2003] and Coulouris [Cou2001]. Aiming our discussion at the application architecture level, we will provide only a brief overview of the most fundamental communication middleware concepts here (including Remote Procedure Calls, Distributed Objects, and Message-Oriented Middleware), followed by a more detailed discussion on the impact that different types of communication middleware have on the application level (including synchrony, invocation semantics, and application coupling).

3.1 Heterogeneity of Communication Mechanisms

Techniques for the distribution of enterprise software components are manifold. As will be seen in the remainder of this book, this heterogeneity is inevitable due to the various communication requirements of enterprises.

The situation is comparable to communication in real life—many forms of communication exist (verbal, non-verbal, written, etc.), and every form has its own purpose. It is not possible to replace one form with another without reducing expressiveness.

Figure 3-1 depicts three possible levels of heterogeneity of distribution techniques:

- Communication mode
- Products
- Additional runtime features

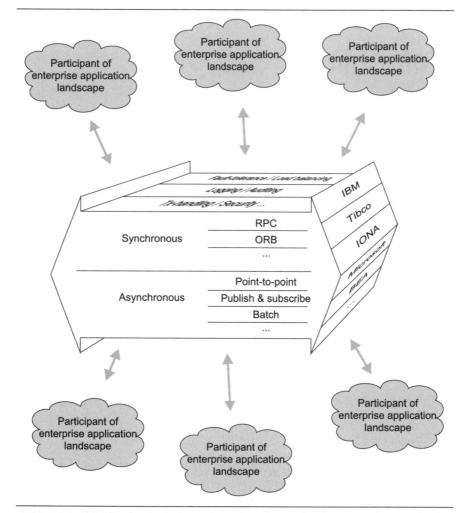

FIGURE 3-1   Distribution techniques for enterprise applications are characterized by manifold requirements and consequently by various dimensions of heterogeneity.

Communication modes are basically distinguished between synchronous and asynchronous mechanisms. Evidently both are required in real-world projects. However, in practice, there are usually numerous variants of these basic modes of communication. Obviously, one can encounter numerous *products* that provide distribution mechanisms. In addition, a concept that is supposed to cover all the distribution issues of an enterprise must also provide a set of _additional runtime features_ such as security support, fault tolerance, load balancing, transaction handling, logging, usage metering, and auditing.

It should be noted that our classification scheme is arbitrary. It is possible to define other classifications or to find additional levels of heterogeneity. However, independent of the classification scheme, it is true that enterprise distribution techniques tend to create heterogeneity at different levels.

From a technical point of view, this scenario leads to three different layers, as shown in Figure 3-2. The first layer contains the core assets of the enterprise application landscape, including all business logic. The second layer provides technology-dependent adapters that connect the core assets to various software busses. Finally, the third layer represents the sum of the enterprise's communication facilities.

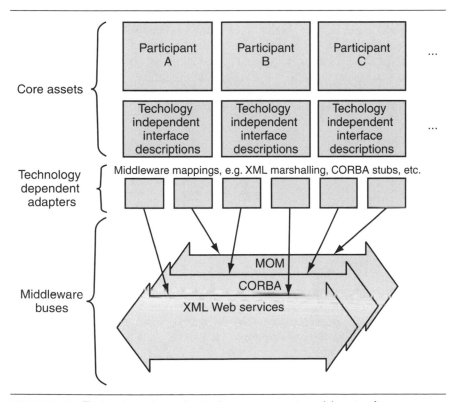

FIGURE 3-2   Technology-dependent adapters connect participants of an enterprise application landscape with its communication infrastructure.

The remainder of this chapter focuses on the second layer. Chapters 4 to 7 provide an in-depth discussion of the first layer, while Chapter 9 discusses the third layer.

3.2 Communication Middleware

A communication middleware framework provides an environment that enables two applications to set up a conversation and exchange data. Typically, this exchange of data will involve the triggering of one or more transactions along the way. Figure 3-3 shows how this middleware framework acts as an intermediary between the application and the network protocol.

In the very early days of distributed computing, the communication between two distributed programs was directly implemented based on the raw physical network protocol. Programmers were involved with acute details of the physical network. They had to create network packets, send and receive them, acknowledge transmissions, and handle errors. Therefore, a lot of effort was spent on these technical issues, and applications were dependent on a specific type of network. Higher-level protocols such as SNA, TCP/IP, and IPX provided APIs that helped reduce the implementation efforts and technology dependencies. They also provided abstraction and a more comfortable application development approach. These protocols enabled programmers to think less in terms of frames at OSI layer 2 or packets at layer 3 and more in terms of communication sessions or data streams. Although this was a significant simplification of the development of distributed applications, it was still a cumbersome and error-prone process. Programming at the protocol layer was still too low-level.

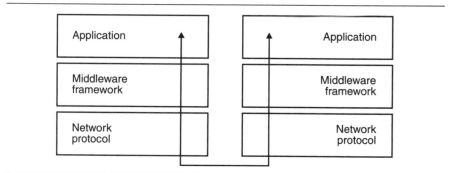

FIGURE 3-3 A communication middleware framework isolates the application developers from the details of the network protocol.

As the next evolutionary step, communication infrastructures encapsulated the technical complexity of such low-level communication mechanisms by insulating the application developer from the details of the technical base of the communication. A communication middleware framework enables you to access a remote application without knowledge of technical details such as operating systems, lower-level information of the network protocol, and the physical network address. A good middleware framework increases the flexibility, interoperability, portability, and maintainability of distributed applications. However, it is the experience of the recent two decades that the developer's awareness of the distribution is still crucial for the efficient implementation of a distributed software architecture. In the remainder of this chapter, we will briefly examine the most important communication middleware frameworks.

3.2.1 RPC

Remote Procedure Calls (RPCs) apply the concept of the local procedure call to distributed applications. A local function or procedure encapsulates a more or less complex piece of code and makes it reusable by enabling application developers to call it from other places in the code. Similarly, as shown in Figure 3-4, a remote procedure can be called like a normal procedure, with the exception that the call is routed through the network to another application, where it is executed, and the result is then returned to the caller. The syntax and semantics of a remote call remain the same whether or not the client and server are located on the same system. Most RPC implementations are based on a synchronous, request-reply protocol, which involves blocking the client until the server replies to a request.

The development of the RPC concept was driven by Sun Microsystems in the mid 1980s and is specified as RFC protocols 1050, 1057, and 1831. A communication infrastructure with these characteristics is called RPC-style, even if its implementation is not based on the appropriate RFCs.

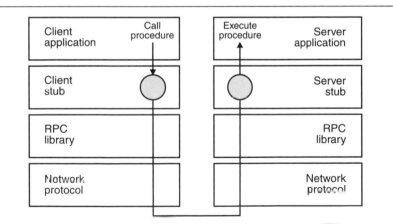

FIGURE 3-4 RPC stubs and libraries enable location transparency, encapsulate the functional code for the RPC communication infrastructure, and provide a procedure call interface.

It is interesting to note that the need to provide platform-independent services was one of the main drivers in the development of RPC-style protocols. Particularly, the widely used SUN RPC protocol (RFC 1057) and its language bindings were developed to enable transparent access to remote file systems. NFS (RFC 1094) was implemented on top of SUN RPC and is one of the most popular ways to enable networked file system access in Unix-like environments.

At the end of the 1980s, DCE (Distributed Computing Environment) emerged as an initiative to standardize the various competing remote procedure call technologies. DCE also adds some higher-level services such as security and naming services. However, for reasons that were mainly political, DCE failed to win widespread industry support.

3.2.2 DISTRIBUTED OBJECTS

In the early 1990s, object-oriented programming emerged as a replacement for the traditional modular programming styles based on procedure or function calls. Consequently, the concept of Distributed Objects was invented to make this new programming paradigm available to developers of distributed applications.

Typically, Distributed Objects are supported by an Object Request Broker (ORB), which manages the communication and data exchange with (potentially) remote objects. ORBs are based on the concept of *Interoperable Object References*, which facilitate the remote creation, location, invocation, and deletion of objects (see Figure 3-5) often involving object factories and other helper objects. By doing so, ORB technology provides an object-oriented distribution platform that promotes object communication across machine, software, and vendor boundaries. ORBs provide location transparency and enable objects to hide their implementation details from clients.

The most common ORB implementations are CORBA, COM/DCOM, and RMI. While RMI is limited to Java and COM/DCOM is restricted to Microsoft platforms, CORBA spans multiple platforms and programming languages.

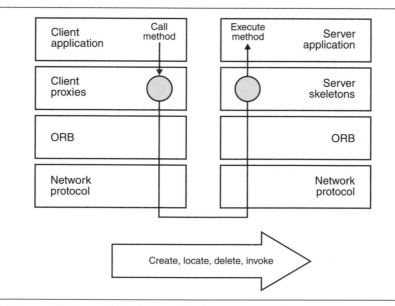

FIGURE 3-5 ORBs enable client applications to remotely create, locate, and delete server objects (e.g., through factory objects) and communicate with them through remote method invocations.

Today, most enterprise architectures embody object-oriented components (such as for the implementation of graphical user interfaces), but there is rarely an enterprise architecture that is built purely on object technology. In most cases, legacy applications based on programming languages such as COBOL or C are critical parts of an enterprise application landscape (some people prefer the term *software assets* over *legacy software*). It is therefore vital that a component that should be reused on an enterprise-wide level provides an interface that is suitable both for object-oriented and traditional clients. This is particularly true for the service of an SOA.

In this context, it is important to understand that object-oriented applications typically come with a fine-grained interaction pattern. Consequently, applying the object-oriented approach to building distributed systems results in many remote calls with little payload and often very complex interaction patterns. As we will see later, service-oriented systems are more data-centric: They produce fewer remote calls with a heavier payload and more simple interaction patterns.

Nevertheless, it is entirely possible to use ORB technology to implement a data-oriented, coarse-grained SOA interface. This leads to a very restricted application of the ORB technology and typically to an RPC-style usage of the ORB (see Figure 3-6).

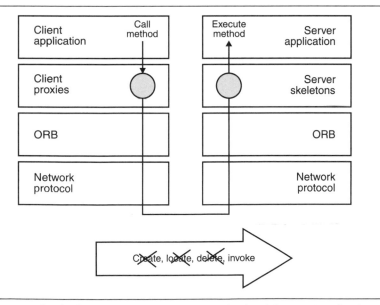

FIGURE 3-6 An ORB can be used as a communication infrastructure for the implementation of an SOA. In this case, the advanced capabilities of the ORB to cope with multiple instances of remote objects are not used.

3.2.3 MOM

With the advent of IBM's MQSeries (now IBM WebSphere MQ) and Tibco Software's Rendezvous in the middle of the 1990s, Message-Oriented Middleware (MOM) technology became popular, and it has since become an integral part of the communication infrastructure landscape of large enterprises.

Although there are alternative implementation approaches (e.g., UDP multicast-based systems), the most common MOM implementations are based on the concept of message queuing. The two key components of a message queuing system are *message* and *queue*.

Typically, a message consists of a header and a payload. The structure of the header field is usually predefined by the system and contains network routing information. The payload is application-specific and contains business data, possibly in XML format. Messages typically relate to a specific transaction that should be executed upon receiving the message. Depending on the queuing system, the name of the transaction is either part of the header or the application payload.

The queue is a container that can hold and distribute messages. Messages are kept by the queue until one or more recipients have collected them. The queue acts as a physical intermediary, which effectively decouples the message senders and receivers. Message queues help to ensure that messages are not lost, even if the receivers are momentarily unavailable (e.g., due to a network disconnection). Email is a good example of the application of messaging concepts. The email server decouples sender and receiver, creating durable storage of email messages until the receiver is able to collect them. Email messages contain a header with information that enables the email to be routed from the sender's email server to the receiver's email server. In addition, email messages can be sent from a single sender to a single receiver (or to multiple recipients, through mailing lists for example), and one can receive email from multiple senders.

Message queuing systems provide similar concepts of connecting senders and receivers in different ways (one-to-one, one-to-many, many-to-many, etc.) (see Figure 3-7). The underlying technical concepts are typically referred to as point-to-point and publish-subscribe models. Point-to-point represents the most basic messaging model: One sender is connected to one receiver through a single queue. The publish-subscribe model offers more complex interactions, such as one-to-many or many-to-many. Publish-subscribe introduces the concept of *topics* as an abstraction, to enable these different types of interactions. Similar to point-to-point, a sender can publish messages with a topic without knowing anything about who is on the receiving side. Contrary to point-to-point communications, in the publish-subscribe model, the message is distributed not to a single receiver, but to all receivers who have previously indicated an interest in the topic by registering as subscribers.

Although the basic concepts of message queuing systems (message, queue, and topic) are relatively simple, a great deal of complexity lies in the many different ways that such a system can be configured. For example, most message queu-

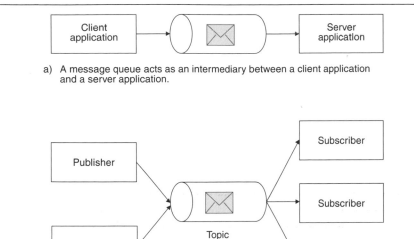

a) A message queue acts as an intermediary between a client application and a server application.

b) Publish-subscribe enables messages to be sent to multiple subscribers.

FIGURE 3-7   MOM decouples the creators and consumers of messages providing concepts such as point-to-point messaging and publish-subscribe.

ing systems enable the interconnection of multiple physical queues into one logical queue, with one queue manager on the sender side and another on the receiver side, providing better decoupling between sender and receiver. This is similar to email, where senders transmit email to their own mail server, which in turn routes the mail to the receiver's mail server, a process that is transparent to the users of email. Furthermore, queues can be interconnected to form networks of queues, sometimes with intelligent routing engines sitting between the different queues, creating event-driven applications that employ logic similar to that of Petri nets [Rei 1992]

Message queuing systems typically also provide a number of different service levels (QoS—quality of service), either associated with specific messages or specific queues. These service levels determine, for example, the transactional capability of the message, the send/receive acknowledge modes, the number of allowable recipients, the length of time a message is valid, the time at which the message was sent/received, the number of times to attempt redelivery, and the priority of the message, relative to other messages.

Generally, <u>MOM encourages loose coupling between message consumers and message producers, enabling dynamic, reliable, flexible, high-performance systems to be built</u>. However, one should not underestimate the underlying complexity of ensuring that MOM-based systems work efficiently, a feature that is not often visible at the outset.

3.2.4 TRANSACTION MONITORS

With the rising demand for user-friendly online applications in the 1980s, trans-action monitors[1] became popular. They provide facilities to run applications that service thousands of users. It is the responsibility of a transaction monitor to effi-ciently multiplex the requirements for computing resources of many concurrent clients to resource pools. Most importantly, they manage CPU bandwidth, data-base transactions, sessions, files, and storage. Today, transaction monitors also provide the capability to efficiently and reliably run distributed applications. Cli-ents are typically bound, serviced, and released using stateless servers that mini-mize overhead by employing a non-conversational communication model. Furthermore, up-to-date transaction monitors include services for data manage-ment, network access, authorization, and security.

Popular examples of transaction monitors are CICS (Customer Information Control System), IMS (Information Management System), Encina, or Tuxedo, which all provide facilities for remote access. A variety of different distribution concepts can be found to support the particular strengths of respective transaction monitors.

Although it is not the intention of this book to discuss current technology and products in detail, a short glance at IBM's CICS and IMS can provide useful insights. CICS is a time-sharing system. Although more than 20 years old, it is still a key element of IBM's enterprise product strategy. It is probably today's most important runtime environment for mission-critical enterprise applications. Even today, there are new applications developed for CICS. Native protocols such as SNA or TCP/IP and various communication infrastructures such as object brokers and messaging middleware can be used to integrate CICS applications with non-CICS applications [Bras2002]. One of the most common ways to con-nect to a CICS application is CICS's External Call Interface (ECI). The ECI basi-cally provides an RPC-like library that enables remote applications to invoke CICS transaction programs. Based on the ECI, the CICS Transaction Gateway (CTG) provides an object-oriented interface for Java. Contrary to the CICS time-sharing concept, its predecessor IMS was based on processing queues. Although IMS appears to be archaic, it is still important in practice due to its base of installed transaction programs. There are also many different ways to remotely invoke an IMS transaction program [Bras2002]. The most popular ways are IMS Connect and MQSeries OTMA-Bridge [Lon1999]. While IMS Connect imposes an RPC-like access to IMS transaction programs, the MQSeries OTMA-Bridge is based on the MOM concept.

---

[1] Often referred to as TP monitors, TPMs, or TX monitors.

3.2.5 APPLICATION SERVERS

With the booming demand for Web applications in the dot-com era of the late 1990s, the application server became extremely popular. An application server mediates between a Web server and backend systems, such as databases or existing applications. Requests from a client's Web browser are passed from the Web server to the application server. The application server executes code that gathers the necessary information from other systems and composes an HTML reply, which is returned to the client's browser.

An application server can be simple, such as Microsoft ASP (Active Server Pages), which comes with IIS (Internet Information Server), or they can be complex and expensive systems that implement load balancing, data management, caching, transaction management, and security.

The basic functions of an application server can be described as hosting components, managing connectivity to data sources, and supporting different types of user interfaces, such as *thin* Web interfaces or *fat* client applications. Taking a closer look at the basic mechanisms of an application server, one can sometimes get the impression that not much has changed from the days of IBM CICS and VT3270 terminals, only that these days, the user interfaces are more colorful.

When looking at the high end of application servers, notably Microsoft .NET Server, BEA WebLogic, and IBM WebSphere, it can sometimes be difficult to find out exactly what is still part of the core application server functionality because these companies have started to use their respective brands to describe a very broad array of products. For example, J2EE, the application server framework from the non-Microsoft camp, started with core application server functionality including JSP (Java Server Pages) for the dynamic generation of HTML and EJB (Enterprise Java Beans) for managing and hosting more complex software components. Within a couple of years, J2EE has become a complex and sophisticated framework (see Figure 3-8).

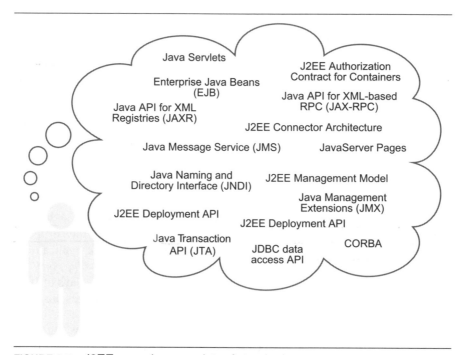

FIGURE 3-8   J2EE comprises a variety of standards.

3.3 Synchrony

Synchronous and asynchronous communications are two different forms of interaction that both require the support of a generic technology for distributed systems.

Synchronous communication is characterized by the immediate responses of the communication partners. The communication follows a request/reply pattern that enables the free flow of conversation, often based on the use of busy waits. Applications with user interaction specifically require this conversational mode of interaction. Synchronous communication requires that the client and server are always available and functioning.

Asynchronous communication is less stringent. Both communication partners are largely decoupled from each other, with no strict request/reply pattern. Typically, one party creates a message that is delivered to the recipient by some mediator, and no immediate response is needed. The sender can store context information and retrieve it when the recipient returns the call, but there is not necessarily a response. In contrast to a synchronous request-reply mechanism, asynchronous communication does not require the server to be always available, so this type can be used to facilitate high-performance message-based systems.

Typically, synchronous communication is implemented by RPC-style communication infrastructures, while asynchronous mechanisms are implemented by MOM. However, it is entirely possible to implement synchronous communication based on MOM, and it is also possible to build MOM-style interaction over RPC. Nevertheless, RPC is more suitable if immediate responses are required, and MOM is the technology of choice for decoupled, asynchronous communication.

Due to the manifold requirements of most real-world scenarios, typical enterprise systems embody both synchronous and asynchronous communication. For this purpose, a variety of different communication infrastructures is used, ranging from simple FTP (File Transfer Protocol) to more advanced middleware platforms, such as RPC and MOM. In addition, there are also communication infrastructures that support both communication modes—for example, pipelining RPC, which supports asynchronous communication in addition to the standard synchronous RPC communication.

To conclude this discussion on synchrony, we will provide an overview of the most common ways of implementing synchronous and asynchronous communication with both RPC/ORB and MOM technology. We will look at the following examples:

- Simulated synchronous services with queues
- Asynchronous one-way: fire-and-forget RPC
- Callbacks and polling services

The first example, *simulated synchronous communication*, can often be found in mainframe environments, where a message queuing system has been chosen as the standard means for remote interaction with the host, such as OS/390 with MQSeries access. This is a common scenario in many large enterprises. Often, these companies have gone one step further, developing frameworks on top of this combination of OS/390 and MQSeries that enable service-like interfaces to the most widely used transactions on the mainframe. This is done by implementing client-service wrappers that shield the underlying MQ infrastructure from the client developer. These service wrappers often simulate synchronous interactions with the mainframe by combining two underlying queues, one with request semantics and the other with reply semantics, using correlation IDs to pair messages into request/reply tuples. Effectively, this relegates the message queuing system to playing a low-level transport function only, not generally leveraging any of the advanced features of the messaging system. Figure 3-9 provides an overview of this approach.

The second example, *fire-and-forget RPC*, assumes an RPC or ORB implementation with asynchronous one-way semantics: The client fires off a request to the server without expecting an answer. This can be achieved either by defining an operation signature that does not include any return values or by using specific features of the middleware, such as a CORBA IDL operation using the keyword oneway. Figure 3-10 provides an overview of this approach.

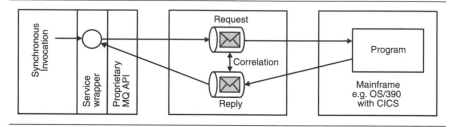

FIGURE 3-9 Simulated synchronous services with queues. A correlation ID maps a reply message to the corresponding request. On the client side, this is hidden by a service wrapper, which gives the caller the impression of synchrony.

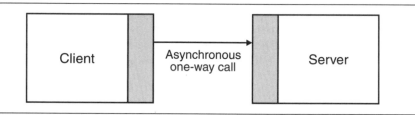

FIGURE 3-10 Asynchronous one-way call implies fire-and-forget semantics. The request is fired off by the client without a reply from the server.

There are two key issues with this approach: The first is that the client has no guarantee that the server will receive and process the request appropriately. This problem reduces the applicability of this method significantly. The second problem is that most RPCs/ORBs typically use a reliable communication protocol such as TCP. Sending a one-way request through TCP generally means that the client is blocked until delivery to the server on the TCP level has been completed. If a server is getting swamped with requests, it might become unable to process all incoming one-way requests on the TCP layer. Effectively, this means that the client is blocked until the server is at least able to read the request from the network. Therefore, it is not advisable to use this approach to implement large-scale event notification. Instead, an appropriate MOM should be chosen.

The third example, *callbacks and polling services*, is the most common way of decoupling clients and server in RPC-style applications, without having to move to a fully fledged MOM solution. The basic idea is similar to the conventional callback, as it is realized in functional programming languages with function pointers, or in OO languages using object references: A client sends a request to the server, and the server stores the request and returns control back to the client (possibly sending an acknowledgment that it received the request). After having processed the request, the server (now acting as a client) sends the result back to the client (now acting as a server), using the standard RPC/ORB invocation mechanism (see Figure 3-11). Sometimes, it is not possible for the client to act as a server (e.g., due to firewall restrictions). In these cases, the client can periodically poll the server for the availability of the result.

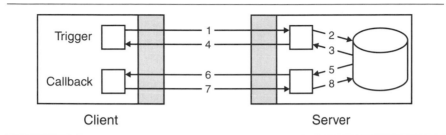

FIGURE 3-11   Callbacks and polling services: A client sends a request to a server ("trigger"). The server stores the requested activity in a database before replying with an acknowledgment to the client. The server has a thread that takes pending requests from the database, processes them, and sends back the result to the originating client using callback.

This approach can sometimes provide a good compromise for satisfying the need to decouple clients and servers without having to add technology such as a MOM. However, often the implementation of such a remote callback can be more difficult than it originally appears. This is especially true if the application requires a high degree of reliability. In these cases, it is necessary to introduce some kind of mechanism for ensuring reliability, such as through combining a server-side database with some kind of custom-built acknowledgment protocol. Also, the server-side logic can become quite complex: To ensure that all requests are eventually processed, the database must be constantly polled for pending requests, potentially adding a huge burden on database performance. For this reason, one should carefully weigh the use of database triggers. Here, it is important to ensure that the execution of the trigger is not part of the same transaction that puts the new request in the database. In this case, you could encounter a situation where the client is blocked because it has to wait not only until the server has stored the request in the database before returning an acknowledgment to the client, but also until the database trigger has been executed. This will effectively eliminate the decoupling effect of the callback implementation.

As shown in Figure 3-12, the server-side implementation can alternatively use internal message queues to ensure an efficient means of storing incoming requests in a reliable and efficient manner, thus avoiding many of the issues with the pure-database approach described previously.

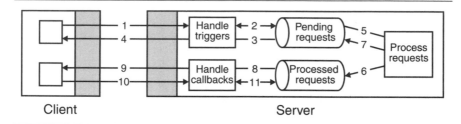

FIGURE 3-12   Callbacks and queues. Similar to the previous example, except that queues are introduced on the server side to ensure better decoupling on the server side.

3.4   Interface Versus Payload Semantics

Typically, an interaction between a client and a server (or a sender and a receiver) results in the execution of a transaction (or some other activity) on the receiving end. In order to determine the type of transaction or activity that was requested by the caller (or sender), it is necessary to specify the operation. This is normally performed in one of two ways: The requested transaction/activity can be encoded in the operation signature of the server component's interface, or it can be embedded in the message itself.

In the first case, the requested transaction (or other kind of activity) is defined by using self-descriptive function names such as `saveCustomer()`, `retrieveCustomer()`, or `transferMoney()`. RPC-style interfaces provide this type of semantically rich interface, which we refer to as *interface semantics* (see Figure 3-13).

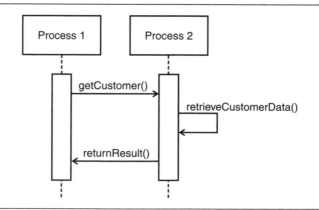

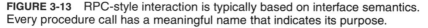

FIGURE 3-13   RPC-style interaction is typically based on interface semantics. Every procedure call has a meaningful name that indicates its purpose.

In the second case, the requested transaction is embedded directly into the message (see Figure 3-14). This can be done as part of the message header (if the MOM provides such a field as part of the message header data structure), or as part of the application specific payload. We refer to this as *payload semantics*.

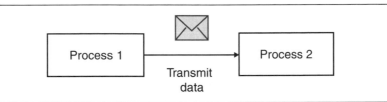

FIGURE 3-14   The name of a remote call with payload semantics has no functional meaning in its own right. The remote functionality required is encoded in the message that is sent. The receiver typically has to determine the function name and the dispatch message to the associated business function.

Payload semantics is widely used in the context of MOMs that provide APIs with functions such as `MQGET()`/`MQPUT()` or `sendMessage()`/`onMessage()`/`receiveMessage()` for the clients and servers to communicate with each other. The semantics of these functions is purely technical (see Figure 3-15).

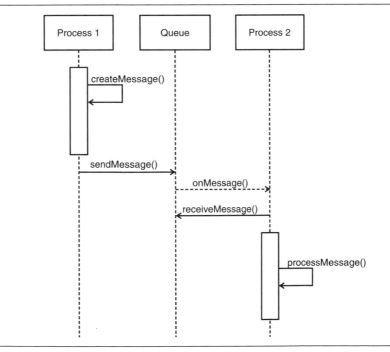

FIGURE 3-15   MOM is generally based on payload semantics. Functions such as `sendMessage()` and `processMessage()` are purely technical, without any business semantics.

Interface semantics provide users with well-defined interfaces that are intuitive and easy to understand. Changes to these interfaces require modifications to all applications that depend on the particular interface, even if they do not depend on the operation or argument that was added or changed. Payload semantics, on the other hand, result in systems where changes to message formats can have a potentially lesser impact on the different components of the system. New functionality can easily be added to a system by creating new messages types. Consumers that are not dependent on the new messages types remain unaltered. Thus, payload semantics results in a weaker coupling at the type level.

The choice of *interface semantics* versus *payload semantics* is not an obvious one, as each approach has its pros and cons. Strongly typed languages, such as Java, limit the flexibility of the programmer by applying strict type checking at compile time. Almost all dependencies caused by the change of a type in the system can be discovered at compile time, thus significantly reducing the number of runtime errors. Weakly typed languages, such as TCL, offer much more flexible data manipulation, often based on string manipulation. These types of languages are generally used for scripting, especially in Web environments, where fast results are required.

However, the application of interface semantics and payload semantics cannot be viewed in black-and-white terms. While RPCs are not restricted to pure functional call semantics, neither are MOMs limited to payload semantics. This can be illustrated with one insightful example. Consider an RPC call such as transferMoney(). The transmitted data can significantly contribute to the determination of the code that is executed:

```
String transferMoney (amount: decimal; cur, accFrom, accTo: String);
{
   switch (cur)
   case 'EUR':
      handleEurTransfer (amount, accFrom, accTo);
   case 'GBP':
      handleGbpTransfer (amount, accFrom, accTo);
   case 'USD':
      handleUsdTransfer (amount, accFrom, accTo);

   . . .

}
```

Going one step further, it is possible to remove all interface semantics from an RPC-style interface. In the following example, a service supports exactly one function, executeService(). This function has only one parameter, a plain string. This string encodes all functional parameters and the requested functionality:

```
String executeService (message: String);
{
   int i = determineFunctionNumber (message);
```

```
switch (i)
   case 1:
      handleCase1 (message);
   case 2:
      handleCase2 (message);
   case 3:
      handleCase3 (message);
      . . .
}
```

3.4.1 DOCUMENT-CENTRIC MESSAGES

With the emergence of self-descriptive data structures such as XML, an approach to handling message types referred to as *document-centric* has become popular. Document-centric messages are semantically rich messages where the operation name, its parameters, and the return type are self-descriptive. However, the passed parameters and returned object can be extremely flexible and can include any number of optional parameters. SOAP (Simple Object Access Protocol) is a technology that is particularly suitable for this type of solution. As long as the underlying XML Schemas impose only loose constraints on the document structure, the parameters can be extended in any manner required without breaking compatibility with previous software versions. Consider the following example that describes the booking of a flight. It is straightforward to enhance the protocol with additional parameters, such as the time of day of the flight, the date and time of arrival, or the verbose names of the airports. As long as these fields are not required, the previous version of the protocol, in addition to all software that relies on that version, remains totally valid. Because this type of communication includes a structured document in both reply and response, it is called document-driven communication:

```
<SOAP-ENV:Envelope xmlns:SOAP-ENC="http://schemas.xmlsoap.org/
soap/encoding/" xmlns:SOAP-ENV="http://schemas.xmlsoap.org/
soap/envelope/" xmlns:xsd="http://www.w3.org/2001/XMLSchema"
xmlns:xsi="http://www.w3.org/2001/XMLSchema-instance">
   <SOAP-ENV:Body>
      <ns1:bookFlight xmlns:ns1="http://www.openuri.org/">
         <ns1:inbound>
            <ns1:flightNumber>LH400</ns1:flightNumber>
            <ns1:flightDate>2003-11-08</ns1:flightDate>
            <ns1:isConfirmed>false</ns1:isConfirmed>
         </ns1:inbound>
         <ns1:outbound>
            <ns1:flightNumber>LH401</ns1:flightNumber>
            <ns1:flightDate>2003-11-17</ns1:flightDate>
            <ns1:isConfirmed>false</ns1:isConfirmed>
         </ns1:outbound>
         <ns1:passenger>
```

```
        <ns1:Passenger>
            <ns1:firstName>Karl</ns1:firstName>
            <ns1:lastName>Banke</ns1:lastName>
            <ns1:birthday>1970-08-05</ns1:birthday>
        </ns1:Passenger>
      </ns1:passenger>
    </ns1:bookFlight>
  </SOAP-ENV:Body>
</SOAP-ENV:Envelope>
```

3.5   Tight Versus Loose Coupling

Recently, a lot of attention has focused on comparisons between *loose coupling* and *tight coupling* approaches to application interactions. On the technology side, this has mainly been driven by the potential of Web services to dynamically discover and bind to other services, such as through UDDI (Universal Description, Discovery and Integration). On the business side, this has been driven by the growing need of enterprises to increase flexibility with respect to changes in their own business processes and the ways in which they interact with partner companies.

Traditionally, business processes have been designed within the boundaries of an enterprise, or even within the different business units of the enterprise. These activities were managed with the help of detailed, real-time information. Processes that span multiple business units or enterprises typically have to deal with a very different set of requirements, needing a higher degree of flexibility. In these kinds of scenarios, one sees a much higher degree of uncertainty, a much more frequent change in terms of participants and their roles, and a constant evolution of the types of interactions required.

There appears to be a consensus that for these types of "in-flux" situations to operate, a loosely coupled architecture is required because loose coupling is seen as helping to reduce the overall complexity and dependencies. Using loose coupling makes the application landscape more agile, enables quicker change, and reduces risk. In addition, system maintenance becomes much easier. Loose coupling becomes particularly important in the B2B world, where business entities must be able to interact independently. The relationships between business partners often change rapidly—alliances are settled and cancelled, and business processes between trading partners are adopted to new market requirements. Two companies that are partners in one market might be competitors in another market. Therefore, it is essential that the underlying IT infrastructure reflect this need for flexibility and independence. Ideally, no business relationship should impact another—new business relationships should be able to be established without any effect on existing ones. Functionality that is offered to one business partner might not necessarily be available to others. A change that is relevant for one business partner should have no impact on other partners. One trading partner may not cause another to block while waiting for a synchronous response, nor may one IT system depend on the technical availability of the IT system of a business partner.

The term *coupling* refers to the act of joining things together, such as the links of a chain. In the software world, *coupling* typically refers to the degree to which software components depend upon each other. However, the remaining question is: "*What are these dependencies, and to what degree can one apply the properties of* tight *and* loose*?*" Software coupling can happen on many different levels. One of the first issues is to differentiate between build time (compile time) dependencies and runtime dependencies. However, this is typically only sufficient when looking at monolithic applications. In a distributed environment, we believe that in order to determine the degree of coupling in a system, one needs to look at different levels. Table 3-1 provides an overview of these levels and shows how they relate to the tight versus loose coupling debate.

Table 3-1 Tight Versus Loose Coupling

Level	Tight Coupling	Loose Coupling
Physical coupling	Direct physical link required	Physical intermediary
Communication style	Synchronous	Asynchronous
Type system	Strong type system (e.g., interface semantics)	Weak type system (e.g., payload semantics)
Interaction pattern	OO-style navigation of complex object trees	Data-centric, self-contained messages
Control of process logic	Central control of process logic	Distributed logic components
Service discovery and binding	Statically bound services	Dynamically bound services
Platform dependencies	Strong OS and programming language dependencies	OS- and programming language independent

In the following, we will examine the items in Table 3-1 in detail.

For distributed systems, the way that remote components are connected is possibly the most obvious technical factor when looking at the problem of "coupling." A physical intermediary enables loose coupling on this level. Therefore, MOM systems are loosely coupled on the physical level, with message queues acting as an intermediary, decoupling senders and receivers of messages. RPC-style applications are tightly coupled on this level because clients and servers interact directly with each other—clients require servers to be alive and accessible in order to interact with them.

The impact of synchronous versus asynchronous communication on the level of coupling is often closely related to the physical linking of the distributed components, as described previously. Asynchronous communication is generally associated with loose coupling. However, this assumes that the underlying middleware is capable of supporting the asynchronous communication in a loosely coupled manner. Assume a one-way RPC call: There is still a notion of tight coupling here, even if the client does not wait for the reply of the server—the client will only be able to send the one-way request to the server if it is directly connected and if the server is up and running. This is a good example for the varying degrees of "coupledness"—asynchronous communication through a proper MOM is more loosely coupled than asynchronous one-way RPC calls.

Looking at the type system of a distributed application as the next level of "coupledness," we find that the stronger the type system, the stronger the dependencies between the different components of the system. This is true not only during the application development phase, but also (and perhaps more importantly) when changing or reconfiguring the running system. Earlier, we differentiated between *interface semantics* and *payload semantics*. Interface semantics provide an explicit interface and operation names and also strongly typed arguments. Effectively, this means components are tightly coupled together on this level because every change of an interface ripples through the entire application, as far as dependent components are concerned. The benefit is that we discover the affected parts of the application that need to be adapted to reflect these changes at compile time, thus avoiding runtime exceptions due to incompatible message formats. *Payload semantics,* on the other hand, enable a looser coupling of components because message formats are generally more flexible. In some cases, message format validation might be applied, such as through XML Schema validation. However, this requires efficient management of the up-to-date schema definitions between participants. Notice that the problems with changes to message formats is not eliminated by employing payload semantics: One must still know those parts of the system that are affected by changes in order to ensure that they can act appropriately on the new format. In many cases, this means that the problem has simply moved from build time to runtime.

Another important factor to examine is the interaction patterns of the distributed components. For example, an ORB-based system will typically impose an OO-style navigation of complex object trees. The client has to understand not only the logic of each individual object, but also the way to navigate across objects, again resulting in a fairly tight coupling. Given that RPC-style interfaces do not enable such complex navigation, the degree of coupling is lower when compared to a distributed object system. MOM-based systems typically impose a much simpler interaction model, where often a single queue is sufficient as an entry point for clients, and all input for server-side transactions is provided in a single message.

Related to this discussion is the question of whether we generally assume that the system is structured around RPC-style services or around queues and topics. Generally, topics and queues provide more flexibility for changing the system at runtime by rearranging the configuration of queues and how they are related to each other. The powerful configuration management of most MOM systems greatly increase the "looseness" of the coupling between system components.

Another important factor is the ownership or control of process logic. If processes are managed centrally, this results in tight coupling between the different sub-processes and transactions. For example, database mechanisms might be used for ensuring referential integrity and general consistency of the data owned by the different sub-processes. This is often the case, for example, with large, monolithic ERP (Enterprise Resource Planning) systems. If business processes are highly distributed, as in a B2B environment, the different sub-processes and transactions are generally more independent of each other, or more loosely coupled, in the context of our current discussion. Often, this means that one must accept the fact that there is no globally defined consistent process state. Similarly, the data owned by the different participants might not always be consistent—one system might have already cancelled an order for which another system still owns an invoice.

Finally, the way in which participants in the system locate each other has a great impact on the level of coupling in the system. Statically bound services yield very tight coupling, whereas dynamically bound services yield loose coupling. Looking up services in a naming or directory server reduces the tightness with which components are tied together, although it still requires the client to know the exact name of the service to which it wants to bind. Services such as UDDI enable a more flexible location of services, using constraints such as "*Find me the next printer on the second floor.*" Notice that dynamic service discovery as provided by UDDI for Web Services is not a new concept; it has previously been provided by other standards such as the CORBA Naming Service. Notice also that past experience has shown that the number of applications requiring completely dynamic service discovery has been fairly limited.

When making architectural decisions, one must carefully analyze the advantages and disadvantages of the level of coupling. Generally speaking, OLTP-style (online transaction processing) applications, as they are found throughout large enterprises, do not normally require a high degree of loose coupling—these applications are tightly coupled by their nature. When leaving the scope of a single enterprise or single business unit, especially in B2B environments, loose coupling is often the only solution. However, in most cases, the increased flexibility achieved through loose coupling comes at a price, due to the increased complexity of the system. Additional efforts for development and higher skills are required to apply the more sophisticated concepts of loosely coupled systems. Furthermore, costly products such as queuing systems are required. However, loose coupling will pay off in the long term if the coupled systems must be rearranged quite frequently.

3.6 Conclusion

Today's enterprise application landscapes are characterized by a variety of different technologies and concepts for distribution. On one hand, this variety arises within the enterprise organization itself for historical reasons, personal preferences of different people, and the dynamics of acquisitions and mergers. As a matter of fact, many redundant concepts exist within the same organizational unit. On the other hand, complementary concepts and technologies also exist. Due to the requirements of different types of distribution problems that coexist in one corporation, different solutions arise as well.

A modern architecture must be able to embrace all these technologies and concepts. Heterogeneity—including heterogeneity of middleware—must be understood as a fundamental fact that cannot be fought but instead must be managed. Furthermore, an architecture must accommodate frequent changes of the underlying distribution infrastructure. As a matter of fact, the lifecycles of today's infrastructure products are largely incompatible with the lifecycles of enterprise applications. Thus, you must protect the assets of an existing application landscape and simultaneously take advantage of the latest infrastructure products.

In this chapter, we have discussed the necessity of carefully choosing the right approach to integrate two distributed software components. Among other issues, you must decide on the appropriate communication infrastructure, synchrony, call semantics, usage of an intermediary, and object-oriented versus data-centric interfaces. All these decisions impact the coupling of the two systems.

References

Braswell, Byron, George Forshay, and Juan Manuel Martinez. *IBM Web-to-Host Integration Solutions*, 4th ed. IBM Redbook SG24-5237-03, 2002. [Bras2002]

Long, Rick, Jouko Jäntti, Robert Hain, Niel Kenyon, Martin Owens, and André Schoeman. *IMS e-business Connect Using the IMS Connectors*. IBM Redbook SG24-5427-00, 1999. [Lon1999]

Tanenbaum, Andrew S. *Computer Networks*, 4th ed. Prentice-Hall, 2003. [Tan2003]

Tanenbaum, Andrew S. and Maarten van Steen. *Distributed Systems: Principles and Paradigms*. Prentice-Hall, 2002. [Tan2002]

Coulouris, George, J. Dollimore, and T. Kindberg. *Distributed Systems Concepts and Design,* 3rd ed. Addison-Wesley, 2001. [Cou2001]

Reisig, Wolfgang. *A Primer in Petri Net Design*. New York: Springer Compass International, 1992. [Rei1992]

URLs

http://www.rfc-editor.org

http://www.omg.org

http://www.microsoft.com/com

http://java.sun.com/j2ee

http://www.bea.com

PART I

ARCHITECTURAL ROADMAP

The first part of this book describes the architectural roadmap to the service-enabled enterprise. We define the term Service-Oriented Architecture (SOA), provide a classification of service types, describe the different expansion stages of a SOA, show how to address key issues such as business processes and transactions, outline a service bus infrastructure, and describe how to use the different SOA concepts in real-world applications.

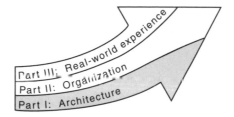

4

Service-Oriented Architectures

This chapter provides a definition of Service-Oriented Architecture and introduces its key concepts—namely, application frontend, service, service repository, and service bus. It lays the conceptual foundation for a more in-depth discussion about the ways in which SOAs help address the specific issues of enterprise applications that are covered in Chapter 5, "Services as Building Blocks," and Chapter 6, "The Architectural Roadmap."

Section 4.1 gives a general definition of the term *architecture* as we use it throughout this book. Section 4.2 defines the term *Service-Oriented Architecture*. Section 4.3 describes elements of a Service-Oriented Architecture, such as application frontends, services, the service repository, and the service bus in detail.

4.1 What Is a Software Architecture?

The literature in our field provides many different definitions of software architecture. Booch, Rumbaugh, and Jacobson [BRJ99] claim that *"An architecture is the set of significant decisions about the organization of a software system . . ."* Brass, Clements, and Kazman define software architecture in [BCK03]: *"The software architecture of a program or computing system is the structure or structures of the system, which comprise software elements, the externally visible properties of those elements, and the relationships among them."* The IEEE Standard 610.12-1990 claims that *"Architecture is the organizational structure of a system."* Fowler characterizes architecture in [Fow02]: *"'Architecture' is a term that lots of people try to define, with little agreement. There are two common elements: One is the highest-level breakdown of a system into its parts; the other, decisions that are hard to change."* You can find even more definitions at http://www.sei.cmu.edu/architecture/definitions.html.

For our purposes, we define software architecture in the sidebar, "Definition of Software Architecture."

> **Definition of Software Architecture**
>
> A software architecture is a set of statements that describes software components and assigns the functionality of the system to these components. It describes the technical structure, constraints, and characteristics of the components and the interfaces between them. The architecture is the blueprint for the system and therefore the implicit high-level plan for its construction.

In this book, we will also use the terms *application* and *application landscape*. An application is a set of software components that serves a distinctive purpose, and an application landscape is the sum of all applications of an organization. Ideally, all applications of an application landscape comply with a single architectural blueprint. However, in practice, they usually don't. We also casually use one particular phrase: *"Software component X belongs to architecture Y."* More precisely, this phrase means: *"Software component X belongs to an application landscape which is designed according to an architecture Y."*

4.2   What Is a Service-Oriented Architecture?

Now we introduce the basic concepts of SOAs as we use them in the remainder of this book. As we previously emphasized, this book focuses on enterprise architectures and their specific characteristics. Consequently, we will also discuss the specific characteristics of SOAs.

As we mentioned earlier, an SOA is based on four key abstractions: *application frontend, service, service repository,* and *service bus* (see Figure 4-1). Although the application frontend is the owner of the business process, services provide business functionality that the application frontends and other services can use. A service consists of an implementation that provides business logic and data, a service contract that specifies the functionality, usage, and constraints for a client[1] of the service, and a service interface that physically exposes the functionality. The service repository stores the service contracts of the individual services of an SOA, and the service bus interconnects the application frontends and services.

---

[1] A client can either be an application frontend or another service.

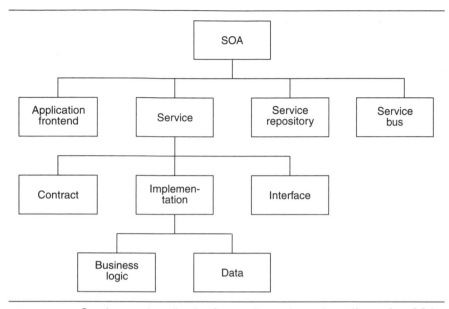

FIGURE 4-1 Services and application frontends are the major artifacts of an SOA. In addition, we also have a service repository and service bus.

> **Definition of Service-Oriented Architecture**
>
> A Service-Oriented Architecture (SOA) is a software architecture that is based on the key concepts of an application frontend, service, service repository, and service bus. A service consists of a contract, one or more interfaces, and an implementation.

The whole concept of an SOA focuses on the definition of a business infrastructure. When we use the term "service," we have in mind a business service such as making airline reservations or getting access to a company's customer database. These services provide business operations such as *get reservation, cancel booking,* or *get customer profile.* Unlike business services, technical infrastructure services, such as a persistency service or a transaction service, provide operations such as *begin transaction, update data,* or *open cursor.* Although this kind of technical functionality is very useful when it comes to implementing a business operation, it has little strategic relevance from the SOA point of view. More generally, technology must not have any impact on the high-level structure of the application landscape or cause dependencies between components. Actually, the SOA must decouple business applications from technical services and make the enterprise independent of a specific technical implementation or infrastructure.

The application frontends are the active elements of the SOA, delivering the value of the SOA to the end users. Nevertheless, you must always take into account that the services provide structure to the SOA. Although the services can often remain unaltered, the application frontends are subject to change, as are the business processes of the enterprises. Consequently, the lifecycle of application frontends is much shorter than the lifecycle of the underlying services. This is why we regard services as the primary entities of strategic importance in an SOA (see Figure 4-2).

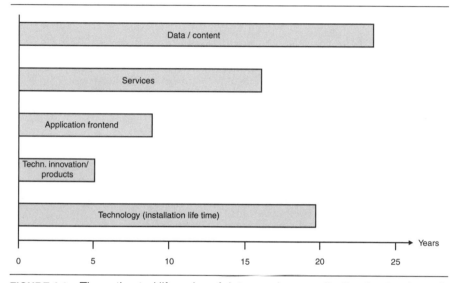

FIGURE 4-2   The estimated lifecycles of data, services, application frontends, and technologies are different.

4.3   Elements of a Service-Oriented Architecture

In this section, we take a closer look at the key elements of the SOA, including the application frontend, services, the service repository, and the service bus.

4.3.1   APPLICATION FRONTENDS

Application frontends are the active players of an SOA. They initiate and control all activity of the enterprise systems. There are different types of application frontends. An application frontend with a graphical user interface, such as a Web application or a rich client that interacts directly with end users, is the most obvious example. However, application frontends do not necessarily have to interact directly with end users. Batch programs or long-living processes that invoke functionality periodically or as a result of specific events are also valid examples of application frontends.

Nevertheless, it is entirely possible that an application frontend delegates much of its responsibility for a business process to one or more services.

Ultimately, however, it is always an application frontend that initiates a business process and receives the results.

Application frontends are similar to the upper layers of traditional multi-layer applications. Although you might expect that services more closely resemble the lower layers, this is not the case. The following chapters demonstrate that services have a different structure, which is characterized by vertical slicing.

4.3.2 SERVICES

A service is a software component of distinctive functional meaning that typically encapsulates a high-level business concept. It consists of several parts (see Figure 4-3).

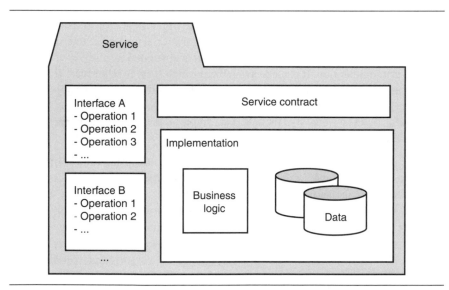

FIGURE 4-3   A service consists of both data and business logic along with interfaces and their descriptions.

Contract. The service contract provides an informal specification of the purpose, functionality, constraints, and usage of the service. The form of this specification can vary, depending on the type of service. One non-mandatory element of the service contract is a formal interface definition based on languages such as IDL or WSDL. Although it is not mandatory, a formal service interface definition adds a significant benefit: It provides further abstraction and independence of technology, including programming language, middleware, network protocol, and runtime environment. However, it is important to understand that the service contract provides more information than a formal specification. The contract can impose detailed semantics on the functionality and parameters that is not subject to IDL or WSDL specifications. In reality, many projects must cope with services that cannot provide formal service interface descriptions.[2] In these cases, the service can deliver access libraries or a detailed technical description at the network protocol level. However, it is important to understand that every service requires a service contract—particularly if no formal description based on a standard such as WSDL or IDL is available.

Interface. The functionality of the service is exposed by the service interface to clients that are connected to the service using a network. Although the description of the interface is part of the service contract, the physical implementation of the interface consists of service stubs, which are incorporated into the clients[3] of a service and dispatcher.

Implementation. The service implementation physically provides the required business logic and appropriate data. It is the technical realization that fulfills the service contract. The service implementation consists of one or more artifacts such as programs, configuration data, and databases.

Business logic. The business logic that is encapsulated by a service is part of its implementation. It is made available through service interfaces. However, programming against interfaces is desirable, whether or not one applies a service-oriented approach.

Data. A service can also include data. In particular, this is the purpose of a data-centric service (see Chapter 5).

As previously discussed, services are not just the encapsulation of some code of the former lower layers of applications. Every service is an entity of distinctive functional meaning that typically encapsulates a high-level business entity. Services impose a strong vertical slicing of the application that defines the coarse-grained structure of the whole system, similarly to component-oriented software design. Therefore, from the client perspective, a service is a black box entity.

4.3.3 SERVICE REPOSITORY

A service repository provides facilities to discover services and acquire all information to use the services, particularly if these services must be discovered outside the functional and temporal scope of the project that created them. Although much of the required information is already part of the service contract, the service repository can provide additional information, such as physical location,

---

[2] Notice that the key task of a project aiming to introduce SOAs at the enterprise level is often not to implement new business functionality, but rather to identify suitable existing application modules and components and wrap them with service interfaces with the appropriate level of functionality and granularity, thus making them available as services in an easier-to-use and better documented manner.

[3] Application frontends or other services.

information about the provider, contact persons, usage fees, technical constraints, security issues, and available service levels.

It should be noted that we focus on service repositories that are mainly used for purposes within the boundaries of a single enterprise. Repositories that are used for cross-enterprise service integration typically have different requirements—in particular, those repositories that are made public through the Internet. These requirements can comprise legal issues (terms and conditions of usage), style of presentation, security, user registration, service subscription, billing, and versioning.

Obviously, a service repository is a very useful element of an SOA. Although you can build an SOA and achieve many of its benefits without establishing a service repository, a repository is indispensable in the long term. An architecture can cope without a repository if the scope of a service is just one project, if it has very few services, or if all projects are staffed with the same team members. In reality, though, most enterprise scenarios are characterized by many concurrent projects, changing teams, and a variety of services.

A service repository can be arbitrarily simple; at one extreme, no technology might be required. A batch of printed service contracts located in an office and accessible by all projects is already a valid service repository. However, better ways exist to provide this information while retaining the simplicity of the repository. Often, you'll find a type of proprietary database that contains some formalized administrative data and a more or less formal service contract for every version of a service.

In some cases, companies have developed their own tools that automatically generate the service description from the formal service definitions (e.g., an HTML generator that takes WSDL as input, similar to a JavaDoc generator). This is particularly useful if the formal service definition is annotated with additional information about the service. Notice that this information is typically very different from the meta-information provided for low-level APIs, such as Java classes. This is due to the different roles that service definitions play in an SOA. Services typically are more coarse-grained, self-contained, and capable of supporting different usage patterns. In particular, services are typically not linked as code libraries but are bound to at runtime. All the preceding results in different documentation requirements. The following are examples of information that should be contained in an enterprise-wide service repository:

- Service, operation, and arguments signatures, such as in the form of WSDL and XML Schema definitions.
- Service owner. In an Enterprise SOA, owners can operate at the business level (responsible for questions and change requests on the functional level), development level (responsible for technical questions and change requests), and operations level (responsible for questions regarding the best ways to link to a service, or operational problems).
- Access rights, such as information about access control lists and the underlying security mechanism, or a description of the process that must

be followed within the enterprise so that a new system can utilize a particular service.

- Information about the intended performance and scalability of the service, including average response times, and potential throughput limitations. This can be summarized as part of a generic SLA (Service Level Agreement) template.
- Transactional properties of the service and its individual operations. This includes information on the read/write/update characteristics, whether the operation is idempotent, and associated compensation logic (see Chapter 8, "Process Integrity," for more details).

Manage Your Service Repository Centrally

To provide a service repository with high quality services, consider setting up an architecture board. The architecture board's responsibility is to perform constant maintenance, monitoring, and coordination from a central location. It must manage the repository and carefully review the service entries it contains. This includes the fundamental design of the service itself, as well as its description in the service repository. Consequently, the architecture board must be involved from the outset of the development of new services in order to coordinate the service specification across different projects and business units, and it must ensure that a good compromise between ease of implementation, usability, and reusability can be achieved.

It is important to distinguish between development time and runtime binding of services. Binding refers to the way in which service definitions and service instances are located, incorporated into the client application, and finally bound to at the network level.

4.3.3.1 *Development-Time Binding.* If services are discovered and bound to at development time, the signatures of the service operations are known in advance, as well as the service protocol and the physical location of the service (or at least the exact name of the service in a directory service). Figure 4-4 describes a process in which services are bound to at development time.

Although development time binding is quite a simple model, it is sufficient for most purposes. It enables projects to identify functionality that has been created by former projects and to reuse these services.

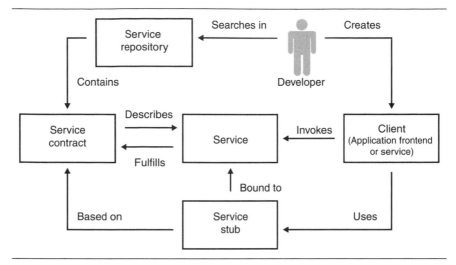

FIGURE 4-4 Development time discovery imposes a fairly simple model. The developer is responsible for locating all required information from the service repository in order to create a client that interacts correctly with the service instance.

4.3.3.2 *Runtime Binding.*

Runtime binding is far more complex than development time binding. One can differentiate between different levels of runtime binding:

Runtime service lookup by name. This is the most straightforward case, and it is also the most commonly used means of dynamically binding to services: The service definition is known at development time, and the client logic is developed accordingly. The client is enabled to dynamically bind to different service instances by looking up services with specific names in a directory. For example, a client application looks up printing services with different names, depending on the printer name selected by the user.

Runtime service lookup by properties. This is similar to the preceding, except that services are discovered by properties, not by name. For example, a printing service can search a service repository for three different predefined printing service interfaces it understands, together with other properties such as location of the printer (`"FLOOR == 2"`) and document formats that the printer is able to print (`"DOCTYPE == PostScript"`).

Runtime service discovery based on reflection. In the final case, the actual specification of the service definition is not known at development time. Assume that a client discovers a service with the right properties (`"FLOOR == 2 AND DOCTYPE == PostScript"`) but with an unknown printing service interface. In this case, some kind of reflection mechanism[4] must be implemented at the client side, which enables the client to dynamically discover the semantics of the service and the format of valid requests. This type of service discovery is the most complex and least widely used because it requires very complex logic to dynamically interpret the semantics of unknown service interfaces.[5]

Runtime service binding that goes beyond the complexity of dynamic service lookup by properties with predefined service interfaces is very rare and is limited to very few application domains. A rare example for a problem domain that really requires highly dynamic service binding is in the wireless world, such as a Bluetooth application: Bluetooth clients dynamically discover services based on location and other properties. But again, even in this scenario, Bluetooth clients typically support a limited set of predefined services.

> ### Make Service Binding as Simple as Possible
>
> Always aim to make service binding as simple as possible because the level of complexity and risk increases exponentially with the level of dynamics in the service binding process. Service lookup by name with predefined service interfaces represents the best trade-off between flexibility and implementation complexity in the majority of cases.

4.3.4 SERVICE BUS

A service bus connects all participants of an SOA—services and application frontends—with each other. If two participants need to communicate—for example, if an application frontend needs to invoke some functionality of a basic service—the service bus makes it happen. In this respect, the service bus is similar to the concept of a software bus as it is defined in the context of CORBA. However, significant differences exist between these concepts. Most importantly, the service bus is not necessarily composed of a single technology, but rather comprises a variety of products and concepts.

An in-depth discussion of the service bus is found in Chapter 9, "Infrastructure of a Service Bus." For the time being, it will suffice to highlight the following characteristics of a service bus:

---

[4] Similar to mechanisms that are used in many object-oriented programming languages, such as Java's reflection mechanism.

[5] Notice that there is a case in between, where systems have to cope with many similar yet different message types, such as 12 different formats of a customer data record. A number of existing EAI tools (e.g., in Microsoft Biztalk Server) enable the user to graphically match fields in different data structures, providing runtime translation between these incompatible data formats. However, these mappings between data structures are provided at development time and are not dynamically determined by the system at runtime.

Connectivity. The primary purpose of the service bus is to interconnect the participants of an SOA. It provides facilities that enable the participants of an SOA—application frontends and services—to invoke the functionality of services.

Heterogeneity of technology. The service bus must embrace a variety of different technologies. The reality of enterprises is characterized by heterogeneous technologies. Consequently, the service bus must be able to connect participants that are based on different programming languages, operating systems, or runtime environments. Furthermore, you will usually find a multitude of middleware products and communication protocols in the enterprise, and all this must be supported by the service bus.

Heterogeneity of communication concepts. Similar to the heterogeneity of technologies, the service bus must also embrace a variety of different communication concepts. Due to the divergent requirements of different applications, the service bus must enable different communication modes. Obviously, you must at least have facilities for synchronous and asynchronous communication.

Technical "services." Although the purpose of the service bus is primarily communication, it must also provide technical services such as logging, auditing, security, message transformation, or transactions.

4.4 Conclusion

In this chapter, we introduced the key concepts of Service-Oriented Architecture.

We began our discussion with a general definition of software architecture: *". . . set of statements that describe software components and assigns the functionality of the system to these components. It describes the technical structure, constraints, and characteristics of the components and the interfaces between them . . ."* The definition of an SOA is based on this definition. It states that *"A Service-Oriented Architecture (SOA) is a software architecture that is based on the key concepts application frontend, service, service repository, and service bus."*

References

Bass, Len, Paul Clements, and Rick Kazman. *Software Architecture in Practice.* Addision-Wesley, 2003. [BCK03]

Booch, Grady, James Rumbaugh, and Ivar Jacobson. *Unified Modeling Language User Guide.* Addision-Wesley, 1999. [BRJ99]

Fowler, Martin. *Patterns of Enterprise Application Architecture.* Addision-Wesley, 2002. [Fow02]

URLs

http://www.sei.cmu.edu/architecture/definitions.html

5

Services as Building Blocks

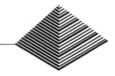

The focus of a Service-Oriented Architecture is on the functional infrastructure and its business services, not the technical infrastructure and its technical services. A business-oriented service in an SOA is typically concerned with one major aspect of the business, be it a business entity, a business function, or a business process. This chapter provides an in-depth discussion of the different types of services.

In Section 5.1, we establish a classification that distinguishes between basic, process-centric, intermediary, and public enterprise services, and we discuss the characteristics of these different classes of services and what this means from a design, implementation, and project management point of view. These service types have significantly different characteristics with respect to reusability, maintainability, scalability, and performance; therefore, it's crucial to understand them in order to implement them efficiently.

Section 5.2 introduces SOA layers for design at the application landscape level. As we will demonstrate, SOA layers are largely independent of the system architecture's tiers, which is a major benefit of the SOA approach.

5.1 Service Types

An important feature of a software architecture is that it breaks down the overall structure of a software system into smaller components. These components are intended to be flexible building blocks.

5.1.1 MOTIVATION

Being able to classify service types is a precondition for the effective design of SOAs.

Common language. Being able to talk about the specific nature of different services at an abstract level will enable the different stakeholders in an SOA project—business analysts, architects, designers, managers, and programmers—to communicate their ideas and concerns more effectively.

Vertical slicing. Classifying services according to their specific nature is a prerequisite to breaking down a complex application landscape into manageable parts. In an SOA, this will naturally lead to a "vertical slicing," which is an important part of SOA-centric project management (see Chapter 13, "SOA Project Management").

Effective estimating. The classification of services is extremely helpful when it comes to making proper estimates on their implementation and maintenance cost. These costs depend on the complexity of the implementation, the level of design for reuse, and the frequency of change. These factors will vary by service type.

Separation of code segments with different reuse characteristics. It is good practice to separate code that is supposed to be reused from other code that is unique to a single project. This separation improves the reusability of the "purified" code because it eliminates any project-specific ballast that would complicate reuse. It also helps you avoid fruitless efforts to make project-specific code fit for a reuse that will never happen. Being able to classify your services according to our classification matrix will enable a cleaner separation between reusable and once-off code.

Choosing the right implementation strategy. Different types of services require different implementation strategies. Choosing an unnecessarily complex implementation strategy for a simple service will naturally lead to inefficiencies. For example, services that maintain conversational state can be very helpful in order to simplify clients. The client implementation can be "thin," and the service can provide all the necessary business logic to support even complex business processes. However, stateful services often have a negative impact on the scalability of a distributed system. It is therefore advisable to identify services that inevitably require conversational state and separate them from other services.

Managing change. Finally, it is important to separate business logic that is exposed to a high frequency of change from business logic that is more stable. Doing so can significantly reduce the costs and risks of maintenance. Once again, our classification matrix will be helpful in identifying services with different change characteristics. It should be noted that this is good practice in any development situation, not just for SOAs. However, SOAs are particularly well suited to enable this kind of code separation.

5.1.2 CLASSIFICATION

We differentiate between four classes of services: basic services, intermediary services, process-centric services, and public enterprise services. Figure 5-1 introduces a basic notion we will use throughout this book.

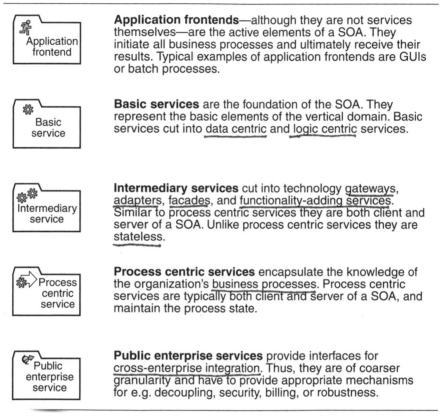

Application frontends—although they are not services themselves—are the active elements of a SOA. They initiate all business processes and ultimately receive their results. Typical examples of application frontends are GUIs or batch processes.

Basic services are the foundation of the SOA. They represent the basic elements of the vertical domain. Basic services cut into data centric and logic centric services.

Intermediary services cut into technology gateways, adapters, facades, and functionality-adding services. Similar to process centric services they are both client and server of a SOA. Unlike process centric services they are stateless.

Process centric services encapsulate the knowledge of the organization's business processes. Process centric services are typically both client and server of a SOA, and maintain the process state.

Public enterprise services provide interfaces for cross-enterprise integration. Thus, they are of coarser granularity and have to provide appropriate mechanisms for e.g. decoupling, security, billing, or robustness.

FIGURE 5-1   We distinguish basic, process-centric, intermediary, and public enterprise services.

In the remainder of this book, we will also use the terms *participant* or *SOA participant*. These terms comprise both application frontends and services. Table 5-1 provides an overview of the different service types and their key characteristics.

Table 5-1   Service types

	Basic Services	Intermediary Services	Process-Centric Services	Public Enterprise Services
Description	Simple data-centric or logic-centric services	Technology gateways, adapters, façades, and functionality-adding services	Encapsulate process logic	Service shared with other enterprises or partner organizations
Implementation Complexity	Low to moderate	Moderate to high	High	Service specific
State Management	Stateless	Stateless	Stateful	Service specific
Reusability	High	Low	Low	High
Frequency of Change	Low	Moderate to high	High	Low
Mandatory Element of SOA	Yes	No	No	No

We now examine the elements of Table 5-1.

5.1.3   BASIC SERVICES

Basic services are the foundation of the SOA. They are pure servers in the SOA and maintain no conversational session state. Basic services cut into data-centric and logic-centric services. However, in practice, there is often a smooth transition from a data-centric service to a logic-centric service. As a matter of fact, many services deal with both data and behavior. Thus, we cannot classify them as either purely data-centric or logic-centric. Fortunately, the mix of data and business logic does not render the SOA unsound. Services that provide both data and business logic can be as agile and reusable as "pure" services. Let's consider, for example, a contract administration service. This service typically stores data sets that represent contracts. In this respect, this service is data-centric. But this service also needs to provide plausibility checks that decide whether any data set represent valid contracts. In the second respect, this service is logic-centric.

5.1.3.1   Data-Centric Services.   It is the purpose of a data-centric service to handle persistent data. This includes the storage and retrieval of data, locking mechanisms, and transaction management. A data-centric service also handles (and utilizes) a physical data storage facility such as a relational database, file system, or tape library. In this respect, a data-centric service behaves similarly to the data access layer of a traditional application. The major difference is the vertical layering of data-centric services. Whereas a traditional data access layer manages data for the entire application, <u>a data-centric service deals with</u> <u>one major business entity only.</u> Furthermore, a data-centric service strictly encapsulates its data entities. Any other service that requires access to this data needs to use the service interface of the corresponding data-centric service (see Figure 5-2). Consequently, <u>an application requires several coordinated data-</u> <u>centric services.</u>

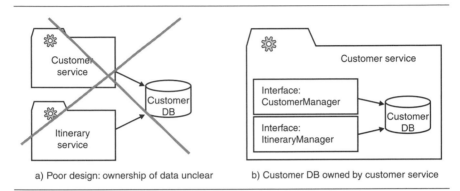

a) Poor design: ownership of data unclear   b) Customer DB owned by customer service

FIGURE 5-2   The SOA strictly defines the ownership of data.

One of the most important tasks of the SOA architect is to identify the relevant business entities that are represented by data-centric services. This task is similar to traditional analysis of the business domain. Methods that are based on entity relationship models (ER) or object oriented-design provide a sound base for the design of services. Notice that these techniques are primarily used for designing the data objects that are either managed by services or that serve as input and output data structures. It is important to understand that <u>cross-service</u> <u>relationships are not allowed,</u> and as such, no cross-service navigation exists as in distributed object technology. This means that the complex value objects managed by the services must be sufficiently self-contained or must contain unique identifiers that enable them to relate one complex value object to another.

Similar to the design of objects or abstract data types, a data-centric service can also encapsulate data behavior. In this respect, SOAs provide many of the benefits of object orientation. However, SOAs do not require object-oriented programming languages for their implementation. The independence of programming languages and the underlying technology is one of the greatest strengths of the SOA approach. In practice, you will often find that programming languages such as COBOL, C, or PL/I and traditional transaction processing monitors are used for the implementation of mission-critical services.

However, the usage of SOAs and data-centric services raises certain issues. Although the vertical layering that is leveraged by SOAs is worthwhile, especially for big applications, benefits such as flexibility and reusability are not without cost. Traditional applications typically access one monolithic data store that has no vertical substructure even if the application is horizontally layered. The functionality of the underlying database or transaction monitor is fully leveraged. Physical transactions often span all parts of the data model and, from the developers' perspective, this is very convenient. There is no need for explicit considerations of data integrity. This is achieved in a transparent fashion by the database or transaction monitor. The downside is a resulting monolithic structure with many implicit and explicit dependencies. The issue of data ownership gains tremendous importance with the vertical layering of applications. Although data ownership has been on the agenda since the very first days of data modeling, it was not really relevant for the implementation of traditional applications due to the monolithic structure of the data access layer. So, this aspect of data modeling was mainly of academic concern and was reflected in naming conventions for database tables and access modules. With the vertical slicing of SOAs, the assignment of entities to data-centric services becomes a design decision with a major impact on many characteristics of the resulting applications. In such a case, explicit efforts are required to overcome these dependencies (see Chapter 8, "Process Integrity").

5.1.3.2 Logic-Centric Services.

Logic-centric services encapsulate algorithms for complex calculations or business rules. In traditional applications, this type of functionality is often encapsulated in libraries and business frameworks.

A very instructive example for a logic-centric service is an insurance product engine. This is a service that encapsulates the knowledge, terms, and conditions of the products of an insurance company. It is capable of computing fees, payments, or refunds and can validate customer applications, suggest new offers, or simulate fee adjustments. This type of functionality is generally part of the back office system for insurance contract/policy management. Consequently, only a back office clerk can provide legally binding information. This is very unfortunate for up-to-date business processes of sales and claims.

Traditionally, people have taken a number of approaches to resolve this problem. The first deals with approximations. In this approach, the front office application provides an approximation of the real value to be validated by the back office using a manual process. Although the front office processes of insurance companies have had to cope with approximations in recent decades, customers nowadays expect accurate data and rapid processing. Particularly for the sales of new contracts, legally binding data that is instantly available is increasingly mandatory.

The second approach is based on duplication of the relevant business logic. On one hand, this approach satisfies the needs of the sales and claims departments, while on the other hand, it can raise many technical issues in traditional environments. Most importantly, you must cope with the deployment of the appropriate functionality and regular updates to potentially thousands of PCs and laptops. You will also encounter heterogeneous technology in front and back office implementations. While back office environments are mostly based on centralized mainframes, the front office systems are usually based on PC technology. This means that every new version of the calculation rules also requires a porting effort before deployment, a process that is both costly and risky.

In the third approach, the users of the front office applications are provided with access to the back office applications. Although this might look like a solution of striking simplicity at first glance, it is not an option for most insurance companies. Many insurance companies have no desire to grant access rights to their back office applications to front office personal—particularly if independent agencies are involved.

A logic-centric service providing the functionality of the product engine would overcome many of the aforementioned challenges. The insurance company could operate this service centrally (see Figure 5-3). Its functionality could also be integrated both with the internal IT systems of the different departments and with business partners. Furthermore, façades (discussed later in this chapter) can be utilized to provide different "views" for different types of users (e.g., independent agencies versus claims department).

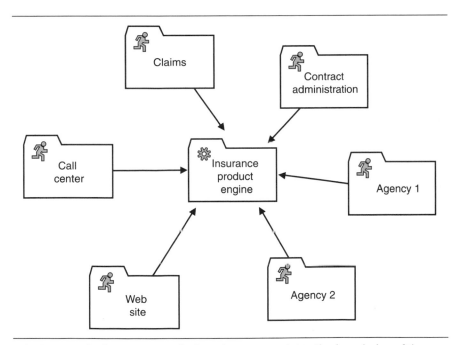

FIGURE 5-3   An insurance product engine encapsulates the knowledge of the insurance company's products.

5.1.4 INTERMEDIARY SERVICES

Intermediary services can be classified as stateless services that bridge technical inconsistencies or design gaps in an architecture. They are both clients and servers in an SOA. They cut into technology gateways, adapters, façades, and functionality-adding services and act as stateless mediators when bridging technological or conceptual gaps. Although many intermediary services seem to be rather technical, we can distinguish them from technical infrastructure services because they provide a business-oriented API, whereas purely technical services provide a technical API. Many intermediary services are highly project-specific.

5.1.4.1 Technology Gateways.   Technology gateways bridge technological gaps (see Figure 5-4). They therefore incorporate two or more technologies for communication or data encoding. Technology gateways act as proxies for their business services and represent the functionality of the underlying services in an environment that is technologically different from the original business service's runtime environment.

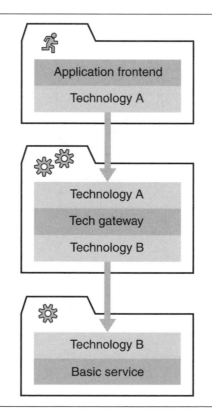

FIGURE 5-4   A technology gateway bridges the gap between different technologies.

They are particularly useful for legacy integration projects where one often encounters the conflicting demands of a need to extend existing legacy application with a requirement not to "contaminate" new components with legacy technology. There are good reasons for both requirements, and a technology gateway can be very useful in such cases.

A typical scenario provides a good illustration of the problem. Assume that a terminal-based legacy application contains valuable business logic. Due to its outdated user interface, a reengineering project is planned for the near future. However, a more urgent project requires the business logic of this application before the reengineering project is completed. The new project is implemented based on a Service-Oriented Architecture and up-to-date technology for distributed computing. In such a case, a technology gateway can act as a mediator between the legacy application and the components of the new project. The new project accesses the technology gateway using a modern technology such as a Web service. The technology gateway translates the Web service requests to terminal data streams in order to communicate with the legacy application. Although it is a monolithic application that serves all requests, it is advisable to distinguish between different services according to service-oriented design principles. It is an irony of enterprise IT that you never know whether the reengineering project of the legacy application will ever take place. However, even if this is the case, the design of the existing services will be very useful. For these services, you only must replace the legacy implementation with the reengineered basic services.

5.1.4.2 Adapters.   An adapter is a special type of intermediary service that maps the signatures and message formats of one service to the requirements of a client.

We can illustrate the concept with an airline booking example. Assume that airline A merges with airline B and that both airlines already have an SOA in place. Apart from other services, both airlines have an established customer service. More than likely, one of the first business requirements after the merger will be to enable access to customer data across the borders of the two former corporations. For the sake of customer service, this feature should be put in place as soon as possible. It is also a very typical requirement that the existing applications of both airlines should remain largely unaltered. A simple solution to this problem is based on two adapters. One maps requests of application 1 to service 2, and the other maps requests of application 2 to service 1.

5.1.4.3 Façades.   The purpose of a façade is to provide a different view (probably aggregated) of one or more existing services (see Figure 5-5). As such, façades often act also as technology gateways and/or adapters.

An in-depth discussion of façades is found in Gamma, et. al. [GHJV95]. Although Gamma describes the encapsulation of object-oriented subsystems, the

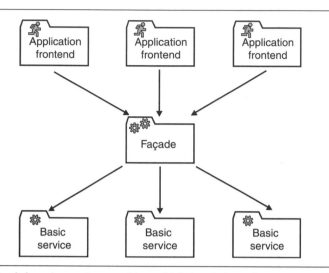

FIGURE 5-5   A façade service provides a high-level view of one or more basic services.

entire concept is widely transferable to SOAs. Gamma defines a façade as *". . . a unified interface to a set of interfaces . . . that makes the subsystem easier to use."*

Façades can be used to provide a specific view of a set of underlying services. As such, a façade can act as a simplifying access layer for a project. It can hide functions that are not needed by the project, aggregate services, or add standard parameters. Furthermore, a façade can hide technical complexity and heterogeneity. Façades can also be very useful in a rather unexpected way—they can serve as a single point of coordination between a project's development team and a maintenance team that is responsible for the SOA.

Contrary to the project-specific view, a common service access layer provides uniform access to the complete functional infrastructure of the organization. Creating one is a very tempting idea because such a layer could provide easy access to the entire functional infrastructure for all projects. You could also add specific value to this layer, such as support for distributed transactions and the capability to hide their complexity from projects. It also would make the development and deployment of services easier because there would be exactly one unified and mandatory process to make the services available. In particular, some current J2EE-based enterprise architectures tend to employ this type of access layer (see Figure 5-6).

In spite of these benefits, the idea of a common service access layer has certain disadvantages. Many similarities exist between service access layers and traditional data access layers. As we have already discussed, a data access layer spans the entire data model of an application. It is very convenient for the development of this particular application, but it results in a monolithic structure that

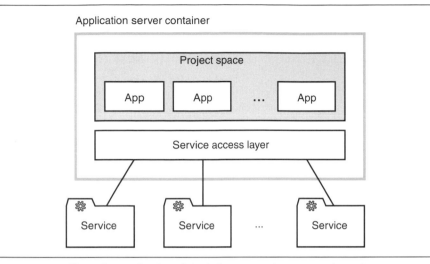

Application server container

FIGURE 5-6 From the project's point of view, a service access layer is a convenient way to access the functional infrastructure of the organization. However, at the enterprise level, these layers have some severe disadvantages. Due to their monolithic nature, they tend to spoil many of the benefits of an SOA.

makes reuse or standalone usage of vertical subcomponents difficult. The technology of the data access layer is also a very strong constraint for the development and for service access layers. Though a common service access layer is very well suited to the development of single projects, it also has many unwanted characteristics at the enterprise level.

Introducing a binding design rule that leverages a common service access layer will probably lead to exceptions, which will outweigh many of the benefits of the access layer. Eventually, these exceptions will establish an uncontrollable shadow architecture that reflects the necessities of real-world heterogeneities. Because the shadow architecture is "officially forbidden," the architecture team cannot openly discuss many important design decisions. This ultimately leads to solutions that are driven by short-term political feasibility rather than by long-term design goals.

A common service access layer impacts both backend and frontend integration. The possible consequences are illustrated in the following example. Assume a large organization has a traditional application landscape based on mainframes, transaction monitors, and COBOL. New applications are required as part of a new J2EE-based strategy. The COBOL application should be reengineered and reused as functional backend services. In this scenario, one generally needs to design vertical slices of previously monolithic mainframe subsystems to create services of reasonable granularity. In practice, the integration of new services becomes a major challenge for the new SOA. As a result of the "common service access layer" design strategy, all aggregations must be performed in the J2EE container at a layer above the service access layer. Although this might look reasonable at first glance, the integration with the Java layer is not acceptable in many cases due to complicated technical designs, maintainability requirements, transaction security issues, development costs, and performance issues. More often, a mainframe-based intermediary service is much more efficient in all these respects. One will also encounter difficulties at the frontend due to different technologies. The enterprise benefits greatly when it can choose the best of breed products from a functional perspective rather than from a technical perspective. For applications based on non–Java-technology such as .NET, the Java layer provides no value. At the same time, it introduces a new element of complexity. While all business logic is implemented in C# and COBOL, the Java layer only passes the calls and parameters from the frontend to the backend—the Java layer adds maintenance overhead without creating any additional business value.

Keep Access Layers Project-Specific

The requirements of projects with regard to access to an underlying functional infrastructure are generally very different. Introducing generic designs leads to a significant overhead in implementation and unwanted dependencies at a technological level. It is therefore highly advisable to design and use access layers for the purpose of a single project only.

5.1.4.4 Functionality-Adding Services. In many cases, you want to add functionality to a service without changing the service itself. In this case, you would establish a functionality-adding service that provides the functionality of the original service and adds the required new characteristics.

There could be several reasons for such a design. If the original service is a third-party product for which there is no source code available, a functionality-adding service can be extremely helpful. The functionality-adding service can also serve as an evolutionary step. If the original service is currently under construction by a different development team, one can decouple both developments with the functionality-adding service. Consequently, a second step is required to reintegrate both development efforts into one service in order to achieve a clean design. The functionality-adding service could also be the first step for reimplementing the original service. This is a particularly good strategy if the original service is of poor quality, if you need the additional functionality as soon as possible, or if you intend to improve the quality of the original service. In this case, you would create a pure façade in the first step. In the second step, you would add the new functionality. Finally, in the third step, you would reengineer all the functionality of the original service and migrate it in small portions to the functionality-adding service until it implements the entire functionality, and then the original service could be decommissioned.

5.1.5 PROCESS-CENTRIC SERVICES

Process-centric services can encapsulate the knowledge of the organization's business processes. They control and maintain their state. From a technical viewpoint, process-centric services are the most sophisticated class of services. They require careful design and deliberate efforts to achieve an efficient implementation. Similar to intermediary services, a process-centric service acts as a client and server simultaneously. A major difference from intermediary services is the fact that process-centric services are stateful because they must maintain the state of a process for their clients.

As with every additional element of an architecture, process-centric services introduce some complexity. However, there are certain benefits:

> **Encapsulate process complexity.** Process-centric services can facilitate application frontends. They can completely hide the complexity of process control from the application. The process-centric service enables different teams to work concurrently on the implementation of presentation and processes. The service interface ultimately leads to a clear encapsulation and facilitates testing and integration. The rich business APIs that process-centric services typically provide facilitates the development of very lean applications.
>
> **Enable load balancing.** Process-centric services enable load balancing naturally. While the application frontend focuses on the presentation, a service can execute the underlying processes on another machine. This division of labor can be particularly helpful in Web applications where user interface responsiveness is a high priority.
>
> **Leverage multi-channel applications.** Multi-channel applications can require process logic that is shared by multiple channels. Features such as channel switching or co-browsing ultimately need an instance that controls the process and that is independent of the channel.
>
> **Separate process logic.** Process logic should be carefully separated from core business logic and dialog control logic. Process-centric services provide appropriate measures to do just that. When process-centric services are in place, you can assign core business logic to basic services, and you can implement dialog control in the application frontend. The separation of process logic is the precondition for efficient business process management (see Chapter 7, "SOA and Business Process Management").

It is noteworthy that properly designing process-centric services and achieving the aforementioned benefits is not an easy task. Many traditional designs suffer from an inaccurate encapsulation of the process logic. You'll rarely find applications with a clear distinction between business logic and process control, and you'll seldom find a clear distinction between process control and dialog control. Individuals must have much experience to design these layers properly. The same holds for process-centric services. Chapter 7 gives an in-depth discussion on this issue and provides valuable design guidelines.

Notice that process-centric services are mostly project-specific. In the airline booking example, the required business logic and data is largely independent of concrete usage. A travel agent requires far more processes than the customer, but both are concerned with the same business entities. Therefore, and despite all obvious benefits, one must bear in mind that process-centric services do not contribute to the functional infrastructure of the SOA due to their marginal reusability.

Process-centric services are not mandatory for an SOA. Because it is highly advisable to keep an architecture as simple as possible, you must carefully balance the trade offs when considering implementing process-centric services. Figures 5-7 and 5-8 illustrate two different approaches. In Figure 5-7, the application frontend makes use of a process-centric service. As an alternative to process-centric service, the application frontend can encapsulate the processes in its process control layer (see Figure 5-8). Process-specific objects or subroutines represent the process definition and control the entire workflow that is initiated by the application. Although this approach appears to be very simple, it can be appropriate for many real world cases.

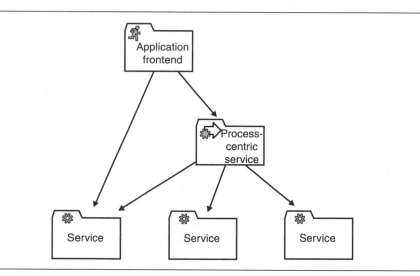

FIGURE 5-7   The application frontend can delegate the entire process control to a process-centric service that executes the process on behalf of the application frontend.

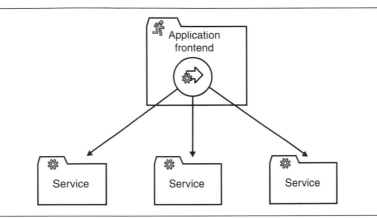

FIGURE 5-8   In many cases, the application frontend controls the entire process. Process objects or subroutines in the process control layer encapsulate the process definition and invoke the actors of the process.

5.1.6   PUBLIC ENTERPRISE SERVICES

Whereas most of the service types described previously are only for use within the boundaries of a particular enterprise, <u>public enterprise services</u> are <u>services that an enterprise offers to partners and customers</u>. For example, a shipping company can offer services that enable large customers to track their shipments as part of their own just-in-time management systems. In another example, a telecom carrier might offer an SMS (Short Messages Service) service, enabling customers to easily add SMS functionality to their systems. Because the consumers of public enterprise services are usually not known in advance and the relationship between consumer and provider is much looser, these services have very specific requirements:

> **Interface at the business document level.** Interfaces at the enterprise level have the granularity of business documents. They have a standalone business meaning and include the complete context that is necessary to be legally unambiguous. Therefore, enterprise services are coarse-grained.
>
> **Decoupling.** Enterprise services need to support decoupling of the business partners. This generally implies asynchronous communication and payload semantics.
>
> **Security.** Crossing enterprise borders raises security issues. Today, many typical SOAs focus on intra-enterprise services, where it is much easier to define a pragmatic security policy. Crossing the organization's borders implies the need for a much higher standard of security mechanisms such as authentication, encryption, and access control.
>
> **Accounting/billing.** While interdepartmental accounting assesses the capability of different departments without the need for cash flow, the billing of

cross-enterprise services implies a real cash flow. It is therefore necessary to put more reliable mechanisms in place.

SLA. The operations of a public enterprise service will probably be regulated by SLAs (Service Level Agreements), which will lead to a different form of treatment for these services. A normal precondition of effective SLA control is service metering.

5.2   Layers on the Enterprise Level

In this chapter, we have already discussed different service types. Now we take a first look at the overall structure of an application landscape and how the services relate to each other.

Traditionally, software layers provide important levels of abstraction. You can assume that layers are sequentially ordered, where layer N is above layer N+1. Code segments within one layer N can use other code segments with the same layer in addition to code segments of the layers N+1. In a distributed environment, the concept of tiers exists, where a tier is a set of contiguous layers that can be deployed separately. Although layers and tiers are extremely useful abstractions for the construction of single applications (or services), neither is suited as an abstraction at the enterprise level. Service-Oriented Architectures provide application frontends and services that are much more suitable for this purpose.

SOA layers, which you must not confuse with these traditional software layers, and tiers provide a conceptual structure at the enterprise level that organizes the application frontends and services (see Figure 5-9). Each layer contains distinct types of services and application frontends:

> **Enterprise layer.** The top layer of SOAs contains application frontends and public enterprise services, which are the end-points that provide access to the SOA. These endpoints facilitate both the communication between end users and the SOA (application frontends) and enable cross-enterprise (or cross-business unit) integration (public enterprise services).
> **Process layer.** The process layer contains process-centric services—the most advanced service type.
> **Intermediary layer.** The third layer contains intermediary services. These services act as façades, technology gateways, and adapters. You can also use an intermediary service in order to add functionality to an existing service.
> **Basic layer.** The bottom layer contains the basic services of the SOA. Basic services represent the foundation of the SOA by providing the business logic and data. The basic layer also contains proxies for other companies' public enterprise services.

As we will see in Chapter 6, "The Architectural Roadmap," many problems can be solved with two or three SOA layers. In these cases, there is no benefit to artificially introducing additional layers simply to have a "complete" SOA.

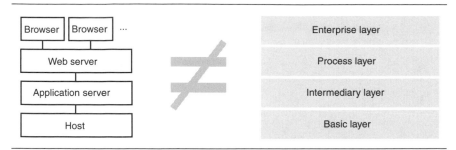

FIGURE 5-9   No 1:1 relationship exists between traditional tiers and SOA layers. These concepts actually are largely independent.

Recall that an SOA is about simplification. As long as a problem can be solved with simple measures, it is best to do so.

Although we will not discuss this matter in great detail, we must briefly consider the deployment of SOAs and the resulting system architecture in order to prevent a common misunderstanding: SOA layers do not correspond to physical tiers. It is not necessary for services, which originate from different SOA layers, to be deployed at different tiers. Nor must all services of one SOA layer be deployed at the same location. The system architecture is driven by matters such as available hardware and system software, system management requirements, and compatibility. These issues are largely independent of requirements such as maintainability or simplicity that drive the design of the services.

Actually, the design of the SOA and the system architecture are largely independent aspects of the application landscape, which is the remarkable strength of the SOA paradigm.

Decouple System and Software Architecture

A major benefit of the SOA paradigm is to be able to design the system and the software architecture largely independently of each other. This results in a high level of flexibility regarding the deployment of the SOA. Do not introduce unnecessary technical dependencies and rules for short-term benefits!

SOAs enable a largely independent design of the system and the software architecture. This results in a high level of flexibility regarding the deployment of the SOA. Do not spoil these benefits by introducing technical "short-cuts" and design rules for short-term benefits!

Figure 5-10 shows an example of how a system architecture and SOA layers can relate. It depicts three tiers at the system architecture level—the Web server, application server, and host. You can see that the SOA layers do not map directly to these tiers.

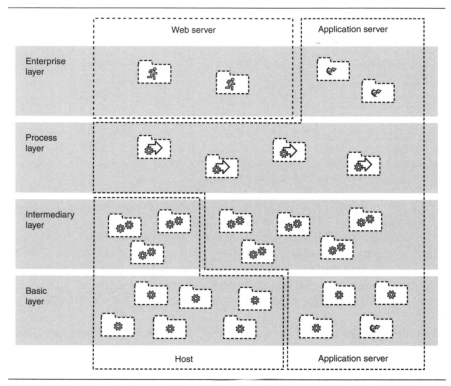

FIGURE 5-10   The deployment of an SOA is largely independent of the SOA layers.

5.3 Conclusion

In this chapter, we have introduced four classes of services: basic, process-centric, intermediary, and public enterprise services. These different services are predominantly used by the application frontends, which are the active elements of the SOA but are not services themselves. It is important for a designer of a Service-Oriented Architecture to be aware of the distinctive characteristics of the different service types because they all have different requirements with respect to design, implementation, operation, and maintenance.

In addition, this service classification is ideally suited to provide an overall structure within the SOA that is expressed by the different SOA layers, including enterprise layer, process layer, intermediary layer, and basic layer.

References

Gamma, Erich, Richard Helm, Ralph Johnson, and John Vlissides. *Design Patterns*. Addison-Wesley, 1995. [GHJV95]

Herzum, Peter and Oliver Sims. *Business Component Factory: A Comprehensive Overview of Component-Based Development for the Enterprise.* OMG Press, 2000. [Her2000]

Reisig, Wolfgang. *A Primer in Petri Net Design.* New York: Springer Compass International 1992. [Rei1992]

6

The Architectural Roadmap

Implementing an SOA at the enterprise level is a significant endeavor that is likely to take many years. During this time, we probably will encounter many obstacles and will have to cope with frequently changing requirements. It is therefore essential that we look at a realistic roadmap for rolling out our Service-Oriented Architecture. It is important that our architecture *and* our roadmap is designed to cope with the complexity and dynamics of an enterprise environment. Chapter 1 introduced an SOA-based *enterprise IT renovation roadmap*. In this chapter, we will focus on the architectural aspects of this roadmap. In Chapter 12 of this book, we will then focus on the political and organizational aspects.

6.1 The Architectural Roadmap

For the architectural roadmap, we have identified three expansion stages that signify different levels of maturity of an SOA. The expansion stages indicate the allocation of responsibility between the application frontends and the services (see Figure 6-1). The first stage is called *fundamental* SOA. In this expansion stage, much of the complexity and responsibility is still allocated at the application frontend. Although a fundamental SOA does not provide all features of a fully leveraged SOA, it is already a useful platform for an enterprise application landscape. The next expansion stage is called *networked SOA*. At this stage, intermediary services aggregate low-level basic services to more sophisticated services. Finally, we have *process-enabled SOAs*. At this stage, the application frontends delegate process control to the SOA.

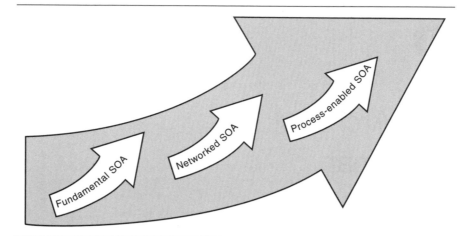

FIGURE 6-1   The expansion stages fundamental SOA, networked SOA, and process-enabled SOA are milestones of the architectural roadmap to the service-enabled enterprise.

In Figure 6-2, we depict the typical development of an application. It shows how permanent change requests and a lack of continuously applied architectural concept diminish maintainability and how an SOA-driven refactoring can reestablish agility. In Part III of this book, we present several case studies that show how different enterprises experienced difficulties when extending their historically grown application landscapes and how a transition to a Service-Oriented Architecture helped to incrementally overcome their difficulties.

It should be noted that the concept of expansion stages cannot be applied in a black-and-white fashion. As soon as the SOA is established, you will probably find areas of differing maturity that are at a different expansion stage fortunately, without any undesired impact on the SOA itself. This reveals a major benefit of Service-Oriented Architectures—they enable enterprises to start small and evolve in manageable steps as required in future projects. Actually, the SOA enables both evolutionary development of technology and functionality. Furthermore, the SOA supports different developments that run in parallel or in sequence. The SOA brings all these developments together in a smooth fashion, without harming a single project or the overall SOA endeavor. However, the expansion stages differ in regard to the distribution of responsibilities between application front-ends and services. With an increasing maturation of the SOA, the services gain more and more responsibilities.

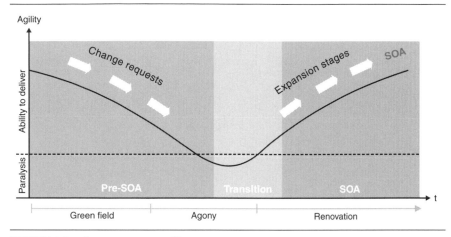

FIGURE 6-2   Agony versus agility.

Allow Different Expansion Stages

Typically, different expansion stages coexist in the same SOA. Do not fight this heterogeneity! Develop different areas of the SOA in parallel to the requirements of business-driven projects.

The definition of your SOA strategy and the required level of maturity strongly depend on the scope of the business integration you are planning to reach. Obviously, implementing an SOA strategy is always a question of budget, and the further you are planning to advance your SOA, the longer you will have to invest (see also Chapter 12, "The Organizational SOA Roadmap," for a discussion on the budget requirements of an SOA).

Identifying the required scope of the business integration is usually a good first step on the way toward the definition of the overall SOA strategy because there is a strong correlation between the integration level one is aiming for on the one hand and the required maturity level of the SOA on the other. Figure 6-3 depicts this dependency.

For example, if the required scope of business integration is only the intra-departmental level, a fundamental SOA will already help achieving good levels of maintainability of the system at hand. Obviously, the limited integration scope effectively limits the amount of flexibility or agility that can be achieved because only a limited view to the overall business processes is studied. In addition, investing in a very advanced SOA (such as a process-enabled SOA) is likely to be costly because the required IT investments would not be justified by the resulting business benefits.

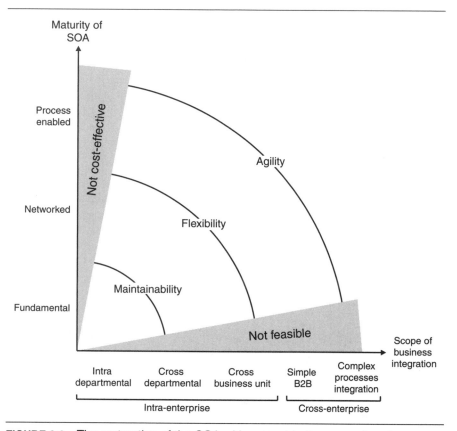

FIGURE 6-3 The maturation of the SOA with respect to the expansion stages often correlates to an enlargement of the scope of business integration.

On the contrary, in a scenario where the scope of business integration to be achieved is broadly defined, an approach based on a networked or process-enabled SOA is much more efficient. However, an extremely complex scenario, including cross-enterprise-integration and complex processes, might not even be feasible on the basis of a fundamental SOA.

When deciding on your SOA strategy, you should always ask yourself how much agility do you really need? Also consider the learning curve in your organization. Are you fit for process-enabled services? Choose an SOA strategy that best matches your agility requirements, your integration scenario, your architectural and development skills, and (obviously) your budget constraints. Your SOA strategy should be based on an evolutionary approach, subsequently developing your SOA expansion stages, taking all of the above mentioned factors into consideration. This approach also allows you to gradually broaden your integration horizon, moving from intra-departmental integration toward cross-departmental or even cross-enterprise integration.

6.2 Fundamental SOA

A *fundamental SOA* consists of two layers: the basic layer and the enterprise layer. Distinguishing these two layers helps single applications to define a proper high-level structure. It also enables two or more applications to share business-logic and live data. Although a fundamental SOA represents a rather simple approach, it provides a strong platform for large enterprise application landscapes. In fact, it is a major improvement compared to many of today's real-world scenarios. It is also an excellent starting point for the introduction of an enterprise-wide SOA because it enables enterprise organizations to start small on the technical side and focus on other critical success factors (see Chapter 12, "The Organizational SOA Roadmap").

A simple example (see Figure 6-4) shows how one application can be divided into meaningful components using an SOA. The Airline Web site utilizes four services that encapsulate the major business entities and their behaviors that are relevant to the business processes that are exposed to the customers.

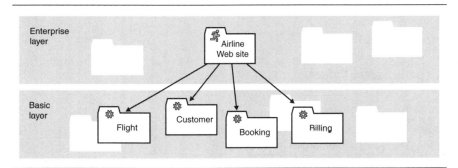

FIGURE 6-4   A fundamental SOA consists of two layers. Application frontends and basic services provide a fully functional base for enterprise applications.

We can now expand the original example by adding another application. A key characteristic of a fundamental SOA is that it enables two or more applications to share live data and business logic. In our example, we consider a traditional billing application that is required to keep track of terms of payment and the handling of demand notes (see Figure 6-5). This type of application is traditionally provided with customer and billing data through nightly batch jobs. Integrating billing and invoicing into a fundamental SOA enables the booking and the billing applications to share live data. In practice,[1] this means that the billing

---

[1]   It should be noted that a real-world scenario would be much more complex, as depicted in Figure 6-5. It would involve a customer care application, a sort of workbasket, and additional business services. However, the aforementioned benefits still apply.

application gets access to the customer service and billing services that, in turn, make batch processes that transfer data between the applications obsolete.[2] In addition, there are clear benefits for the booking system. As a result of up-to-date billing, the booking system also has access to precise, up-to-date data at any time. This increases the capability of the booking system to treat customer requests in a more appropriate manner. For example, a change in the credit rating of a customer, which is detected by the billing system, is instantly available for the booking system. As previously mentioned, in many traditional environments, this information is only available to the databases of the booking application after nightly batch updates.

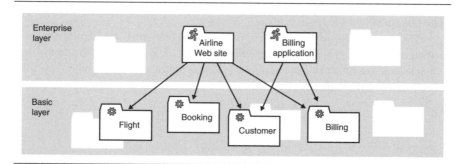

FIGURE 6-5   Enterprise application integration becomes obsolete if several applications share live data.

The introduction of a fundamental SOA is the first important step toward a truly SOA-enabled enterprise. The following summarizes the main characteristics and scope of a fundamental SOA:

- A fundamental SOA is an appropriate base for an enterprise application landscape.
- Due to its simplicity, it is technically easy to implement.
- It is a good starting point for an SOA that enables the introduction of more advanced expansion stages in the future.
- The application frontends are still complex. They must cope with the control of business processes and the full integration of the backend.
- A fundamental SOA increases the maintainability of an enterprise application landscape.
- Shared services can make data replication (enterprise application integration) largely obsolete.

---

[2] Note that an update in one application is instantly visible in the other application. In a traditional EAI scenario, you should consider decoupling the original data change from notifying the second application due to throughput and performance considerations. In the SOA world, these notifications are obsolete.

6.3 Networked SOA

The next expansion stage is called *networked SOA*, and it deals with backend complexity in addition to technical and conceptual integration. It includes a layer of intermediary services that can include *façades, technology gateways, adapters,* and *functionality adding services.*

We start our discussion with *façades*. As we discussed in Chapter 5, "Services as Building Blocks," façades can serve various needs. Most importantly, they encapsulate some of the complexity of underlying basic services by providing an aggregated API that enables clients to more easily utilize the functionality of the basic layer. In Chapter 8, "Process Integrity," we will discuss one aspect of this complexity—the challenges of achieving process consistency. Introducing a façade is one possible solution to this issue. Figure 6-6 provides an example of the booking and the billing services that must update their databases in a coordinated manner. Depending on the detailed requirements and the concrete technology upon which the booking and the billing services are built, it is not always simple to guarantee consistency. Actually, you will want to shield client developers from this kind of complexity. It is often necessary to apply particular skills in server-side development to master the challenges of the design and implementation tasks. Moreover, if multiple clients require similar functionality, there should be no duplication of workload. Thus, in our example, this complexity is encapsulated by the intermediary service "BookAndBill."

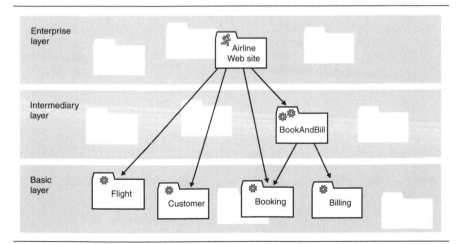

FIGURE 6-6   The intermediary service BookAndBill encapsulates the handling of distributed transactions that span the services Booking and Billing.

Utilizing *technology gateways* is a handy technique to enable one service to be used in different technical environments.[3] In Figure 6-7, we describe a scenario in which the flight service that is implemented on CICS is exposed to EJB, .NET, and MQSeries environments by technology gateways. This enables developers to specify, design, develop, test, operate, and maintain exactly one instance of the flight service, including live data, and reuse it in many heterogeneous environments at the same time.

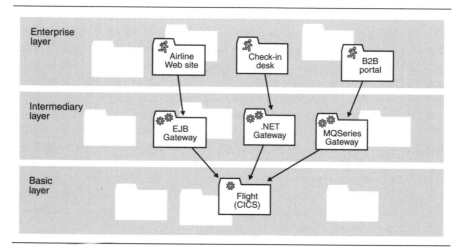

FIGURE 6-7   Technology gateways expose the functionality of services in technologically different environments.

The perfect world does not need technology gateways. In the first place, you would not encounter heterogeneous technologies. Secondly, given that the clients are heterogeneous in the real world, you would choose a single uniform bridging technology to integrate all clients. In our example, you might want to implement a type of XML RPC interface directly as part of the CICS-based service and use this interface in all client environments. Unfortunately, the ongoing evolution of

---

[3] Note that from a purely technical point of view, there is no difference between a technology gateway and an additional interface to the underlying basic service. Thus, it is possible to add some Java classes to an existing PL/I based service in order to provide an additional interfacing technology. The communication between the Java code and the PL/I code would become an internal matter of the service. The main difference between these two approaches is at the project management and team organization level. Most often, it is advisable to separate these technically different artifacts. In practice, you will find different subteams working on the different areas anyway. Separating their work by means of a service contract, configuration management, and distinct entries in the service repository is generally preferable. The same discussion applies to the adapters discussed in the following paragraphs.

technology can raise many unforeseen issues and new requirements. You might want to adopt current improvements without reimplementing existing services. Furthermore, you cannot predict which technologies you will need to integrate in the future. It is also unclear which political or commercial constraints will have an impact on a technology decision at a specific point in time. As a matter of fact, the SOA paradigm enables the creation of clear designs that cope with this kind of heterogeneity. Although it is not desirable to have multiple technology gateways that provide access to the same service, these technology gateways do no real harm to the architecture.

Figure 6-8 depicts a typical chronology. It shows the major milestones of a check-in application after its launch in 1986. The first milestone was the integration with partner airlines. Besides other requirements, the partner airlines needed access to flight data. This integration was accomplished by extending the dialog control layer that previously supported only the 3270 presentation. After integration with the partner airline, the dialog control layer also had to communicate with message queues that integrate the partner airlines. The integration code between the dialog control and the message queues simulated terminal sessions. This resulted in the fact that every change in the control flow of the application—such as new masks—required a change in the integration code. Although this dependency reduced agility, it was still acceptable. The next milestone was the launch of an online portal. This was implemented in Java and also required access to flight data. The integration with the existing message queues seemed to

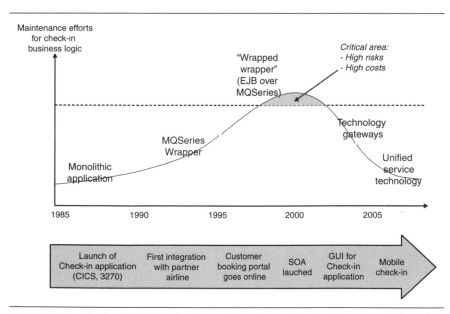

FIGURE 6-8 The typical lifecycle of an enterprise application traverses different development stages.

be the easiest and cheapest solution. However, this decision was rather short-sighted because any change in one system had a potential impact on other systems, and maintenance became a nightmare. It was at this point that a new requirement was specified. A graphical user interface was needed to replace the 3270 representation. Because this GUI required a completely new dialog control, the new project turned out to be infeasible. Driven by the requirement to implement a modern user interface, an SOA was put in place. Based on the SOA and technology gateways, the GUI became feasible and the maintainence costs could be significantly reduced. Finally, it provided the base for future developments such as mobile integration.

Adapters are useful in integration scenarios. They bridge conceptual gaps between a service and its clients. In the simplest case, an adapter maps signatures and transforms parameters. You must not underestimate the importance of such adoptions. As a matter of fact, much of the complexity of enterprise architectures results from small differences in how similar entities are handled in different parts of the architecture. Although many of these differences do not result from logical considerations, they are constraints that you must accept in real-world projects. For example, the booking application can regard any person that has registered at the Web site as a customer, whereas CRM might require that a person has purchased at least one ticket in the last three years in order to be considered a customer.

Figure 6-9 depicts three different scenarios in which you can operate a booking and CRM application in parallel. The first scenario represents the traditional architecture. Two distinct applications are integrated through nightly batch runs. As a result, two separate databases contain redundant data that is synchronized overnight. The second scenario is service-enabled. Although this might already have several benefits, two separate databases are still involved, along

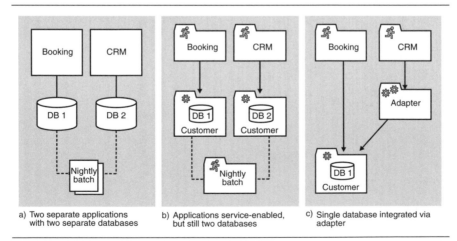

a) Two separate applications with two separate databases

b) Applications service-enabled, but still two databases

c) Single database integrated via adapter

FIGURE 6-9 Adapters bridge conceptual gaps between services and their clients, and they map signatures and adopt semantics. Adapters are a very powerful tool for enabling application integration according to the SOA paradigm.

with the associated issues. The final scenario abolishes one redundant database. The CRM application utilizes the Customer service of the Booking application using an adapter. This is the scenario of choice because it provides the simplest structure, abolishes batches, enables live data sharing, reduces maintenance costs, and guarantees data consistency.

There are various situations in which *functionality-adding services* can be very useful. Let's consider three different examples (see Figure 6-10). In the first example, a new client uses an existing legacy application. It is a common requirement that the legacy application remains untouched while the functionality is expanded. In our example, an additional service maintains additional attributes for data entities stored by the legacy application. Similar to database views, the data of both sources is transparently joined by a functionality-adding service in the intermediary layer. From the client's perspective, a single service delivers all the data. The second example involves a packaged application. Because you typically have no source code available, any changes or enhancements to existing functionality must be done by the vendor of this package or by an intermediary service. The third example uses a traditional client/server application. This application has a client that requires a specific communication protocol to be functional, which suspends the possibility of simply changing the existing server application. If a new client requires additional functionality, you either must modify the existing client or add this functionality with an appropriate service in the intermediary layer.

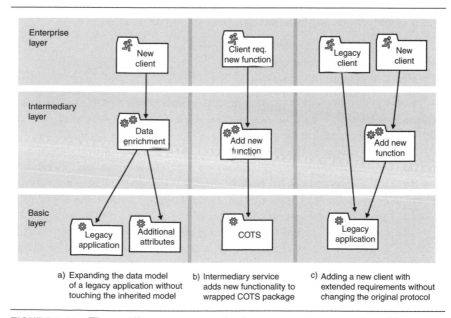

a) Expanding the data model of a legacy application without touching the inherited model

b) Intermediary service adds new functionality to wrapped COTS package

c) Adding a new client with extended requirements without changing the original protocol

FIGURE 6-10   Three different examples for the usage of functionality-adding services in the intermediary layer.

The introduction of a networked SOA represents the second step toward the evolution of an SOA-enabled enterprise. The following summarizes the main characteristics and scope of a networked SOA:

- Application frontends can be more lightweight when compared to a fundamental SOA. However, they remain complex because they must cope with the business processes.
- Intermediary services bridge technical and conceptual gaps.
- The application frontends are shielded from the complexity of backend systems.
- A networked SOA enables the enterprise to flexibly integrate its software assets independently of underlying technology.

6.4   Process-Enabled SOA

The third expansion stage is the fully leveraged SOA. The key feature of the *process-enabled SOA* is the maintenance of process state in process-centric services.
Similar to intermediary services, a process-centric service is both client and server in an SOA. The major difference between these service types is the fact that process-centric services are stateful. This is a crucial difference because handling state is a critical issue for server-side software. There are several possible reasons for introducing a process-centric service:

- Encapsulating the complexity of processes
- Sharing state between multiple clients
- Handling long-living processes

Encapsulating process state in a process-centric service enables application frontends to be simple and lightweight and at the same time very user-friendly with an elaborate handling of the user session.

Figure 6-11 extends the booking example first introduced in Figure 6-5. A new service "Booking process" encapsulates the business process "Booking." The Booking process utilizes the BookAndBill service and the Customer service. Although most of the work is carried out by the Booking service, the application frontend has access to all layers of the SOA.

The scenario in Figure 6-11 is the straightforward evolutionary step arising from the scenario in Figure 6-5. However, a green-field design would be different. In our example, the BookAndBill façade could become part of the process-centric service. Omitting the BookAndBill service (see Figure 6-12) reduces our scenario to three layers. Because one of the primary goals of SOAs is simplicity, this is a desirable step. Furthermore, reducing the number of tiers between the application frontend and basic layer reduces the system's latency and the number of elements that can potentially fail.

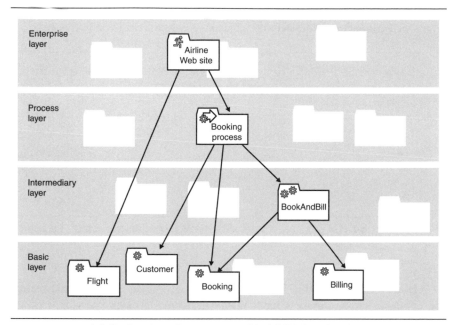

FIGURE 6-11   A fully developed process-enabled SOA has four layers.

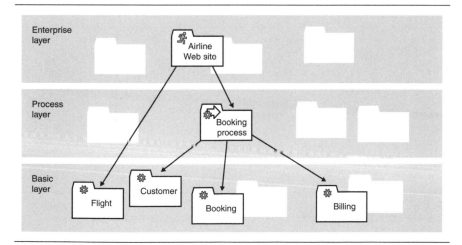

FIGURE 6-12   The Booking process encapsulates all functionality necessary to book flights. It also maintains the session state.

But there are also possible scenarios where our BookAndBill service can be beneficial. Assume that several clients, such as a Web site, a B2B gateway, and a mobile application, are running simultaneously (see Figure 6-13). Typically, these applications require a distinct process-centric service. Factoring out the BookAndBill functionality becomes a reasonable design decision in this case.

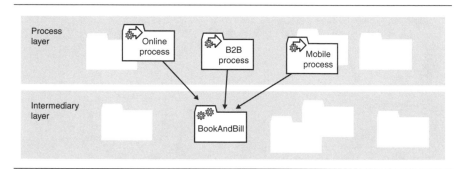

FIGURE 6-13   Several processes can utilize the BookAndBill service at the same time.

However, as depicted in Figure 6-14, an alternative design exists that factors out common booking process functionality to a process-centric service that can incorporate the BookAndBill functionality. The shared process-centric service both maintains a channel-independent process state and shields the channel-specific process-centric services from backend complexity.

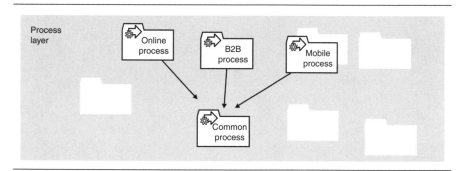

FIGURE 6-14   In general, every channel of a multichannel architecture requires channel-specific process logic. Nevertheless, different channels also share behavior.

Finally, process-centric services can handle long-living processes—in particular if user interaction or asynchronous backend services are involved. Obviously, one requires a location that maintains the state of a process for the duration of its execution.

Assume that the booking process supports waiting lists. This means that a customer can register a seat in a fully booked flight. If cancellations occur, the customer is notified using email or SMS (mobile phone text messages), or he can retrieve the status of his registration in a later session at the Web site. This kind of functionality implies that the booking process is long-living. External events (here, cancellations of other customers) change the state of the process.

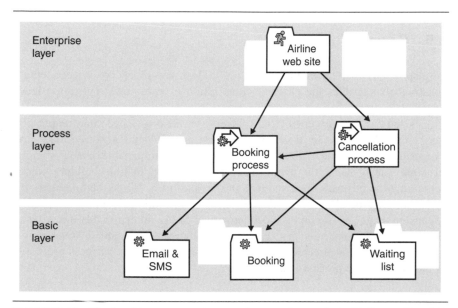

FIGURE 6-15   The booking process is asynchronously coupled with the waiting list service.

A possible implementation scenario would assume that the cancellation process is another client of the booking process, as depicted in Figure 6-15. If a cancellation is made for a flight for which the waiting list is not empty, the cancellation process starts the appropriate booking process. The booking process notifies the waiting customer and converts the entry in the waiting list into a proper booking.

A process-enabled SOA represents the endpoint of the evolution we have described in this chapter. A process-enabled SOA

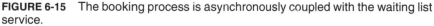

- Enables lightweight application frontends that "only" need to worry about user interaction
- Encapsulates complexity of business processes and handles their state
- Encapsulates complexity of backend systems in intermediary services and process-centric services
- Enables the process logic located in the process layer to be clearly separated from other types of code including dialog control that is located in the application frontends and the basic services' core business logic

- Represents the most sophisticated expansion stage and is therefore more difficult to implement than other expansion stages
- Is required for integration of highly independent organizations and the implementation of complex processes. However, it is not as cost effective in well-controlled environments such as intra-departmental integration scenarios.

6.5 Conclusion

In the previous chapter, we introduced four SOA layers that serve as a conceptual construct that enables the efficient organization of enterprise application landscapes.

Based on the concept of SOA layers, we distinguished three expansion stages that define the level of sophistication an SOA has achieved. The first expansion stage—fundamental SOA—delivers a maintainable business infrastructure that provides the application landscape with flexible building blocks, containing the business logic and data of the enterprise. While the integration of these building blocks is still allocated at the application frontend in the first expansion stage, the second stage—networked SOA—encapsulates this kind of complexity in an intermediary layer. Finally, the process-enabled SOA depicts the truly SOA-enabled enterprise, leveraging support for the business processes of the enterprise in process-centric services.

7

SOA and Business Process Management

In previous chapters, we discussed the general "renovation roadmap" that describes the evolution of an enterprise IT infrastructure toward a more agile Service-Oriented Architecture. We examined fundamental and networked SOAs as the initial stages in great detail. According to our roadmap, the final stage in this evolution are process-enabled SOAs. Although process-centric services can be realized in many different ways (and can thus take many different shapes and forms), *business process management* (BPM) represents possibly the most consequent approach to process-enabling an SOA. Consequently, we provide a general introduction to BPM in this chapter, followed by a discussion on how BPM fits into the SOA landscape. In this chapter, we focus more on the technical (computational and architectural) aspects, while Chapters 12, "The Organizational SOA Roadmap," and Chapter 13, "SOA-Driven Project Management," concentrate on the IT strategy and project-management aspects.

7.1 Introduction to BPM

Business process management has a number of predecessors. Following the *Total Quality Management* wave of the late 1980s, a new paradigm emerged in the early 1990s: *Business Process Reengineering* (BPR). In 1993, Michael Hammer and James Champy published their New York Times bestseller *Reengineering the Corporation* [HC93], which was followed by a plethora of other management books on the topic of process-orientation and reengineering. The promise of reengineering was to deliver dramatic business performance improvements in a relatively short period of time by completely reinventing existing business processes, that is, starting from scratch with new, optimized ways of doing business, throwing out the old, encrusted, inefficient procedures of the past.

However, after the initial BPR boom (and millions of dollars spent on management consultancies to lead BPR projects in Fortune 500 companies), the process movement became idle. Many projects resulted in complete failure, with experts claiming that between 60% and 70% of reengineering efforts failing to achieve expected results. Hammer and others attribute these failure rates to resistance to change, lack of understanding of the business models and underlying processes, and failure of nerve on the part of the client companies.

Almost ten years after BPR, you can observe a revival of the process movement under the umbrella term *business process management* (BPM), as advocated by Howard Smith and Peter Fingar in *BPM: The Third Wave* [SF03]. When comparing BPR and BPM, it appears as if one thing has fundamentally changed: While in the 1990s *reengineering* meant "starting from scratch," *process management* builds on and transforms that which already exists—it recommends incremental change and evolutionary optimization. However, BPM is still about processes, which are the main competitive differentiator in all business activity.

BPM is a general management topic that focuses on the strategic and operational aspects of *process orientation* in a given business area. Mapping a BPM model onto an enterprise IT landscape is a challenging task, which has some interesting technical as well as IT management-related aspects.

7.1.1 BPM VERSUS BPMS

When discussing BPM, it is important to differentiate between the business and IT sides. When looking at the business side of BPM, you will often find related keywords such as ISO 9000 and Six Sigma. The IT side of BPM is often accompanied by keywords such as process modeling and workflow management (see Figure 7-1).

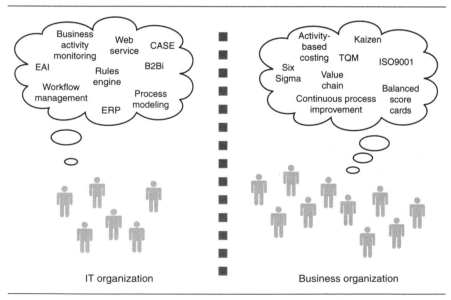

FIGURE 7-1 IT and business people have different views of the processes of an organization.

A BPMS (Business Process Management System) provides the technical platform for realizing BPM management initiatives. It comprises several parts including a BPM engine, facilities for business process monitoring, design tools and facilities for simulation. A BPMS installation can include several products or custom made software components. Closing the gap between the business and IT sides of BPM (or other process-oriented approaches) has been something of a holy grail in IT for two decades. Currently, it seems that the solution might be a conversion between more software engineering approaches such as CASE (Computer Aided Software Design) and MDA (Model Driven Architectures) on one hand, and workflow management and BPM approaches on the other (see [Fra03]).

BPM introduces the concept of "process processing" and stresses that this concept is not limited to the automatic execution of digital process models, but *"encompasses the discovery, design, and deployment of business processes, as well as the executive, administrative, and supervisory control over them to ensure that they remain compliant with business objectives"* [SF03]. This describes at a high level the features that are typically included in BPMS, a new software category that supports the entire lifecycle of modeling, executing, and monitoring business processes.

7.1.2 WHEN TO CHOOSE A BPMS

The cost and complexity of introducing a BPM engine or platform should not be underestimated. Most BPM products are fairly complex and require a mixture of highly skilled developers and administrators for installation, implementation, and maintenance. Thus, the decision for a BPM solution is a critical one. When does it actually make sense to consider a technical BPM solution, and what are the decision criteria?

IT and business must work hand-in-hand. You must understand that the introduction of a BPM software solution will not enable the process-oriented enterprise on its own. If the enterprise is not prepared for a process-oriented operation at the business level, a BPM platform will always be limited to covering very small sections of the enterprise. On the other hand, if an enterprise has gone through the process of defining and documenting key business processes, for example as part of an ISO 9000 certification or a Six Sigma quality management project, it is likely that the introduction of a BPM engine will be widely accepted at both the technological and business levels. See Chapter 12 for a more detailed discussion.

Utilize process templates. It is interesting that some BPM vendors are starting to bundle their BPM platforms with process templates for several different vertical industries, such as banking, insurance, and manufacturing. Although a process definition, such as claims processing in insurance, is likely to be different for every single company, the provision of a template for specific processes as a starting point can be extremely valuable. This can be particularly interesting if you consider that the BPM concepts are not about starting from scratch (like in business process reengineering) but rather are about incremental changes: starting a project for defining and implementing process definitions from scratch imposes significantly higher risks than a project that can start from a working process template, even if this template must be adapted to fit the individual needs of the enterprise. **Match the right technology to your problem.** To determine whether it makes sense to choose a BPM engine to support a particular business process, you should understand the nature of the business process itself—different types of processes are best addressed using different types of technologies. Two key characteristics of a business process are its complexity and dynamism (frequency of change) on one hand, and the degree of coordination the particular process requires on the other (see Figure 7-2). **Adopt the development model.** A BPM platform can also provide significant benefits at the level of software development processes: It provides a complete development model that enforces a clean separation between business logic and low-level technical code. This can be a major benefit, especially if a team has highly heterogeneous skills. BPMs are also particularly useful in situations where people have made many ad-hoc changes to the business model and a transparent runtime management of process instances is required.

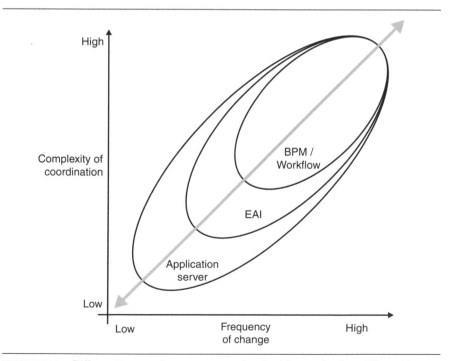

FIGURE 7-2   Different types of processes are best addressed using different types of technologies, such as EAI, application servers, or BPM/Workflow.

However, given the high resource requirements of a BPM introduction, you must carefully evaluate the real need for BPM. Generally, <u>you should avoid using BPM if the workflows or business processes are of a simple to moderate com-plexity</u> because a team with knowledge of an existing development platform would be significantly faster in developing developing these workflows or business processes using an ordinary programming language.

7.1.3 OVERVIEW OF A BPM SYSTEM

A BPM software product should enable business analysts, software developers, and system administrators to model and deploy business processes (at development time) and to interact with, monitor, and analyze process instances (at run-time). The following looks at actual modeling and execution of business processes in a BPMS.

7.1.3.1 Modeling Languages.
A number of competing modeling languages have been proposed by a variety of different industry consortia, although the final shoot-out has yet to happen. However, almost all these process modeling languages are based on or at least influenced by the theoretical concepts of Petri [Rei 1992] and or the more recent work of Milner [Mil80].

Two of the most popular approaches are Business Process Execution Language for Web Services (BPEL4WS) and Business Process Modeling Language (BPML). BPEL4WS is based on IBM's Web Service Flow Language (WSFL) and Microsoft's XLANG. BPML is developed by the Business Process Management Initiative (see BPMI.org), which is supported by vendors such as Intalio, SAP, SeeBeyond, Sun, and others.

While process definition languages such as BPEL4WS and BPML are designed to enable the exchange of process definitions between process engines from different vendors, graphical modeling languages exist that enable human users to understand, create, and modify process definitions more easily. The BPMN (Business Process Modeling Notation) is a language that has been defined by the BPMI in order to support a standardized, graphical representation of business process diagrams. In a way, the BPMN approach is similar to the UML approach, in that it provides a graphical representation of object models that is independent of the implementation language. In fact, many similarities exist between UML activity diagrams and BPMN. However, BPMN is specifically designed with BPM engines in mind. Consequently, it includes a mapping of its graphical objects to BPML. We use BPMN at various points in this book to graphically illustrate business processes.

Figure 7-3 shows how BPMN is positioned at the interface between business and IT: While UML is widely used within the IT organization as a means to communicate abstract concepts and models, BPMN aims to become the *de facto* standard used between IT and business to discuss the scope and functionality of processes and applications.

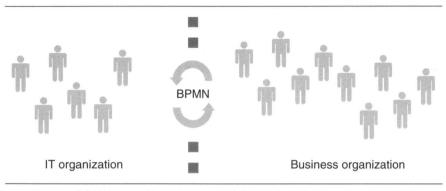

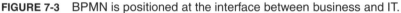

FIGURE 7-3   BPMN is positioned at the interface between business and IT.

Another feature of many modern BPM systems is the capability to provide different views of a process definition, including a more abstract view designed for business analysts and a much more detailed view for technical staff.

7.1.3.2   Architecture of a BPM System. Depending on the BPM product at hand, processes are usually modeled graphically (e.g., based on a graphical notation such as BPMN), stored in a block-structured model (e.g., in BPEL4WS or BPML), and executed by a process engine. What is common to most pure-play BPM engines is their foundation on a mixture of Pi-Calculus [Mil80] and Petri Net models [Rei1992]. BPM tools vary in their support for different modeling languages, application integration, process monitoring, and so forth. However, we provide an overview of a generic BPM system architecture in Figure 7-4. At the heart of a BPM is the process engine, which creates and interprets runtime instances of formal process definitions. Process definitions (development time) and process instances (runtime) are stored in repositories, and the system provides appropriate interfaces to design, deploy, and configure process definitions and to monitor and manage process instances.

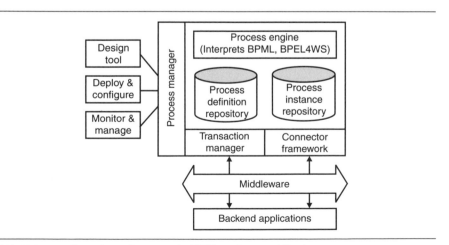

FIGURE 7-4   Overview of a generic BPM system architecture.

7.1.4 VISION AND CAVEAT

The BPM vision is a strong one—instead of hard-coding information and rules regarding important business processes directly into the application code, we take this information out of the application systems and put it under the control of a BPM system. The BPM facilitates the modification, reconfiguration, and optimization of process definitions with graphical tools that can be used by less technology-oriented business analysts.

As depicted in Figure 7-5, this BPM vision and our SOA vision are a very good fit. The SOA provides the backend functionality that is required by a BPMS in order to implement its process functionality. All the concepts discussed with respect to SOA—including the evolutionary development of basic, intermediary, and process layers—make sense in light of this picture. SOA becomes the enabling infrastructure for the process-oriented enterprise.

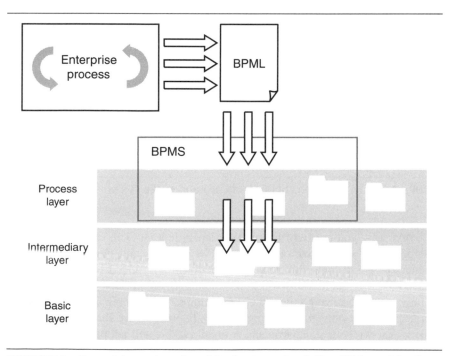

FIGURE 7-5 Roundtrip engineering at the business level: The SOA provides the enabling business infrastructure.

However, there is one caveat to all this: Remember the hub-and-spoke model as it was proposed by late-nineteen-ninetieth EAI-products? In the hub-and-spoke model, a centralized hub connects a variety of different applications, enabling the seamless interplay of different transactions in these sub-systems. A picture similar to the central hub is the famous "software bus" promoted by the CORBA community. This never worked out in your enterprise? There was never *one* centralized software bus or hub, but rather a multitude of competing integration and EAI products and projects? Does this BPM vision not resemble the central hub/bus vision and cause a major concern? Would this BPM vision not require the centralization of all business process definitions, as depicted in Figure 7-6?

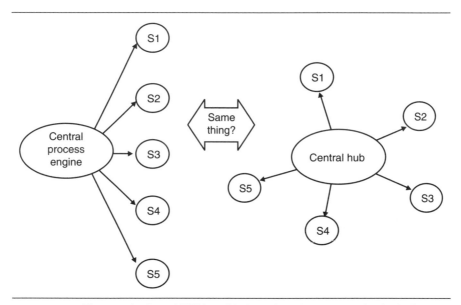

FIGURE 7-6   The topologies of BPM and hub-and-spoke systems look similar.

In a way, you are right if you experience déjà vu. The chances that your enterprise will standardize on just one BPM platform and migrate all its core business processes onto this centralized platform are indeed fairly slim. However, we believe that there is still light on the horizon and that BPM could play an important part in your enterprise's transition toward a more agile and flexible IT infrastructure with an underlying SOA. In Figure 7-7, we show a more realistic scenario: Individual departments or organizations will adopt SOA and BPM. The integration across these organizational boundaries will not be based on centralized hub, bus, or BPM architectures for a variety of reasons. The cloud in the figure represents the void between the different organizations, a void that will not be filled by a centralized technology standard controlled by a single political unit. Instead, the connections between the different organizations will continue to be ad-hoc and often short-lived. A number of common (sometimes conflicting) standards, such as SOAP and CORBA IIOP, enable basic communication between the different organizations. In some cases, higher-level protocols such as ebXML or RosettaNet might play a role. However, organizations will have to cope with the fact that the integration with external organizations (or other business units, subsidiaries, etc.) will still need protocols and logic that require more flexibility than within a well controlled, intra-organizational environment. If the organization hooks into this "cloud" using a BPM, the organization receives a very powerful tool for reacting to frequently changing requirements for integration with third parties.

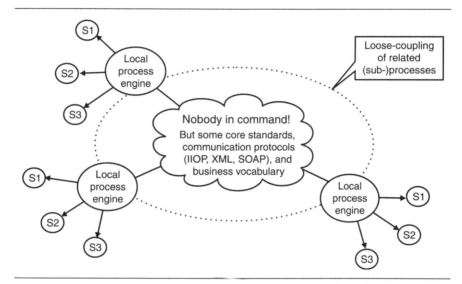

FIGURE 7-7 The scope of a BPMS is generally limited to a single business unit. Crossing the borders of the organization requires distributed process control and largely heterogeneous standards.

Although this vision does not promise to unravel the enterprise system integration "spaghetti," it provides a chance for individual organizations to react to the realities of intra- and extra-company system integration in the most flexible manner, shielding the systems under their own control from outside dynamics and at least providing a cleaner architecture that is extensible and adaptable.

7.2 BPM and the Process-Enabled SOA

Having introduced the foundations of BPM and its long-term vision, we now take a closer look at what this means for the SOA architect.

7.2.1   THE PAST: DATA AND FUNCTIONS VERSUS OBJECTS VERSUS SERVICES

This chapter focused on BPM and process-orientation, which comes at the very end of our "enterprise renovation roadmap." We should now step back and look at the origins of SOAs and what can be learned from their evolution.

In the early days of functional programming, data and functionality were strictly separated. With the emergence of object orientation, people began to merge data and functionality into encapsulated, reusable object implementations. This worked particularly well for large, monolithic applications, such as complex graphical user interfaces. In the middle of the 1990s, people started to apply the concepts of object orientation to distributed systems. CORBA and a number of other standards for distributed object computing emerged. However, when applying distributed object technology in large-scale projects, it eventually became clear that this approach had some severe limitations. As a result, Service-Oriented Architectures emerged, with supporting technology platforms such as XML Web services.

So what problems with distributed objects led to the emergence of SOAs? The first problem that we usually cite is the fine level of granularity of distributed objects, which often leads to performance problems due to latency and other issues. An SOA addresses these performance issues by adopting patterns of more coarse-grained objects, which require less frequent interaction between clients and servers, thus reducing the number of network roundtrips, marshalling overhead, and so forth.

However, a second and potentially more critical problem exists: Due to the complicated interaction patterns that result from the fine-grained nature of distributed objects, the reuse of distributed objects became increasingly complex. The complex dependencies between different objects prevented efficient reuse and made these systems very inflexible and hard to maintain because few people really understood these dependencies and the impact that changes to individual objects and their interfaces would have on overall systems.

With SOAs, we take a deliberate step back from the highly complex, fine-grained, highly dependent distributed object models toward less complex, relatively coarse-grained, loosely coupled (i.e., less dependent) component interfaces.

7.2.2   THE FUTURE: CORE BUSINESS LOGIC VERSUS PROCESS CONTROL LOGIC

Rather than revert to a paradigm that separates data and functionality, the SOA should develop an architecture that differentiates between core business logic and process control logic. Both of these concepts comprise data and functionality, although in very different ways. Unfortunately, these concepts are not as clean as the concepts of data and functionality, but we believe that they are still essential for the successful implementation of an SOA-based "enterprise IT renovation roadmap." Let's take a look at each concept using concrete examples.

Core business logic comprises *basic data access services, complex calculations, and complex business rules*. Data access services represent core business logic because they make core business entities available to different systems. An example is a service that enables different applications to read and update shared customer data. An example of a complex calculation would be the calculation of an insurance premium based on statistical data that is encapsulated by the service. Different processes such as sales, premium adjustment, and risk assessment require this core business logic. It is not always clear whether business rules represent core business logic (residing in a basic service) or whether they should be a direct part of the process logic (e.g., residing in a BPMS or process-centric service). Often, this will depend on the level of complexity of the business rule. The simple rule that "all orders over USD 100,000 must be manually validated" might well be part of the process control logic. However, a complex claims validation engine that incorporates legislative data to check the validity of insurance claims would clearly fall into the category of core business logic.

Related core business logic usually resides in a single service. As we stated before, these services are relatively coarse-grained and loosely coupled (or independent) and do not have complex interfaces (even though they might encapsulate a very complex piece of logic such as a claims validation engine). In particular, services that represent core business logic control their own transactions; they do not participate in externally controlled, potentially long-lived transactions. The interaction with services representing core business logic is usually OLTP-style, based on underlying short-lived transactions. However, services representing core business logic might participate in complex processes "orchestrated" by a BPM or a process-centric service.

Process control logic, on the other hand, has very different characteristics. As discussed at the beginning of this chapter, many processes are dynamic in that they are prone to frequent change and often require complex coordination with the process participants. Often, these processes are related to non-tangible assets, in service industries for example. Other examples include contract management, supply-chain management, sales of complex tailored products, or software outsourcing processes.

Services managing process control logic, such as process-centric services, do not usually have application state such as currency exchange rates, customer data, or airline seat availability. However, they do have state related to the process itself. This process state includes information regarding process participants (people and services), input from participants, the actual position within the process flow, and basic rules. Process-centric services are highly dependent on other services, in particular those services that represent the core business logic. Such services provide the glue to bind the core business services. In particular, process-centric services must coordinate complex activities that can span more than one person, several major business entities, multiple locations, or long periods of time.

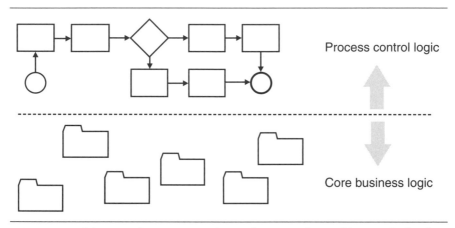

FIGURE 7-8 A key requirement toward an agile enterprise architecture is that it clearly distinguishes between process control logic and core business logic.

The benefits of cleanly separating SOA services (see Figure 7-8) into services containing core business logic (with a potentially long lifetime) and processes containing control logic (with a usually much shorter lifetime) are manifold. In particular, this approach should benefit the overall goal of our "enterprise renovation roadmap," which is increased agility. If the separation is thorough, changes to existing processes and the introduction of new processes should happen relatively smoothly because changes will be limited to services that represent process control. Furthermore, the approach supports the encapsulation of critical stateful code—in particular, this means that changing one process does not affect another process. Finally, business logic will be implemented only once, thus helping to reduce redundancies and inconsistencies.

7.2.3 DESIGN IMPLICATIONS FOR SOA ARCHITECTS

Decomposing an SOA into services that represent core business logic and those that represent process control does not simply mean moving back from a distributed object paradigm toward a functional paradigm. Services representing core business logic go far beyond simple data access services. Similarly, process control logic is not limited to pure functionality. Although process control logic does not usually own large amounts of core business data, such as the customer database, it still can manage a lot of internal data, such as user input, input from basic services, and so forth.

The challenge for the SOA architect is to identify and categorize services accordingly, taking many aspects into consideration, including business and process requirements, the existing application landscape, make-versus-buy decisions, resource availability (e.g., development skills), SOA design considerations, and budget constraints. However, if an enterprise is serious about the long-term renovation of its IT landscape, this decomposition process will represent an important cornerstone in the overall process.

7.3   Conclusion

As we saw in this chapter, an SOA represents a good foundation for adopting a process-oriented approach in the long term. You can introduce process orientation at different levels in an SOA, with the most powerful level being represented by a Business Process Management System (BPMS). However, migrating to a process-enabled SOA is a long process that can easily run for a number of years. In the meantime, enterprises must find ways to deal with processes and, in particular, process consistency in the short term. This issue is the focus for the next chapter.

References

Frankel, David S. *BPM and MDA: The Rise of Model-Driven Enterprise Systems*. Business Process Trends, http://www.businessprocesstrends.com/, June 2003. [Fra03]

Hammer, Michael and James Champy. *Re-engineering the Corporation*. London: Nicholas Brealey, 1993. [HC93]

Milner, Robin. "A Calculus of Communication Systems." *Lecture Notes in Computer Science*, volume 92, 1980. [Mil80]

Reisig, Wolfgang. *A Primer in Petri Net Design*. New York: Springer Compass International, 1992. [Rei1992]

Smith, Howard and Peter Fingar. *BPM: The Third Wave*. Tampa: Meghan-Kiffer Pr., 2003. [SF03]

URLs

http://www.bpmi.org

http://www-306.ibm.com/software/solutions/webservices/pdf/WSFL.pdf

http://www-106.ibm.com/developerworks/library/ws-bpel/

http://www.gotdotnet.com/team/xml_wsspecs/xlang-c/default.htm

http://www.businessprocesstrends.com/

8

Managing Process
Integrity

Achieving consistency in the execution of complex business processes that span
multiple subsystems is one of the most challenging problems in IT. The first part
of this chapter provides an overview of the problem scope, common solutions for
achieving process integrity, and how they fit into an SOA. The second part of the
chapter provides a set of concrete recommendations for SOA architects, based on
an extension to our airline example.

8.1 Data Versus Process Integrity

Process integrity is not necessarily a well-established or well-defined concept.
The core building blocks of *process integrity* are based on the widely established
concepts of *data integrity*. However, as we will see in the following, *data integrity*
is insufficient for addressing all integrity requirements of complex business
processes spanning multiple IT systems, which is why it is necessary to introduce
process integrity as a concept that helps to address these more complex and
demanding requirements.

8.1.1 DATA INTEGRITY

Data integrity is an umbrella term that refers to the *consistency, accuracy,* and
correctness of data. The classical mechanisms for ensuring data integrity are
often closely tied to the concepts of relational databases. The primary types of
data integrity include *entity, domain,* and *referential integrity.* Entity integrity
requires that each row in the table be uniquely identified. Domain integrity
requires that a set of data values fall within a specific range (domain)—for example,
a birth date should not be in the future. Referential integrity refers to the

validity of relationships between different data tuples. Finally, *user-defined* data integrity refers to types of data integrity that usually cannot be enforced by commercial database tools. User-defined data integrity is typically enforced using a data access layer, triggers, and stored procedures. These are all fairly technical concepts, and typical business requirements for data integrity go far beyond technical concepts. These are all fairly technical concepts, and typical business requirements for data integrity go far beyond technical concepts. These concepts are typically limited to a single database. As you will see in the following, more flexible concepts for ensuring process integrity are required if you are leaving the domain of a single database or application system.

8.1.2 PROCESS INTEGRITY

The problem with complex business processes that span multiple IT systems goes beyond the issues of traditional data consistency. In these kinds of situations, we are not dealing with short-lived updates of data contained in a central repository, but instead with long-lived processes that cross multiple systems. These processes do not often have a well-defined state because it is not possible to obtain access to all the participants all the time, a requirement necessary to determine the process state. This is particularly true for processes that span the boundaries of business units or enterprises. Take the example of a manufacturer who receives product parts from a supplier. If the manufacturer receives a last-minute cancellation for an order, there will be time intervals where the internal systems reflect this cancellation while the order for related parts is still with the supplier. This is what we refer to as a *process inconsistency*.

8.1.3 TECHNICAL FAILURES VERSUS BUSINESS EXCEPTIONS

The key to maintaining process integrity is to ensure that failures within or between the execution of the different steps that comprise a complex business process are captured and the necessary steps taken to resolve the problem. It is necessary to differentiate between technical failures on one hand and exceptions and special business cases on the other:

> **Technical failures.** Technical failures include database crashes, network problems, and program logic violations, among many others. Often, these problems can be addressed in their respective context, for example through backup and recovery mechanisms (provided by the DBMS; e.g., transactions), retries (in the case of network problems), exception handlers (e.g., a Java `catch` clause), or process restarts (e.g., after a process terminated because of a C++ NULL pointer exception). However, in many cases, technical failures must be addressed using more complex, often custom-built solutions. For example, systems must cope with network problems by temporarily storing a process state locally until the subsystem to which it attempted to connect can be reached again.

Business exceptions. Business exceptions can range from very simple exceptions to arbitrarily complex ones. An example of a simple exception is an attempt by a customer to book a flight on a date that lies in the past. Such a simple *domain inconsistency* (see the previous discussion on data inconsistencies) can be addressed at the database level. For the sake of usability, it can be handled directly in the user interface (e.g., Java script in the browser). However, simple domain inconsistencies have local impact only. An example of a more complex business exception—with a more proliferating impact—is an *out of stock* exception, for example in an online Web shop. A straightforward solution is to tell the customer that the requested item is not available. However, in the real world, this is unacceptable. A better option is to trigger a process such as *reorder item* to ensure that the item is available the next time a customer wants to buy it. However, this might also be unacceptable because the customer is still lost. The best solution might be to constantly monitor inventory and reorder in advance. This avoids or at least minimizes *out of stock* situations and leads to the discussion on *special cases*.

Special cases. In almost all complex business processes, the complexity lies not in the *happy path* case but in special cases that are dependent on the context of the process. For example, a trading system might choose completely different execution paths, depending on the type and size of trade and the customer's risk profile. The business process, under consideration, could comprise a credit check of the customer. A negative result of the credit check could be either an exception (resulting in a refusal of the trade) or a special case requiring a different approach (e.g., resulting in another subprocess asking the customer to provide additional collateral). In many situations, the entire business process is a "special case" from a process integrity point of view. A good example is that of airline seat reservations: in order to ensure maximum utilization of airplanes, many airlines deliberately overbook flights, making the assumption that a certain percentage of bookings will be canceled or that some passengers will not show up. Such systems are constantly optimized to find the optimum level of overbooking, based on recent flight statistics. Although at first sight, it appears inconsistent to overbook a flight, achieving process consistency in this case requires finding the "right" level of overbooking.

The boundaries between business exceptions, special cases, and complex processes such as a flight booking are not black and white. Often, each problem scenario requires its own specific solution. In this chapter, we concentrate mainly on problems that are on the *exception* or *failure* side of the equation and not so much on *special cases*. However, in many cases, problems (exceptions or failures) at the technical or business level lead to process inconsistencies that cannot be immediately addressed and that must be treated as special cases.

8.1.4   WHO OWNS THE PROCESS LOGIC?

Process logic is rarely centralized but instead is spread across different systems, which makes it hard to devise generic strategies for ensuring process integrity. Although in the ideal world, all key process definitions would be managed by a central BPM (Business Process Management) or Workflow Management System (WMS), this is rarely the case. Although centralized management is reasonable in the B2B world because each company wants to retain control over its own processes, even a single company is unlikely to have centralized processes (or at least process implementations captured in a central system).

Take the example of a manufacturing company that has two systems, one for order processing and one for billing. This is quite a common scenario in many companies. The two systems are synchronized through nightly batch updates, where the order processing makes all the changes and additions that came in during the day available to the billing system using FTP (File Transfer Protocol). Assume that a customer makes an order one day and cancels the order the next day. The information about the order has been passed from the order processing system to the billing system during the nightly batch. The next day, the customer cancels the order, and the order processing system is able to stop the delivery of the order to the customer. However, the billing system cannot be notified until the following night, when the next batch run is executed. In the meantime, the billing system might already have debited the customer's account. Upon receiving the cancellation the next day, the billing system now must provide the customer with a credit note or take alternative steps to undo the debit. In the real world, the special cases caused by the decoupling of such systems are much more complex and have often led to a situation where individual systems have grown to a tremendously large size with a huge internal complexity. Of course, we now have a wide range of middleware technologies to enable real-time data exchange between systems where process logic is split between different subsystems, but this type of batch scenario is still a reality for most companies.

By examining the many enterprise IT architectures that have grown over decades (the famous Gartner *Integration Spaghetti* comes to mind), we will see that the majority of enterprises have no centralized, enterprise-wide workflow systems but rather that workflows are deployed more implicitly. Instead of a clean separation of application logic and business rules, you will often find that the logic comprising a particular logical workflow or process is scattered across a multitude of systems and subsystems, buried in new (e.g., Java-based) and old (e.g., COBOL-based) applications, tied together using point-to-point integration or middleware hubs. Even within a single application system, business logic is likely to be spread across the presentation tier (fat clients or presentation servers such as ASP or JSP), the middle tier (EJBs, Web services), and the database tier (e.g., stored procedures).

All this makes it very hard to realize consistent processes. Regardless of how implicit or explicit processes are realized in a distributed system (and how deliberate the decision for using or not using a dedicated BPM or workflow product), process integrity is one of the most difficult problems to solve.

8.2 Technical Concepts and Solutions

You can choose from a wide range of solutions to implement process integrity. These solutions range from simple technical solutions such as distributed logging and tracing to advanced transaction concepts. BPM systems provide the facility to address process integrity on a less technical and more business-oriented level. BPMs are used to model and execute business processes, as we discussed in Chapter 7, "SOA and Business Process Management." They enable us not only to explicitly model special cases but also to provide definitions for the appropriate countermeasures in case of exceptions. We look at each of these solutions in turn, followed by recommendations for their application in an enterprise SOA.

8.2.1 LOGGING AND TRACING

Logging and tracing—at different levels of sophistication—is probably still the most commonly used approach for providing at least rudimentary levels of process integrity on an ad-hoc basis.

Log traces are commonly used for debugging but are also used in production systems in order to identify and solve problems in day-to-day operations. Particularly in the case of complex systems that integrate large numbers of nontransactional legacy systems, logging is often the only viable approach to providing a minimum level of process integrity, especially if processes or workflows are implemented implicitly (i.e., there is no dedicated BPM system). Often, the operators of these types of systems employ administrators that manually fix problems based on the analysis of log files. If the log file provides a complete trace of the steps executed in a particular process until the failure occurred, the administrator has some chance of fixing the problem, even if this often requires going directly to the database level to undo previous updates or fix some problem to enable the process to continue.

A key problem with logging based problem analysis and repair is the lack of correlation between the different log entries that relate to a particular logical process instance, especially for processes that are implemented implicitly. If a process fails due to a technical fault, someone must identify what has happened so far in order to complete or undo the process. To do this, you must find the log entries that relate to the process, possibly across different log files from different systems. Ideally, some kind of correlation ID (related to process instances) should exist for each log entry because this helps with the log consolidation (as depicted in Figure 8-1). However, often the only way to correlate events is by comparing timestamps, which is a difficult task, especially with systems that use distributed log files. For example, how is it possible to relate a JDBC exception written into a local log by an EJB application server to a database deadlock event that was written to a database log (both log entries are potentially relevant for identifying and fixing the problem in the application)? In this case, a significant chance exists that both exceptions occurred at the same time. The problem becomes even more difficult if processes are long-lived and you are trying to find out which customer account was modified earlier by a process that failed later, such as when updating a shipping order.

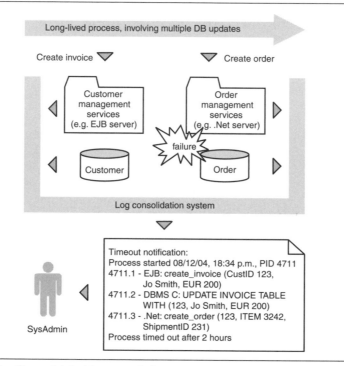

FIGURE 8-1 Consolidated logs can help system administrators deal with error situations in distributed, long-lived processes. Log consolidation can be performed across systems (e.g., providing the ability to relate updates in one database to updates in another), as well as within systems (e.g., relating database logs to application server logs).

Nevertheless, logging and tracing is still important in many operational systems and is often the only possible way to achieve at least minimum process integrity. Many projects have therefore invested heavily in building a sophisticated infrastructure that helps with distributed logging and log analysis. Often, this infrastructure is built on or tightly integrated with system management platforms such as IBM Tivoli or HP Openview.

Chapter 9, "Infrastructure of a Service Bus," provides a detailed overview of how this can be achieved in an SOA environment. Notice that distributed log consolidation can only partly address technical failures and does not address process inconsistencies that relate to business-level problems at all.

8.2.2 ACID TRANSACTIONS

Online Transaction Processing (OLTP) has been a key element of commercial computing for several decades. OLTP systems enable large number of users to manipulate shared data concurrently. For example, in an online flight reservation system, sales agents around the world share access to flight booking information.

In order to support shared manipulation of data, OLTP systems are based on the concept of transactions. Traditionally, the term *transaction* has been used to describe a unit of work in an OLTP system (or database) that transforms data from one state to another, such as booking a seat on a particular flight. The term ACID (atomicity, consistency, isolation, durability) has been coined to describe the ideal characteristics of concurrently and possibly distributed transactions, which ensure the highest level of data integrity. It is described in ISO / IEC 10026-1: 1992 section 4.

ACID (handwritten in right margin)

We will use the simplified example of a money transfer with a debit and a credit update to illustrate the properties of ACID transactions:

Atomicity: ACID transactions are atomic "all or nothing" units of work. If any one part of a transaction fails, the entire transaction is rolled back. If the debit update works but the credit update fails, the original debit update must be rolled back.

Consistency: ACID transactions transform data from one consistent state to another. In our example, the sum of all account balances must be the same as before the transaction. Of particular importance is the stipulation that a transaction ensures referential integrity: if a customer account is deleted, orphan address records originally related to the customer must also be removed (see the discussion on data integrity in the previous section).

Isolation: The internal state of a running transaction is never visible to any other transaction. This is usually achieved through locking. In our example, there is a window of time between the debit and the credit, during which the sum of all accounts will not add up. However, nobody outside of the transaction can see this inconsistency.

Durability: Committed updates of a transaction are permanent. This ensures that the consistent, up-to-date state of the system can be recovered after a system failure during the execution of the transaction. If we have a crash after the debit but before the credit, we can still recover the state before the start of the transaction.

Almost all commercial DBMS products support the concept of transactions enabling concurrent access to a database, albeit with varying degrees of "ACIDity." The DBMS must provide an appropriate concurrency control mechanism in order to deal with the concurrent execution of transactions. The transaction performance and behavior in case of access conflicts depends strongly on the choice of optimistic versus pessimistic concurrency control strategies, the choice of locking (exclusive or shared locks) versus timestamps versus versioning, and the locking/versioning granularity (tables, pages, tuples, objects). Most DBMSs can be programmed or configured to use different concurrency control policies (isolation level) in order to enable different types of applications or transactions to chose the appropriate mix of performance versus transactional integrity.

8.2.3 TRANSACTION MONITORS AND DISTRIBUTED 2PC

Building applications with ACID properties becomes more difficult if you operate outside the domain of a single system. Transaction Processing Monitors (TPMs) can be used to ensure the ACID properties of a transaction that spans multiple databases or other transactional resources (as depicted in Figure 8-2). A *resource manager* typically manages these resources, which include DBMS and transactional queue managers.

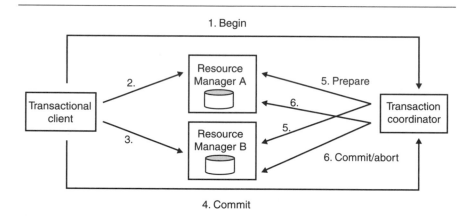

FIGURE 8-2   Example for 2PC: A client begins a new transaction (1), executes two updates (2 & 3), and attempts to commit the changes (4). The transaction coordinator sends prepare requests to both resource managers (5). The final step of the transaction (6) either commits or aborts all updates. If both resource managers agree to commit the transaction, the transaction coordinator sends a commit to all participants. If one participant wants to abort, the transaction coordinator asks all participants to abort.

Most commonly, the so-called Two-Phase Commit Protocol (2PC) is used to ensure ACID properties for transactions that span more than a single resource manager. Transactions are coordinated among different resource managers through a *transaction coordinator*, which is part of the transaction monitor. At the end of each distributed transaction, the transaction coordinator will coordinate the commitment of the transaction across the participating resource managers:

- In the first phase (prepare), all participating resource managers must ensure that all relevant locks have been acquired and that the "before" and "after" state of data that has been modified in the context of the transaction has been persistently captured.
- Depending on the outcome of the first phase ("voting"), the transaction coordinator informs all participating resource managers whether to commit or rollback the changes.

▪ A single "abort" vote will cause the entire transaction to be rolled back, helping to ensure the atomicity property of the transaction. Only if all participants vote to "commit" will they also be asked to make the changes permanent and visible.

The 2PC protocol assumes a very tight coupling between all the components involved in the execution of the transaction. All participants must "play by the rules" in order to ensure that the outcome of each transaction is consistent. If a participant does not abide by the rules, the result will be a so-called "heuristic" outcome, that is, a transaction whose final state is undefined. Furthermore, deadlocks become an issue that must be handled with great care.

The most important standard in the area of transaction monitors and 2PC is the X/Open standard for Distributed Transaction Processing (X/Open DTP). Among other protocols and APIs, the X/Open standard defines the so-called XA interface, which transaction monitor use to interact with a resource manager, for example to execute the "prepare" and "commit" calls. Most commercial RDBMS and queue managers provide support for the XA interface, enabling them to participate in distributed transactions. Well-established transaction monitors include CICS, IMS, Encina (IBM), and Tuxedo (BEA). In the Java world, JTS (Java Transaction Service) is widely established, and its counterpart in the Microsoft world is MTS (Microsoft Transaction Server).

8.2.4   PROBLEMS WITH 2PC AND TIGHTLY COUPLED ACID TRANSACTIONS

Although ACID transactions are a good theoretical concept for ensuring the integrity of a single database or even a distributed system, in many cases, they are impractical in real-world applications. We will now cover the key limitations of tightly coupled ACID transactions in more detail.

8.2.4.1   Performance.   Even in a non-distributed system, ensuring the isolation property of a concurrently executed transaction can be difficult. The problem is that the higher the isolation level, the poorer the performance. Therefore, most commercial DBMSs offer different isolation levels, such as *cursor stability*, *repeatable read*, *read stability*, and *uncommitted read*.

In distributed systems, the execution of a distributed 2PC can have an even more negative impact on the performance of the system, in some cases due to the overhead of the required out-of-band coordination going on behind the scenes. Finding the right tradeoff between performance and a high degree of concurrency, consistency, and robustness is a delicate process.

8.2.4.2   Lack of Support for Long-Lived Transactions.   Another big problem with systems based on transaction monitors and ACID properties is that most database management systems are designed for the execution of short-lived

transactions, while many real-world processes tend to be long-lived, particularly if they involve interactions with end users. Most OLTP systems (and transaction monitors and underlying databases) use pessimistic locking to ensure isolation for concurrent transactions. If a lock is held for long, other users cannot access the resource in question during that time. Because some RDBMS-based applications still prefer page-level locking to row-level locking, a lock can block resources that reside within the same page but that are not directly involved in the transaction. The problem is made worse if the lock is held for a long time. A typical solution to the problem with pessimistic locking is the application of an optimistic, timestamp-based approach. However, this must often be performed at the application level (e.g., by adding a timestamp column to the relevant tables) due to a lack of out-of-the-box support from many DBMSs for timestamp-based versioning. If the application is responsible for ensuring consistency, we now have a problem with our transaction monitor: the transaction monitor assumes that all these issues are dealt with directly between the transaction monitor and the DBMS during the 2PC. The XA-prepare and -commit calls implemented by the resource manager are expected to manage the transition from the "before" to the "after" state and locking/unlocking of the involved resources. Effectively, this means that we must include customized logic into the 2PC that deals with these issues at the application level by checking for timestamp conflicts before applying changes. Even if some transaction monitors support application-level locking through callbacks, which can be inserted into the two-phase commit, this approach severely limits an "off-the-shelf" approach because work that should originally have been split between the transaction monitor and the DBMS must now be performed at the application level (at least partially).

8.2.4.3 Problems with the Integration of Legacy Systems and Packaged Applications.

Perhaps the biggest problem with transaction monitors and 2PC is the lack of support for two-phase commit using an XA interface from legacy systems and packaged applications, such as an ERP or CRM system. Even if an ERP such as SAP uses an XA-capable database such as Oracle or DB2 internally, this does not mean that SAP can participate in a 2PC: all access to the SAP modules must go through an SAP API, such as BAPI, which is a non-transactional API.

This lack of support for 2PC in many legacy systems and packaged applications severely limits the application scope of distributed transactions and TP monitors because we normally need to integrate applications instead of databases into complex workflows.

8.2.4.4 Organizational Challenges.

If used at all, the adoption of 2PC has traditionally been limited to tightly coupled, well-controlled intra-enterprise environments or perhaps single application systems with short-lived transactions. Transaction coordinators are the control center for the orchestration of the 2PC amongst resource managers. Not only is tight coupling required at the protocol level, but also successful orchestration amongst participants requires that everybody "plays by the rules" in order to avoid frequent heuristic outcomes that leave transactions in an ill-defined state. Such tight control over databases, applications, transaction frameworks, and network availability is usually limited to intra-enterprise environments, if it can be achieved at all.

Conducting inter-organizational transactions between autonomous business partners is a completely different situation. In an inter-organizational environment, we cannot assume total control over all aspects of transaction processing. Relationships between trading partners are typically loosely coupled, and the nature of intra-business transactions reflects this loose coupling. The technical implementations of these transactions must deal with this loose coupling and also with the fact that the level of trust between the transaction participants is different from that of a tightly coupled, well-controlled environment. For example, security and inventory control issues prevent hard locking of local databases: Imagine a denial of service attack from a rogue partner that results in a situation where locks are taken out on all available items in your inventory database, preventing you from doing business while the locks remain in place.[1]

8.2.4.5   2PC Is Not Suited for Discontinuous Networks.   When integrating B2B systems over the Internet, the discontinuous nature of the Internet with its lack of QoS (quality of service) properties must be taken into account. This applies to the execution of the actual business logic of a transaction across the Internet in addition to any out-of-band interactions between transaction participants that are part of the transaction coordination because they are also executed over the Internet. Relying on a potentially discontinuous medium such as the Internet for execution of the two-phase commit could lead to situations that increase the time between the prepare and commit calls in an unacceptable way, with the potential for many heuristic outcomes.

8.2.5   NESTED AND MULTILEVEL TRANSACTIONS

The complexity of many business transactions and the fact that business transactions are potentially long running has led to the development of advanced transaction concepts such as multilevel and nested transactions.

A multilevel transaction T is represented by a set of sub-transactions $T = \{t_1, t_2, t_3, ..., t_n\}$. A sub-transaction t_i in T can abort without forcing the entire transaction T to abort. T can, for example, choose to rerun t_i, or it can attempt to find an alternative means of completion. If t_i commits, the changes should only be visible to the top-level transaction T. If T is aborted, then so is t_i. Multilevel and nested

---

[1] Even with optimistic concurrency control, this would be a risk because a participant could block access during the normally short time period of the transaction resolution (prepare/commit), during which all participants must lock the updated data, even when applying optimistic concurrency control policies for transaction execution.

transactions are slightly different in the way in which they deal with releasing locks on the completion of a sub-transaction.

Although some commercial transaction monitor implementations support the concept of nested or multilevel transactions, the problem with their adoption lies in the lack of support from resource managers (database and queue managers). Very few commercial resource managers provide sufficient support for nested transactions.[2] Unfortunately, this lack of support from the major commercial resource managers makes these good theoretical concepts somewhat unusable in the real world.

8.2.6 PERSISTENT QUEUES AND TRANSACTIONAL STEPS

Persistent queues can increase the reliability of complex processes. They can even create transactional steps in a more complex process: when combined with transactions, persistent queues can guarantee consistency for the individual steps of a process or workflow. An application can de-queue messages in the context of a transaction. If the transaction aborts, the de-queue is undone, and the message returned to the queue. People usually use abort count limits and error queues to deal with messages that repeatedly lead to an aborted transaction.

Figure 8-3 shows an example of a transactional process step with persistent queues. Notice that if the queue manager is not part of the database system (i.e., is an independent resource manager), the transaction effectively becomes a distributed transaction and requires a transaction monitor that can coordinate the two-phase commit between the database and queue managers.

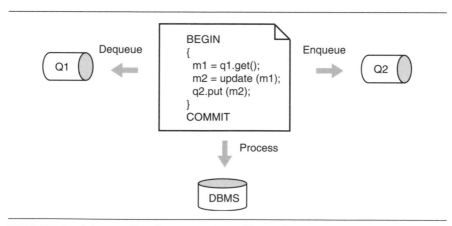

FIGURE 8-3   A transactional process step with persistent queues.

---

[2] More commonly, RDBMS offer support for Savepoints or similar concepts, which define a point in time to which a partial rollback can occur.

> **Leverage the Concept of Transactional Steps**
>
> A transactional step is a set of closely related activities, executed in the context of a single transaction. At the beginning of the transaction, an input token or message is read from an input queue. The result of the related activities is written into an output queue. Transactional steps are a key concept for ensuring process integrity because they facilitate the decomposition of complex, long-lived business processes into individual steps with short execution times and high transactional integrity. Transactional steps dramatically increase the robustness and flexibility of distributed systems.

8.2.7   TRANSACTION CHAINS AND COMPENSATION

The concept of *transactional steps* provides a great way for ensuring the integrity of individual process steps. You can create complex workflows or processes by chaining or linking together individual steps ("transaction chains"). However, the remaining issue is to ensure the integrity of the overall process or workflow. Although abort count limits and error queues provide a good means of ensuring no loss of information upon failure of an individual step, it is still necessary to fix these failures after detecting them.

One possible way to deal with failures in individual process steps is to identify compensating transactions that logically undo a previous transaction. For example, the compensation for a debit transaction would be a transaction that credits the same amount. An implementation of a distributed money transfer between two banks could be split into different steps that debit an account A at bank X and pass a message to the receiving bank Y using a transactional queue. If a problem occurs at bank Y (e.g., the account does not exist), bank X would have to execute a compensating transaction, such as crediting the appropriate account A (admittedly, this is a simplified example, ignoring the complexity of intermediary clearinghouses, end-of-day settlements, etc.).

Notice that, unlike nested or multilevel transactions, chained transactions effectively relax the isolation properties of ACID transactions because the results of each link in a chain of transactions is made visible to the outside world. For instance, assume that we have credited an account A in the first step of a transaction chain. When attempting to execute the corresponding debit on another account B in the next step, we discover that the target account B does not exist. We could now launch a compensating transaction to debit account A and undo the previous changes. However, a time interval now exists between the credit and subsequent debit of account A, during which the funds resulting from the credit transfer could have been withdrawn by another transaction, leading to the failure of the compensating transaction because the funds were no longer available.[3]

In order to apply compensating transactions in a workflow, we need to log the input and/or output of the individual steps of a workflow because we might need this data as input for compensating transactions.

> ### Combine Transaction Chains with Compensating Transactions
>
> ACID properties are usually too strong for complex workflows. Instead, chained transactions with compensating transactions offer a viable means of dealing with process integrity. Transaction chains combine individual transactional steps into more complex workflows. Compensating transactions undo previously executed steps if a problem is encountered during the execution of a particular step in a transaction chain.

8.2.8 SAGAS

SAGAs are formal workflow models that build on the concept of chained transactions (steps). A SAGA describes a workflow wherein each step is associated with a compensating transaction. If a workflow stops making progress, we can run compensating transactions for all previously committed steps in reverse order. Although formal SAGAs are still at the research stage, the concept of using a compensating transaction for dealing with specific failure situations in a complex workflow is valid.

A number of problems exist with SAGAs and compensations in complex workflows, particularly with the complexity of workflow graphs and the corresponding compensation graphs. Typically, the complexity of compensation graphs increases exponentially with the complexity of the actual workflow graph. Thus, it is generally impossible to define complete compensation graphs. In addition, the need to deal with failures during the execution of compensating transaction chains adds even more complexity.

Even if formal SAGAs and compensations for each possible combination of failures are unavailable, it often makes sense to apply the concept of compensating transactions for individual failure situations that have been specifically identified to fit this approach, such as failures that we expect to happen frequently, perhaps because they are caused by business conditions such as "out of funds."

8.2.9 BPM AND PROCESS INTEGRITY

As introduced in Chapter 7, Business Process Management platforms provide features to enable business analysts and developers to design, execute, and manage instances of complex business processes. Many BPM platforms are in fact based on or at least incorporate some of the features described previously, such as chains of transactional steps. In the following discussion, we examine how the

---

[3] Of course, in this example, the problem could be easily solved by reversing the order of the debit and the credit (starting with the debit first). However, the example still illustrates the problem.

formal introduction of a BPM will help to increase the process integrity aspects of an enterprise application.

Firstly, explicitly modeling workflows and processes and separating them from low-level technical code will have a positive impact on what process integrity actually means with respect to a particular process because the BPM approach provides a comprehensible separation between "technical integrity" and "process integrity."

Secondly, if the BPM engine provides a mechanism for monitoring and managing process instances at runtime, we receive a powerful mechanism for controlling the integrity aspects of individual process instances at no extra cost.

Finally, some BPM engines support the concept of compensating transactions, which is a key concept for managing the rollback of partially executed processes after a failure situation. A key question is whether compensating transactions are sufficient to ensure process integrity, given that the compensation-based model is less strict than, for example, the ACID properties of a distributed transaction. In particular, it is useful to examine how to handle failures of compensating transactions. Do we actually introduce compensations for failed compensations? Although in some rare cases this might be required (some transaction processing systems in financial institutions have sophisticated meta-error handling facilities that cope with failures in failure handling layers), this will not be the case in most systems. Thus, the support for compensating transactions as offered by some BPMs often presents a sound and flexible alternative to platforms that require very tight coupling with applications and resource managers, such as transaction monitors.

8.2.10 RELATED WEB SERVICE STANDARDS

This book takes on the position that Web services are only one possible technical platform for SOAs (see Chapter 9, "Infrastructure of a Service Bus"). However, we want to take a quick look at standards that relate to Web services and process integrity, because this subject is likely to become very important in the future, as Web services become more pervasive. Unfortunately, the area of standards for Web service-based business transactions (see Figure 8-4).

It is important to realize that most of this is still at an early stage. Simply defining a new transaction standard is usually insufficient for solving process integrity problems. Even if a standard emerges that is supported by a number of commercial transaction managers or coordination engines, it is insufficient: The real problem is not to implement a transaction or coordination engine that is compliant to a specific protocol, but rather to find widespread support for such a new coordination protocol from resource managers. Without the support of commercial databases, queue managers, and off-the-shelf enterprise application packages, a new transaction standard is not worth much to most people. Recall that it took the X/Open standard for Distributed Transaction Processing almost ten years from its initial specification to its adoption by the most widely used commercial data-

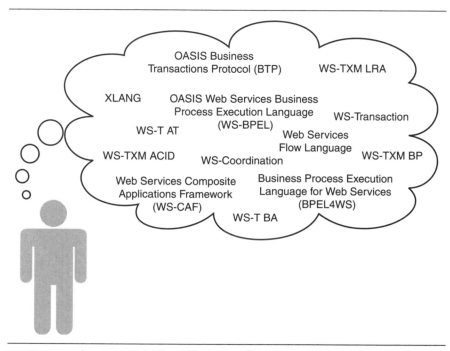

FIGURE 8-4 A number of different industry alliances and standardization bodies are currently working on different Web services-based transaction protocols. However, much of this work is still in the early stages, and no dominant standard has emerged yet.

base products such as Oracle, IBM DB2, and SQL Server. Even today, the support found in these products for the critical XA interface (which is the DB side of the X/Open standard) is often weak.

Some of the more recent (pre-Web services, post X/Open) transaction standards, such as the CORBA Object Transaction Service (OTS) and Java Transaction Service (JTS), were designed to fit into the widely adopted X/Open framework, which also applies to some of the previous Web services-based transaction standards. However, as we discussed in the first part of this chapter, X/Open-based 2PC transactions are not suited to the long-lived business transactions that you are likely to encounter in most Web service cases, which is why the need exists for a new transaction or coordination protocol. It remains to be seen which of the contenders will eventually become the dominant standard for loosely coupled transaction coordination and at what point in time commercial resource managers will support this standard. Until then, we must cope with ad-hoc solutions.

8.3   Recommendations for SOA Architects

Having discussed the concepts of data and process integrity on a more conceptual level, it is now time to examine concrete recommendations for SOA architects. In order to make this discussion as hands-on as possible, we will first introduce an extension to our airline example, which will serve as a basis for the discussion that follows.

8.3.1   EXAMPLE SCENARIO: TRAVEL ITINERARY MANAGEMENT

The management team of our airline has decided to expand the current online offering by providing airline customers with the ability to not only book individual flights but also to create complete itineraries for their trips, including multiple flight, hotel, and car reservations.

The new itinerary management system will reuse and build upon several of the airline's existing IT systems, in particular the customer management and billing systems. In addition, the customer database will be expanded to support the management of complex itineraries. Management decided that two different frontends are required for the new system: a Web-based online frontend and a call center for telephone support of customers. A further decision was to use different technologies in each of the two frontends: the Web-based frontend will use thin HTML clients, whereas the frontend for the call center agents needs more complex functionality and will thus be implemented as a VB GUI (fat client).

The high-level architecture of the system is based on three backend services: customer management (including itineraries), billing, and complex processes (in order to manage customer complaints regarding itineraries or invoices). In addition, a number of partner systems will have to be integrated, including partner airlines' flight reservation systems and hotel and car reservation systems (although this is not a key aspect of this discussion). Figure 8-5 provides an overview of the system architecture.

We will look at two key transactions throughout the rest of this chapter: *confirm itinerary* and *create invoice*. *Confirm itinerary* is an important transaction of the customer management system, which is responsible for confirming the individual flight, hotel, and car reservations on an itinerary, involving potentially complex interactions with partner systems. This transaction is potentially irreversible, in that the system might require a cancellation fee when attempting to cancel a previously confirmed booking (assuming that a cancellation is possible). *Create invoice* is a transaction of the billing system. Assuming that a customer has proven creditworthiness, the system creates an invoice, calculates the total amount and taxes for each individual item on the itinerary, and sends a letter with a printed version of the invoice to the customer by mail.

These two transactions are interesting for several reasons. First, they are closely related at the business level because the confirmation of an itinerary

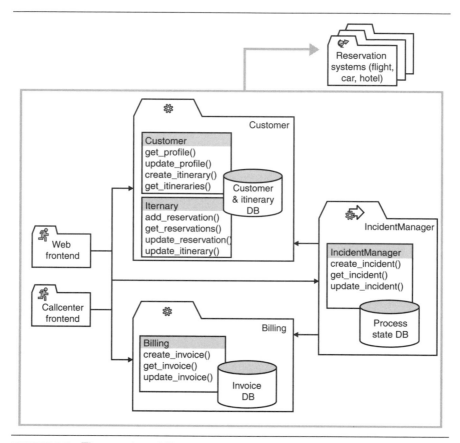

FIGURE 8-5 The new travel itinerary management system provides services to manage customers, itineraries, invoicing, and complex incidents.

inevitably causes costs and therefore must be accompanied by a valid invoice under all circumstances. Second, these transactions cross several organizational boundaries because they use two services provided by different departments (customer management is a marketing function, and invoicing is a back-office function) and even involve several different companies (other airlines, hotels, and car rental companies). Finally, these transactions also cross several technical boundaries. Notice in particular that in our airline example, these two transactions are related to two independent databases.

8.3.2 OPTIMISTIC CONCURRENCY CONTROL SHOULD BE THE DEFAULT

To begin with, it is necessary to explain how to deal with concurrent access to shared data in an SOA. Two widely established models for managing concurrent access to shared data by multiple users exist: *optimistic* and *pessimistic concurrency control*. Both come in multiple flavors, but the general characteristics of each model can be summarized as follows:

Pessimistic concurrency control. This model gives users exclusive access rights to a set of data that they intend to modify, usually through the acquisition of a lock, which is associated with the data in question. Other users are locked out—they cannot perform actions that would conflict with the lock until the lock owner releases it. This model is predominantly used in situations where heavy contention for data exists. The two key problems with this model are lockouts and deadlocks. For these reasons, pessimistic concurrency control assumes that lock times are short, which is normally only the case in automatic processing of data records.

Optimistic concurrency control. In this model, no locks are acquired during the transaction execution. Optimistic concurrency control permits different transactions to read the same state concurrently and checks for potential write conflicts and data inconsistencies only at the end of the transaction, when changes are actually written to the database. Because this implies that the danger of losing one's changes at the end of the transaction exists, this model is most effective in environments with low contention for data.

Each approach has its own advantages and disadvantages, depending on the specific problem context. As we will show, optimistic concurrency control is the preferable model in an SOA.

> ### Apply Optimistic Concurrency Control
>
> Optimistic concurrency control is the model of choice for long-running transactions, in particular those requiring interactions with human users or other sub-systems. In addition, optimistic concurrency control supports a more loosely coupled approach because resources are less dependent on clients, for example with respect to lock duration. For these reasons, optimistic concurrency control is the model of choice in an SOA because it significantly reduces dependencies between different service components.
>
> Of course, this is assuming that you are not limited by existing concurrency control policies, as would be the case if a legacy system had to be incorporated into an SOA. In that case, a flexible way to incorporate the existing policies into the overall concurrency policy of the SOA is required, and you might have to look at introducing intermediary services for bridging incompatible concurrency control policies.

8.3.2.1 Implementing Optimistic Concurrency Control.   Given the importance of optimistic concurrency control in an SOA, it is useful to examine specific implementation models. In order to determine write conflicts, the optimistic concurrency model must, at the end of each transaction, determine whether a competing transaction has changed the data after it was initially checked out. There are different ways to achieve this: using *timestamps*, *version counts*, or *state comparison* (directly or using check sums).

When using timestamps or version counts with relational databases, the most popular approach is to add a column for the timestamp or version number to each table that must be controlled (alternatively, you can add only a column to the top-level data structure). In order to determine write conflicts, you must add the timestamp or version number to the primary key used in the WHERE clause of the UPDATE statement. This minimizes the interactions required with the DBMS. If our timestamp or version number does not match the number correlating to the primary key, this means that somebody has changed the data after our initial read. In this case, no rows will be updated, and the user must reread the data and reapply the changes.

The benefit of state comparison is that you don't need to alter the structure of the database. Microsoft .NET provides an elegant implementation of these concepts in its ADO.NET framework. *ADO DataSets* contain complex data objects that you can easily read and write to and from databases, transform into XML, expose through Web services, and version through *ADO DiffGrams*. However, in environments that do not provide direct support for state comparison, the update logic is more complex, and we must maintain two versions of data throughout the transaction, which complicates the data structure used in our application. In these cases, timestamp or version number-based concurrency control is preferable.

When choosing timestamp or version number-based concurrency control, it is necessary to design service interfaces accordingly. This is best achieved by extending the root level elements of the data structures used in the service definitions to include the timestamp or version number. Notice that these data structures are typically fairly coarse-grained or even document-oriented. The different elements in such data structures are usually stored in different tables in a database. The assembly and disassembly of these complex data structures into different rows in a database is hidden from the user. In an SOA, we can deal with these data structures in an elegant manner that does not require operating at the database level. Specifically, it is possible to employ optimistic concurrency control with a level of granularity that best fits individual services. Conceptually, you can view this as a check-in/check-out mechanism for related data. It is only necessary to focus on version control at the level of root elements of these coarse-grained data objects, not at the level of individual rows.

Notice that when embedding version information in data structures that are passed between services in an SOA, you assume that you can trust clients not to attempt to modify the version information. If you cannot trust your clients, it is necessary to revert to the *state comparison* approach.

8.3.2.2 Use of Optimistic Concurrency Control in the Example. A good example of an entity that is accessed concurrently is the customer profile. Assume that a customer is examining his profile online while simultaneously talking to a call center agent by telephone, discussing a question related to his profile. While waiting for the agent's answer, the customer changes the meal preference to vegetarian. At the same time, the agent updates the customer's address details as instructed by the customer during their telephone conversation. Both read the profile at the same time, but the customer submits his changes just before the agent hits the Save button. Assume that the customer profile is protected by an optimistic concurrency control mechanism, based on timestamps or version numbers, for example. The agent now loses his changes because the system detects a write/write conflict based on the version number or timestamp of the agent's copy of the customer profile and thus refuses to apply the agent's changes. The agent must now reread the profile before reapplying the changes—an annoying situation, from the agent's point of view.

So far, we have made the implicit assumption that the customer profile is protected by an optimistic concurrency control mechanism. Does this still make sense in the light of the previous conflict situation, which resulted in the loss of the agent's changes to the customer profile? That depends on the concrete usage patterns of the system. Recall that optimistic concurrency control is predominantly used in situations with low contention for data. If one assumes that the chances of two users (such as customer and agent) accessing the same profile at the same time are extremely low (which seems likely in our overarching example), the optimistic approach might still be an acceptable solution. This decision will typically be made on a case-by-case basis, looking at different entities in a system individually.

Still, it is usually safe to assume that for all entities in an SOA, optimistic concurrency control is the default implementation strategy, unless we know from the outset that we are looking at an entity with very high contention. However, it is usually hard to predict realistic contention levels, and therefore the optimistic approach should be used as the default to start with. Over time, you will learn more about the critical entities of the deployed system, and you will react accordingly, by migrating the access to these highly contentious entities to more suitable concurrency control strategies. This evolutionary approach helps to dramatically reduce implementation complexity, enabling you to focus on those few entities that actually require a more sophisticated concurrency control mechanism.

Assume in our customer profile example we discover over time that conflicting write access is more common than initially anticipated. In this case, we can offer a number of different solutions.

First, we could implement a "merge" routine, which would enable an agent to merge his changes with those of the customer in the case of a conflict (see Figure 8-6). This would work as long as both are updating different parts of the customer profile, as in the previous example, where one changed the address and the other changed the meal preferences. This approach would require a move from a version or timestamp-based approach to a state comparison-based approach.

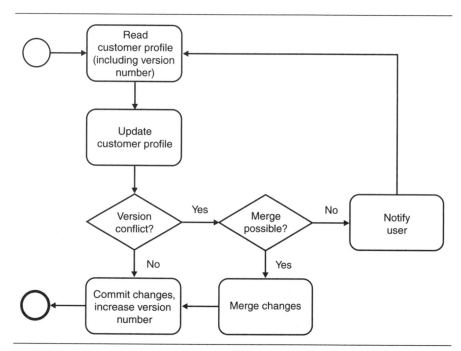

FIGURE 8-6 Normal version conflict detection can be combined with "merge" routines to enable more effective handling of version conflict situations.

Second, we could split the customer profile into finer-grained entities. For example, instead of having one data structure containing all customer profile data, we could have one for general data (such as name and date of birth), one for address information, one for customer preferences, and so on. This should also help reduce the potential for write/write conflicts.

Finally, pessimistic concurrency control enables us to avoid entirely conflict situations that result in the loss of updates by determining potential read-for-update conflicts when reading the data, far before we apply our changes (at the cost of locking out one of the users with write intentions). However, notice that such pessimistic strategies in an SOA usually come at much higher implementation costs and thus should be kept to a minimum. The next section provides an appropriate example.

8.3.2.3 Use of Pessimistic Concurrency Control in an Example.

Given the generally higher implementation complexity, pessimistic concurrency control in an SOA is usually limited to situations where a write/write conflict with resulting loss of changes is extremely critical. This situation can arise, for example, when updates are performed manually and require a considerable amount of time but a merger with another user's updates is almost impossible.

Recall that we are discussing pessimistic concurrency control at the application level, not at the database level—database locking mechanisms are generally not designed for long-lived transactions! This means that the locking mechanism that is required for a pessimistic concurrency control strategy must be implemented at the application level—that is, all services in our SOA that manage or manipulate data (which would be mainly *basic* and *intermediary* services, according to our service classification in Chapter 5, "Services as Building Blocks") must be implemented in a way that supports the pessimistic concurrency control strategy. As a result, we would significantly increase the implementation complexity (and hence the cost) of our SOA. In addition, application-level lock management usually results in fairly complex workflows because it requires much interaction with human users. For example, we need to provide a management infrastructure that deals with situations where a user takes out a lock on a critical entity but then fails to release it, for example because the user is out sick for a couple of days during which the entity remains locked. Examples of systems providing this kind of sophisticated infrastructure include document management systems and insurance claims processing systems (often combined with the concept of work baskets, which assign pending claims to individual clerks).

In our itinerary management example, we introduced the concept of an "incident," such as a complaint about an itinerary or an invoice. In our example, call center agents process these incidents. An incident can be a very complex data structure, including information about the customer, the itinerary, the invoice, a change history, a contact history (including copies of emails and faxes), a working status, and so on. Incidents are allocated on a per-agent basis, meaning that a single agent is responsible for the resolution of an incident. Thus, the customer only has to deal with one person, who has full knowledge of the incident.

In order to achieve this exclusive association between incidents and agents, we need to implement a pessimistic concurrency control strategy based on locks, which prevents an agent from updating an incident owned by another agent. The implementation of the basic locking strategy is relatively straightforward. For example, the incident table in the database can be expanded to include a "LOCKED BY" column. If a row contains no "LOCKED BY" entry, it is not locked. Otherwise, the "LOCKED BY" field contains the ID of the agent claiming the lock. Notice that all application modules accessing the incident must play by the rules, checking the "LOCKED BY" field. In our example, the incident table is encapsulated by an incident service interface, which takes care of ensuring that only requests from clients with the right credentials are allowed to access a particular incident.

Although all this sounds relatively straightforward, it is still considerably more complex than a simple optimistic concurrency control strategy. In addition, we now need a management infrastructure that enables us to deal with the allocation of locks on incidents. The allocation of locks will most likely be embedded in some kind of higher-level work-allocation system, based on the availability of agents with the right skills, combined with a work load distribution algorithm. Each agent might own a personal work basket containing all incidents allocated to him or her. Furthermore, we need a management function that enables managers to manually reallocate incidents to other agents, in case a customer calls with an urgent request when the original agent is unavailable, for example. Figure 8-7 provides an example design for the logic that would be required.

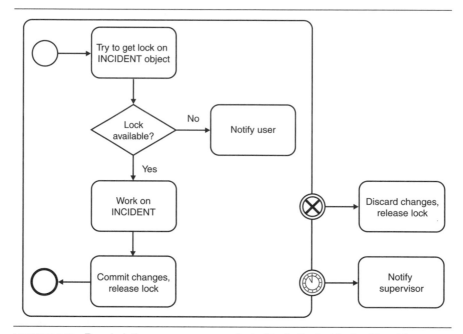

FIGURE 8-7 Pessimistic concurrency control with dedicated locks. Read-for-update conflicts are detected earlier, and only one user can access the incident object at the time.

All this significantly increases the cost and complexity of the solution. What was initially a relatively simple concurrency control problem has suddenly grown into a complex workflow and task management system.

8.3.3 MAKE UPDATE OPERATIONS IDEMPOTENT

Having discussed strategies that enable us to handle update conflicts in an SOA using concurrency control, the next requirement is to look at problems arising from failures during update operations. These occur because clients remotely invoke update operations on the server housing the service for the transaction. Handling failures during remote update operations in a distributed environment is a challenging task because it is often impossible for a client to determine whether the failure on the remote server occurred before or after the server executed the database update. Therefore, in the ideal world, service operations that change the database (update transactions) should be idempotent—that is, if they are invoked repeatedly, the corresponding function should only execute once. For example, suppose a service implementation encapsulates a database update. A client invokes the service, triggering the execution of the local transaction. If the service implementation crashes before it has sent the reply back to the client, the client can't tell whether the server has committed the transaction. Thus, the client does not know whether it is safe to resubmit the request (or to call an appropriate compensation operation).

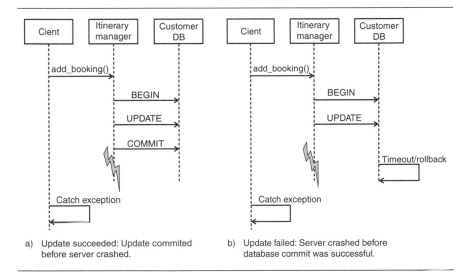

a) Update succeeded: Update commited
    before server crashed.

b) Update failed: Server crashed before
    database commit was successful.

FIGURE 8-8   Fatal failures at the server side make it hard for clients to detect whether an update was executed—that is, whether the fatal failure occurred before or after the database update was executed successfully.

Figure 8-8 shows two scenarios for a failure during the remote execution of an `ItineraryManager::add_booking()` operation. In the first version, the update is successfully executed, but the server fails before returning the reply to the client. In the second version, the server fails before actually committing the changes to the database, which will eventually lead to a rollback of the changes. In both cases, the client sees only that a problem occurred on the server side; he has no easy way of finding out whether the additional booking was added to the itinerary. This represents a problem for our client implementation because we cannot safely reinvoke the operation without the risk of adding the same booking twice (our implementation is not idempotent).

Notice that this type of problem applies only to certain types of update transactions: we need to differentiate between update operations with "set" semantics on one hand and "create/add/increment" semantics on the other. Typically, it is safe to reinvoke an operation with "set" semantics because in the worst-case scenario, we simply override the first update and don't actually change the overall outcome. "Create/add/increment" semantics are a bigger problem.

Thus, there are two possible solutions for these kinds of problems: The first approach is to change the semantics of an operation from "create/add/increment" to "set," which usually will not be possible for "create" semantics, but in many cases will be possible for "add/increment" semantics. The second approach is to make the non-idempotent transactions idempotent by slightly restructuring the transaction. We can achieve this by adding unique sequence numbers, as we will now discuss.

8.3.3.1 Use Sequence Numbers to Create Idempotent Update Operations.

In the previous section, we discussed different failure scenarios for the `Itinerary::add_booking()` update operation (refer to Figure 8-8), an operation with "add/increment" semantics. Changing the semantics of this operation to "set" is not easy because it would require reading the entire itinerary, adding the booking on the client side, and sending back the entire itinerary to the server—resulting in an undesirably coarse level of granularity. Instead, we can use unique sequence numbers to make the `add_booking()` operation idempotent.

Sequence numbers can be passed either implicitly (as part of the message header or some other place for storing request context information) or explicitly (as a normal request argument). This is a design choice, and it depends on the flexibility of the SOA infrastructure in the enterprise. The following example shows a possible solution for the `add_booking()` problem with explicit sequence number passing:

```
interface Itinerary {
  SQN getSequenceNumber();
  void add_booking (in SQN s, in Booking b);
}
```

If performance or latency is an issue (we are potentially doubling the number of remote interactions, at least for all update operations), we can assign sequence numbers in bulk—that is, a client can ask for a set of sequence numbers in a single call. Assuming the number space we use is fairly large, this is not a problem—if clients do not use all the sequence numbers, they can simply discard the ones they don't need.

Sequence numbers should generally be managed at the server side and assigned to clients upon request. You could think of ways in which clients could manage their own sequence numbers, by combining unique client IDs with sequence numbers for example. However, this increases the complexity of the problem, and rather than providing a server-side solution, it places the burden on potentially multiple clients.

8.3.3.2 Idempotent Operations Simplify Error Handling. A key benefit of using only idempotent operations in an SOA is that we can handle errors in a more easy and elegant fashion. Firstly, we can reinvoke operations a number of times, potentially minimizing the number of problems related to once-off error situations (e.g., a server crash due to a memory corruption).

In addition, we can group related remote calls into a single block for error handling purposes. This block can be executed repeatedly, regardless of where the failure occurred in the block, because it is safe to reinvoke previously executed idempotent operations. The following pseudo-code shows an example for the execution of two idempotent operations, `confirm_itinerary()` and `create_invoice()`, in a single block:

```
while (retry limit not reached) {
  try {
     itineraryManager.confirm_itinerary();
     invoiceManager.create_invoice();
  }
  catch (FatalError e) {
    // manage retry limit counter
  }
}
if (not successful) {
  // we now have a number of possible error scenarios
  // which we must address
}
```

Of course, we are not saying that you should not catch all possible error situations. In particular, a client implementation should handle user-defined exceptions individually on a per-call basis. However, this approach makes sense for handling fatal failures in more complex processes that are managed through recovery frameworks based on distributed log consolidation (see the previous section). In this case, the framework is responsible for determining, for example, if an itinerary has been confirmed but no corresponding invoice created. A system administrator could detect this problem description and manually fix the problem, by using an SQL console, for example.

8.3.4 AVOID DISTRIBUTED 2PC

In many cases, the adoption of log-based or other simple solution (as described in Section 8.2.1) is insufficient, such as when two operations must be executed together with "all or nothing" semantics (atomicity), and a failure of one operation would lead to a process inconsistency that cannot be handled by simple recovery routines.

Examine the `confirm_itinerary()` and `create_invoice()` operations described previously. Because it is absolutely critical for our airline not to confirm an itinerary without creating a corresponding invoice, the logging-based manual recovery framework described in the previous discussion on idempotent operations might not be acceptable. The airline might fear that the antici-pated volume of problems could be too large for a systems administrator to resolve manually in a timely manner, or the airline simply might not want to rely on a systems administrator to deal with problems that are directly related to a potential loss of income.

An intuitive solution is to use a transaction monitor and distributed 2PC to ensure the atomicity of our two update operations, `confirm_itinerary()` and `create_invoice()`. However, as we have discussed in Section 8.2.4, there are many problems with the distributed two-phase commit. In general, you should try to avoid using 2PC on the SOA level (i.e., across multiple service instances). In the following, we will present a number of potential solutions based on our itinerary management scenario and discuss their respective benefits and drawbacks.

8.3.4.1   First Iteration: Client Controlled Transactions.   A possible alter-native to the simple error handling mechanism would be the introduction of a transaction manager, which enables the grouping of both critical operations into one distributed transaction, as depicted in Figure 8-9.

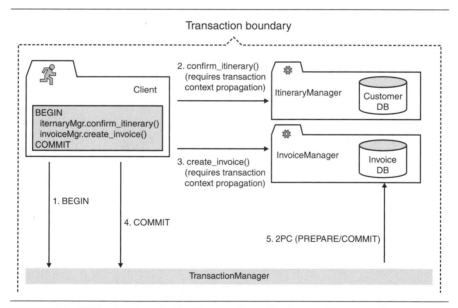

FIGURE 8-9   With client-controlled transactions, the transaction boundary spans the entire system, including transactional clients, all service implementations, and resource managers.

Technically, this approach would solve our problem because we could now ensure that no itinerary is finalized without creating a corresponding invoice. However, there are severe problems with this approach:

- The approach requires that we enable our clients to deal with distributed transactions. This is generally a bad idea, especially for lightweight user interfaces and Web servers, because it dramatically increases the complexity of service usage.
- Other issues that were identified during the discussion on distributed 2PC and tightly coupled ACID transactions at the beginning of this chapter can arise, including the very tight coupling at the technology and protocol layers, low performance, lack of support for long-lived transactions, and problems with integrating legacy applications and application packages.

Essentially, we are in danger of creating a solution that is complex to implement and administer and that severely limits the reuse potential of our backend services because now only transactional clients can use them. For these reasons, we need to look at alternative solutions.

> ## Avoid Exposing Transaction Logic to Service Clients
>
> In 99% of cases, exposing transaction control to service clients is a bad idea. Distributed 2PC relies on extremely tight coupling of clients and server-side services on many levels, which is fundamentally against the design principles of Service-Oriented Architectures, which are about independent, loosely coupled services.

8.3.4.2 Second Iteration: Server Controlled Transactions.
Rather than expose transaction logic to service clients, you should consider moving transaction control to the server side. Transactions that involve multiple updates (or even that span multiple resource managers) should be encapsulated inside a single service operation, where possible.

In our example, we could consider combining our `confirm_itinerary()` and `create_invoice()` operations into a single `confirm_itinerary_and_create_invoice()` operation. This would eliminate the need to expose transaction logic to our service client because we have now moved the management of the distributed transaction to the server side, as depicted in Figure 8-10.

Although in this approach we can now hide the complexity for distributed transaction processing from our service clients, there are still some issues with this design:

- Possibly the biggest problem with this approach is that our itinerary manager has now become a monolithic service that assumes control over another service's database and that is hardly reusable. By letting one service implementation access another service's database directly, we have failed to achieve the most important design goal of an SOA, namely, the creation of loosely coupled, independent services.

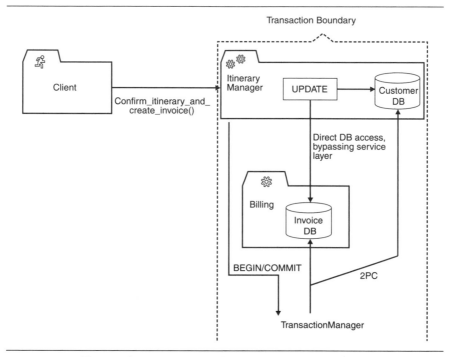

FIGURE 8-10 Transactions spanning multiple resource managers (databases and queues) can be encapsulated inside a single service operation. However, the danger of creating monolithic services that are not reusable exists.

- This approach requires that both databases participate in a 2PC. Ignoring the previously described design issues, this might also represent a technical problem: recall that the billing system that is responsible for invoice management is a legacy system. This system might not be designed to participate in a 2PC, either because the underlying database is not 2PC enabled (i.e., XA-compliant), or because the billing application relies on total control over the database (a common scenario) and cannot handle transactions that bypass it.
- Finally, this second iteration of our design still requires an infrastructure for handling a transaction that spans two databases. This means that we still incur the potentially high license cost for a transaction monitor, plus the additional overhead for implementation and maintenance, which should not be underestimated. Not only is our implementation complex, but it also requires higher-skilled developers and systems administrators.

8.3.4.3   Third Iteration: Implicit Application Level Protocol.   Given   the problems with the first two iterations of our design, the third design iteration could consider   moving   the   process   integrity   issues   that   we   have   with   our `confirm_itinerary()` and `create_invoice()` operations to the application level. We could agree upon an implicit application level protocol as follows:

- We split the creation and actual sending of the invoice into two operations (so far, we have assumed that `create_invoice()` would create and send the invoice).
- The invoice is created before the itinerary is finalized. This helps to ensure that no itinerary lacks a corresponding invoice.
- If we can create the invoice successfully, we can next confirm the itinerary and call `send_itinerary()`.
- Because `send_invoice()` can still fail, we create a background task in the process engine that checks every night for inconsistencies between itineraries and invoices. If this process detects a confirmed itinerary for which the invoice has not been sent, the process ensures that this takes place.

Figure 8-11 provides an overview of this approach. Although it solves all the issues related to distributed transaction processing, it is somewhat limited. In particular, it requires that clients now adhere to a complex yet implicit protocol at the application level. For example, no client can confirm an itinerary without previously creating an invoice. We are not only relying on our clients to play by the rules, but we are also dramatically increasing the complexity for our clients by forcing them to implement complex business logic. Chapter 7 provides a discussion of the disadvantages of putting complex business logic into application frontends.

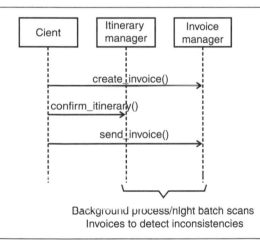

FIGURE 8-11 An implicit application-level protocol could be agreed upon in order to ensure consistency between invoices and finalized itineraries.

8.3.5 BUILD TRANSACTIONAL STEPS

Having discussed the issues with distributed 2PC and implicit application-level protocols in the previous section, we have still not arrived at a completely satisfactory solution for our `confirm_itinerary_and_create_invoice()` problem. In this section, we look at how the concept of transactional steps might provide a better solution than the previous design iterations.

Recall that a transactional step is a set of activities that are closely related to one another, executed in the context of a single transaction, with a queue as an input feed for these activities and another queue as a store for the output of that step. We now look at how this concept can be applied to our problem.

8.3.5.1 Fourth Iteration: Fully Transactional Step.

If we apply the transactional step concept to our `confirm_itinerary_and_create_invoice()` problem, a possible solution might look as follows:

- The `confirm_itinerary()` operation simply stores a message in a "pending confirmations" queue.
- This queue serves as the input for a background thread, which represents a transactional step. This thread uses the "pending confirmations" queue as an input queue. For each pending confirmation, the appropriate steps (confirmation and invoice creation) are executed in the context of a transaction, and the result is stored in an output queue of "confirmed itineraries."
- The system notifies the customer as soon as the itinerary has been successfully finalized. Alternatively, in the case of a problem, a dialogue with the customer begins, aimed at solving the problems with the itinerary.

Figure 8-12 shows a possible implementation architecture.

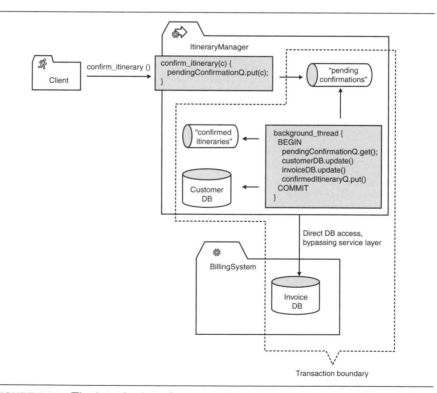

FIGURE 8-12   The introduction of a transactional step on the server side enables us to decouple the client's `confirm_itinerary()` call from the actual server-side processing of the confirmation request.

This approach solves a number of the problems with the first couple of design iterations and also provides additional benefits:

- We remove complexity from the clients and instead place it into a service under our own control.
- We no longer risk losing income due to the system confirming itineraries without sending out a corresponding invoice because the interactions with the input and output queues are transactionally secured.

However, there are also some significant drawbacks:

- This approach is not much better than the second design iteration with its `confirm_itinerary_and_create_invoice()` approach because this design also requires that the ItineraryManager accesses the billing system's database directly, thus bypassing the service layer, which was designed to provide service-oriented abstractions from this database in the first place.
- Finally, we have now reintroduced the need for a transaction monitor, which coordinates the 2PC between different queues and databases, with all associated costs and complexities.

8.3.5.2   Fifth Iteration: Semi-Transactional Step.   Rather than adding complex logic to the itinerary manager service and accessing the billing system's database directly, we now create a new ConfirmationManager service. This is a process-centric service (see Chapter 6, "The Architectural Roadmap") that implements a "less" transactional step to encapsulate the required functionality. Figure 8-13 provides an overview of the implementation architecture. The confirm_itinerary() operation stores only a request in the "pending confirmations" queue, which serves as an input queue for background threads. This thread processes pending confirmations in a transaction. The transaction calls the basic services ItineraryManager and InvoiceManager. Notice that these calls are part of the transaction—that is, we do not assume that a transaction context is propagated to these services—these services execute their own transactions to update their databases but are not part of the ConfirmationManager's transaction.

This final design iteration based on a "less" transactional step solves our most pressing problems:

- We are now back to a clean separation between "basic" and "process-oriented" services (see Chapter 5 on service types), significantly enhancing the reusability and maintainability of the system.
- The basic services (customer and invoice manager) now fully encapsulate their databases, and we do not bypass these services as part of the itinerary confirmation. Instead, they retain their reusability potential.
- The new ConfirmationManager service now contains the specialized (and probably less reusable) business logic, which is required to finalize itineraries.

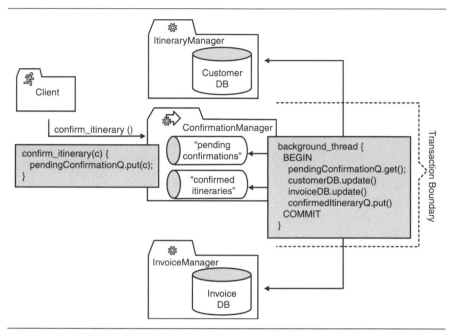

FIGURE 8-13   Introducing a dedicated ConfirmationManager in combination with semi-transactional steps enables us to limit the transaction boundary to the `confirm_itinerary()` implementation. We are thus no longer forced to access another service's database directly, as this is a fundamental violation of SOA design principles.

- We do not require a 2PC across multiple resource managers (we rely on the queue manager's built-in transaction mechanism), and thus we do not need a transaction monitor, which reduces complexity and costs.

However, there is one outstanding issue with this design: The transactional brackets around the in-queue and out-queue only offer a limited guarantee of non-approval of itineraries without creating a corresponding invoice. These brackets provide only a guarantee that we do not lose any itinerary confirmation requests due to the transactional nature of the queues. However, we still need to deal with the scenario in which the transaction logic fails because it is possible to confirm the itinerary even when the subsequent creation of an invoice fails. Because the requests to the itinerary and invoice manager are not transactional, aborting the confirmation manager's transaction will not undo the changes already applied to customer and invoice databases.

Instead of aborting the step's transaction in case of a problem, we should create an error token, place the token into an error queue, and commit the transaction—we are still guaranteed not to lose any information because the error queue is part of the transaction. However, we must deal with this problem, and we will look into these issues in the next two sections.

8.3.5.3 Sixth Iteration: Choosing the Right Level of Granularity for Individual Steps.

The basic idea of transactional steps is that we can combine them to create chains or even graphs of relatively independent yet logically related steps.

Choosing the right granularity for individual steps is difficult. On one hand, we do not want to clutter the system with meaningless micro-steps. On the other hand, the more fine-grained the individual steps, the more flexibly they can be rearranged to address changes in the business logic or to enable better error handling. In the case of the itinerary management example, we need to anticipate two basic problems: a problem with the itinerary itself (e.g., a confirmed seat on a flight is no longer available due to cancellation of the flight) or a problem with the creation of the invoice. Each case must be addressed individually by invoking the matching compensation logic.

We could also have achieved this by adding appropriate error handling logic. For example, we could have individual try/catch blocks for each remote invocation, as follows:

```
BEGIN
{
    pendingConfirmationQ.get();
    try {
      itineraryMgr.confirm_itinerary();
    }
    catch (e1){
      errorQ.put(e1)
  COMMIT;
     return;
    }
    try {
      invoiceMgr.create_invoice(r1);
    }
    catch (e2) {
     errorQ.put(e2)
  COMMIT;
  return;
    }
    confirmedItineraryQ.put();
}
COMMIT;
```

However, this approach limits the flexibility of rearranging the executing order of each individual step because code must be modified to change the order of execution.

Another approach is to change the design by splitting this step into two independent steps, which are then linked together. Each step is now responsible for handling only a single part of the overall transaction. In the case of a problem with each of these steps, we can put the resulting error token into a separate error queue. The first error queue is responsible for handling problems with itineraries, while the second is responsible for handling problems with invoices. Figure 8-14 provides an overview of how the initially large transactional step can be broken down into two more fine-grained steps.

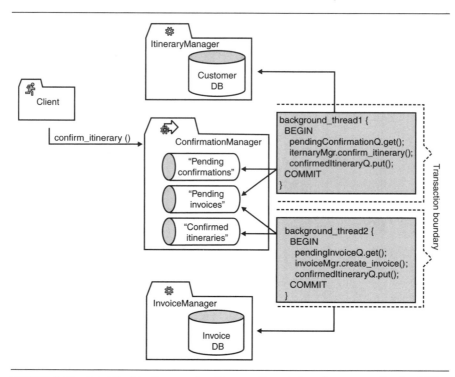

FIGURE 8-14 Introducing finer-grained transactional steps increases the flexibility of the system, especially with respect to error handling.

Assuming a sufficiently generic system design (in particular the message formats passed between the different queues), the use of more fine-grained transactional steps facilitates the reconfiguration of the execution order by changing the configuration of our input and output queues. This permits us to change the system on the fly to improve the way in which we handle error situations. For example, we might want to change the order of steps to create the invoice before confirming the itinerary. Notice that even if this reordering does not happen completely "on-the-fly" (which is the likely case—often the "on-the-fly" reconfiguration fails due to some minor data conversion or configuration issues), we will be pretty close to a completely flexible solution. In particular, this approach eliminates the need to set up a large project to implement the required changes because such a reconfiguration represents much lower risks compared to a major change in the application code.

Another benefit of this approach is that we limit the number of error scenarios in individual steps, and we can associate more meaningful error queues with each step—each problem type is reported into a separate error queue.

8.3.6   USE SIMPLE YET FLEXIBLE COMPENSATING LOGIC

In the theory of SAGAs and chained transactional steps, each step in a chain is associated with a compensating transaction. In case of failure during the processing of a transaction chain, we simply call the compensating transactions for each of the steps executed so far. In our itinerary management example, `confirm_itinerary()` and `create_invoice()` could be associated with compensating transactions, which would aim to undo the previous changes, as shown in Figure 8-15.

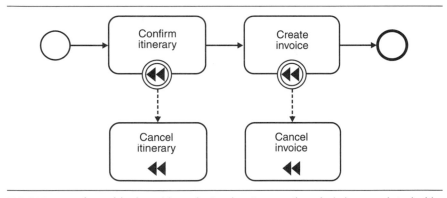

FIGURE 8-15   In an ideal world, each step in a transaction chain is associated with a compensating transaction. In case of failure, the compensating transactions for all successfully executed steps are called to undo all previous changes.

This works in theory, but in practice, there are several limitations to this approach. First, in many cases, a specific operation will have no simple compensating transaction. Take our `confirm_itinerary()` operation: If an itinerary has been confirmed once, real costs have been created because we will have made reservations for flights, cars, and hotels, which cannot simply be canceled—in many cases, a fee will be associated with a cancellation.

Second, many business processes are not linear—that is, they are not simple chains of transactions but are based on complex, context-sensitive decision graphs—where context refers to technical as well as business-related information and constraints. Although in theory the concept of compensation should not only apply to linear chains but also to complex graphs, this dramatically increases the complexity of compensations, especially due to the context sensitivity of many decision trees, which often will have an impact on different ways to compensate particular nodes.

Finally, we are likely to encounter problems not only in the transactional steps but also in the compensating transactions. How do we deal with a problem in a compensating transaction? Is there a compensation for a failed compensation?

In many cases, all of this means that a 1:1 mapping between transactional steps and compensating transactions is not feasible. Recall our discussion on exceptions versus special cases at the beginning of this chapter. For example, is an "out of stock" situation an exception or simply a special case that must be dealt with at the business level?

In our itinerary management example, it seems very likely that an overly simplistic compensation approach is not going to work. For example, we will most likely have to take into account cancellation fees resulting from a complete or partial cancellation of an itinerary. Figure 8-16 shows how a revised, more realistic workflow for itinerary finalization and invoice creation might look.

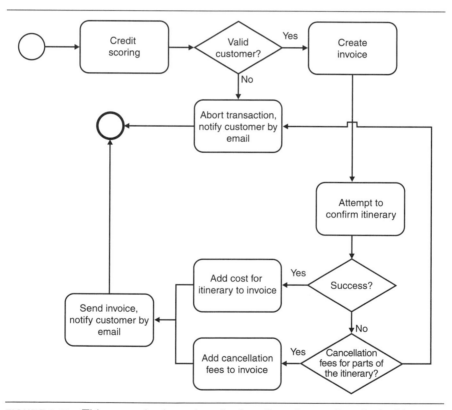

FIGURE 8-16 This example shows how the handling of exceptions in the itinerary finalization becomes part of the workflow. Thus, we are no longer dealing with exceptions or compensating transactions. Instead, we treat these situations as "special cases" within the normal workflow.

> ### Consider BPM If It Is Getting More Complex
>
> If the complexity of your process definitions, including special cases and com-pensation logic, is getting out of hand, you might want to consider using a BPM platform. Make sure that this platform provides you not only with suffi-ciently rich graphical tools for modeling your standard and special case pro-cesses but also the ability to model compensating transactions and a framework for automatically mapping these associated compensating trans-actions to a transactional execution environment.

8.3.7 COMBINE SOA, MOA, AND BPM TO INCREASE FLEXIBILITY

When examining projects with very complex process logic that spans the bound-aries of enterprises or other organizational barriers, it makes sense to look at the combination of SOA, MOA, and BPM to increase the flexibility with which pro-cesses can adapt to changes on either side of the organization's boundary, as depicted in Figure 8-17.

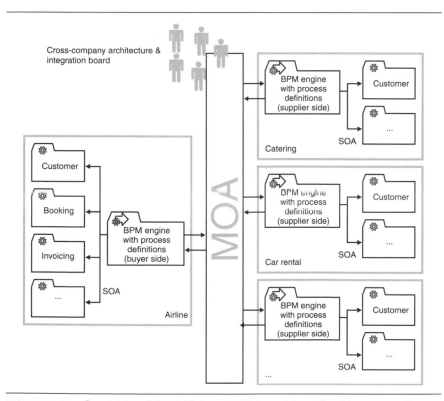

FIGURE 8-17 Combining SOA, MOA, and BPM provides a flexible means of integrating complex processes that cross enterprise boundaries.

In such a case, the SOA would provide basic services and process-oriented services within each individual enterprise, as we discussed in Chapter 4. The basic services provide the core business logic, while the process-centric services (e.g., implemented by a BPM engine) provide the actual business process logic.

Using an MOA rather than an SOA to provide integration across enterprise boundaries makes sense in many cases. Firstly, an MOA can provide greater flexibility with respect to message formats and different types of messaging middleware. In addition, inherently asynchronous MOAs are better suited to protect an enterprise against time delays on the partner side, which are outside the control of the issuing side. In addition, the SOA usually provides store and forward functionality ("fire and forget"), which eliminates some of the issues we discussed earlier on with respect to making operations idempotent. Finally, an MOA in combination with a BPM is well suited to represent Petri-Net-like communication trees with multiple branches, which can often be required in these types of integration scenarios.

8.4 Conclusion

Ensuring process integrity is often more a project management issue than a technical issue—the available technical solutions are relatively well known, but how and when to select each solution is often a key problem. Finding the right tradeoff between integrity requirements from a business perspective and sophistication of the technical solution is a task that requires careful analysis from responsible architects and project managers.

It is important for project managers to understand that a very clear tradeoff exists between the level of process integrity and implementation costs. For example, while the two-phase commit protocol potentially provides a very high level of integrity (at least in homogeneous, tightly coupled environments), it comes with very high implementation costs because it requires highly skilled architects and developers and very expensive software. However, transactional steps incur lower costs and offer reasonable process integrity properties. They often provide a very good cost/integrity tradeoff (Figure 8-18 categorizes several approaches to process integrity in regard to their cost integrity ratio).

If technical project managers can communicate these tradeoffs clearly to the decision makers at the business level, they enable them to make judgments regarding the level of consistency requirements they have and the money they are prepared to spend on them. Chapter 13, "SOA Project Management," adds to this discussion by providing concrete tools for project managers to enable them to find the right tradeoff between implementation costs and integrity requirements.

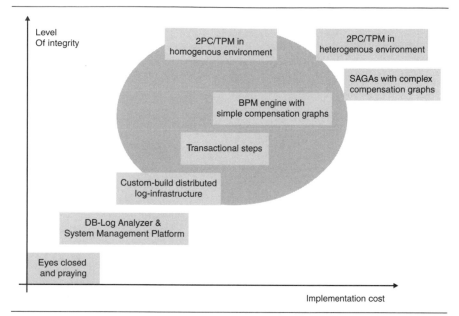

FIGURE 8-18   It is key for project managers to realize the tradeoff between the level of process integrity provided by a particular technical solution and its implementation costs.

References

Codd, E.F. *A Relational Model of Data for Large Shared Data Banks*. ACM Communications, Volume 13, No 6, June 1970. [Co70]

9

Infrastructure of the Service Bus

In this chapter, we describe the different elements that constitute an SOA-enabling infrastructure, referred to in the following as a *service bus*. One of the fundamental principles that this chapter is based upon is the assumption that it is impossible for large organizations to enforce standardization on a single technical architecture. We believe that this is especially true with respect to communication middleware, application platforms, or interface technology. Consequently, this chapter is not about describing specific technical standards for a service bus. Instead, we propose to look at a service bus as a kind of *meta bus*, which is comprised of the different existing software buses and middleware platforms that you will find in your organization. The job of the service bus is not only to enable basic interaction with different service components across the different platforms, but also to tie together the different higher-level infrastructure functions of these platforms.

After a general overview of the service bus concept in Section 9.1, Section 9.2 looks at logging and auditing, followed by scalability and availability in Section 9.3, and security in Section 9.4.

9.1 Software Buses and the Service Bus

People often use the term *software bus* to refer to the technical infrastructure of the distributed environment. We consider a software bus to be analogous to the well-known concept of a hardware bus. Much as a hardware bus enables the integration of hardware parts from different vendors, for example when assembling a desktop computer, a software bus is the standardized way of hooking together any software components.

9.1.1 BASIC CONCEPTS OF A REAL-WORLD SERVICE BUS

The most widely known software bus is OMG's CORBA, essentially a communication infrastructure for individual object instances. The CORBA infrastructure enables an object to locate any other object on the bus and invoke any of that object's operations. The CORBA model does not make a strict distinction between clients and servers and is essentially a symmetrical bus. CORBA is a very mature technology, but unfortunately, its underlying concept leans itself to a very fine-grained communication infrastructure that created a history of maintenance and performance problems in many projects.

Whereas CORBA is very generic bus technology with a focus on object orientation, another concept of a software bus recently emerged called the *Enterprise Service Bus* [DC2004]. Although as of this writing, it cannot be considered anywhere near a standard, its main elements are a coarse-grained XML communication protocol together with a message-oriented middleware core to perform the actual message delivery.

A number of other software buses are on the market, among them the Enterprise Java Beans as part of the J2EE specification, Microsoft's .NET, and various messaging products, including IBM MQSeries and Tibco Rendezvous. All these buses require standardization on a single interaction and communication model, as shown in Figure 9-1. For example, CORBA and EJB promote synchronous object-oriented communication, whereas messaging products such as MQSeries support asynchronous document-oriented communication.

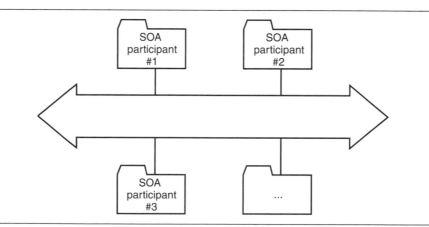

FIGURE 9-1   Ideal software bus that supports a single communication model. All applications must conform to the same standard, such as CORBA or MQSeries.

In a real enterprise application landscape, a single communication model will hardly suffice. Instead, you will need various communication models based on the requirements of the individual application. Vendors have long understood this point, and they provide environments that support multiple communication models at the same time. The J2EE environment, for example, supports various communication types, as shown in Figure 9-2. EJBs provide synchronous object-oriented communication, the Java Message Service (JMS) provides messaging, the system supports communication using email and SOAP, and the Servlet specification provides general support for HTTP applications.

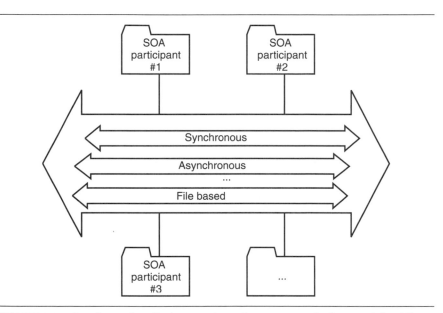

FIGURE 9-2   A software bus that supports various communication models at the same time, such as synchronous, asynchronous, or file-based communication.

In the real world, the situation is usually even more complicated because products from different vendors that support similar communication models are often in use at the same time. This situation can arise when different departments of the company introduce competing technology or when a new technology enters the environment as the result of a merger or acquisition. A typical enterprise "software bus" will usually look like that depicted in Figure 9-3.

Of course, single applications might use various communication models when communicating with each other. For example, an application might call another one using a synchronous technology if an immediate answer is required and might use an asynchronous communication model if it requires guaranteed and reliable delivery.

However, no matter what technology you use, an enterprise SOA infrastructure must conform to certain standards across the board in order to achieve certain goals, such as security and auditing that is independent of the product or the network protocol. In this respect, a service bus is not like a general software bus. An enterprise must create a higher-level entity, some kind of *Über bus* or *Meta bus* that endorses all the various products and technologies of the enterprise.

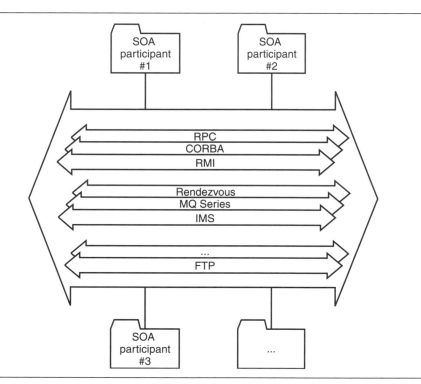

FIGURE 9-3   The infrastructure of a real-world enterprise will normally consist of various products that support similar communication models.

Create a Meta Bus

Do not enforce the usage of a single product, even one that supports many communication models, as the sole service bus of the organization. Plan for a service bus on a meta level that supports technical services at a higher level and adds flexibility that can be critical for the business during acquisitions or major restructuring.

This is why most of the products available on the market cannot be considered service buses in their own right. Instead, they fall into one—or both—of two categories: communication frameworks and execution containers. Communication frameworks are essentially infrastructures that only facilitate communication without many additional infrastructure services. Practically all communication frameworks are built around the concept of a stub and a dispatcher. Typical communication frameworks are MOM products and plain remote method invocation frameworks. Execution containers provide much more sophisticated infrastructure support, including support for transactions and security. Typical execution containers are CORBA and the EJB container.

However, do not develop this meta bus in isolation from concrete application projects. Avoid keeping the concepts too abstract; do not build too many technical features into it initially. Chapter 12, "The Organizational SOA Roadmap," describes how and why you should develop an SOA infrastructure gradually, hand-in-hand with concrete business application projects. Chapter 16, "Credit Suisse Case Study," discusses a case study, outlining how a company introduced a synchronous Information Bus (CSIB), an asynchronous Event Bus Infrastructure (EBI), and a file transfer-based Bulk Integration Infrastructure (BII), all driven by the demand from application projects, which in turn were driven by concrete business demands.

9.1.2 SERVICE STUB AND DISPATCHER

A service stub is a piece of software that is located at the client side of a service (see Figure 9-4). It provides a local API that presents a convenient access method for the remote service. The service stub encapsulates technical functionality such as handling of the network and application protocol, marshalling and unmarshalling of data, and standard security mechanisms.

The service dispatcher is the counterpart of the service stub. It receives incoming network requests that are generated by the service stub. The service dispatcher analyzes these requests technically and invokes the requested operation with the appropriate data.

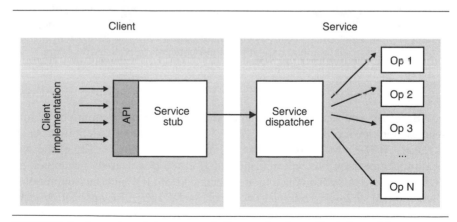

FIGURE 9-4   A service stub represents the service for a client. It provides a convenient API that the client developer can easily use. The service stub encapsulates the complexity of the technical access of the service such as network protocol, marshalling and unmarshalling of data, standard security mechanisms, etc.

9.1.2.1 Code Generation. Code generation is a powerful technique that can be applied to SOA projects in an efficient manner. In such a scenario, the code generator encapsulates all technical knowledge regarding distribution and service invocation. The application developers can focus on the business aspects of interface definition, while the code generator covers technical issues.

Code generation decouples the functional code from the technical code. It provides support for different programming languages, various network and application protocols, and different operating systems with a single code base. Code generation can be used to generate test clients and test servers—a handy feature that can prove beneficial for the overall development process. Last but not least, code generation typically increases the quality of the technical code. Contrary to handcrafted code, the generated code will be uniform. Improvements in generated code (e.g., better marshalling or connection management) can be made without causing an impact on current applications if the changes are restricted to the inside of the API of the generated code.

Projects that do not use code generation often suffer from a cut-and-paste syndrome. In this scenario, developers of business functionality integrate one functioning version of the technical code into their implementation of the business logic. This code will be repeatedly reused, while slight changes to that code can lead to many different implementations of the same technical functionality.

Successful Use of Code Generation

Use code generation to automate repetitive tasks that cannot be resolved using code libraries, such as generating type-safe service interface stubs, which provide high-performance marshalling code. Avoid changing generated code manually at all costs! You cannot regenerate code without losing your changes, which will be a nightmare if you use generated code across many different interfaces. Instead, modify the code generator if possible. Alternatively, use smart scripts that can differentiate between handcrafted and generated code within a single file.

Basically, you can use code generation in a top-down or bottom-up fashion. Whereas top-down code generation is based on formal interface definitions such as IDL or WSDL, the bottom-up approach analyzes the source code of the service implementation. A typical candidate for top-down code generation is CORBA, where stubs and skeletons are generated from IDL interface definitions. Many modern Web service frameworks, such as .NET or J2EE application servers, support bottom-up mapping of existing APIs (e.g., Java classes) to Web service interfaces (WSDL), often using a combination of internal code generation and reflection.

9.1.2.2 Top-Down Approach. The precondition for top-down code generation is the usage of a formal interface definition language such as IDL or WSDL.

Using a formal interface definition language has a great impact on the development process. It decouples the formal description of interfaces from the actual coding. As illustrated in Figure 9-5, this decoupling enables development teams to simplify the coordination of the service programmers and their clients.

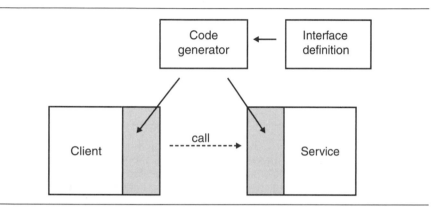

FIGURE 9-5 Code generation is a powerful mechanism to increase development productivity and quality. The code generator encapsulates the technical complexity of the communication between client and service. This enables the developers of both client and service to focus on the functional code.

9.1.2.3 Bottom-Up Approach. Code generation can also be performed using low-level implementation APIs (e.g., Java classes or CICS transaction programs) rather than from abstract, implementation-independent interface definitions (see Figure 9-6).

This technique is particularly useful when transforming legacy applications into services. If existing code must be exposed as a service, the generation of the service interface can save a lot of development time.

The caveat is that we get service interfaces that are programming language-specific, technology-focused, and very fine-grained. This is particularly true for the transformation of the traditional application with terminal-based user interfaces such as VT3270. The user screens, which are the natural structural elements of these applications, might be of an inappropriate granularity for a service interface.

The bottom-up approach can also be applied to the development of new applications. Although there is no explicit representation of the interface in a formal document, the careful design of the interface is still pivotal and cannot be omitted. With the bottom-up approach comes the danger of ad-hoc design, although there are also benefits to this approach. For example, no additional development tools are required for the design of the service. The developer of the service can use the preferred development environment and modeling tools that are used for the development and design of the original code. If the code generator is integrated into this environment, you can achieve very short turn-around times.

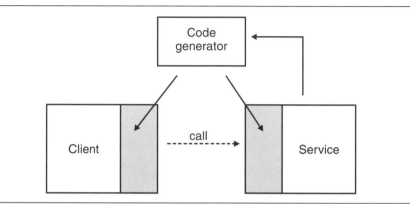

FIGURE 9-6 Bottom-up code generation is based on the service implementation. It is therefore dependent on a specific programming language and the details of its runtime environment and implementation technique. The code generator can use a service description language such as WSDL as an intermediate representation.

The bottom-up approach leverages a development model that is driven by the implementation of the services. Very efficient development environments exist that support the bottom-up approach such as Microsoft's Visual Studio .NET. The downside of such efficiency is a high degree of technical dependencies that could result in a technology lock-in that jeopardizes all the flexibility that should have been leveraged using the SOA approach. Therefore, you should take care when deciding whether to employ a bottom-up or top-down strategy.

> ## Top-Down Service Design Is the Preferred Approach in an SOA
>
> Service definitions are probably the single most important artifacts in an enterprise SOA. Therefore, it is important that you put a lot of thought into the specification of each individual service. Ensure that all service definitions
>
> - Meet business requirements
> - Are designed at the right level of granularity
> - Provide potential for later reuse
> - Can be implemented in a way that ensures scalability and integrity
> - Are independent of any underlying implementation
> - Provide appropriate service level specifications
>
> Service definitions should be designed explicitly; they should not be generated from lower-level APIs automatically.

9.1.2.4 Code Generation With MDA. Model Driven Architecture (MDA) is a contemporary approach to managing technology-independent service specifications, and implementing and managing "SOA meta-bus" architectures, as described in Section 9.1.1.

MDA is the umbrella-term for a number of specifications that are currently standardized by the Object Management Group (OMG), including UML, XMI, and MOF. MDA leverages UML to specify Platform Independent Models (PIMs) and Platform Specific Models (PSMs). In MDA terms, a PIM is the formal specification of the technology-neutral structure and function of a system, while a PSM adds the technical details which are needed for the concrete implementation of a software component. The Meta-Object Facility (MOF) is at the heart of the MDA concept. MOF-based meta-models allow the implementation of model repositories, the exchange of models (via XMI), and the transformation between different models, e.g. from a PIM to a PSM. While not limited to code generation techniques, MDA is well suited to using these techniques by generating the mapping from an abstract model to a concrete model implementation. MOF is particularly well suited to define and implement model transformations. A number of tools and standards support the transformation of MOF meta-data, e.g. transformation of UML models into XML, CORBA IDL, Java, and lately into WSDL. This allows for the implementation of very sophisticated code generators, which can generate highly targeted code, as shown in Figure 9-7.

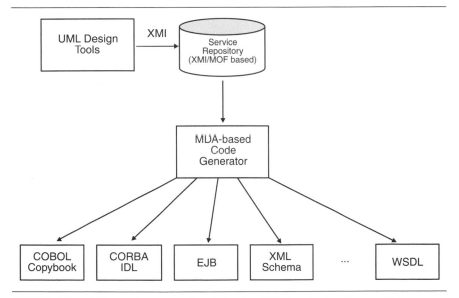

FIGURE 9-7 MDA can be a good basis for the "SOA meta-bus," providing platform-independent service definition and model transformations that support a wide range of middleware and SOA infrastructure platforms.

In the light of our discussion on "top-down" versus "bottom-up" code generation (refer to the previous section), technology-independent service definitions would be usually defined in a top-down fashion as a PIM, representing only business functionality. MDA tools can then be used to generate platform specific service interfaces, e.g. in CORBA IDL or WSDL.

In many cases, MDA tools will be used in combination with existing code generators, e.g. CORBA IDL compilers or WSDL compilers. However, most MDA tools go beyond the generation of service stubs by supporting the generation of prototypical service implementations, GUI descriptors, SQL code, etc.

While MDA is a very powerful concept, it is clearly not a "silver bullet": Like any other technology, MDA depends on a specific set of standards and tools. However, with its focus on model transformation, MDA in combination with SOA could help especially those enterprises which are suffering particularly badly from application and middleware heterogeneity.

9.1.3 EXECUTION CONTAINERS

The execution container is the runtime environment for the service implementation. Most runtime environments for enterprise software also provide appropriate containers for services, mainly because they can provide guidance—and sometimes solutions—when catering for the technical challenges that we describe in this chapter.

Although the formal definition of *container* was coined with the emergence of the Enterprise Java Beans (EJB) standard, many older application platforms provide similar features for efficient, secure, and transactional execution of service requests. These include transaction monitors such as CICS, distributed object systems such as CORBA, Web application servers (Servlets), and database management systems (stored procedures). The following summarizes the generic feature set of an execution container:

Dispatching and servicing. There are different possibilities for routing an incoming service call to the implementation of the corresponding service operation. The necessary dispatcher could either be part of the service implementation or an integrated part of the container.

Transaction management. An execution container should include built-in facilities for the management of transactions. For example, data-centric services needing access to databases and files under transaction control require these facilities. Process-centric services that invoke a variety of other services while executing one instance of a business process also need transaction management.

Security. The security requirements for execution containers are similar to those for many other server environments. An execution container must provide facilities for authentication, authorization, and transport encryption.

Logging. Contrary to many monolithic architectures with applications that run completely under the control of one single transaction monitor and use one database, an SOA must cope with various issues of vertical and horizontal distribution and decoupling. Logging is a particular measure to address many of these issues. The execution container must provide facilities to keep track of all service invocations. For the sake of performance or due to legal considerations, one must be able to configure the scope of the logging. At a minimum, it must be possible to switch on and off the logging of a service invocation's payload. Furthermore, the execution container must be able to provide facilities for the retrieval and consolidation of log entries.

Billing. The development, maintenance, and operation of a service are not free. Therefore, it is a valid approach to charge for the usage of a service. This can be performed both within an enterprise (cross-departmental billing) and between different organizations. In order to do billing, the execution container must provide usage metrics and it must meet Service Level Agreements (SLAs). Furthermore, you will need user accounts that keep track of accumulated costs and that allow service usage only under defined commercial conditions.

Systems management functionality. It is often necessary to run a service in a highly automated operation environment. In such an environment, the service must provide facilities to cooperate with systems management tools. At a minimum, it must provide functionality for starting and stopping services. Furthermore, it is beneficial to have statistical functions that connect to these systems management tools and report errors, average (or minimum or maximum) processing times, resource consumption, currently active operations, uptime, and many more details. In this context, it is worth mentioning that many traditional runtime environments such as transaction monitors running on a mainframe provide a certain subset of this functionality out-of-the-box. More sophisticated systems management functionality could be easily added to the base operations. Both development teams and operations are aware of systems management necessities and are used to the associated issues. As a result, traditional environments are still a reasonable choice for today's mission-critical applications.

Message transformation. Message transformation is a feature that you typically find in an EAI or B2B scenario. Here, you might have a heterogeneous set of clients that potentially use different formats to represent the payload of a service invocation, such as different flavors of SOAP messages. In such a case, it is very convenient if the execution container provides preprocessing facilities that transform all incoming calls to a single unified format.

In Sections 9.2 to 9.4, we discuss some of the aforementioned aspects in more detail.

9.1.3.1 Cross-Container Integration. Individual execution containers often provide a rich out-of-the-box functionality that makes the development, deployment, and management of individual services reasonably straightforward. However, almost all enterprises suffer from "middleware overload." They must deal not only with a multitude of incompatible applications but also with the existence of many different application platforms and communication middleware systems. In most enterprises, many different types of execution containers can be found, ranging from modern .NET, Java Servlets, and EJB containers to mainframe transaction managers such as CICS and IMS.

The key challenge of an enterprise SOA is to define an architecture that enables applications to use different services independently of their container. Although simple service interoperability can be achieved relatively easily through interoperable messaging protocols such as IIOP or SOAP, the challenge is to connect services that reside in different containers beyond simple request/response interoperability, including security and transactionality. Figure 9-8 provides an example of a customer and flight booking system deployed across multiple service platforms.

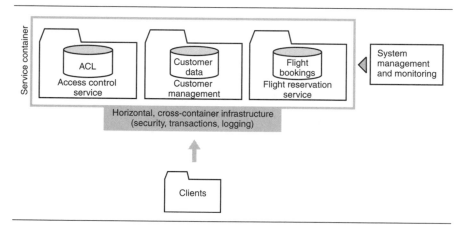

FIGURE 9-8 In a system where services are implemented on incompatible execution containers, one must introduce a horizontal infrastructure layer that manages technical cross-container integration of services. If this cannot be deployed as a technology layer, it is necessary to incorporate appropriate design principles and procedures to each container in order to address the related problems.

In some cases, the introduction of an external horizontal infrastructure layer can automate some of the tasks of integration services across container boundaries at the technical level. However, this is often impossible, and more flexible solutions must be incorporated into the system.

In particular, the problem of data and process integrity across container boundaries is a difficult one. Although technologies such as X/Open-based transaction monitors can enable transaction processing across multiple distributed and heterogeneous systems, these technologies are often impracticable due to the many technical and organizational limitations (see Chapter 8, "Managing Process Integrity").

9.2   Logging and Auditing

In this book, we provide technical and organizational tools to build a system that is not prone to failures. Yet it is of course virtually impossible to rule out all failures. A lot of the measures described elsewhere in this book are potentially costly, and for this reason, they are often omitted in practice. For example, in real-world situations, the budgets for infrastructure investments to set up a fail-safe database cluster or a redundant network setup simply might not be approved. Hence, you sometimes must rely on measures such as logging. Chapter 8, "Managing Process Integrity," has already given an in-depth discussion on process integrity for which logging is a crucial building block.

Another reason for operation disruption might be that one of the services that the application depends on must undergo unplanned maintenance. Consider an airline booking application that—among others—relies on a pricing service to determine the price for specific flights on a given date. Consider a serious bug within the module that performs flight price calculation. No company wants something like this to happen—especially if the calculated prices are far too low—and the corresponding service will often be shut down immediately to prevent further damage.

The bottom line is that even if you have planned for the system to handle a lot of error conditions automatically, unplanned and unrecoverable errors can still happen. We will call such errors *failures* in the remainder of the chapter. As depicted in Figure 9-9, failures require activities at different levels, including: user interaction, logging, and systems management.

When coping with failures, the concepts and techniques discussed in this chapter are not only relevant to SOAs. Most of them are simply good coding practices or design patterns. However, in a distributed and loosely coupled architecture, they are of much greater importance than in a standalone monolithic application. The distributed nature of the architecture and the fact that the source code or core dumps of the actual services are not available for debugging make explicit failure-handling measures essential.

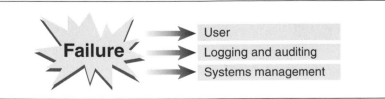

FIGURE 9-9   An error must be reported to the user, to a log file or database, and to a systems management system.

In case of such failures, it is usually necessary to perform certain manual activities to return things to normal. In lucky circumstances, this might be as easy as resetting a power switch. On the other hand, it might result in a number of employees browsing millions of rows in multiple database tables. It is not hard to see that resolving problems is a lot easier if we know where and when the error occurred and which users were involved in it. It is, therefore, mandatory that every SOA has a reliable logging and auditing infrastructure. Although logging and auditing are quite similar from a technical point of view, they differ considerably at the requirements level.

Usually, runtime output from a system is mapped to different log levels. These levels are—among other things—used to distinguish auditing, logging, tracing, and debugging output. They are usually identified by a number of a text warnings, such as "DEBUG," "TRACE," "INFO," "WARN," "ERROR," "AUDIT," etc.

Auditing is normally put into place to satisfy some legal requirements, such as documenting that a credit card was actually charged because the client ordered flight tickets, or to document that the ticket actually did get printed and that it was sent to the address given by the client.

Auditing creates a new subsystem that by itself impacts system operation. When normal logging fails, for example, if the log file or disk partition is full, you can usually carry on merely by halting the logging process. However, if auditing itself fails, it must be considered a failure, and the system must stop its operation. After all, continuing to run without auditing in place might violate some legal obligation, and no company wants that to happen.

Tracing is usually disabled while a system is in production and is only enabled in case of a major problem because it is often so detailed that it significantly degrades system performance. Tracing is usually switched on explicitly to track down a particular error. In case of intermittent errors, this will of course result in a degradation of system components for a potentially lengthy interval until the error can be identified.

Finally, debugging consists of statements that are only significant to application developers. Therefore, debugging code is often excluded from the production code altogether. In the rest of this chapter, we will focus on logging and auditing. Both are treated in a largely similar fashion.

9.2.1 ERROR REPORTING

One of the most common issues with error reporting is that failures can go unnoticed. Unfortunately, it is all too easy to build a system where failures are not reliably detected. A common mistake is when a program catches all exceptions during development and discards them silently. As the project moves on—usually toward an overly optimistic deadline—developers move on to their next tasks, and the RAS (Reliability/Availability/Serviceability) features are never completed. Of course, cases like this should be avoided in any kind of software development by employing proper coding standards. In an SOA, they become an even greater problem because of the loosely coupled nature of the application.

Similarly, an error that is logged but not reported to the customer can cause a lot of confusion. For example, if the airline ticket printing service is temporarily unavailable, an error might not be reported to the customer. Instead, it might be discovered and fixed during a routine log screening at the end of the week. By that point, the customer is likely to have called in and opened a customer service case, causing expenses that might otherwise have been avoided.

It is crucial for the business owners to clearly define both to developers and software designers what their requirements are for logging, auditing, and reporting. Likewise, it is mandatory to report an error each and every time it occurs. When using distributed services, this can be achieved using the technologies of the underlying platform. For example, when using SOAP, you can utilize the SOAP error mechanism. Similarly, if you are using a distributed object technology such as EJB, you can use remote exceptions to report an error.

9.2.2 DISTRIBUTED LOGGING

Using a framework of potentially distributed services does little to make logging easier. In fact, using distributed services for logging is rarely appropriate. Usually, the requirements for logging are that it must be both reliable and lightweight.

Additionally, it should be easy to use in order to encourage programmers to log whenever they think that there is something worth logging. Given these requirements, it is astonishing how often one comes across a central logging service. Granted, the idea to set up logging as a service in a distributed environment is very tempting, but it is easy to see that such an approach is not lightweight by thinking in terms of the network load and latency involved. If logging is implemented using object-oriented technologies, the cost of marshalling and unmarshalling log record objects adds to this overhead. It is also not reliable because many things can go wrong when storing the individual log records. This starts with network failure and ends with storing the actual log records in a file or database table. Finally, it is out of the question to use distributed transactions to make entries in a log facility because this is probably as complex a process as one could encounter.

> ### Log Locally but View Globally
>
> Local logging is essential due to the need for a logging facility to be lightweight and reliable. Global viewing of logs is required for the analysis of errors in distributed processes.

To ensure that logging is both reliable and lightweight, the best approach is to log locally and consolidate the logs as illustrated in Figure 9-10. Whether log data is written to a file or database does not really matter, nor does the format of the log records itself. What matters, however, is that each and every log entry carries some common information to enable log consolidation. This information includes the time-stamp, the origin of the log (method or procedure), and the name of the user who made the call (if legally possible). Additionally, each service call should include a unique token that can be used during log file consolidation to build a distributed stack trace.

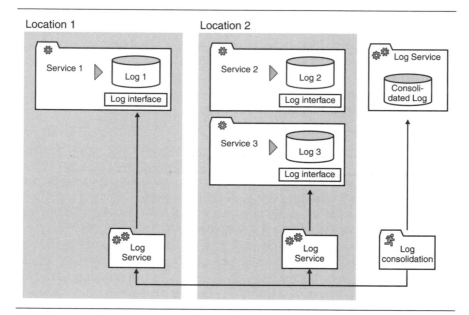

FIGURE 9-10   Structure of a distributed logging environment. The individual services write to dedicated logs of arbitrary format that are consolidated to form a common storage. The log services that are available at the various locations should ideally have identical interfaces. An audit trail service can be used to query the consolidated storage and request consolidation from the various log services.

Session and Transaction Tokens

A good service-oriented logging facility needs to ensure there are tokens such as session-tokens and transaction-tokens, which can be used to consolidate the log files as they are constructed and for searching after an exceptional event.

Consider the example of purchasing an airline ticket, shown in Figure 9-11. The airline ticket service itself logs to an XML file. When called, it generates a unique request ID that is logged with all entries to that file and passed to other necessary services. The billing service logs to an RDBMS, while the flight reservation uses a record-based log file. The three log sources are then all accessible using a log service for that particular location. Ticketing takes place at a different location. It logs using a line-oriented file, again using the unique request ID. The contents of the logs for that location are also made available using a log service. If engineered properly, the interfaces of the two log services should be identical. The log services store the consolidated log information in a centralized data store. This operation does not need to be overly reliable because it is intrinsically idempotent. The common data store can then be queried using an audit trail service.

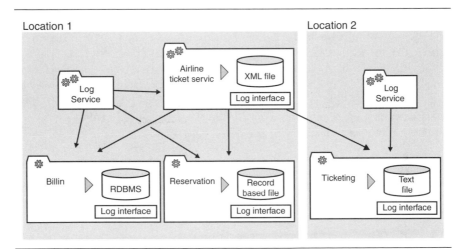
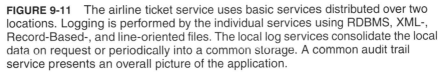

FIGURE 9-11   The airline ticket service uses basic services distributed over two locations. Logging is performed by the individual services using RDBMS, XML-, Record-Based-, and line-oriented files. The local log services consolidate the local data on request or periodically into a common storage. A common audit trail service presents an overall picture of the application.

9.2.3   LOGGING AND TRANSACTION BOUNDARIES

As we mentioned previously, logging is a lightweight activity, and as such, log data should not be written to the same database as the transaction being logged. The reason is obvious: In case of an error, not only will transactions get rolled back, but the logs will also be rolled back. It can be very hard to determine the cause and precise circumstances of the failure, especially when using an environment that has sophisticated container-provided transaction management. For example, when using an EJB container, the user must be aware of the restrictions imposed. If, for some reason, it is infeasible to use the logging facilities provided, logging to a file usually does the trick. If you need to log to a resource, such as a transaction message queue or an RDBMS, it is necessary to manage all resources manually.

Never Log Under the Control of a Transaction Monitor

Never log under the control of a transaction monitor. Ensure that each completed call to a logging system yields an entry in the appropriate log data store. Prevent rollback mechanisms of a transaction monitor from extinguishing log entries.

Logging to a file can also show some unwanted behaviour. File systems such as Linux ext3 or NTFS use a write buffer. This means that data is not written persistently until the operating system synchronizes the file system. This might require that the file system be synchronized manually after each call.

In the case where there are multiple explicit updates using a transactional resource, logging should be performed before and after each of these activities, as shown in Figure 9-12 when making a flight reservation with two flight legs. This situation occurs commonly when EJB Entity Beans are used as the persistence mechanism of the service.

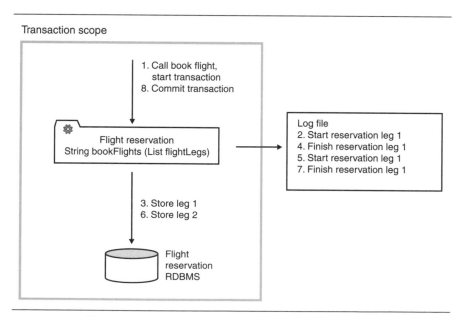

FIGURE 9-12   Transaction log.

Naturally, one of the occasions where logging is mandatory is before calling a remote service and after that call returns. This makes sense not only because making a remote call is more error-prone, but also because an error can often be fixed by running the remaining services in the call chain again. Consider the example in Figure 9-13, where the billing and flight reservation succeeds but the ticketing call never returns. After we determine that no ticket was printed, all we must do is rerun the ticketing service.

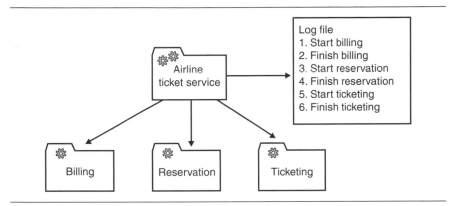

FIGURE 9-13   Call chain.

9.2.4   LOGGING FRAMEWORKS AND CONFIGURATION

A common activity is to build the consolidation part of the system and provide services for remote retrieval of log entries. However, a normal project should not be concerned with building the part of the system that writes the actual log records in the first place. Normally, the execution and development environment will provide some form of logging services. Many containers provide logging in their own right; EJB or CORBA containers often include logging consolidation facilities. A development environment might be able to weave logging into the source code based on well-defined rules. Furthermore, a runtime environment might provide a high degree of logging in any case, based on automatic interception of certain activities, such as making a HTTP request or obtaining a database connection from a pool.

Finally, there are software products and libraries available for the sole purpose of logging. The Apache log4j framework is probably the most prominent example in the Java programming language. Since the arrival of Java 1.4, the JDK itself contains similar libraries for logging [GS2003].

That being said, there is no way to avoid the fact that logging is ultimately the programmer's responsibility. Too much business logic is coded by hand instead of being automatically generated. The input and output for this business logic usually provides the most valuable insight into the cause of an error. With the advent of Model Driven Architecture (MDA) and highly sophisticated code generation, this might be automated in the future. Of course, it is very unlikely that even generated code is completely bug-free. Thus, an important part of code generation is sensibly placed log and audit statements.

Traditional midrange and mainframe applications usually provide a robust built-in logging infrastructure. For example, IBM's CICS offers logging using the CICS log manager. This infrastructure is used for all logging purposes, from basic user-level logs up to CICS transaction logging and recovery. This logging facility connects to the system-level MVS log streams. One of its most powerful features besides its robustness is its ability to consolidate log messages from different physical and logical machines that use IBM's Sysplex technology. Furthermore, logs can be automatically placed into different archive stages so that accessing and searching the most recent logs becomes easy, while at the same time, the full historical information is preserved.

Logging should ideally be configurable in a fine-grained manner. For example, frameworks such as log4j enable users to define how to handle a particular log event based on its origin and severity. Usually, this is used to log into different target files based on the origin, to turn logging off for low severity, or to turn logging off completely for a particular origin. This is sensible from a performance perspective, but it can have the opposite effect in certain scenarios. Assume that the flight reservation service has the nasty behavior that—just sometimes—flight legs are not reserved properly. Fortunately, the programmers have included a high degree of logging in their code. Given the data, it is quite easy to determine why this happens. The flight reservation service is currently configured to log only events of severity "error" and above, but information of the level "trace" is needed to really figure out what is happening. Unfortunately, the system does not allow for runtime configuration. This means that the entire flight reservation service must be taken offline, the configuration must be changed, and then the system must be brought back online. This can cause an unwanted disruption of service because (a) it's the holiday season and (b) it's 5 P.M., and customers—a lot of customers—just want to use this system.

Runtime Configuration

If there is a requirement for fine-grained log configuration, take care to ensure that the settings can be changed at runtime. Otherwise, everything should be logged.

9.3 Availability and Scalability

It is mandatory for any enterprise architecture to provide functionality in the way it has been commissioned to do so. In this context, we consider a system as providing availability if it is operational for 100% of planned uptime. In other words, we consider a system to be 100% available if it prevents any unplanned downtime. Note that we do not include planned downtime in our concept of availability. For example, if an application becomes unavailable because a database is taken offline for backup every night, it does not reduce the availability of the application. Instead, it limits the service level that the application supports.

Scalability in the context of this book means that an enterprise architecture provides some way to increase its capacity beyond initial planning. Capacity designates the work a system can perform in a given amount of time, commonly measured in transactions per second (TPS). Other measures of capacity are the number of concurrent users a system can support and the amount of storage space it provides. Ideally, scalability should provide a linear solution, meaning that if the capacity of the system is doubled, the resources available—memory, CPUs, network and management overhead—should at most need to be doubled. In practice, systems can scale linearly only to a given point. For most practical purposes, scalability means that a clean and defined path exists to increase the capacity of a system by a requested amount. In general, scalability is only considered up to a certain boundary. For example, a requirement might be that an application must be scalable from an initial load of 100 to 10,000 users.

One of the most common confusions that arise surrounding issues of scalability and availability is that they are often not rigorously defined or that they are defined based on insufficient information. The so-called Service Level Agreement (SLA) lies at the heart of this matter. An SLA typically defines a set of performance figures that are an integral part of the contract between one organization that provides an IT service and another that consumes that service.

The most common performance figure is the guaranteed operation time. The operation time (commonly referred to as uptime) states the time that the system must be available, along with an acceptable amount of unplanned downtime. The SLA also states the capacity of the system. This includes storage capacity, number of concurrent users, and TPS. Often, an SLA also states the response times that are acceptable for a certain percentage of requests.

Care must be taken when the requirements for any IT system are defined. Further care should be taken for any system that relies on other systems to function properly. Far too many so-called "SLAs" in the industry only state the wishful thinking of the people who originally "defined" them during a sales pitch. As a consequence, they also state requirements that far exceed what the systems actually needs to deliver in the worst-case scenario. For example, it is unacceptable to require an airline booking system to support a number of concurrent requests that is equal to all airline seats available for the entire year. Even if the booking system could fulfill this requirement, there would be no benefit for the business. Therefore, such requirements must be based on known values, such as the current number of transactions and the actual number of users that are concurrently connected to the system, where possible. If such numbers are not available, extrapolation from currently known values is required. It is both valid and commonplace to add a safety margin, but you must take into consideration that the requirements for the system's availability ultimately impacts engineering efforts. At the same time, it is valid to question whether any business process needs to operate unaffected in the cases of nuclear war or an alien invasion. Finally, you should be wary of the concept of guaranteed response times for as yet unspecified and unimplemented business functionality. It is fairly easy to plan for capacity and availability; it is almost impossible to plan for an unknown computational algorithm.

By now, it should be clear that availability and scalability come at a price. A number of applications exist in which you should be prepared to spend a large amount of money to guarantee availability. Consider air traffic control systems or a control system for a nuclear power plant. In these cases, not only the functioning of the economy but also human lives depend on these systems remaining permanently operational. In other cases, the systems that are affected by your IT system might be very expensive or very hard to replace, such as a multi-billion dollar spacecraft whose IT systems enter unplanned downtime just as it enters the atmosphere of one of the moons of Jupiter. However, for a large number of systems, some amount of unplanned downtime is inconvenient but acceptable. One example is an online banking system where most users might not even notice a downtime of a couple of hours every month. A second example is an airline check-in system. Although downtime is very inconvenient and large queues form in front of the check-in desk, fallback procedures exist that allow for a manual check-in process.

The stronger the requirements, the higher the price tag. Building an extremely fail-proof system that is scalable from initial hardware setup to software development to operating procedures is very expensive.

On a different note, you must never forget that the overall performance of the system is ultimately limited by the weakest link in the technology chain. This has an important effect on any integration or service-enabling effort because the impact that legacy systems and databases have on overall system performance is regularly underestimated. In principle, the service layer scales linearly to support unlimited capacity, regardless of the underlying technology. However, the supporting systems stop scaling at some point, such as when the number of connections a database server can support is exceeded, when the storage area is full, or when transactions occurring at a certain rate create concurrency problems at the database level. Often, this is not a technical but an administrative problem: hardware must be bought, database configurations must be changed, host computing power must be ordered, and so on. Because these things typically take time to progress to the proper channels in an enterprise's IT operation, it is important to stress test the entire application stack as soon as possible in the project to allow enough time for uncovering any backend scalability issues.

Stress Test Early

Often, simple measures on IT system level will improve performance and scalability radically. However, time is required to implement these changes. To buy yourself this crucial time, do not be afraid of using stress testing early in the development process.

Finally, note that session state should be placed in the application frontend. If the application frontend is not suitable, you should create lean process-centric services, which should be carefully separated from non-conversational services.

9.3.1   SCALABILITY AND AVAILABILITY USING WEB SERVICES

Web services are generally built on one of the widely available technologies to deliver dynamic Web pages, most notably Microsoft .NET and J2EE. In principle, these technologies provide easy scalability. You can use a load balancer to forward the requests to any number of framework instances or containers that are configured identically. If needed, you can add additional hardware to host more instances of the container in order to increase system capacity until the network is saturated. Most off-the-shelf load balancers provide the concept of sticky sessions, where a request that originates from a certain IP address is always forwarded to the same container. This will enable the container to preserve conversational state with the client. As we discussed in Chapter 8, limited resources such as open database connections or transaction contexts should never be part of this conversational state. Newer load balancers even analyze the request for information about the server on which the session relies instead of using only the IP address. In general, failure of the container will result in the loss of the conversational state. Strictly speaking, from the preceding definition, this does not limit availability—the load balancer will notice that a system has come down and will forward the request to another machine. It might nevertheless prevent the uninterrupted operation of the system. Again, this presents additional motivation to make service interfaces stateless and idempotent wherever possible. Most frameworks support some notion of preserving session state. The actual implementations vary widely: state might be stored in a database or in a shared file system, or it might be replicated to all members of a cluster using multicast or to a single dedicated server. Similarly, session state replication might or might not be transactional. In any case, preserving session state creates a noticeable overhead. For example, state that is convenient to store but that is easily re-created should not be replicated. You might even consider the complete abandonment of conversational session state, even if this requires its re-creation with every service invocation. The simplicity and scalability obtained can easily outweigh the extra costs for hardware.

However, the best solution is to store the session state in the application frontend. This makes most of the challenges of maintaining server-side state irrelevant.

As an example, consider checking in for a flight using a self-service terminal. Consider the stage of the check-in service where the seat is assigned (see Figure 9-14). The call signature can easily be crafted to be both idempotent and stateless. In this case, no session replication is required. If the first try to assign a seat fails because the system has gone down, the terminal retries the call. The load balancer has noticed that it has lost connection to the first instance of the service and uses another instance to retry the call. This call subsequently returns the required information to print the boarding card.

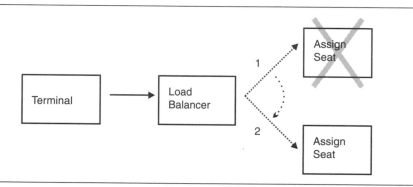

FIGURE 9-14   Failover using a hardware load balancer and a service that uses no conversational state.

Interoperability with Off-the-Shelf Load Balancers

Always aim for a coarse-grained service interface. Use idempotent methods wherever possible. These measures will provide optimal interoperability with off-the-shelf load-balancing routers.

9.3.2   SCALABILITY AND AVAILABILITY USING EJBS

Creating scalable applications using EJBs is fairly simple because most EJB servers support clustering. This enables an administrator to add additional server instances and hardware until the capacity requirement is reached. Usually, the clients' EJB home interface implementation makes a decision based on certain algorithms as to where to create the required EJB. In case of a stateless session bean, the remote stub itself might load balance on a call-by-call basis. Typical algorithms include random, load-based, and round robin. Some EJB containers also facilitate the provision of custom algorithms.

Most EJB containers will bind a specified remote client to a single server instance to limit the amount of transaction coordination needed if multiple EJBs take part in the same transaction. If they do not, you can easily emulate this behavior by using a façade pattern to push down the transaction boundary.

Regarding availability, the same concepts discussed in the previous section on Web services hold true. Stateless session bean stubs will detect the failure of a server and try to connect to a different server. Stateless session beans should be used wherever possible to avoid conversational state. If conversational state is a firm requirement, some EJB containers provide data replication and failover for stateful session beans. Likewise, entity beans that are not part of a transaction can be reloaded from a different server. Because the latter is quite specialized behavior, and because it is also highly vendor-specific, it is again best to try to maintain as little conversational state as possible. Some EJB containers also support the idea of an idempotent method in a bean. This is a powerful concept because it enables the stub to transparently re-create a call if the original call fails in flight. These features of EJB containers often lead to performance problems in a tightly coupled environment with a fine-grained object model. However, they are very useful in the face of the scalability and availability issues of an SOA.

Avoid Stateful Beans' Fine-Grained Interaction Patterns

Using stateless session beans with coarse-grained interfaces will enable you to make effective use of your application server cluster. Avoid fine-grained object interaction patterns. The striking simplicity of this concept will improve not only the availability and scalability of the system but also its robustness and maintenance-friendliness.

As an example, consider booking an airline ticket, as illustrated in Figure 9-15. An examination of that part of the booking process contains the following three steps:

1. A reservation is entered into the system.
2. The customer's credit card is charged.
3. The reservation is marked paid and closed.

If the client notices that the call fails, it can retry the call using a replicated instance of the booking service. The key data to be replicated is the primary key of the reservation record and the credit card data, along with the state of the payment. If a reservation key exists and the state of payment is "charged," then the implementation of the booking service can continue with closing the reservation. If there is no primary key for the reservation, it can retry the whole process. If the state of payment is "not attempted" and a reservation primary key exists, it continues charging the credit card. Note that due to the transaction boundaries, a state might arise that cannot be handled automatically—if the payment fails in flight and the payment state in the replicated data is attempted. In this case, the implementation can run checks using service methods of the payment service to determine the outcome of the attempted call.

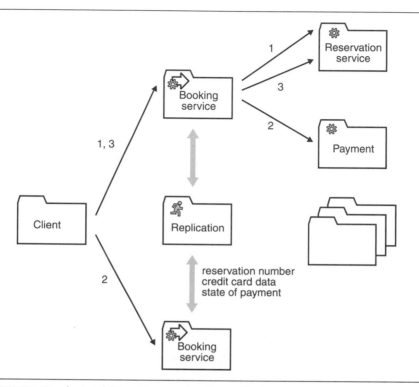

FIGURE 9-15 A stateful booking service that calls the reservation and the payment service. The reservation number, credit card data, and state of payment are replicated in order to support failover.

9.3.3 SCALABILITY AND AVAILABILITY USING CORBA

With CORBA, most of the concepts discussed in the previous section hold true. The CORBA specification defines requirements for "fault-tolerant CORBA." Among other things, this specification is concerned with detecting communication faults, providing transparent failover, and replicating the object state of distributed object instances. Load balancing within CORBA is usually performed by the individual vendor implementations using low-level functions of the CORBA GIOP (General Inter-ORB Protocol).

Because CORBA fault tolerance is a relatively new specification, various vendor-specific implementations for availability and object state replication exist.

9.3.4 SCALABILITY AND AVAILABILITY USING CICS

Even though it might seem old-fashioned, IBM's Customer Information Control System (CICS) remains widespread for mission-critical services. Basically, CICS is a transaction server that provides very efficient facilities for loading, initializing, and executing programs.

While CICS servers usually run on mainframe or midrange computers, a variety of tools is available to connect to a CICS server. For example, the CICS Transaction Gateway (CTG) enables Java programs to act as a CICS client using the Java Connector Architecture (JCA). Other programming languages, such as COBOL, C++, and Visual Basic, can use the CICS universal client to access the CICS server. Connectivity to IBM's messaging product, MQSeries, is also available. In this way, any client of an MQSeries server can make use of existing CICS programs. Finally, CICS programs can be directly exposed as SOAP Web services using SOAP for CICS.

To ensure a seamless operation with existing CICS programs, any CICS-based service should ensure that no conversational state is held. One transaction should map to exactly one service call. CICS programs can run for an arbitrarily long time interval. If the service implementation breaks while the CICS call is in flight, it can be very hard to determine the result of the transaction. Therefore, extra care must be taken to ensure that CICS programs used in services are small and that they execute quickly.

Scalability and availability of CICS itself is provided by IBM's CICSPlex and SYSPlex technologies.

CICS can even participate in distributed transactions, for example using JCA. However, as discussed in Chapter 8, distributed transactions must be handled with care. Because CICS programs usually execute on systems with very high load and transaction density, using distributed transactions with CICS is often inefficient and might have a significant impact on other CICS jobs accessing shared resources.

9.3.5 SCALABILITY AND AVAILABILITY OF WRAPPED LEGACY APPLICATIONS

It is often desirable to use an existing terminal-based legacy application within a service. Just as often, it is not possible to make changes to the existing application. In these cases, one of the most popular and effective ways of using legacy applications in newly developed applications is screen scraping. The character stream that is used to build the terminal user screen, such as on a VT100 terminal, is analyzed. Effectively, the application mimics a VT100 terminal client.

This approach has several benefits. It is a fairly cheap and straightforward way to include some of the existing functionality into a service. Specifically, it is a low-impact solution because no changes to the original application are required. There are also downsides to this approach, mainly in relation to scalability and availability. First, a lot of existing VT100 systems will have daily maintenance windows—usually at night—when the application and thus the service are not available. This must be incorporated into the relevant SLAs for the service. Second, any changes to the application terminal screen require maintenance work in the service application. Furthermore, granularity of a typical stateless service call can easily span multiple terminal screens. This will lead to rather high latency when invoking such a service. On the other hand, a design that performs multiple fine-grained service calls requires a stateful service, which is generally not advisable, particularly because such systems normally work on a pooled resource, in this case, terminal connections. Furthermore, the service can only scale to the amount of transactions and sessions that are supported by the legacy application.

A business that aims for this type of reuse must be prepared to face the consequences of this decision. It will usually save a large amount of money, but this comes at the cost of somewhat limited scalability and robustness with increased maintenance [TDM2000].

9.3.6 SCALABILITY AND AVAILABILITY IN A HETEROGENEOUS SOA

Ultimately, services in most SOAs that run on different platforms are likely to be integrated. For example, the flight booking EJB might call a SOAP Web service to charge the customer's credit card. Because many SOA initiatives start out providing a whole new enterprise IT infrastructure, it is easy to lose sight of this fact. However, if properly deployed, an SOA supports the concept of heterogeneous service platforms working together. The individual services are only loosely coupled and share no common transaction contexts. Therefore, if all individual services are designed to be available and scalable, the overall system will be available and scalable in principle.

However, the situation is not quite so simple. For example, increasing scalability on the top of the service stack might not increase overall scalability of the system because services down the application stack might be overloaded. Thus, changing an SLA for a frontend service usually requires changing SLAs for backend services as well. As an analogy, imagine a call center that relies on a single database to operate at its maximum user load. Simply adding more agent seats and phone lines to the call center does not increase its capacity unless the database system is also upgraded.

The uptime of services that run within a heterogeneous infrastructure does not amount to the lowest uptime of the service chain. If three services provide an uptime of 98%, the resulting uptime is the product of the individual uptimes:

$$UT = 98\% \times 98\% \times 98\% = 94.1\%$$

However, the weakest link in the service chain still has the highest impact on availability in addition to scalability. Therefore, project management must first focus on bringing the weakest technology in line with the SLA's requirements.

9.4   Securing SOAs

In SOAs, security is certainly of primary concern and should have solid foundations in the infrastructure. Before you take any technical steps to implement a
specific security structure, you should capture the security requirements for all
relevant pieces of software during a risk analysis. Based on this analysis, you
build the software architecture to incorporate the defined security requirements.
Performing a risk analysis is beyond the scope of this book, but details on the
subject can be found in [PT2001]. Instead, based on a number of implementation
projects carried out by the authors, we discuss here some technical issues that
you must address when designing a security infrastructure in a distributed software architecture.

The main issues of a basic security infrastructure are authentication, authorization, and confidentiality. The focus broadens where the infrastructure is
exposed on the outside of some well-controlled environment, such as a specific
department or geographic location. In these situations, concerns such as non-
repudiation, message integrity, and legally binding identity assertion become
increasingly important [GS1997].

In this section, we discuss these principles and provide examples of how
they relate to platforms that are commonly used to create SOAs. The guiding
principle is that we want to use security as a tool to foster and encourage the use
of our enterprise architecture, rather than security simply being a means to prevent incidents.

9.4.1   AUTHENTICATION

Authentication means that a service caller is using a mechanism to prove its identity to the called resource. The caller must provide credentials such as a username
and password or a digital certificate. Often, security requirements for authentication include an implicit authorization requirement. The typical scenario is that
callers must authenticate themselves before being allowed to use the environment.

Three levels of authentication can be readily distinguished. First, it is possible for the caller to authenticate against the application frontend, second, authentication against the SOA framework is possible, and finally, authentication
against a single service is also a possible option. Figure 9-16 illustrates authentication at different levels of the application.

Authentication against the application frontend is generally straightforward
and quickly deployed. Often, it will be a vital business requirement to protect
access to the application itself. Authentication against individual services is
often desirable in order to limit access to these services and to create a clean
audit path within service invocations. However, when authentication becomes
part of each individual service, a significant amount of code cluttering results. If

the authentication mechanism and storage change, a significant amount of reengineering might be necessary to propagate these changes into the various services. In addition, different services probably rely on different types of storage and authentication mechanisms in the first place.

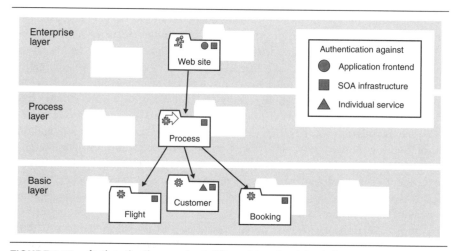

FIGURE 9-16 Authentication against different levels of the infrastructure. In this case, the Web site supports authentication. Authentication against the infrastructure is also supported. Individual services, such as the customer service, might also require or support authentication.

Therefore, it is generally better to insist that the user be authenticated against the infrastructure rather than against individual services. It is a prerequisite for SOA-wide authorization and identity assertion, as we discussed in the following. However, some very important advantages are available. For example, having a common user for subsequent operations in an SOA makes monitoring the environment a lot easier. Common types of attacks—such as password guessing or denial of service attacks—can be prevented or at least treated in a standard way throughout the SOA. In addition, maintenance benefits greatly because changes in the underlying authentication mechanism can be performed across the board rather than against individual application frontends or services.

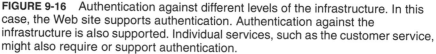

Authenticate Against the SOA

Authentication against the SOA facilitates cleaner and easier-to-maintain code with a comparably small overhead.

Authentication against the SOA is usually based upon the framework that is used to build the SOA infrastructure or a common framework on top of the basic infrastructure—for example, a J2EE-compliant server that can be extended using a pluggable authentication provider.

An authentication framework usually consists of at least an authenticator and a context. Technically, a context is often associated with conversational state in a session (see Chapter 8). The authenticator is a software component that checks a user's credentials, such as a username and password or a digital certificate. The infrastructure then creates a context that is accessible from the business domain in order to obtain the authenticated user, commonly known as the principal. The predominant middleware frameworks all support authentication mechanisms that can be leveraged in an SOA and that can be readily extended to satisfy individual enterprise needs. For example, a company might create an authenticator within a newly created SOA that uses usernames and passwords from an existing mainframe application. The J2EE environment provides JAAS (Java authentication and authorization service), a mechanism that describes the process of authentication and authorization of client interactions.

One drawback of such specifications is that they tend to be at least partly proprietary. Contexts that originate from different frameworks are usually incompatible. Even when they support a common client API such as JAAS, their implementations can differ significantly, and they might support different and incompatible extension mechanisms.

Such systems share the fact that the actual authentication process is fully transparent to the individual service. A service might decide to check the current principal and thus reject any operation, but it will not perform the actual login process. This isolates the service implementation from changes in the authentication mechanism. For example, it is possible to change authentication credentials from username/password to digital certificates without the need to change the service implementation. In short, the service needs only to know the context, not the authenticator.

If authentication against the SOA itself is not practical—perhaps because individual services are engineered in a way that requires individual authentication, possibly using different credentials—single sign-on frameworks can be used to relax the problems of integration. Typical single sign-on frameworks—such as Netegrity Siteminder, Oblix NetPoint, and Citrix Metaframe—plug into the authentication hooks of the various software components used, including middleware, Web servers, and mainframe applications. They provide a consistent view of an authenticated principal within all these environments. The individual systems might—on their own—rely on different authentication mechanisms that have their own storage mechanisms and different credentials. A single sign-on framework can provide credential mapping, providing the correct logon credentials for each invoked service or even backend applications. Single sign-on is generally straightforward and transparent to implement for programmers but needs a significant effort to introduce and maintain, especially when credential mapping is involved. The general principle of a single sign-on framework is illustrated in Figure 9-17. Note that most single sign-on products are not limited to simple authentication and credential mapping; they usually offer mechanisms and storage for authorization, too. Some frameworks even provide hooks to include biometric equipment such as retina scanning or face recognition.

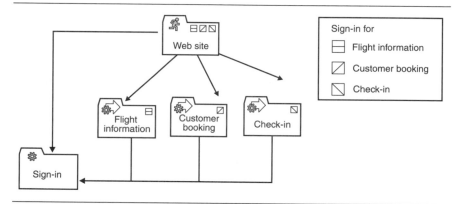

FIGURE 9-17   Principal of a single sign-on infrastructure. The user is originally authenticated against a single application that interfaces to the single sign-on framework. The framework provides login contexts and tokens for the other applications and the application frontend.

9.4.1.1 Authentication and Middleware.

Authentication is fairly straightforward to implement when standard middleware such as J2EE, CORBA, or .NET is used as the basic runtime foundation. Most of these frameworks support some notion of authentication and caller identity.

Of course, the process of passing credentials might not be very secure. For example, it is common practice to use unencrypted passwords when logging in to a remote EJB container. Therefore, most distributed environments use the notion of a login session. Once logged in, a session ID is passed between the participants. A frequently used technique for session creation is the server-side session management in Web applications where HTTP cookies or URL rewriting is used to maintain a session. Similar techniques apply to CORBA and to authentication when obtaining a J2EE naming context.

There is also the notion of a login context in the Java Authentication and Authorization Service (JAAS), now a standard in the J2EE application environment. This login context provides callbacks that enable the called runtime environment to query the caller identity using the callback:

```
...

import javax.security.auth.login.LoginContext;
...
```

```
LoginContext loginContext = null;
try {
  // Create LoginContext with username, password and
      // login url
  loginContext = new LoginContext("AirBookers",
      new AirBookersCallbackHandler(username, password, url));
  loginContext().login();
} catch (Exception exc) {

}
```

The callers then pass their identity on each subsequent invocation using an implementation of the `PrivilegedAction` interface, in this case `Flight-BookingAction`:

```
Subject subject = loginContext.getSubject();
FlightBookingAction flightAction =
    ➥new FlightBooking-Action(url);
Security.runAs(subject, flightAction);
System.exit(0);
```

After the user has completed the interaction, the login context can be discarded by calling `loginContext.logout()`. Note that the client interface for JAAS authentication is rather complicated to handle. However, the actual service implementation is usually not concerned with the details of the authentication mechanism. The implementation does not directly call any of the available callbacks. Instead, the framework provides the current caller within a context object, for example a `SessionContext` object in case of stateless and stateful session EJBs. The caller principal can then be obtained from the session object:

```
...
Principal principal = ctx.getCallerPrincipal();
System.out.println("Called by "+principal.getName());
    ...
```

More sophisticated frameworks protect the login session by varying the session ID during the session by issuing new session IDs or transaction numbers for every service invocation.

Creating authentication as part of an SOA is easy because of its limited impact on the underlying applications. Remember that services are often created from existing applications. Service enablement of such applications includes obtaining the caller principal from the service infrastructure. Even if the application does not support anything similar to a pluggable authentication module (PAM), it is fairly easy to create something similar in almost every application. For example, if the legacy application has an existing data store of users that it has a strict requirement to use, you can always create shadow users for every principal in the infrastructure security store and map them to the existing users of the legacy application.

Sometimes, you might see the concept of authentication as a service. Several frameworks are available that provide identity services that require a certain amount of infrastructure to be available. Although they are very powerful, there is also some resistance to adoption of these frameworks. Deploying such systems in any large organization is generally a costly exercise that must be based on a strategic decision made at the enterprise level. Even then, individual project teams might show a certain resistance to using them because they can create additional risks in projects in terms of software development skills or adherence to their SLAs. In the end, using these frameworks can help an SOA effort as well as kill it. Within the enterprise, the best option is to standardize on a single storage facility to access enterprise-wide user data. Directory services such as LDAP servers provide a very efficient means of storing and looking up such data.

When designing an authentication architecture from scratch, you should take care to make it "pluggable." This makes it possible to change the implementation as well as the underlying concept of an authentication mechanism, such as changing user stores or switching from username/password authentication to certificate-based authentication.

9.4.1.2 Authentication and SOAP.

Web services using SOAP are one of the most popular ways of building a Service-Oriented Architecture. Although various techniques exist to secure a Web service environment [H2003], SOAP provides only limited standardized support to satisfy the most basic authentication needs.

SOAP 1.2 does not include a standard means of passing credentials, nor does it support the concept of a caller context. Although both can be built easily using simple SOAP calls and the SOAP header, this amounts to a proprietary approach. Any bindings into the application to access the context and caller principal must be handcrafted.

There are specifications that offer solutions, most notably the WS-I Basic Security Profile and SAML, a framework for exchanging authorization and authentication information. Both define a means for authentication at the protocol level, but unfortunately, that is all they do. No stable standard bindings are available into common programming languages such as Java or C++ that can be leveraged in a project. Hand coding support that strictly adheres to the specifications is by no means trivial. It is not so much a problem for service implementation but for the client applications. For application developers, an SOA using SOAP that does not adhere to some standard is likely to discredit the SOA initiative in the first place. For the moment, the best compromise might well be to use only a small and clearly constrained subset of the specifications that either are available or that can be easily provided for the client environments of the SOA. Unfortunately, at the time of writing, this process can result in a somewhat weak security model. The WS-I Security Profile of the Web Services Interoperability Organization is likely to provide a more consistent and thorough toolset for securing Web services in the future. It will—among other things—support user authentication using various technologies.

The Security Assertion Markup Language (SAML) developed by OASIS can be used to include authentication and authorization-related statements in addition to signed messages into a SOAP document. In SAML, security statements are packaged into assertions that are issued by assertion providers. There are three basic types of assertions: authentication, attributes, and authorization. Similarly, there are three matching assertion providers, although a single entity might well act as assertion provider for all three types. An application can request a security assertion from an assertion provider, such as using username and password. The assertion provider will return an (optionally signed) assertion that always contains a timestamp, an assertion ID, and the subject of the assertion, typically the application user. It can contain conditional information; for example, about the length of time the assertion remains valid. The assertion or the assertion ID can be included with other SOAP messages and can be automatically verified by the called application. Single sign-on frameworks are obviously prime candidates to act as assertion providers. The following is an example of an authentication assertion:

```
<saml:Assertion
      MajorVersion="1" MinorVersion="0"
      AssertionID="235CX364-7654-9876-5474-00A41E354H0D"
      Issuer="www.dolphinair.com"
      IssueInstant="2003-07-01T12:00:00+01:00">
      <saml:Conditions
       NotBefore="2001-07-01T12:00:00+01:00"
       NotAfter="2001-07-01T12:00:00+01:00"/>
   <saml:AuthenticationStatement
        AuthenticationMethod="password"
        AuthenticationInstant="2001-05-31T13:21:00-05:00">
      <saml:Subject>
      <saml:NameIdentifier>
         <SecurityDomain>"www.dolphinair.com"</SecurityDomain>
         <Name>"cn=Dirk,co=travel,ou=check-in"</Name>
      </saml:NameIdentifier>
      </saml:Subject>
   </saml:AuthenticationStatement>
</saml:Assertion>
```

9.4.2 AUTHORIZATION

Authorization is the mechanism used to grant a caller access to a specific resource. In the simplest case, the caller might have the right to generally use a certain service, but more often, the authorization decision is much more dynamic. For example, a user may alter only certain data sets that belong to that particular user. Consider a flight planning example, where cockpit crews may change their own flight plans but not the flight plans of other flights. In authorization, no common abstraction principle lies at the core of the authorization process, other than allowing or denying certain actions. As with authentication, authorization can be performed at several levels, such as the application frontends, the individual services, and the SOA infrastructure.

Authorization within the application frontends is one possibility. However, if used on its own, this creates a severe security flaw because the underlying services would not offer any authorization protection at all. The ease of implementation comes at the high price of reduced security, as well as inconsistent authorization policies for the same business activity due to the implementing application. Mirroring authorization decisions at the application level might appear sensible in order to reduce round trips to a remote server, easing the load on the remote server and the network while at same time providing a better user experience. Consideration for the maintenance of the system is an issue during the design phase.

As with authentication, the level for authorization might not necessarily be the SOA infrastructure level. Instead, both the storage of the authorization data and the level of dynamism in determining caller permissions determine the preferred location for an authorization decision in an SOA.

The parameters used to determine the access decision can be complicated, and several approaches can be identified. They mainly differ in the way in which the authorization relevant information is stored and the way the authorization decision is determined:

- **Store access data with the authorized resource.** This is a modular approach where the actual data that determines the authorization decision is stored with the resource itself. As a common example, consider the file access rights in the Unix file system. No central registry stores the read, write, and execute rights in addition to the owner and group information for a file. This data is stored with the file itself. The benefit of such an organization is that the authorization decision is very effective from a performance viewpoint. An obvious disadvantage is that the introduction of a new authorization policy can be a rather complicated exercise.
- **Store access data centrally.** This approach is for the example used in the access control system of the Windows NT operating system family. Often, authorization information is stored and accessed by means of access control lists (ACLs), whereby a resource is identified by a certain path. Each resource features certain capabilities, such as read, write, delete, or execute. Access to these resources can be either granted or denied.

Both of these mechanisms basically define a static binding between a resource and either a user or a mapping of users into a group or role. In a real-world scenario, this is rarely sufficient. The following types of access decisions can be readily distinguished:

- **Static authorization decision based on the current user or a static group membership.** This is easily determined by a resource external to the actual business process providing access to the authorization data is guaranteed.

- **Dynamic authorization decision based on a dynamic group membership (role).** This might be based on any factor external to the application but accessible for the authorization framework. Popular examples are decisions that grant access during a certain period of the day or based on the value of session variables that are only temporarily available.
- **Dynamic authorization based on an attribute of the authorized resource.** This is the type of decision that is often at the core of business processes. As an example, consider the authorization of a credit card that is based on the card number, expiration date, and customer address. Another example is the authorization of a banking transaction that is based on the user entering a valid transaction number from a list.

Often, business requires the auditing of authorization and authentication processes. This particularly includes both forms of dynamic authorization decisions. A fair amount of authorization can be performed using standard technologies, such as the authorization mechanism in frameworks such as .NET or the Java Authorization and Authentication Framework (JAAS). Language bindings are also available that enable authorization at the message level of SOAP, even though these are, at the time of writing, mostly proprietary solutions. CORBA enables declarative authorization using the CORBA security service.

Authorization can in principle be performed by an external service. Technologies such as SAML and the upcoming WS-I security support it out of the box.

Although frameworks and APIs are available to support authorization using declarative mechanisms or even rule-based decision frameworks, you must bear in mind that SOA is fundamentally about the integration of existing applications. Applications that are to be integrated might very well use authorizations mechanisms that cannot be mapped easily onto a common system.

This is because at least some part of the authorization procedure will generally be part of the service implementation, instead of residing on the service infrastructure level. For example, the authorization scheme within a certain service implementation might not easily map to the one in another service implementation. Often, the authorization decision is buried deep within the service implementation. At the same time, it is often at the heart of the business process. Requiring externalization of the authorization procedure in the business process also creates a risk for service enablement in integration projects and poses an entry barrier for applications to join an integration initiative.

All this makes it rather unusual to perform authorization completely within the service framework itself because it is genuinely hard to move authorization out of technology. However, a refactoring of code during service enablement to make specific parts of authorization pluggable can provide a good compromise with limited impact and high flexibility. This can include decisions that depend on the principal's static or dynamic group membership. It can also include rule-based decisions, where the parameters for these decisions are available at infrastructure level. Later in the service lifecycle, security frameworks can provide or replace the authorization implementation well within the lifecycle of the application.

9.4.3   ENCRYPTION AND TRANSPORT SECURITY

When talking to people who cover security for business clients, one is often confronted with the requirement of encryption. The general impression is that if something is "encrypted," it is safe, as long as decryption cannot be performed easily and swiftly. To understand the pitfalls of this perspective, it is necessary to distinguish between two different forms of encryption: encryption at the message level and encryption at the transport level. The former can be employed to create real end-to-end security and is generally the preferable method. Furthermore, because encryption can be performed at the message level, it is possible to encrypt only the payload or payload segments of the message. If such a message uses the SOAP protocol and the W3C's recommendation for XML encryption syntax and processing, a section of the message using encryption might look like this:

```
<PaymentInfo xmlns='http://www.dolphinair.com/booking'>
    <Passenger>John Smith</Passenger>
    <Itinerary >ae12345-fght</Itinerary >
    <EncryptedData Type='http://www.w3.org/2001/04/xmlenc#
        Element'
     xmlns='http://www.w3.org/2001/04/xmlenc#'>
      <CipherData>
        <CipherValue>A23B45C56</CipherValue>
      </CipherData>
    </EncryptedData>
</PaymentInfo>
```

The benefit of this approach is that it not only provides superior security but that certain rules can still be applied to the otherwise encrypted messages. This makes it possible to use message-based routing, to perform advanced audit checks on the unencrypted parts of the messages, and to perform analysis to detect denial of service attacks, attempts for message replay, or similar attacks that might otherwise go unnoticed. Of course, this comes at a price in that the necessary infrastructure to support message-level encryption must be in place. In the preceding example, the payment information that might be sent as part of a ticket purchase includes the name of the customer as well as the itinerary ID in clear text. Only the actual payment information is encrypted. This has the same basic challenges one faces when creating a thorough authorization infrastructure, both organizational and technical.

Because of this overhead, it is often a sensible alternative to apply security at the transport level. The preferred way to accomplish this is to use the Secure Socket Layer (SSL) protocol. The benefits of this approach are obvious because SSL works almost everywhere, from mobile phones to mainframe computers. It requires little overhead to initialize, and resource usage is limited. Where resources are at a premium, it can be made faster using special cryptographic devices. When two-way SSL is employed, it can even be used to pass user credentials and to perform transparent user logon. The main advantage, however, is that it is widely understood. This is a very important issue because many failures in security infrastructure are due to accidental misconfiguration that in turn occurs because the implications of the infrastructure parameters are not fully understood.

However, there are also downsides to this approach. Intrusion detection becomes practically impossible because there is no way to "listen in" to the occurring traffic. When no end-to-end network connection can be employed, this setup is a potential target for a man-in-the middle attack because messages must be decrypted somewhere along the transport chain. This can be a simple network "hop," or messages need to be decrypted by some part of the SOA architecture, such as a MOM server that encrypts them again when forwarding to the recipient. Furthermore, two-way SSL for authentication is no longer usable because the original certificate does not retain a value beyond the first network hop.

In summary, encryption at the message level is definitely more desirable than encryption at the transport level. Yet more often than not, the latter will be the only feasible solution due to the lack of standards for creating message-level security and fundamental technical considerations; for example, with systems where performance is at a premium, you often cannot afford the computational and memory overhead of message encryption and decryption.

9.4.4   TRUST DOMAINS

A layered architecture such as an SOA often employs the concept of trusted domains. Authentication and authorization is located in the application frontend and in the high-level process-centric services. Other backend services and applications might require no security at all or might support a very limited set of security features. For example, no authorization or user-level security might be required by the backend services. Often, minimal security is imposed using a firewall setup, where connections to the insecure backend services are allowed only from specific hosts.

This is somewhat analogous to common setups using a Web server or an application server and a backend database. In this situation, not every user is authenticated against the database; instead, the server uses a pool of connections to the database that are all associated with a single database user.

It is evident that such a setup is applicable only within a closed and secured computing network. For a typical enterprise computing setup, this maps to certain network segments in a closed data center environment.

One benefit of this approach is the ease of setup and development of the backend services. The development effort associated with authentication is simply omitted. In addition, the backend services can be independent of any enterprise single sign-on infrastructure, making them simpler and ultimately more robust.

The greatest benefits of the approach are also its greatest weaknesses. For example, all auditing within the backend services must be performed manually. It is thus more error-prone and harder to maintain. This can lead to enormous efforts if legal regulations require in-depth changes to auditing. It is often desirable to make a backend service publicly available. In the case where the required security infrastructure is missing in these services, they usually must be proxied by another service that adds no business value at all. This adds an additional level and introduces a maintenance effort if the original service changes. For example, an airline might decide to expose their booking process to a partner airline, as in Figure 9-18.

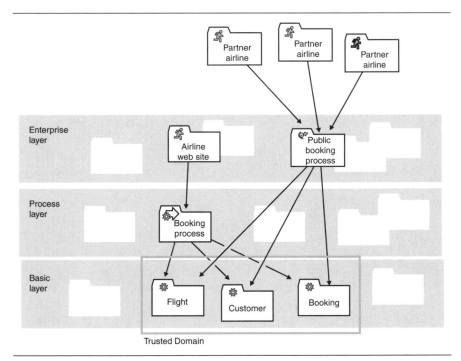

FIGURE 9-18   A trusted domain can be convenient but can introduce overhead and entropy if a service in the trusted domain must be promoted for third-party use. In this example, an airline is offering its booking service to a partner airline.

Trust Domains

Trust domains require a controlled, closed environment. Individual securing of even basic services is likely to save money in the long run and reduce maintenance efforts.

9.4.5 SECURITY AND HETEROGENEITY

Typical IT landscapes in the enterprise are very heterogeneous. For security considerations, the same rule applied to SOAs holds true: Do not fight heterogeneity but rather embrace it. More often than not, it is impractical to bind a backend service, let alone an entire legacy implementation, completely into the global enterprise security framework. On top of that, heterogeneity also exists among different client devices to your SOA, as well as the difference between the infrastructure inside and outside the enterprise or the department running the SOA.

For the outside world, it is important that the SOA appeals to as many potential clients as possible. The general rule is to secure the services exposed to the outside world as much as possible. It might be an option to provide certain services in multiple versions for different environments and to ensure that access takes place through the correct device.

Within the SOA, it is a good idea to provide a unified security framework. However, no possible participant of an SOA should be alienated by the required participation in a security framework that one does not want or cannot support. Thus, it should be an option rather than a requirement.

In addition to providing an SOA security framework, the infrastructure should be well protected using firewalls and trip wiring between the different layers of the application, as illustrated in Figure 9-19.

> ### Secure the Outside—Police the Inside
>
> Use off-the-shelf technology, such as firewalls, to lock out intrusion at the network perimeter. Use monitoring and trip wiring at system boundaries inside the enterprise to detect and report any suspicious activity.

Let us study the practical implications of such a setup with the customer booking process. The booking process originates on the airline Web site. At this level, customers will usually authenticate themselves with the system. The ability of the customer to book a flight is decided within the Web layer. The booking process then calls into the customer booking service using a single privileged user. A firewall ensures that no call with that user identity is made from anywhere but the Web application. The process-centric service checks authorization of the caller and calls out in turn to the different backend services passing the user. They in turn call out to the actual legacy implementations. Although two of these share the same user store with the application, credential mapping is performed in order to access the customer information system on the mainframe. None of the business services perform any authorization because these decisions are made within the legacy applications themselves.

If the process originates from a travel agent application frontend, authentication is performed directly within the application. The application is also bound into the general authorization scheme, presenting the travel agent with only the authorized options. Each travel agent is authorized as a separate user.

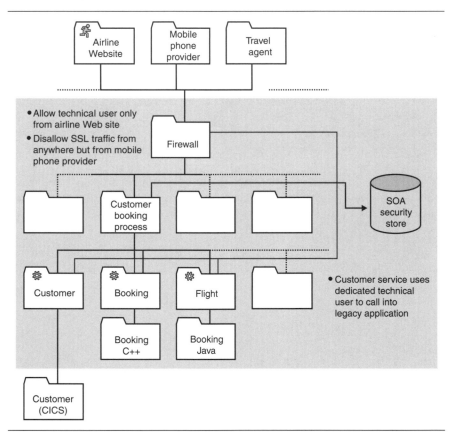

FIGURE 9-19   Illustration of security infrastructure that is catering for heterogeneous frontends and backends alike. In this example, a number of service implementations participate in a common security infrastructure, which uses a common security store. The customer implementation is part of a trust domain with respect to the SOA infrastructure. Access to this domain should be policed in a clearly defined way.

9.4.6 OTHER SECURITY TOPICS

When a service is offered to third parties outside the enterprise, matters of non-repudiation and message integrity are vitally important. Both technologies are directly related to concepts of asymmetric encryption, often using a public key infrastructure [GS1997].

   For message integrity, it is sufficient to digitally sign the message using a symmetric or asymmetric key, provided the key is known only to trusted parties. For most practical purposes, the message will be signed using the private key of a message sender, and the receiver will check the signature using the public key of the sender (see Figure 9-10). Note that the sender and receiver need not be the original sender and final receiver of the message but that the signature can be added to a sent message only for certain parts of the route, for example between two trusted domains. Furthermore, the keys need not be maintained by an independent third party. It is perfectly feasible and often easier to use a PKI that is hosted within the service provider for this purpose, especially where the service provider engages in business only with entities that are well known to the original service provider.

Non-repudiation means that the service provider and service user assume legal responsibility for the actual message contents (see Figure 9-10). For example, if the airline orders a certain number of menus from the caterer, the caterer might want to ensure that the airline has actually placed this exact order and not something different. Likewise, the airline can use the signed order confirmation of the caterer in case there is a dispute between the airline and the caterer. For messages to be non-refutable, it is usually required that a trusted entity manages the public keys of the parties engaged in the actual business transaction. Moreover, these entities will usually be licensed by some government agency to conform to certain standards, processes, and service levels. Message signatures can then be considered suitable for usage in a legal dispute or multimillion dollar contracts, for example the gross purchase of fuel or the ordering of an aircraft.

Technically, message signing can be easily accomplished if the message is in plain text format and can easily be manipulated. The best example is signing XML snippets that can be placed inside the body of a SOAP message.

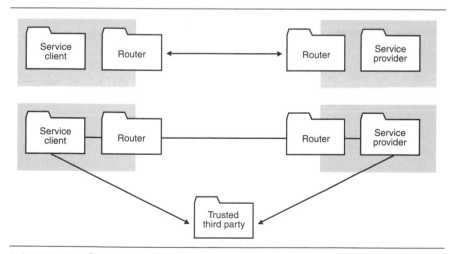

FIGURE 9-20 Communication scenario for message integrity (top) and non-repudiation (bottom). For message integrity, the routers sign the message and check the signature to ensure message integrity after leaving and before entering the trusted domains. For non-repudiation, a trusted third party is needed.

9.5 Conclusion

In this chapter, we looked at the different elements that constitute an SOA-enabling infrastructure, which we refer to as a service bus. Based on our conviction that middleware heterogeneity is an enterprise reality that can't be solved by introducing yet another set of interfaces and communication protocols, we described an approach which is based on loose coupling on the infrastructure level, effectively allowing the co-existence of multiple, heterogeneous middleware platforms within a higher-ranking meta bus which is designed to tie together these different platforms. We also stressed the fact that this meta bus should not be developed in isolation from concrete application projects in order to avoid working on an overly abstract level. Practical experience has shown that one can work for many years on the perfect enterprise infrastructure, without ever reaching a truly stable result. Consequently, a pragmatic, project driven approach should be taken.

The different application execution containers that we find in an enterprise represent the basis for building services in an SOA. We discussed the general nature of these containers, specific implementations, and how to integrate across multiple containers.

To maximize the robustness of our SOA, we discussed dealing with system failures with the main objective of gathering as much knowledge as possible about critical parts of the service. This enables recovery from a service failure to be as seamless as possible, both automatically and manually.

To minimize failures in the first place, we discussed concepts for scalability and availability. Both can be addressed using standard products and procedures and sometimes hardware components such as balancers are a good option. On the other hand, most frameworks for distributed objects such as EJB and CORBA support the basic building blocks needed.

Proper planning is essential for providing an available and scalable system. This holds true for the initial definition of the SLAs up to any subsequent exercise to scale a system by adding additional hardware and software.

It is fairly easy to accomplish availability at the system level and between individual requests. Guaranteeing in-request availability is considerably harder. It is not required nor appropriate for a vast number of application scenarios, and it introduces a significant overhead into system performance, very much comparable to the problems of distributed transactions. For practical reasons, the easiest way to accomplish availability is to maintain request cycles and transactions that are as short as possible.

Always consider the weak points in your application first. Keep in mind that the application is only as strong as its weakest link, both for availability and scalability.

Finally, note how much easier it becomes to cope not only with availability and scalability but also with service failures if your business logic becomes stateless or even idempotent. The strategies that deal with stateful systems are more complex and tend to impact on the overall system performance and ultimately on scalability and availability.

On top of providing reliability and availability, any IT infrastructure must support certain security features. Although technologies and tools are available that can be used to provide transparent, enterprise-wide authentication and authorization for an SOA, it is very likely that a first step will provide only authentication as part of the SOA framework itself. The reasons are mainly rooted in the fact that authentication can be introduced in most legacy systems with very little effort, while refactoring the authorization aspects of an application requires more effort. Also, it will be far easier to implement from an organizational perspective. Legacy applications are likely to be placed within trusted domains to allow for integration into the SOA without disturbing the ongoing operation of the application.

References

Chappell, Dave. *Enterprise Service Bus.* O'Reilly, 2004. [DC2004]

Garfinkel, Simson, et al. *Practical UNIX and Internet Security.* O'Reilly, 1996. [GS1996]

Garfinkel, Simson, et al. *Web Security and Commerce.* O'Reilly, 1997. [GS1997]

Gupta, Samudra. *Logging in Java with the JDK 1.4 Logging API and Apache log4j.* Apress, 2003. [GS2003]

Hartman, Bret, et al. *Mastering Web Services Security.* Wiley, 2003. [H2003]

Peltier, Thomas R. *Information Security Risk Analysis.* Auerbach Pub, 2001. [PT2001]

Piedad, Floyd and Michael Hawkins. *High Availability: Design, Techniques and Processes.* Prentice Hall, 2000. [PH2000]

Tardugno, Anthony, Thomas DiPasquale, and Robert Matthews. *IT Services Costs, Metrics, Benchmarking and Marketing.* Prentice Hall, 2000. [TDM2000]

Schmeh, Klaus. *Cryptography and Public Key Infrastructure on the Internet.* Wiley & Sons, 2003. [SK2003]

URLs

http://www.redbooks.ibm.com/redbooks/SG242234.html

http://www.oasis-open.org/committees/tc_home.php?wg_abbrev=security

http://www.w3.org/Encryption/2001/

http://www.omg.org/technology/documents/formal/corba_2.htm

10

SOA in Action

This chapter shows how a service can be implemented in the real world to serve the needs of different usage models. You can provide the same service using different protocols and different granularity according to the context in which you use it. As is the case with traditional software, it is impossible to design a service based only on abstract principles. However, you can employ careful planning and refactoring of a service to make an implementation suitable for many different usage scenarios.

To illustrate the different design considerations applicable to different usage models, we employ a passenger check-in scenario. A passenger might check in with a mobile phone or PDA, using an electronic (or physical) ticket at an airline booth. Alternatively, the passenger might be checked in with one airline on behalf of a second airline, perhaps if the second flight leg is operated by a different carrier. In some scenarios, the same service might be accessed using multiple channels at the same time.

In its most generic form, multiple services are at work. At the heart of everything is the check-in service, assigning seats to passengers on airplanes and keeping track of the seat occupation in individual planes. As input, it takes any number of passenger ticket coupons and returns the appropriate number of boarding passes. Usually, other services will also be involved. Prior to performing the check-in, the ticket service can be used to determine which tickets are available for a passenger and to validate the tickets before check-in, in addition to marking the ticket coupons after check-in has been completed.

The customer information service might be contacted to read data regarding the preferences or frequent flyer account of the customer. Preferences for seating can be used in the booking itself. A meal preference can be used with services available from the airline's caterer to prepare only the required amount of special food, thus decreasing the airline's overhead. Personal data regarding the passenger might be forwarded to the customs or immigration office at the passenger's destination. For the time being, this discussion will be limited to the services mentioned previously, although more services might be involved for issues such as baggage handling and airport services.

As a prerequisite, it is worthwhile to determine if the provided services are aggregation-friendly. The ticket service's sole purpose is looking up tickets and checking their validity. These calls can be considered idempotent at the semantic level. If they fail, the caller can reattempt the call and expect the same result as the previous call. Invalidating the coupon is an operation that will change some persistently stored data. The call to this operation is logically tied with the assign seats call of the check-in service itself. The latter is likely to live in a local transaction and can be rolled back upon failure. In this event, there will not be any attempt to change the state of the ticket voucher, even though such changes can be easily reset in a compensating call. Finally, setting the meal preference is an operation that might also be considered idempotent. However, in an operational system, this type of process is more likely to be implemented in an asynchronous manner. In general, it is necessary only to guarantee that the caterer gets the information about meal preferences well before takeoff rather than at some specific point in time.

Throughout this chapter, we will use the same example in a set of different scenarios. In Section 10.1, we discuss a Web application. In Section 10.2, our example takes the form of an EAI integration scenario. We employ a B2B model in Section 10.3. In Section 10.4, we discuss a fat client scenario, and in Section 10.5, we deploy it by using a small mobile device such as a cellular telephone. Finally, in Section 10.6, we discuss the multi-channel scenario.

10.1   Building Web Applications

As previously discussed, Web applications are particularly suited as clients for a Service-Oriented Architecture because they offer a natural means of storing context or state information when making calls to a mainly stateless service architecture. In addition, they offer a rich user interface, and users of Web applications are accustomed to a high degree of interactivity. Although the interaction model in Figure 10-1 remains a possibility for providing check-in functionality using a Web interface, it is likely that an airline will provide the user with a richer set of choices during the booking process.

These choices will at least include the selection of seats and meals available on the flight. On the other hand, some of the options that were originally present might not be applicable. For example, checking in online is often only possible if a registered user has purchased the ticket because logging in to the airline's Web site is required in order to perform the check-in operation. On top of that, two people traveling together must check in separately if they purchased their tickets separately.

In a Web application, users will authenticate themselves against the Web tier, usually through a Web page form with username and password or client-side certificates. Users can then be stored within the Web tier of the application. For subsequent calls to services, there are two possible models: principal propagation or trust. Principal propagation is trivial and uses frameworks that are built to support this feature. For example, within the J2EE framework, the same principal object used in the Web tier can directly be used to call other J2EE services such

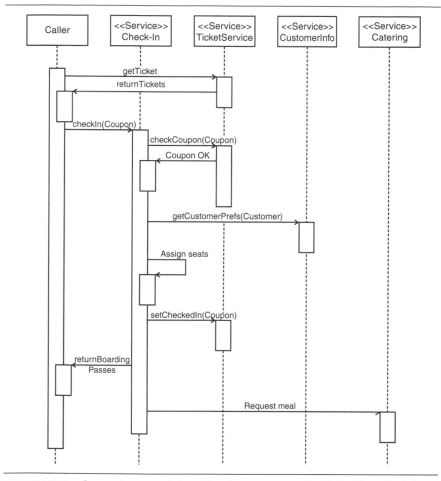

FIGURE 10-1 General service interaction for passenger check-in. The check-in service takes tickets as input parameters and creates boarding passes as output parameters, invalidating the relevant coupon of the ticket. Note that all services are basically stateless.

as Enterprise Java Beans. For other service types, such as CORBA or SOAP, the process is not as straightforward. It might include the need for mapping credentials from the Web tier to the service layer in a specific way. As mentioned in Chapter 9, "Infrastructure of the Service Bus," SOAP does not support a standardized means of passing credentials. Because Web sites can operate within a controlled corporate environment, trust between the Web tier and the service layer is a common scenario. All calls to the service layer are then carried out using a common identity—or no identity at all—and the actual caller principal is just passed as a parameter using call parameters. Of course, this requires that the Web application is not exposed directly to a sensitive network segment.

The interaction diagram in Figure 10-2 illustrates the need to expose the "assign seats" functionality to the outside client. In addition, displaying the available seats to the user for a given plane's seating configuration is also necessary. Although it is tempting to provide this type of layout in an ad-hoc manner within

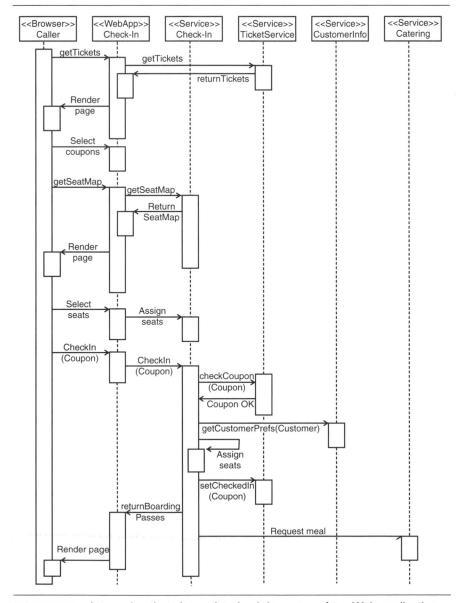

FIGURE 10-2   Interaction that shows the check-in process for a Web application. The state of the application is maintained in the Web application.

the Web application, perhaps as a number of configuration files, this implementation would soon become unmanageable. Airlines often change their seating configurations and add new planes, and it is important to provide this information to customers. In addition, the seat configuration of the airplane and the listing of available seats can be transferred within a single call, providing a good example of a coarse-grained data structure.

Figure 10-2 shows the full interaction diagram for the Web application invocation. Note that we made use of the results from Chapter 8, "Process Integrity," by pushing state as far up the chain as possible. In fact, all state is stored in the Web application itself. This enables a rich interaction between customer and application without the need for any stateful services. Note that the transaction boundaries of the original example have not changed. There is no need to expose transactions directly to the client.

A reasonable amount of interaction takes place between the client and the Web application directly without any need to involve the service layer. This is the result of a well-defined location for storing conversational state along with an optimistic concurrency model (see Chapter 8). After the available tickets have been retrieved from the TicketService, users may choose any selection of flight coupons for which they want to check in. Any logical checks, such as whether a check-in for the coupon can be performed at the current date, can be easily carried out at the Web tier. This is achievable because one person generally handles a single coupon at a time. Of course, race conditions can still occur, such as if someone tries to check in using the telephone and a Web application simultaneously. The same holds true for seat selection. While making the seating selection, one user might select some seats that are already reserved by another user. However, given the time available for check-in and the total number of passengers on a plane, this is rather unlikely. In the event of an error when assigning seats, the user can be prompted with an updated seat map to perform a reselect.

Although the service calls for reserving seats and invalidating a ticket are technically idempotent, this fact cannot be exposed to the customer. One reason is that you shouldn't expose a recoverable error to the customer in the first place. The other is that although changing the state of a ticket is idempotent, the creation of boarding passes might well not be. In that case, it is usually necessary to prevent the customer from making the same call more than once. In Web applications, this is a common scenario that can happen easily if the customer impatiently hits the reload or submit button repeatedly. If not handled properly, such behavior can at worst stall the application. The solution is to apply a one-time transaction pattern (OTT). This involves storing a transaction ID with associated states such as running, finished, and failed. If a customer reattempts an operation, the system retrieves the state of the one-time transaction ID and forwards the customer to an appropriate page. Figure 10-3 illustrates this behavior.

As we mentioned before, service calls can be either synchronous or asynchronous and can be long running. The one-time transaction pattern is a suitable technology for handling such an invocation scenario. Here, the invocation returns a status page immediately after dispatching the asynchronous call. The status page checks periodically for available results using the OTT token. This is a common technique for complicated and long-running processes such as purchasing airline tickets.

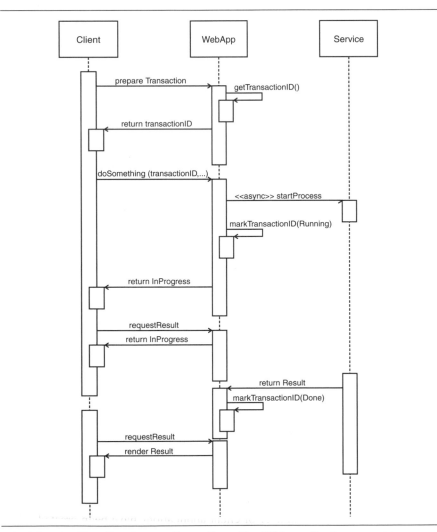

FIGURE 10-3 One-time transaction pattern. The Web application manages a number of transaction tokens and serves requests based on the state of the tokens. For example, a token can start precisely one operation. While the token is in the running state, some meaningful information is returned to the client.

It is worth mentioning that the creation of a Web application can justify implementing an SOA. In many Web applications, it is necessary to interface with an organization's operational core systems, which can be anything from mainframe systems or relational databases to CORBA or J2EE servers. Thus, the creation of Web applications often involves the integration of multiple types of enterprise systems. Usually, this is achieved by using various vendor-specific APIs to connect to the different systems and exposing some consolidated API to the application. Because this integration effort must be performed one way or another, the implementation of these integrations as services presents relatively small overhead and manifests itself mainly during design time in the way transaction boundaries and principal propagation are addressed in the application. This will at least lead to an internal API that is "service-ready" and that can be exposed as a service using appropriate tools.

Web applications can be created using a number of tools, including Perl, PHP, Python, Java Server Pages (JSP), and Microsoft's ASP.NET. When creating a Web application that is simply a client to existing services, any environment that fosters access to the technology used to implement these services can be a reasonable choice. For example, if your SOA is built using Enterprise Java Beans, then using Java Server Pages and Servlets for the Web application is the natural choice. Likewise, if the SOA is implemented using XML over HTTP, perhaps with SOAP, you can use any platform with support for the latest Web service technologies for the Web application. For effectively employing an OTT pattern, the platform should also facilitate the easy creation of request interceptors. J2EE Servlet filters provide one such mechanism.

Many Web applications involve not only the use of existing services but also the direct integration of existing systems. It is usually a good idea to focus on a common skill set for the creation of such an application. The J2EE platform and Microsoft .NET are suitable to that end, not least because components created on these platforms can easily be turned into Web services.

10.2 Enterprise Application Integration

At first glance, Enterprise Application Integration (EAI) appears to be the perfect environment to employ an SOA: In fact, plenty of reasons to use an SOA as a driver for EAI exist, and vice versa. However, EAIs pose a certain set of requirements in addition to profound non-technical issues that you must consider.

Today, most large organizations have a highly fragmented application infrastructure, in which a vast number of client applications have been created using multiple programming platforms and communication infrastructures from multiple vendors. A recent example of the endeavor to solve all application integration problems is the introduction of a corporate "standard" ERP (Enterprise Resource Planning) suite. This process failed in most organizations due to the relatively low flexibility such a solution provides and the fact that businesses have a need for tactical IT solutions, as opposed to strategically planned applications.

This example of failure provides a reason to be wary of addressing EAI problems with an SOA. Nevertheless, if an SOA is properly deployed, it will address many technical and core concerns related to EAI. There are two ways of looking at EAI in a service-oriented world: as a service provider and as a service consumer. As a service consumer, you typically want a service that is easy to access, highly available, functional complete, and stable over an indefinite period of time. As a service provider, you might want a service that is easy to deploy and to upgrade; in an EAI environment, quality of service, single sign-on, and other attributes become paramount.

At the outset, it is worth noting that so-called EAI product suites are generally unsuited to tackle the aforementioned EAI challenges. Most provide a clear integration path that is usually supported by accompanying tools, some of which provide for quality of service and ship pluggable security modules, but they usually fail to provide a stable view of the result of the integration process. Furthermore, because they only partly adhere to open or industry standards, they are very unlikely to be stable for a reasonable period of time. This is one of the prime reasons that organizations that take SOA seriously almost always choose to build their core service architecture themselves while employing standards wherever possible (see the case studies in Chapters 14 through 17).

10.2.1 SERVICE ENABLEMENT

In order to provide EAI functionality in a service-oriented environment, the most common task is service enablement. Service enablement is the process that creates a service to encapsulate the functionality provided by an existing application. The type of application encapsulated can be anything from a monolithic mainframe application to a distributed application built on top of CORBA or DCOM.

Of course, service enablement is more than just wrapping and exposing an existing programming interface. As an example, consider the movement of an existing check-in application in a service-oriented domain. Assume that—as shown in Figure 10-4—the original application is a typical client/server application. As a first step for service enablement, the application is separated into a visual and a non-visual part. Communication between both parts is grouped based on their business domain. Access to the non-visual layer is defined by one or more interfaces. If possible, the implementation of the interfaces and the persistent data upon which they act can also be separated. Finally, the application is moved to the service infrastructure.

Depending on the application, one or more services might emerge from this analysis. For example, when analyzing a real-world check-in application, it is quite likely that services such as ticketing, baggage handling, and actual check-in will surface during such an analysis. After this analysis is complete, consolidated interface descriptions for the communication can be derived. This should include provisions for undoable actions and idempotency wherever possible. The implementation and possibly the interfaces need to be changed to include infrastructure services such as user management and security as well as internal changes for server-side resource handling. Now the visual layer and the service layer can actually be separated.

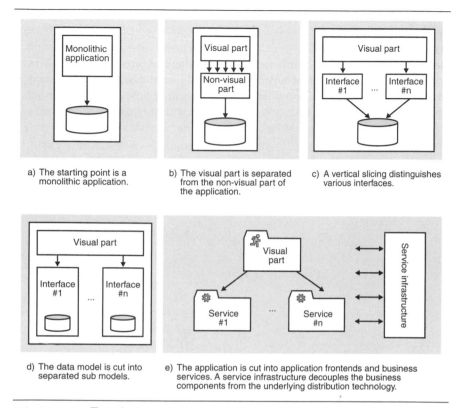

a) The starting point is a monolithic application.

b) The visual part is separated from the non-visual part of the application.

c) A vertical slicing distinguishes various interfaces.

d) The data model is cut into separated sub models.

e) The application is cut into application frontends and business services. A service infrastructure decouples the business components from the underlying distribution technology.

FIGURE 10-4   Transformation of a monolithic application into a service-oriented application.

It is evident from the check-in example that the examination of a single application is unlikely to yield fully reusable services. Although it is reasonable to assume that one can obtain a fairly complete description of the check-in service itself, it is rather unlikely that sufficient information about the baggage handling or the ticketing service can be obtained.

If more than one application exists that relies on common underlying principles, immediate reuse benefits can be obtained from the service enablement. For example, many applications share the concept and even the persistence mechanism for entities, such as customer or contract in a business scenario. Factoring these out into services not only provides instant benefits for reuse but also acts as a successful demonstration of the suitability of the Service-Oriented Architecture that is likely to empower other departments to use the newly created services and contribute new services.

When service-enabling applications for EAI in the way we have described, it is essential that a service registry be available. This can be used to identify those remaining services that are already available in the application and that can be factored out of the existing application.

Another common scenario is to provide services for an already distributed architecture. Recall that a distributed architecture alone does not necessarily consolidate an SOA. Often, the interaction patterns between the application frontend and the distributed components are too fine-grained. A sensible approach is to define façade services that sit between the application and the distributed objects. The application is stripped of all knowledge regarding items such as distributed objects and uses the service as its sole communication channel to the backend logic (see Figure 10-5). The service then aggregates the functionality available in the distributed computing environment. At the same time, coupling in the distributed object layer can be replaced by explicitly coupling services. It will also use a common service infrastructure, as you have seen previously. It is often desirable to replace the distributed object implementation with a more localized implementation to reduce network load and latency. Because the implementation has been encapsulated in the service layer, it can easily be replaced without having an effect on the applications that use the service. The service façades to the distributed computing environment should be cut in a way that enables them to act as the sole owner of the data upon which they operate.

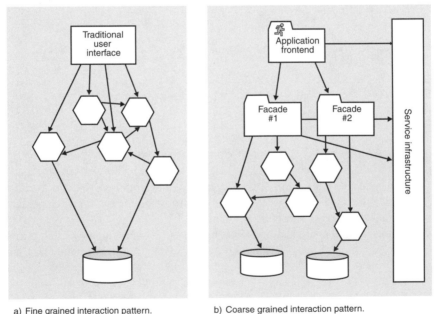

a) Fine grained interaction pattern.   b) Coarse grained interaction pattern.

FIGURE 10-5   Creating a service layer that replaces direct interaction with distributed objects.

There are, of course, other scenarios that can be used to enable transformation toward an SOA. For example, rich applications that rely on backend services (see Section 10.4) greatly benefit from the creation of a service layer.

EAI Can Drive an SOA

EAI is an excellent driver for service-enabling existing applications. From a business perspective, EAI is introduced to simplify the application infrastructure and to foster reuse—providing good motivation for creating an SOA.

10.2.2 STABILITY AND UPGRADE ABILITY

Service stability and the ability to upgrade are two of the most desirable features in an EAI environment. The reason is that the service consumer might reside in a different department or even in a different country from the service provider. The service provider must be able to upgrade a service without having an impact on current applications that integrate this service. You can use various methods to solve this problem, with the two main styles being backward compatibility and the provision of different versions. Backward compatibility is illustrated in Figure 10-6. Effectively, this means that service interfaces can only be extended

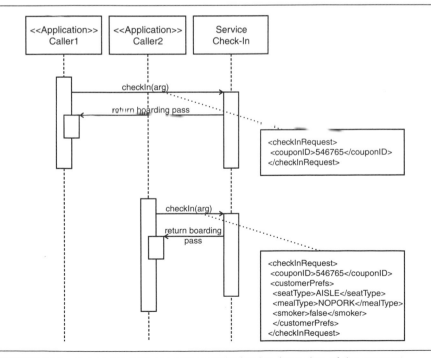

FIGURE 10-6   A service that supports versioning by extension of the request document format. Although this is easy to achieve with pure payload semantics, it can be difficult in other environments.

without violating existing interface contracts. This is similar to the discussion on payload semantics in Chapter 3, "Inventory of Distributed Computing Concepts." Unfortunately, this approach tends to weaken the interface contracts over time, which in turn makes it difficult to enforce a specific usage style.

Although it is fairly straightforward to achieve this using XML communication such as SOAP, it can be arbitrarily hard to do so using CORBA or DCOM without reverting to pure payload semantics.

On the other hand, you can easily provide different production versions of a service by deploying the service in different locations. These locations can be looked up in a registry that also contains information regarding the most up-to-date service available. Although this creates significant overhead in managing the SOA, it completely decouples service upgrades from existing applications. It is also straightforward to provide this using any available communication model. The out-of-date services are continuously monitored and can be shut down when no more applications are accessing them. Moreover, it might be desirable to reimplement the old services in terms of the new services. By keeping the contract unchanged, the old service clients can communicate transparently with the new implementations. Figure 10-7 illustrates two versions of the check-in service working with an online registry. Using the online registry for binding to the actual service implementation at runtime makes it possible to migrate older services to different, less capable hardware.

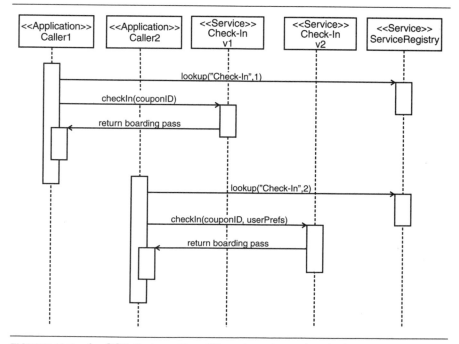

FIGURE 10-7 An SOA that enables different versions of a single service to be productive at the same time.

EAI Requires Repositories

EAI scenarios should use service repositories because this is the best way to ensure stability and upgrade ability. It is crucial to give your internal clients peace of mind when using the SOA.

10.3 Business-to-Business

In a business-to-business (B2B) environment, a corporation offers some service to another company over public networks such as the Internet. In a B2B scenario, both the service consumer and the service provider benefit greatly from standard communication protocols. The service consumer profits from the increased flexibility gained when changing to another provider or when using several providers at the same time. The service provider can also profit—for example, depending on the type of communication, it might be possible to eliminate the necessity to ship software to the client.

The same goes for the security infrastructure. Because security infrastructures can get very complicated, the client and server must be certain to use a mechanism that can be trusted, where both ends of the communication chain can identify a security violation using their standard system management tools. Standards are also desirable because many interactions create a legal obligation between the parties.

In addition, it is attractive to define a standard format for the actual data being transferred. This saves both sides time and money in service development and integration. UN/CEFACT (ebXML) and RosettaNet provide examples of initiatives to establish data standards.[1] Although the resulting standards are not yet mature and they are not appropriate for *all* B2B problems, it is worthwhile to see if they are applicable in specific cases.

Most initiatives that define standard protocols result in the creation of rather large documents that are exchanged in a business transaction. This is basically analogous to a service-oriented approach with very coarse granularity. Because of the latency that can be experienced on a public network connection, it is far more efficient to send a single large document instead of making short procedural interactions.

Although the business process itself can be stateful, it pays to create stateless service invocations. In a B2B scenario, the most common way to achieve this is to pass a token along with every service invocation. These tokens can be used once or on a cyclical basis if the number of tokens is large compared to the frequency of interactions.

---

[1] See the URLs list at the end of this chapter.

Go Stateless for B2B

Stateless semantics are especially important in B2B scenarios. They enable interaction with remote customers over connections with high network latency. They also create much fewer constraints for the calling applications.

Although the authors do not believe that a runtime-naming service or repository is mandatory in an SOA environment, it is of great use in a B2B scenario. The pressure for a service to provide location transparency is far higher than in a controlled enterprise environment. After a business partner uses a service, it might require significant effort to switch to a different version. Even if it can be achieved by configuration only, it still creates an overhead that might result in unwanted downtime. Both service user and provider can be separated by large distances—as much as thousands of miles. This makes location transparency a necessity in order to provide disaster recovery capabilities. If a customer uses a service of a company whose main computing center goes down in a fire, the customer expects to be transferred to the secondary site automatically. Of course, this also includes the service repository itself being failsafe.

Location Transparency for Stable B2B Services

B2B scenarios require real location transparency using service repositories. This enables customers to securely establish long-term relationships regardless of changes to the supplier's infrastructure.

B2B scenarios can include online billing mechanisms, although they are more common in a business-to-consumer (B2C) scenario. A B2B scenario will generally log only access information on the side of the service provider. This information can later be used to create a monthly invoice.

In a B2B scenario, the check-in service can be used by partner airlines to check in customers on a flight leg that is operated by the service provider. In contrast to the examples considered so far, the main difference is that the service provider cannot validate the actual request against its own ticket database. There are several options for handling this situation.

The first option is to trust the remote system because it is well established that the business partner is trustworthy and provides only valid requests. Here, the remote check-in service does not have any information about the tickets that are used on individual flight legs, nor does the service have any information regarding the respective passenger. Data that directly relates to customer service quality—such as the customer's meal preference—must therefore be passed in the check-in call itself. This is shown in Figure 10-8.

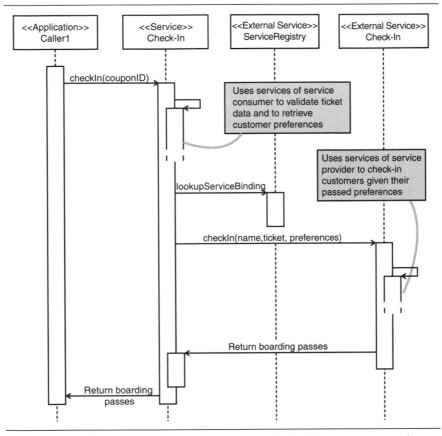

FIGURE 10-8   One-way communication scenario. The ticketing company performs the check-in using the operator's service, passing all the relevant data during the call itself.

The second option is to synchronize all relevant ticket and customer data between the partner companies on a regular basis. The ticketing company forwards the ticket data to the operating airlines, and the operating airlines in turn forward the flight information back to the ticketing companies. Although the check-in process is similar to the ones discussed in earlier chapters, service access within a single corporation is all that is needed during the actual check-in operation.

Finally, the third option in the B2B scenario is that the service provider becomes a service consumer at the other airline's ticket information service. In this situation, both businesses create an effective two-way communication scenario. Because the clients trust each other, the operating airline can validate the tickets of the partner's customers and retrieve some part of the customer preferences. This scenario is shown in Figure 10-9.

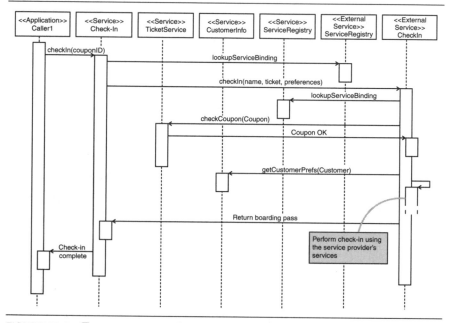

FIGURE 10-9 Two-way communication scenario during the check-in process. The flight's operator uses the services of the ticketing company to validate flight coupons and retrieve customer preferences.

When using external services, care must be taken to cope with the breakdown of the external service. Even if SLAs exists that guarantee a certain availability of the external service, network failures or failures of equipment on the client side should be anticipated. The error should be handled gracefully using the same general principles outlined in Chapter 9.

In general, the best type of service for this scenario depends on both the level of customer service one wants to provide and the technical capabilities and geographical locations of the airlines.

If the partners have weak connectivity, it might be best to use the first option and provide the necessary accounting information separately from the actual process. A common reason for choosing this type of solution is when latency is so high that any additional server-side processing introduces unbearable risks on system performance. Another strong reason for this scenario is when only certain partners are technically capable of operating as service providers.

If the partners are separated by a large distance—consider a European and a South American carrier—an infrequent synchronization mechanism might offer the best solution.

If the partners are located close together and can use a stable connection with sufficient bandwidth, they can use the third scenario. This offers customers the best service, enabling them to buy a ticket from one airline and check in with another airline easily. It also results in the best data quality.

10.4   Fat Clients

The term "fat client" is a common synonym for an application type that provides a lot of its core processes on the client machine and usually relies on a single backend system, which can be a relational database or a host system that provides some procedural capabilities.

Fat clients have a bad reputation in IT departments mainly because they created real challenges for deployment and maintenance. Because they aggregate a lot of computational logic, they require frequent rollouts of the whole application package throughout the enterprise. On the other hand, fat client applications have enjoyed a good reputation among many end users. They provide swift operations compared to many poorly built Web applications that have been created to replace them. They also provide complex interaction models and advanced graphical capabilities that are very hard to re-create using Web interfaces. Therefore, in many usage scenarios, fat clients are regarded as more user-friendly.

Although fat client applications need a considerable amount of deployment and maintenance effort, they also help to save bandwidth and increase response times compared to typical Web applications. Another strong advantage of fat clients is that they offer easy access to local hardware devices such as printers and smart card readers, which makes them particularly well suited for use in a controlled environment with medium to long release cycles.

You can use services together with fat clients to transform fat clients to rich clients, in which the client application directly accesses different services and keeps track of any necessary state information. This works in much the same way as for the Web application layer in Section 10.1. The core advantage is that the rich client application can be completely decoupled from the backend implementation. It thus remains robust in the face of alteration in the data model and ultimately against a possible change in the overall backend infrastructure, such as the gradual replacement of host systems with integrated services.

> ### Build Rich Clients, Not Fat Clients
>
> Usage of thin clients does not necessarily mean reduced functionality. Services can enable you to build rich clients rather than fat clients.

Fat clients can differ in their authentication schemes. Whereas a Web application user needs to authenticate itself to the server—e.g. using username and password—fat clients might be trusted clients or might be authenticated using a certificate. Where backend systems do not support this type of authentication, the service might present some default username and password as a proxy user.

When using a proxy user, you must take care to minimize the resultant security risk (see Chapter 9). In particular, the proxy user credential should not be stored in clear text; they must be configurable, and the allowed origins of proxy user request should be restricted to a well-defined set of network addresses.

> ### Proxy Users Protect Backend Systems
>
> Proxy users can isolate backend systems from physical users. Because this also involves a security risk, you must take extra care to prevent the misuse of proxy users.

In the check-in example, rich clients include check-in kiosks and workstations of check-in clerks. These rich clients access printers for boarding passes and baggage tags and are usually equipped with card readers for electronic tickets, credit cards, or frequent traveler cards. Advanced check-in kiosks might also connect to baggage scales and conveyors. They provide interfaces that make it as easy as possible to navigate across the seat map of the airplane and to choose seats for check-in. Yet they do not perform the actual check-in process and do not directly manipulate data. Instead, they use a service layer that is usually identical to the one used by Web applications. Figure 10-10 shows a typical rich client setup.

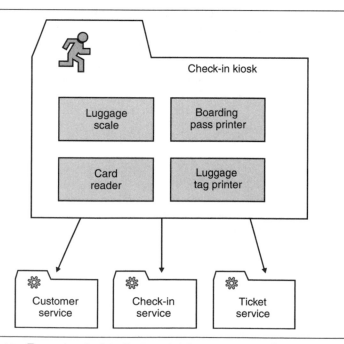

FIGURE 10-10   Example of a fat client containing a smart card reader, luggage scale, luggage tag printer, and boarding pass printer. The fat client uses standard services that in turn rely on relational databases and host systems.

10.5   Designing for Small Devices

For the foreseeable future, the design of services for small devices effectively means designing for a specific device. (For the purpose of this chapter, a small device is one with a small screen of about 150 × 100 pixels, limited processing power, memory often far less than 256kB, and limited data entry support although with a capability to create network connections to facilitate participation in an SOA.) One of the most important points is that the interaction pattern must match the capabilities of the device. Rich interaction patterns for different classes of applications often fail with small devices because of the physical characteristics of the device and also because of additional cost and longer interaction time for the user imposed by these patterns. Because network connectivity might be at a premium, the service implementation itself will usually be as lean as possible to minimize latency.

It is likely that security will be limited to mostly transport security because processing power and available memory might not allow for the encryption and signature of messages as defined in Chapter 9.

Although J2ME MIDP 2.0 supports transport security using HTTPS, there is no support in version 1.0. This means that you must use some other means to prevent passing extensive credentials between server and client. Authentications can be performed in ways such as using the telephone number, using username/password, or using certificates stored in the client. Although using the telephone number might seem like the best scenario, there are a number of reasons to avoid it.

For security reasons, runtime of environments such as J2ME MIDP do not enable access to telephony functionality, including the phone number. Furthermore, unless the delivery path is controlled, the potential for abuse of the telephone number for authentication is very high, both because it is easy to tamper with and because it is basically a public number that can be readily obtained. However, the phone number can be an excellent means of authentication when using SMS-based services, as we discuss at the end of this chapter.

One way or another, this information will be stored persistently at the client. This is mandatory due to the limited data entry support on small devices. A requirement to repeatedly enter a username and password with a clumsy keyboard obstructs usability. Alternatively, it is possible to envisage interaction without the user actually logging in to the system at all. The invocation might be triggered by a unique ID such as a reservation number.

Lightweight Security

Security features often require rather large computational and memory resources. Use only security measures that have little impact on both the device and the user.

Some small devices can use SOAP (or even CORBA) for remote invocations. However, you must carefully consider whether this is a good idea. For example, SOAP requires resources at almost every level of the small device, and a significant amount of processing power and memory is used for XML parsing. In addition, SOAP libraries that are not native to the device must be bundled with the application, which often increases the size of the application beyond what is possible for the target device. When using SOAP, you must also take into account that the specification is still evolving. Because implementations for mobile devices lag back behind the current standard, often by more than a year, it is unlikely that a state-of-the-art small device can properly address state-of-the-art SOAP services in the organization.

Therefore, it is sensible to decouple the service invocation in the device from the actual service using an adapter that resides at a gateway server. This setup enables the client to connect to the service using the least common denominator in technology, usually connecting using HTTP or HTTPS. If—as with MIDP 1.0—only HTTP is available, the server can establish a session that prevents the repeated passing of users' credentials over the wire. The session token (or login token) can be stored in the SOAP header or can be sent using a SOAP parameter. In the authors' experience, moving from lightweight J2ME SOAP implementations, such as kSOAP, to a HTTP-POST style interaction can reduce the client size by approximately 20kB. Given that the footprint allowed by J2ME MIDP Midlet Suites can be as low as 64kB or less, this is effectively a huge reduction in size that in turn creates the opportunity for a of richer and more user-friendly application.

Minimize Resources for Communication

In small devices, use resources for the application rather than the communication. It is better to create a protocol translator on the server side than to withhold functionality from the customer due to resource constraints.

In the check-in example, most users will not be ready to select the seats using a small screen and a hard-to-handle keyboard. Using a small device, it is more likely that the user will check-in right away after the proper flight coupon has been selected. Because interaction using mobile phones is somewhat cumbersome, it might even be possible to check in by simply typing the coupon number for which to perform the check-in and hitting "continue." A typical interaction scenario is shown in Figure 10-11. In this example, this process is achieved by eliminating the need to query the customer service and the caterer. Note that service granularities used by small devices tend to be coarser than services used by Web applications.

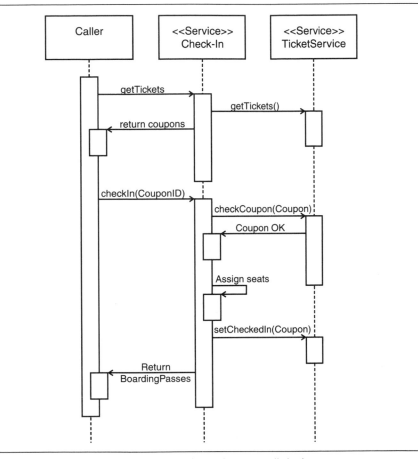

FIGURE 10-11   Typical service interaction using a small device.

As we discussed previously, there are various ways to authenticate the user. In the check-in example, it is hard to board the plane without being the actual ticket holder. Thus, it is possible to check in a single flight coupon based on an ID that is printed on the coupon, as illustrated in Figure 10-12. In such a scenario, only the person holding the physical flight coupon can perform the check-in.

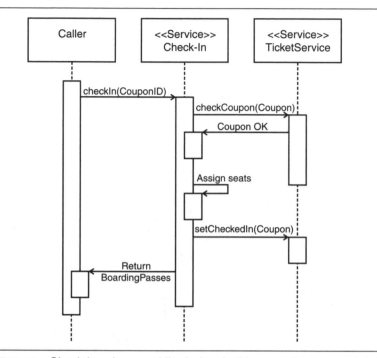

FIGURE 10-12   Check-in using a mobile device. In this example, the check-in is performed solely using the coupon ID.

An alternative scenario with a richer interaction pattern is shown in Figure 10-13. It uses a Web application to store some conversational state, and in the example, this is leveraged to reduce latency for the actual check-in call. To that end, just after login, it dispatches an asynchronous request to the potentially costly operation that obtains the customer's of preferences.

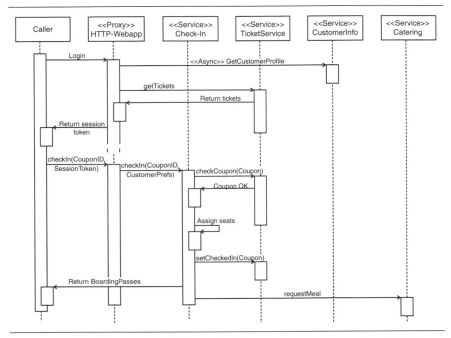

FIGURE 10-13 Using a proxy Web application as a service proxy. As with Web applications, the proxy can be used for state aggregation. It can also dispatch some asynchronous calls, such as requesting a certain type of meal, to reduce latency within the actual check-in calls.

When targeting mobile phones, it might also be an option not to actually install the service on the mobile phone. Mobile phone technology supports options such as short message service (SMS) or its succeeding technology, multimedia message service (MMS), that can also be used to connect to a service. To check in, the user can utilize the coupon number on the ticket along with a dedicated telephone number for checking in. An immediate advantage might be that the user can be uniquely identified using his phone number. However, this communication model has certain security restrictions, although it might well be the best option for deploying consumer services such as multiplayer role playing games or dating services (see Figure 10-14).

Due to their coarse-grained structure, services that are used from small devices are an excellent option for other usage scenarios whenever some resources are at a premium. An example is a check-in terminal that needs to function using limited network connectivity.

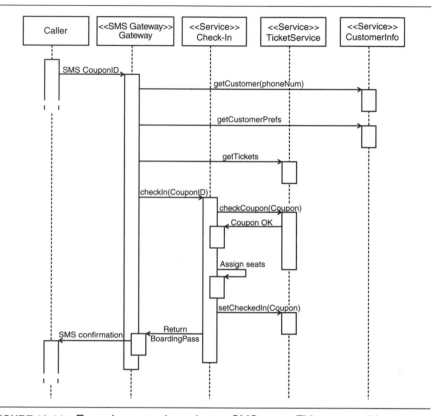

FIGURE 10-14   Engaging a service using an SMS proxy. This can provide a clean—yet potentially insecure—way to identity the customer.

10.6   Multi-Channel Applications

SOAs are extremely effective at implementing multi-channel applications. Strengths such as building a reusable, functional infrastructure, mastering heterogeneity, and providing easy access to data and business logic are key factors for successful multi-channel projects.

A multi-channel application is characterized by a functional core that can be accessed through different channels by either human users or programs, as shown in Figure 10-15. Each channel typically has its own characteristic variant of the basic business processes and specific access technology. These specifics depend directly on requirements of the channel's users such as sales department, back office, or service center. Due to the different requirements, you will often find significant differences in the channels' business processes. For example, a sales representative will require a different view of customer data from a back office clerk or from a service center agent. The processes also depend on the access technology. As we have already discussed in the previous section, you will probably find that the processes on a mobile device with a low bandwidth connection to the functional core and a small display are different from the processes that can be supported by a Web application.

Typical multi-channel applications can provide channels such as the Internet, various mobile channels such as WAP, B2B, fat clients, call centers, or voice applications. They also provide cross-channel functionality, such as co-browsing or channel switching.

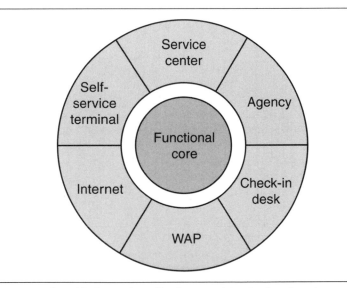

FIGURE 10-15 A multi-channel application consists of a functional core that is shared by several channels. Each channel provides a specific view of core functionality, according to the requirements of the channel user and the channel technology.

10.6.1 FUNDAMENTAL SOA

A fundamental SOA represents the simplest model of SOA-based multi-channel applications (see Chapter 6, "The Architectural Roadmap"). In many cases, this simplicity makes it the preferred choice of model. In this scenario, you have services neither in the aggregation layer nor in the process layer. Consequently, you can also abandon extra tiers and the appropriate hardware, which can lead to reduced latency and improved application response times.

The authors recommend the usage of this minimal approach where possible. This advice does not apply only to multi-channel applications, either. It is beneficial for *every* SOA to keep operations as simple as possible. Abandoning complexity should be a permanent effort. Every tier that can be avoided is a valuable contribution to the system's maintainability and performance (see Figure 10-16).

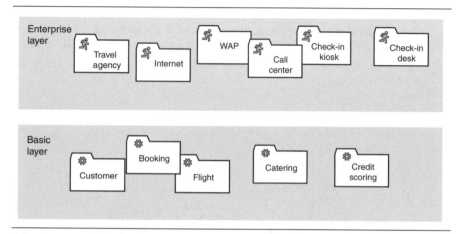

FIGURE 10-16   The fundamental SOA represents a lean service approach that basically implies the usage of application frontends and basic services. No services in the aggregation layer or process layer are involved.

Although a lean approach is desirable, you might find reasons to apply a more complex approach in practice. Requirements such as co-browsing or channel switching, highly complex processes, heterogeneous backend systems, load balancing, and other reasons can force the usage of façades or process-centric services.

10.6.2 SERVICE FAÇADE

A service façade represents a unified interface to the basic service layer for a specific project and encapsulates the functionality of the underlying services. In the airline example, this is particularly useful in order to handle the heterogeneity of the underlying basic services. The façade encapsulates the different technologies and concepts and provides a convenient view of the functionality (see Figure 10-17).

Ironically, façades provide only limited benefits for multi-channel applications. It is true that multi-channel applications suffer worst from the heterogeneity of the application landscape. A unifying layer that encapsulates the heterogeneity of the backend systems should be very helpful at first glance. Unfortunately, the frontend of a multi-channel application is also heterogeneous. Thus, a unified façade for access to the backend can only support a subset of channels directly, or it must provide specific operations for some channels. More often, some channels

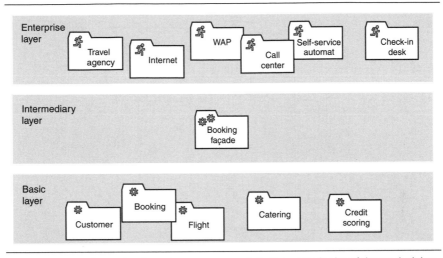

FIGURE 10-17   A service façade can encapsulate the complexity of the underlying service infrastructure. In particular, heterogeneous application landscapes can benefit from service façades.

will require a technically different access to the backend, which will require additional technology gateways or extra efforts in the process layer.

There is a benefit however, because this façade approach decouples the individual project-specific code from general domain code. If nothing else, this creates better maintainability due to decoupled release cycles in the basic layer and the enterprise layer. It can also provide an easier way to manage delivery responsibilities within a project.

Service façades are highly project-specific. Although the idea of one unifying layer might be tempting, it is not realistic. In practice, it's usually better for every project to use its own service façade if it requires one (see Chapter 6).

10.6.3   PROCESS-ENABLED SOA

Choosing whether to introduce a process layer is an important design decision. You should consider a process-centric service if several channels have similar processes and the according process logic can be shared. A process-centric service is also useful if features such as channel switching or co-browsing are required. Last but not least, you can consider process-centric services to handle load-balancing issues (see Chapter 6).

However, keep in mind that the implementation of process-centric services introduces an additional element to the architecture that could increase latency, could make the overall design more complex, and might need additional maintenance. Therefore, you should know the exact benefits before deciding to implement a process-centric service. In our airline example, we introduce the booking process service in order to provide channel switching (see Figure 10-18).

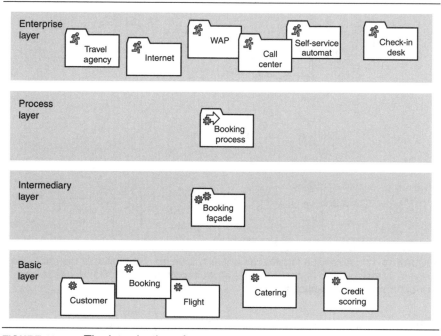

FIGURE 10-18   The introduction of a process-centric service is a major design decision that requires careful consideration.

Although a process-centric service can cover the generic behavior of the business process booking, the application frontends that represent the different channels must add channel-specific behavior. In general, every channel has certain specifics that differentiate it from other channels. This pattern is typical for multi-channel applications. In fact, it is their nature to provide "similar" processes using different channels. At this point, the process layer is rather thin, only exposing the processing steps that are common to all—or most—clients that retain their channel-specific logic.

As soon as you have introduced a process layer, the next potential step is the implementation of channel-specific process logic in distinct services that can also serve as technology gateways (see Figure 10-19).

Another decision applies to the booking façade. If you already have a generic process-centric service, then the functionality of the booking façade can be included in the process-centric service. Every tier inevitably increases the system's latency. As a distinct entity, it also requires additional attention in the maintenance phase.

Consider a user who attempts to book a specific flight using the airline's Web site. The user can access the flight search functionality, select the flight, and even book a specific seat. However, the actual booking operation fails due to a temporary failure or due to an error in the billing engine. A normal airline simply

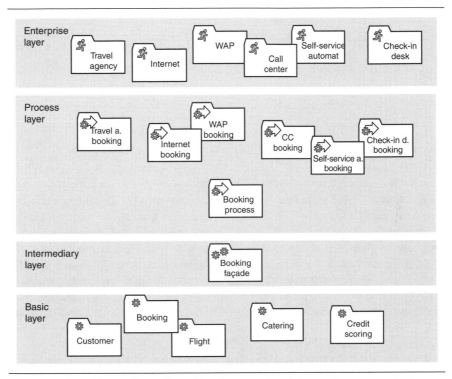

FIGURE 10-19   Every channel requires its own channel-specific process logic.

presents the customer with a message indicating that there is a problem and that it is okay to try later—at which time the booking might or might not work. The actual details of the error might well be far beyond anything the user can easily understand. As a practical example, all credit cards of the brand "Eurocard" ceased to work in 2004 with a major airline's Web site, even though the actual card did not change. The problem was that all the users needed to change the identification of this type of card to "Mastercard."

To cope with such issues, the service-enabled airline goes a step further. A ticket is automatically created for a service center agent indicating the type of failure. The service center agent can complete the booking, using the very same service that the original Web site uses. If needed, the agent can contact the ticket purchaser to request additional information. The Web site, however, might still be unable to access the service due to a network problem or an availability constraint. After the booking is completed, the user is sent an SMS or email indicating that the flight has been successfully booked and payed for. The message includes a link to an appropriate Web or WAP page. This page again uses the same service to access the required information.

Co-browsing is another feature that requires similar implementation techniques. It is a very powerful feature if you want to provide highly interactive portals. You can enable a customer to contact a service center agent at any time within a session by clicking on a button in an Internet form. This click opens a voice and video channel to the agent. The agent gets access to the same application and can support the customer to finish the session. The customer and agent can work with exactly the same user screens to make their dealings as interactive as possible.

10.7 Conclusion

We have discussed several scenarios where an SOA can be beneficial. The requirements for the granularity that a service must provide depend on the usage scenario. The same goes for the security constraints that can be imposed upon a service. Scenarios such as a mobile one might require coarse-grained and rather insecure services, whereas scenarios such as Web-based and fat client ones will usually benefit from a somewhat smaller—yet still coarse—granularity and a tighter security infrastructure. Much the same goes for the technology. Although SOAs internal to the enterprise can be based on well-understood and mature technologies, such as transaction monitors or EJBs, others such as B2B need a technology such as SOAP to offer maximum reusability and the possibility for true location transparency. Furthermore, mobile devices need the simplest protocol available to cope with the resource constraints at hand. Although it is tempting to strive for the lowest common denominator in service design, this will most likely lead to failure. It might be better to provide a service with a number of different interfaces and protocols and carefully design the required service in conjunction with the customer.

References

Erl, Thomas. *Service-Oriented Architectures*. Prentice Hall, 2004. [Erl04]

Fowler, Martin. *Patterns of Enterprise Application Architecture*. Addison-Wesley, 2002. [Fow02]

Harrison, Richard. *Symbian OS C++ for Mobile Phones*. John Wiley & Sons, 2004. [Ha04]

Riggs, Roger, Antero Taivalsaari, Jim van Peursem, Jyri Huopaniemi, Mark Patel, and Aleksi Uotila. *Programming Wireless Devices with the Java2 Platform*. Addison-Wesley Professional, 2001. [Ri01]

Shaw, Mary and David Garland. *Software Architecture: Perspectives on an Emerging Discipline*. Prentice Hall, 1996. [SGG96]

Bass, Len, Paul Clements, and Rick Kazman. *Software Architecture in Practice*. Addison-Wesley Professional, 2003. [BCK03]

McGovern, James, Sameer Tyagi, Sunil Mathew, and Michael Stevens. *Java Web Service Architecture*. Morgan Kaufman, 2003. [Mc03]

URLs

http://www.rosettanet.org

http://www.unece.org/cefact/

PART II

ORGANIZATIONAL ROADMAP

Part II of this book outlines the organizational roadmap to the service-enabled enterprise. We discuss the benefits of an SOA at the organizational level and look at the perspective of the individual stakeholders in SOA. Furthermore, we provide advice on how to introduce an SOA in the organization, and we provide best practices for SOA-driven project management.

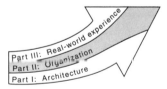

11

Motivation and Benefits

Previous chapters discussed what SOAs are and provided technical details of their implementation. We now focus on the challenge of actually introducing an SOA into the enterprise. This chapter addresses the general motivation and the main benefits to be expected. Subsequent chapters discuss strategies for successfully introducing an SOA into an enterprise and for project management.

This chapter consists of two major parts. Section 11.1 begins with a discussion on enterprise-level goals in order to round off this topic that we saw first in Chapter 1, "An Enterprise IT Renovation Roadmap." The pressure on organizations to become more agile and efficient is a major driving force in the introduction of an SOA, as is the inflexibility of existing IT infrastructures composed of monolithic applications. Section 11.2 describes the viewpoints of the individual stakeholders and considers the interests of the actual people and roles involved in the endeavor of introducing an SOA.

11.1   The Enterprise Perspective

As described in Chapter 1, the main motivation for creating an SOA is the desire to increase agility of the enterprise IT systems. In addition, SOAs offer benefits at several levels, ranging from a reduction of technology dependency to a simplification of the development process to an increase in flexibility and reusability of the business infrastructure.

The ultimate goal of the additional reusability and flexibility provided by an SOA is the Agile Enterprise, in which all processes and services are completely flexible and can be rapidly created, configured, and rearranged as required by business experts without the need for technical staff (see Figure 11-1). Among other things, this facilitates a superior time-to-market for new business initiatives. This vision of an Agile Enterprise reconciles the growing demands of a global and rapidly changing business environment with the limitations of current technological and organizational infrastructures. Consequently, the Agile Enterprise is not so much characterized by a fixed state of the enterprise but rather by an ongoing change process within the enterprise.

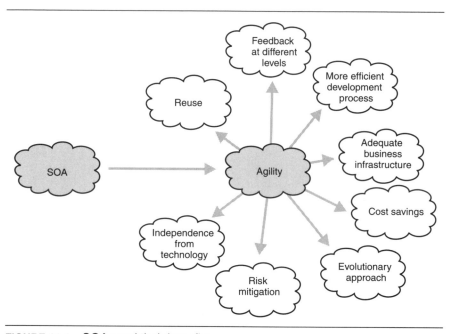

FIGURE 11-1   SOAs and their benefits.

Several sources contribute to the pressure on enterprises to instigate ongoing changes. Enterprises are continually forced to reinvent themselves by offering their customers new or better services to stay ahead of or keep pace with competitors. In order to remain as cost effective as possible, partners and suppliers must be regularly evaluated and, if need or opportunity arises, substituted by alternatives offering better quality, prices, or conditions. In addition, mergers and takeovers often require the integration of new systems, applications, and processes into the enterprise's IT and business infrastructure.

However, as unrelenting as this pressure toward constant change is, it is often obstructed by technological and organizational obstacles. For example, replacing a partner or supplier might be straightforward in theory, but it could require major efforts in reality. These efforts could involve a complete redevelopment of technical interfaces and a major redesign of business processes. Similarly, integrating a newly merged or acquired company's IT infrastructure and processes might call for a large-scale integration project. In addition, although offering new or better services might be desirable from the business perspective, it often proves to be technologically or organizationally infeasible. Typically, this can arise for two reasons:

Too time consuming. In some cases, developing the desired functionality might take too long to be of any use. For the introduction of a new product or service, there often is a window of opportunity (time-to-market) that must not be missed.

Too resource intensive. In most cases, the main risk to feasibility is the cost incurred in achieving the desired functionality. For example, replacing a supplier is only profitable if the long- and short-term costs for doing so do not exceed the savings obtained by the replacement.

For an enterprise to become an Agile Enterprise, it is therefore necessary to construct a technological and organizational infrastructure guaranteeing as much flexibility as possible. SOAs provide the means for achieving this flexibility by leveraging an appropriate architecture. In the following subsections, we describe the benefits of introducing an SOA at the level of the enterprise in detail.

11.1.1   AGILITY

One of the primary motivating factors for using SOAs is the potential increase of agility they offer. In order to fully understand this benefit, we must identify the different levels at which enterprise projects are threatened by *complexity*. Inevitably, complexity diminishes the enterprise's agility. The following elements of complexity can be distinguished:

Technology. Technical products and solutions used in enterprise projects are usually complex. Sometimes, they result from yearlong efforts to capture more and more functionality and lean towards the baroque in size and manageability. Sometimes, they are early versions of some new trend and bring with them all the teething problems of immature technology such as the bad performance of XML parsers or incompatible SOAP implementations in the early days of Web services. Consequently, technology used in enterprise projects can have complex deployment and installation procedures that work against smooth introductions. In particular, finding staff qualified for handling the technology can be a major obstacle.

Business processes. Often less obvious but at least as critical as technological complexity is complexity related to business processes. This complexity might be harder to grasp because processes tend to be much less visible and concrete than specific software. Ultimately, however, a complex business process results in a complex implementation. Sometimes, it is only during the project or even during implementation that the real complexity of the processes to be implemented becomes apparent.

Business functionality. Even if the basic elements of the business functionality are not complex, they can become complex when considered in their entirety. Sometimes, business functionality also contains conflicting elements due to different perspectives or application contexts, which adds to the overall complexity. Let's consider, for example, insurance products and tariffs. Each individual tariff is not particularly complex. However, the various permutations of these tariffs can result in an extremely complex insurance product portfolio.

Integration. Another source of complexity arises from the integration of applications. More often than not, enterprise projects will use and combine functionality from existing applications. Even if the individual applications are stable and well maintained, using them in a new context and integrating them with other applications is generally a complex task.

Maintenance. After an application is launched and running, it might seem that complexity is no longer an issue. However, maintenance of a complex system is far from trivial. Usually, components must be updated regularly, such as when additional functionality has been integrated or when new versions of software have been released. Such updates can cause complex issues similar to those encountered during the initial integration of the application.

Without an appropriate architecture, the risk of complexity preventing agility is very serious because changes might be infeasible or so expensive that the costs exceed the benefits. SOAs can help to significantly reduce complexity at all levels. This is of particular importance for enterprises, given their need to become more agile in order to react as quickly as possible to changing business environments and offer new services to customers, suppliers, and partners that make a difference with respect to competition. SOAs achieve their simplicity by the following means:

Decomposition. SOAs decompose large, complex systems into application frontends and services.

Appropriate granularity. The granularity of services is well suited to gain a high-level understanding of the entire system. Unlike other approaches, SOAs do not confuse practitioners by presenting too much detail.

Decoupling from technology. SOAs can be well understood without in-depth knowledge of technology.

Reuse. SOAs result in the high-level reuse of existing components. This streamlines the code base and reduces complex redundancies.

Documentation. Due to the service contract, every service is well documented, which adds to the comprehensibility of the SOA.

11.1.2 COST SAVINGS

We have already seen that agility and efficiency are the primary benefits of an SOA. This is mainly due to the fact that a commercial organization's agility and efficiency should help increase profit and foster savings. In this section, we discuss possible sources for cost savings. In particular, in price-sensitive, low-margin, mature markets in which the possibility of product innovations is rather limited, cost efficiency plays a key role. In these markets, often the price of the product makes the difference and hence provides the competitive advantage.

In general, we distinguish between direct (saving IT costs) and indirect contributions (saving business costs).

11.1.2.1 Cost Savings at the Business Level.

SOAs can help to reduce costs in the enterprise's core business. These cost savings are largely related to the SOA's agility. There is a number of obvious examples:

> **Choosing the Cheapest Supplier.** In low-margin markets, suppliers do not differ much. Nevertheless, even the slightest difference might make for competitive advantage in the long run. A major obstacle that can jeopardize the positive effect of constantly choosing the cheapest supplier is the inability of IT to support these changes within reasonable time and costs. An SOA solves a couple of issues that are related to a supplier change. Most importantly, an SOA provides an easy-to-use integration infrastructure that reduces the efforts for both business partners.
>
> **Streamlining Business Processes.** SOAs—particularly process-enabled SOAs (see Chapter 6, "The Architectural Roadmap")—are very well suited to support ever changing processes (see Chapter 7, "SOA and Business Process Management"). This enables the enterprise to make use of internal resources in the most efficient way. In traditional environments, however, costly adoptions of existing applications typically prohibit rapid change of business processes.
>
> **Improving Financial Reporting.** Finally, SOAs contribute to more precise and up-to-date financial reporting. Due to its ability to make different parts of the architecture share live data, an SOA can enable financial reporting on the spot, which could mean that the most important business data becomes available on a daily basis. As a result, management decisions that were previously based on quarterly reports could be made more promptly, and longer-term trends could be taken into account in day-to-day business.

It should be noted that the possibilities of cost savings enabled by SOAs are not limited to the examples stated here.

11.1.2.2 IT Cost Savings.

In principle, three major sources for IT cost savings can be distinguished:

> **Reduced project costs.** In general, using an SOA in an enterprise project will considerably reduce project costs because it allows for more efficient implementation and deployment. However, for these cost savings to become effective, the SOA must be already in place. In the introduction phase, overhead usually outweighs reductions. In this phase, you must establish the fundamental development processes and put the technical infrastructure—that is, the service bus and the service repository—in place. However, you will achieve lower costs at several levels, particularly with respect to resources needed for updating or modifying code, integrating modules, and testing. One of the major benefits of an SOA consists of

its significant simplification of both design and configuration of business processes. As a consequence, new business processes can be developed more simply, and the expenditure for modifying or optimizing existing processes remains justifiable.

Reduced maintenance costs. You can significantly reduce the long-term cost of IT systems by introducing an SOA. Due to the simplification of the application landscape, the streamlining of the code base, and technology independence, future changes can be made more easily. Maintenance efforts can be targeted to business functionality. Side effects can be reduced, and comprehensibility can be increased due to a clear decomposition of the application landscape in reasonable components (i.e., application frontends, services) and an up-to-date documentation of the purpose and interface of these components (service contract). A good example is the encapsulation of complexity covered in Chapter 8 with a discussion on process integrity. Applying the recommendations of Chapter 8, you can make an application fit for efficient and targeted maintenance by separating critical code sections from less critical ones. The critical code sections (encapsulated in distinct services) can then be handled with special care.

Future proof solutions. Finally, correctly employing an SOA guarantees future proof solutions. This is mainly due to three reasons. First, an SOA abstracts from the underlying technology and is hence not tied to any idiosyncrasies or shortcomings. Thus, it can be used in conjunction with other technologies, which is particularly useful in cases where the underlying technology becomes obsolete. Second, an SOA guarantees protection of investment because it enables you to integrate functionality from extant systems in an enterprise instead of replacing them. The SOA endeavor creates a functional infrastructure that can be reused in future scenarios independently of its original purpose.

Most of these benefits are more or less directly related to the high degree of reusability provided by SOAs, which we will now discuss in more detail.

11.1.3   REUSE AND THE RESULTING BENEFITS

Reuse has long been a holy grail of the IT industry. The initial idea focused on reusing code through class libraries or code templates. However, within an enterprise, code reuse often has less far-reaching impact than the reuse of runtime components. Being able to reuse a component at runtime by linking it into a number of different sub-systems means not only that we are sharing a common code base, but more importantly that the different sub-systems are now sharing the same application data. This significantly reduces redundancies and inconsistencies in business data, which is a huge benefit.

It is important to point out that it is a key benefit of an SOA that it contributes to runtime reuse.

The use of a service is not confined to the project for which it is initially developed—it can also be reused in other applications. This allows for a holistic IT strategy in which projects are not separated activities but instead contribute to each other and can be combined to achieve an overall synergy.

Moreover, usage is not tied to the technical infrastructure on which the service has been deployed. The service interface provides an abstract layer that can be used in the context of arbitrary technical infrastructures. Therefore, the service itself can be used in different technological contexts that guarantee protection of investment.

Another major benefit of reusability concerns design, modification, and optimization of the implemented business processes. When using an SOA, a business process can be composed directly from services or individual service operations. On one hand, it is possible to create a new service—that is, an intermediary or process-centric service (see Chapter 5, "Services as Building Blocks")—simply by arranging or "choreographing" existing building blocks. On the other hand, modifying or optimizing an existing service is also straightforward because it only requires a rearrangement of the operations used in the service.

Finally, reuse of existing code significantly reduces the risk of failure in enterprise projects. Using proven components, that is, code that has already been in operational use, eliminates time-consuming debugging and functional testing. It also enables the project to proceed iteratively in small steps. Enterprise projects can start with a comparatively small scope implementing the basic functionality. Based on this initial implementation, new functionality can be added step by step, reusing the functionality that has already been proven.

11.1.4 INDEPENDENCE FROM TECHNOLOGY

As previously stated, SOAs—in particular the service contracts that describe services—provide an abstraction from the underlying technology.

This independence offers several benefits for an enterprise. Most importantly, business considerations can assume their natural role as the driving force for decisions.

Focus on technology can be a major problem in IT projects. This is not to say that technology is irrelevant, but often, discussions about "the right technology" threaten to tie up resources that could be better spent designing and optimizing business functionality. SOAs help to shift the attention from technological issues to questions of service functionality and service design. In other words, the question of which services to offer is separated from the question of how to implement the services.

Independence from technology also increases independence from software vendors. The opposite of a service-oriented approach can be caricatured as a project in which the functionality and features of a particular software product or technology determine the scope of the project. Applying an SOA enables choosing the best of breed products and combining them as required by the particular application, not as stipulated by software vendors.

However, contemporary application landscapes are characterized by a variety of different incompatible technologies (e.g., J2EE versus .NET). This heterogeneity makes it particulary hard to create and maintain cross-departmental business processes. Due to the tight coupling of business functionality to specific technology, it can be arbitrarily difficult to force different parts of the architecture to work together. SOAs mitigate these obstacles by decoupling the technologies of the provider and consumer of specific business functionality. SOAs do not eliminate the heterogeneity itself but rather its impact on agility and efficiency. It is the very nature of big application landscapes to tend toward heterogeneity. Fighting this heterogeneity is infeasible, and SOAs therefore embrace heterogeneity as a given fact and cope with it in the best way possible.

Independence from underlying technology permits a decoupling of technology lifecycles from the lifecycles of business services. Thus, the introduction of a new technology within an enterprise does not require a makeover of the business processes and services. Similarly, new business services can be introduced without the need to wait for new, innovative technology to become mature, stable, and affordable.

Although an SOA provides a lot of technological independence, you will never completely eliminate technology dependencies. In fact, every SOA requires a certain amount of technical infrastructure (see Chapter 9, "Infrastructure of a Service Bus"). Distributed logging and data transport are two prominent examples. However, if the SOA is properly deployed, this technical infrastructure is largely encapsulated.

11.1.5 ADEQUATE BUSINESS INFRASTRUCTURE

The traditional IT infrastructure of enterprises is characterized by a strong focus on technology and monolithic applications with fixed functionality. Technology, processes, business rules, and core business logic as well as data are tightly coupled. These applications are usually inflexible and can only serve as an appropriate business infrastructure in their original context. Thus, as the business context of the enterprise evolves over time, these applications often do not keep up with the enterprise's business strategy, which might have evolved in an entirely different direction.

SOAs, if applied correctly, can correct the mismatch between the demands of the ever-changing business environment and the constraints imposed by a rigid IT infrastructure. The business infrastructure of enterprises that implement an SOA will differ from traditional infrastructures. Instead of carefully planning and executing large-scale projects spanning several years, a step-by-step approach becomes feasible.

The scope of enterprise projects will thus become twofold: on one hand, projects will create new services and functionality for immediate use, while on the other hand, the services developed will later serve as building blocks for future projects. More importantly, SOAs decouple technology, processes, business rules, and data. This implies that if one of these becomes obsolete, the others can still remain in use.

Consequently, an SOA-enabled enterprise will create a sustainable business infrastructure over time that consists of flexible building blocks that can be continually reused.

11.1.6 MORE EFFICIENT DEVELOPMENT PROCESS

Using an SOA in an enterprise project also impacts the development process considerably. Chapter 13 will describe in detail how project management should be conceived when applying an SOA. At this point, we concentrate on how an SOA can help to reduce the complexity of the development process in general.

One obvious advantage of the contract-driven SOA approach is a natural relationship between business-oriented project artifacts such as use case descriptions and technical deliveries such as interfaces or even services. From the perspective of the development process, the main benefit of using an SOA is that it allows for a high degree of modularity, which in turn makes it possible to decouple the development process. Let us more closely examine what this means.

First, it means that the services to be developed in an enterprise project can be implemented independently of each other. By its very definition, a service is self-contained and can be used autonomously. In other words, it is not implicitly tied to the environment in which it has been implemented. If the service needs other services to perform correctly, all these dependencies are explicitly modeled and implemented as service calls with well-defined interfaces.

As a consequence, development teams in an SOA-based enterprise project can be decoupled, such that each team is responsible for implementing a specific list of services. Interaction between the teams is then reduced to a minimum, focusing mostly on the agreement of service interfaces. However, the definition of interfaces is one of the main design tasks in any development. An SOA provides a guideline for the interface definition and simplifies the process of achieving them. Project management can focus on managing small development teams and can employ efficient techniques not applicable for large teams with highly interconnected tasks. The overhead of project management is thereby significantly reduced.

A critical phase in most development projects is the integration of code developed by different teams. Problems that had not been apparent when developing the individual modules often surface in the integration phase. One major reason for the integration phase becoming a bottleneck is the inability to separately test and debug code. Once again, the SOA helps to reduce complexity in this respect because it enables the independent testing of individual service operations to a certain degree.

11.1.7 EVOLUTIONARY APPROACH

SOAs can be distinguished from other architectures because they explicitly address many of the enterprises' non-technical constraints. One of the most important constraints is based on the fact that large organizations tend to evolve in small steps. The organization's IT infrastructure should enable a similar evolution. There are several reasons for this:

> **Risk of failure.** The most important reason is that IT systems are at the heart of modern enterprises. They are in many respects mission-critical. On one hand, they enable the enterprise to fulfil its obligations, while on the other, they are essential to conduct its business. A major failure could lead to serious financial and operational consequences for the corporation. This implies that any change to the enterprise IT systems must be performed with great care.
>
> **Capacity of change.** The rollout of new business functionality is not only a technical problem but also a major challenge for the business organization. Every organization has a limited capacity for change due to the need for training and the day-to-day adoption of new business processes. In practice, a number of manual amendments to the electronic processes must be carried out, and the time required for these adjustments must be taken into consideration.
>
> **Involve stakeholders.** In practice, you must convince key players and decision makers to support an endeavor such as the rollout of new business functionality. It becomes increasingly difficult to achieve this support when a large number of departments (or even business units) is involved.
>
> **Feasibility.** The size of a new piece of functionality is a major criterion with regard to its feasibility. The bigger the piece, the more cross-dependencies there are to be considered. You also have to involve more people in order to cover the range of functionality.

SOAs are particularly well suited to enable a step-by-step approach due to two major characteristics.

First, SOAs enable an efficient decomposition of large segments of functionality into largely decoupled components of manageable size—i.e., application frontends and services. A project organization can directly follow this decomposition. Big projects that appear to be too risky, too difficult to rollout in the business organization, or technically infeasible can be broken down into subprojects that can individually be brought to success. Even if a single subproject fails, there is no overall threat to the enterprise. Second, unlike other architectures, SOAs are not tied to any specific technology. This enables an enterprise to be very flexible while introducing new functionality. More importantly, SOAs can make changes or amendments to technology and business functionality by treating them in an independent manner.

However, the real world is even more complex. Endeavors such as the introduction of a new architecture paradigm do not follow a long-term project plan.

Instead, it is a fact that the requirements of day-to-day business have a higher priority. This implies that the introduction of an architecture will be more like an ongoing effort that accompanies the major business projects. As discussed in Chapter 6, SOAs reflect this requirement by their very nature. They enable an increase in both the scope of the SOA's technical foundation and its "content"—the business functionality—in small steps.

11.1.8   SOA ENABLES FEEDBACK AT DIFFERENT LEVELS

It is undisputed that the enterprise architecture impacts all levels of the enterprise's organization with a variety of different stakeholders involved. It is therefore essential that the enterprise architecture address the key needs of these stakeholders (we will discuss the appropriate benefits from the perspective of the individual stakeholders in Section 11.2.).

However, it is not only the architecture that impacts their stakeholders—it also works in reverse, or at least it should. All stakeholders should be able to influence the architecture in order to make the full range of knowledge of the entire enterprise available to create an architecture in the best way possible. Many previous approaches have been comprehensible only to IT experts and therefore do not reflect this essential requirement. Consequently, only a few people have been able to contribute to the architecture, with the effect that valuable knowledge has not been used to make decisions crucial for the entire enterprise.

SOAs provide useful abstractions at different levels. They are not only comprehensible to IT experts but also to representatives of the functional departments. This characteristic of an SOA opens up vast knowledge from many people to contribute to its success and, incidentally, enables the management of the IT and business departments to gain appropriate influence on the main architectural decisions. It can also facilitate buy-in from the department members consulted.

11.1.9   MITIGATING RISK

The risk-mitigating effect of an SOA is a key benefit. Depending on the concrete business of an enterprise, this could even be the most important benefit of an SOA. According to the Standish Group [Sta2001], the key reasons for problems in IT projects are:

- Weak specifications of project objectives
- Bad planning and estimating
- Inadequate project management methodologies
- New technology and insufficient senior staff on the teams

At a minimum, some key characteristics of an enterprise SOA can help to partially address these issues in a number of ways.

Service documentation helps to clarify project objectives. The documentation of business-oriented, coarse-grained services is an invaluable tool for project managers to help close the gap between business requirements and technical specifications. Service specifications not only represent a contract at the technical level, but also between business and technology. This is a crucial part of the ongoing alignment of business and IT objectives. It is critical to ensure that the high-level documentation of services is suitable for the entire project team. Only then it ensures that the technology meets the business objectives.

Service orientation leverages involvement of business departments. The concept of the service contract enables the involvement of the business department. It enables domain specialists to drive the development process, and by doing so, you can significantly reduce the risk that the project outcome does not match business department expectations.

Service orientation helps planning and resource estimation. The abstraction level at which business services are designed (or at least should be) is exactly the right level of granularity at which they can be used as a powerful tool for planning and estimating project resource requirements and duration. Service-orientation helps to decompose large and complex systems into manageable sub-systems, which can be more effectively planned and estimated.

Service orientation can be leveraged at the project management level. Service orientation is not a replacement for sound project management strategies, but when incorporated into established project management methodologies, it can provide a powerful complementary tool. The loosely coupled nature of SOAs supports divide-and-conquer strategies. The decomposition of complex systems into manageable services is an essential tool for effective project management strategies. Service orientation enables you to roll out functionality in small steps, which dramatically reduces project risks because potential problems can be identified early in the development process. This is described in detail in the discussion of the *thin-thread approach* in Chapter 13.

SOAs facilitate the integration of existing and new functionality—independent of the underlying technology. This enables projects to reuse proven core functionality of mission critical sub-systems, such as billing or invoicing. Relying on proven functionality significantly contributes to risk reduction.

A well-managed SOA can reduce the need for senior technical staff. As SOAs support simple yet flexible service components, which encapsulate the underlying technology of the service implementations, SOAs can help to reduce the need for senior technical staff. The decoupling of service components enables developers to stay in their respective technical domains, such as Java or COBOL development. In order to achieve this, services must be well designed and properly documented. In addition, the process for designing, documenting, implementing and rolling out services must be standard-ized and documented, too. SOAs do require senior technical staff for implementing this properly. Chapter 12 describes the role of an SOA *architecture board*, which should be responsible for these types of processes.

Finally, we must add that even failed projects can contribute to the business infrastructure of the SOA by amending business services or service operations that can be reused in future projects. As a consequence, the enterprise can benefit from at least a fraction of failed project efforts in the long term.

11.2 The Personal Perspective

It should not be surprising that it is insufficient for an enterprise architecture such as an SOA "just" to be beneficial to the enterprise in order to become a success. In practice, you must also convince the individual stakeholders to support the SOA. More importantly, you must enlist the key decision makers and domain experts.

An SOA certainly can provide tremendous advantages for the individual people involved in the enterprise architecture. This section provides the most important arguments for an SOA from the perspective of the different roles in an enterprise. This information will help you "sell," the SOA to each individual in an organization, adopting each individual's role and accommodating personal requirements. In particular, we consider the following roles:

- CEO
- CIO (department for IT strategy)
- Architect
- Project Manager
- Functional department
- Developer
- Vendor of standard software (sales or product management)

Table 11-1   CEO

Benefits	Challenges
Agile Strategy SOA helps businesses better react to environments. IT does not limit business strategy, but instead enhances it.	**Make It Happen** Introducing an SOA means change. It inevitably requires coping with some resistance. A clear strategy and firm commitment are needed to overcome this resistance.
Short-Term Planning The planning horizon can be reduced drastically because SOA enables step-by-step approaches.	**Initial Overhead** In its initial phase, the introduction of an SOA creates overhead, for which it is important to allocate a sufficient budget.
Budget Reduction The budget allocated to the IT department for pure maintenance tasks can be reduced and is, thus, freed for business-oriented development projects.	**ROI Consideration** The benefit of the SOA must be quantified.
Technology and Vendor Independence The dependency of business functionality on the technological infrastructure is reduced as is dependence on software vendors.	**Reporting** Reporting to the board is a possible requirement.

Table 11-2   CIO

Benefits	Challenges
Independence from Technology The dependency on the underlying technology is reduced and planning can be focused on business requirements.	**Migration to SOA** The existing IT infrastructure has to be migrated towards an SOA.
Positive Role of IT Department With an SOA the IT department can take the role of an enabler and move closer to the business units.	**Decoupling** Existing functionality has to be decoupled and made available as services. This is far from trivial.
Cost-Reduction The CIO often has a cost-reduction target agreement.	**Change of Attitude** Usually, a change of attitude is required within the IT department when changing to a service-oriented approach. Members of the IT department must be convinced that an SOA is beneficial for the enterprise as a whole and for them as individuals.
Manageable Project Size An SOA enables small projects and step-by-step development.	
Manage Heterogeneity SOA helps to cope with the heterogeneity of existing infrastructure and application systems.	**Change of Relationships** Usually, relationships to suppliers of standard software and infrastructure solution must be reconsidered.
Long-term Renovation Roadmap SOA provides an evolutionary and sustainable approach to modernize existing IT systems without re-implementing them.	

Table 11-3   Architect

Benefits	Challenges
More Attractive Job An SOA allows the architect to focus on more interesting tasks.	**SOA Adherence** Architects have to establish structures and processes ensuring SOA adherence.
Disentanglement An SOA frees the architect from the entanglement typical in monolithic IT infrastructures. This limits the scope of architectural decisions and changes them to become more manageable.	**Reuse** Architects have to make sure that services are designed with reuse in mind to fully leverage the potential of a SOA. **Open-Minded** The architect must be open-minded to amend and change the SOA itself if needed.
Loose Coupling Architecture specification is simplified as the degree of coupling is reduced significantly.	**Missing Technical Standards** The technical standardization of SOA-related technologies is not yet complete.
Code Reuse Implemented functionality can be reused and need not be coded over and over again.	

Table 11-4   Project Manager

Benefits	Challenges
Smaller and Shorter Projects Projects become smaller and shorter and are, therefore, easier to manage.	**Service-Orientation** Adherence of developers to the service-oriented approach must be ensured.
Technology Independence Projects are less dependent on the underlying IT infrastructure—i.e., planning can focus on the functional aspects of the project.	**Potential Overhead** Reusability must be taken into account in the design process. Sufficient budget should be allocated to cover the potential overhead this creates.
Parallel Development Fixed service interfaces help to decouple development and allow for parallel development.	**Program management** The manager of a SOA project has to cope with cross-project dependencies due to the intended reuse of services
Reduced Project Risk Due to project size and limited technology dependency, project risk is reduced significantly.	
Easier Testing and Integration The resources necessary for testing and integration are reduced because of decoupling.	

Table 11-5   Functional Department

Benefits	Challenges
Independence from Technology Dependency on the underlying IT infrastructure is reduced so that business departments can focus on functional requirements.	**Service Orientation** Business functionality has to be made available as services. Service contracts must be fixed and adhered to.
Shorter Time to Market Business departments can achieve a shorter time to market for new functionality.	**Reuse** Implemented services must be designed with reuse in mind. This creates some overhead and the requirement to co-ordinate requirements across different departments.
Reduction of Development Costs The costs for developing new functionality are significantly reduced.	**Sharing of Responsibilities** Potential service users must be involved in the design process and will have influence on the service design.

Table 11-6   Software Developer

Benefits	Challenges
More Attractive Jobs An SOA allows the developer to focus on more interesting tasks.	**Respect Service Interfaces** Developers have to adopt a service-oriented approach. Service interfaces must be respected. This in turn requires a clear specification before coding.
Reduction of Dependency An SOA reduces dependencies. Within a single service, developers can change implementations without affecting external functionality.	**Processes** Developers have to accept rigid processes.
Rapid Prototyping Once a substantial number of services are available, developers can easily test approaches.	**Shared Responsibility** In particular for well-established developers it might be a major change in responsibility for an application because it must be shared between different development teams.
Better Defined Requirements The interface driven SOA-based development process provides the developers with better-defined requirements.	**Learning New Skills** Developers have to learn new skills regarding the specifics of SOAs. This includes, for example, the handling of distributed transactions or the assignment of the ownership of data.
Simplified Testing Decoupling and service interfaces simplify distributed testing.	

Table 11-7   Vendor of Standard Software

Benefits	Challenges
Sell Components SOA opens up a new market segment for standard software packages. Domain specific services can become a great market.	**Customer More Independent** A core characteristic of SOA is that it disentangles dependencies and makes enterprises independent of specific components or technologies.
Reduced Integration Costs Unlike contemporary software packages SOA components do not require high integration costs on the customer side. Due to the lower project costs and risks, it becomes much easier to sell such components.	**Limited Secondary Business** SOAs are not well suited to generate much secondary business around standard components. Integration and migration efforts are particularly low.
Low Entry Barrier Regarding the limited scope of a single service it becomes much easier to create sellable standard software components.	**Missing Technical Standards** The technical standardization of SOA technologies is not yet complete.
Provide Future Proof Solution Customers are increasingly demanding SOA-compliant products.	

11.3   Conclusion

In this chapter, we explained the motivation for an SOA introduction and the main benefits related to such an introduction. Many enterprises adopt an SOA in order to increase agility. SOAs are seen as a means of breaking up inflexible IT infrastructures, which are usually characterized by monolithic applications. The flexibility of an SOA, its modular and decoupled development process, and in particular its potential for application reuse enable enterprises to reduce their project risks and to achieve a faster time-to-market.

Obviously, SOAs are not a magic bullet, solving all problems of enterprise projects with a single strike. Only if the environment is right can an SOA yield the maximum effect. However, SOA does, if applied correctly, minimize the risks of enterprise IT by providing a sound architectural basis.

Introducing an SOA will in general be a long-lasting process, and its beneficial effects will become apparent not all at once but steadily during this process. Only at the end of the process will the Agile Enterprise become a reality.

References

Standish Group. *Extreme Chaos*. http://www.standishgroup.com/sample_research/PDFpages/extreme_chaos.pdf, 2001. [Sta2001]

URLs

http://www.de.cgey.com/servlet/PB/show/1004690/ 07.16.02%20Studie%20Web-Services_G.pdf

http://www.standishgroup.com/

12

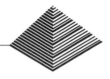

The Organizational SOA Roadmap

This chapter describes the organizational aspects of introducing an SOA on the enterprise level. We take a close look at the political aspects of SOAs, such as the obstacles that block their successful adoption in an enterprise, and strategies and tactics to overcome these obstacles. Because every enterprise is unique, there is no universal guide to cover all eventualities in the course of an SOA introduction. However, certain patterns have emerged that are sufficiently widespread for us to discuss on a generic level. This chapter discusses these patterns and illustrates them with real-world examples of successful and unsuccessful attempts to establish enterprise-wide standards.

It should be noted that much of this chapter's content is not SOA-specific but concerns the general challenge of introducing new methodologies, or processes, at the enterprise level. The presentation in this chapter will, therefore, oscillate between SOA-specific aspects and generic aspects.

We start by providing a generic overview of the main stakeholders involved in managing an organization's IT infrastructure in Section 12.1. Because these stakeholders are relevant for all aspects of an IT strategy, they are also the main actors involved in the introduction of an SOA. Consequently, Section 12.2 looks at the role that each of the different stakeholders plays in the implementation of the roadmap to the service-enabled enterprise. We discuss pillars for success in Section 12.3. Later, in Section 12.4, we describe an ideal world for the introduction of an SOA, while in Section 12.5, we provide some real-world examples of the introduction of SOAs—demonstrating both success and failure. In Section 12.6, we conclude with a series of recommendations for introducing an SOA into the enterprise.

12.1   Stakeholders and Potential Conflicts of Interest

Before introducing SOAs at the enterprise level, we need to examine who the different stakeholders in the SOA are within an enterprise and the potential conflicts of interest that you must overcome to ensure a successful introduction of new standards and architectures at the enterprise level.

Figure 12-1 provides an IT-centric view of key roles and relationships in an enterprise. The CEO and the board of directors are responsible for high-level strategic decisions, which often will have a direct impact on IT as well. Similarly, business units drive functional requirements, and we can often observe that they present the IT department with conflicting requirements because their interests are not necessarily aligned.

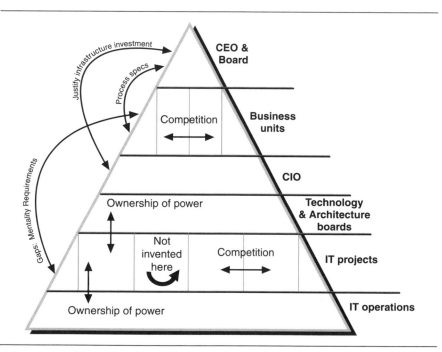

FIGURE 12-1   Enterprise hierarchy and potential conflicts.

The CIO is often caught between these conflicting interests because investments in infrastructure are often harder to justify to business people than concrete business applications that have a measurable return on investment. CIOs thus need good arguments to defend these investments—because IT is typically a cross-sectional function, it is limited by other business decisions.

There is a number of obstacles to investments in IT infrastructure such as SOA, including:

- The difficulty of providing predictable and verifiable returns of the investment that are plausible to the top management and other non-technical stakeholders
- Frequent changes in functional requirements and business strategy, which have a direct impact on the IT strategy
- Divisional interests and the mentality gap between IT and operative units
- The "not invented here syndrome" often found in IT organizations

The *return on investment* (ROI) is a major key performance indicator (KPI) for the board to approve major investments, including IT infrastructure expenses. This is typically a hard sell for three reasons:

- The return of infrastructure investments materializes in higher process efficiency and smaller future investments. However, many of today's controlling systems are not able to attribute efficiency gains to the infrastructure measures, and you can never be sure what your investments would have earned if you hadn't made the major investment.
- IT infrastructure projects have a history of unfulfilled promises, so decision makers are very critical to any kind of return calculation. For example, initiatives such as CASE, EAI, or workflow management that claimed various measurable benefits often failed to achieve them.
- Management often tends to favor short-term benefits over long-term investments.

After executives have made the most strategic decisions, it is up to the business units and the related IT projects and departments to implement systems that meet business requirements. The day-to-day interaction of business and IT people has traditionally been difficult. Business people might have a hard time understanding why technical issues are so complicated, while IT people often struggle with understanding not only certain business decisions but also the actual business itself. You can often observe a "conceptual gap" between the business and IT worlds. Typically, business requirements and the underlying technologies are extremely complex and dynamic, requiring a large number of specialists who have slightly different understandings of the environment and often differing agendas and perspectives. External consultants (strategic, business, and IT consultants) and product and service vendors with their own agendas add to this complexity. All of this increases the difficulty of matching functional requirements to a technology platform.

CIO and technology architecture boards often have different interests from individual projects, and different business units might have different IT organizations with conflicting interests as well. These conflicts can have various reasons. A good example is that of a large retail bank (name withheld), which bought a small investment bank in the late 1990s. Whenever the global CIO tried to define a company-wide standard, for an application server or a communication middleware for example, the CIO of the investment bank found a reason to use a different technology—mainly due to reasons of ego rather than good technical reasons. These disagreements took place at the executive level. The global CEO was prepared to allow the investment banking unit to take certain liberties and bought into the investment bank CIO's argument that the investment business had very different technical requirements from the retail bank. The results were incompatible systems, increased project costs, and increased software license costs.

Technology and architecture boards aim, for example, to introduce standards that allow for reuse of technology and applications. Project managers, on the other hand, often have a bigger interest in getting their projects out the door instead of investing the time to examine reusability. In these cases, it is often not a matter of reasonable decision-making but rather a question of who has the power to enforce a particular course of action.

Similarly, project managers and operations managers can have conflicting interests. How fast the project delivers certain business functionality often measures the success of a project. Consequently, speed is the major concern of a project manager. Looking into the Total Cost of Ownership (TCO) is the responsibility of an operations manager. The TCO is largely determined by characteristics such as systems management integration, exception handling, maintainability, and CPU resource consumption. Obviously, none of these characteristics that contribute to a reduced TCO have any positive impact on project costs or development time. On the contrary, all these characteristics require time and money from a project point of view.

Finally, a word on the "not-invented-here" syndrome. A significant portion of IT projects fail to deliver the required business functionality because they reinvent their own middleware (the famous "let's just quickly build an object-relational wrapper" comes to mind). There seems to be a tendency among IT people not to trust other people's technology, which hinders the successful introduction of technology standards. Furthermore, many IT people seem to feel more comfortable focusing on complex technical concepts rather than on complex business logic, thus distracting them from the more pressing issues at hand.

To conclude this discussion on stakeholders and conflicts of interest, it is necessary to examine projects that cross enterprise boundaries, as depicted in Figure 12-2. After all, this vision underlies many of the current trends in the development of enterprise software—an agile enterprise that is closely connected through technology and business with suppliers, partners, and customers in a completely flexible manner.

This basically means that processes, structures, and standards developed to establish an SOA within an enterprise ultimately also have to be applied to projects reaching across the enterprise boundary. If it is already challenging to align all departments of an enterprise in this respect, it is clear that problems are likely to proliferate if several enterprises are involved.

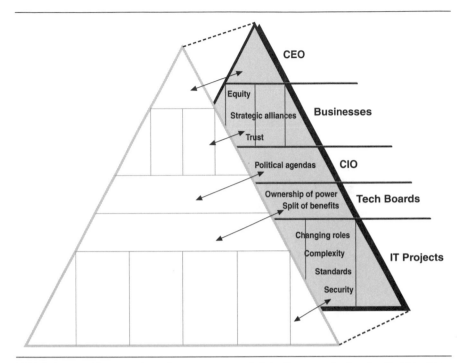

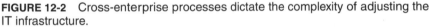

FIGURE 12-2   Cross-enterprise processes dictate the complexity of adjusting the IT infrastructure.

However, the basic picture does not change much, regardless of whether different departments or different enterprises are involved. One major distinction is the lack of a well-defined hierarchy across organizations. If there is substantial disagreement among different departments within an enterprise, the dispute can usually be resolved by a management decision at the lowest hierarchical level responsible for both departments. In these cases, commitment from top-level management is crucial to the success of an SOA.

If similar differences occur between departments of separate enterprises, though, there is usually no common management level with the authority to resolve the issue. Nevertheless, the establishment of clear processes and structures, such as boards spanning several enterprises, is a good strategy for the minimization of potential disagreements.

12.2   The Organizational SOA Roadmap

Having introduced the architectural roadmap in the first part of this book (for example, see the different SOA expansion stages we discussed in Chapter 6), we will now take a closer look at the organizational aspects of the SOA roadmap. Figure 12-3 provides a general overview of this organizational roadmap.

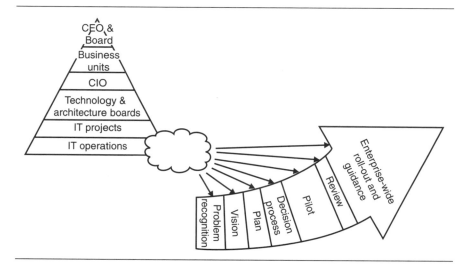

FIGURE 12-3   The organizational SOA roadmap.

The first step on the organizational roadmap is problem recognition. In Chapter 1, we provided a discussion of the reasons that lead to a phase of agony in the development of enterprise software, manifested by a decrease in development productivity and general inefficiency. If your organization is in this position, it is important to recognize this fact. You will have to determine the reasons that the IT organization is in this situation and discuss them with stakeholders before you can define a strategy for getting out of it.

Next, a number of key people have to get together and agree on the vision for the *enterprise IT renovation roadmap* and which role an SOA will play in it. Often, it can make sense to formulate a vision statement, which describes the ultimate goal, and how it should be achieved. People from both the business and technology side should be involved in formulating the vision. Although a visionary technology architect often drives such an undertaking, it is equally important that business people who can validate the concepts of the vision from the business point of view are included because they play a key role in the development processes and boards that are required to set up an SOA (see Sections 12.3 and 12.4).

Having agreed on the vision, the next step is to define a plan that outlines how the goals defined in the vision can be achieved. This will most likely not be a detailed project plan including concrete details about implementation resources, and concrete delivery dates, but more of a high-level roadmap document that highlights the key milestones to be achieved. As we will outline in the next section, the four pillars of a successful enterprise SOA strategy include budget, backers, a team, and a project to start with. These should be included in the plan.

The development of this plan will most likely go hand in hand with the decision making process, which will eventually lead to the go/no-go decision. Assuming a decision for the execution of the plan is made, the typical next step is to start with a suitable pilot project, as identified in the plan. The next section will provide more insights into the ideal characteristics of this pilot.

Finally, it is important to realize that in order to successfully establish an SOA on the enterprise level, you must constantly keep track of the project's status in order to fine-tune and steer the overall strategy. The introduction of an SOA is not a once-off project but instead requires constant efforts to ensure that future development projects will adhere to the architectural principles of the SOA. As we discussed in Chapter 1, enterprise architects constantly must fight the battle between tactical, short-term development and strategic refactoring and architectural compliance (see Section 1.3 for more details). Thus, the enterprise-wide rollout of the SOA should really be seen as an activity that runs in parallel to the day-to-day project business of the IT organization, including as much motivation work as technical guidance.

12.3 Four Pillars for Success

Although a wide variety of factors determines the success of an enterprise's SOA strategy, four main pillars for success can be highlighted: securing a budget, choosing a suitable project to start with, setting up a strong SOA team, and finding backers and buddies (see Figure 12-4).

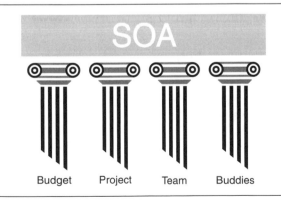

FIGURE 12-4   Four pillars of an SOA's success: budget, project, team, and buddies.

12.3.1 BUDGET

Obviously, *securing a budget* is a sine qua non for any successful introduction of new technology and standards within an enterprise. For one thing, this budget will be needed to *finance one or more initial projects* acting as pilot applications of the SOA. Because the success of these projects will have a considerable impact on the perceived success of the overall SOA introduction, they should be chosen with great care, as we will explain in detail later. It is also crucial that they are equipped with sufficient budget to meet the challenges inherent in the use of new technologies, methodologies, and processes.

In addition, a budget is needed to *compensate for initial overheads* caused by applying an SOA. Such overheads are caused by different factors. For one thing, employees have to familiarize themselves with new standards and processes. More important, however, is the initial overhead caused by efforts required to increase reusability. Instead of merely focusing on immediate requirements, potential future applications must be taken into account to ensure that the implemented service is reusable.

Even if a business department is supportive of an SOA in principle, it might have problems providing the resources needed to account for this overhead. In such a case, it is good to have a budget available to cover the necessary resources.

12.3.2 INITIAL PROJECT

The second pillar is the *choice of a suitable project* piloting the implementation of the enterprise SOA.[1] You must take into account several criteria to determine good candidates. First, the chosen project should be as *visible* as possible. This does not necessarily mean that it has to be particularly prestigious. On the contrary, choosing a less prestigious project might be advantageous because it diminishes the immediate pressure during the project's realization. However, the functionality provided by the implemented services should be widely used in the enterprise. On one hand, this ensures that the results achieved in the project will be highly visible. On the other hand, it will guarantee a significant reuse potential of the implemented services, which in turn will contribute to the validation of the benefits of the SOA and will help to sell it.

Ideally, the project should run no longer than two or three years, with a first delivery after six months. There should be a clear technological scope based on equally clear business requirements. In fact, it is crucial that the project have a business focus with measurable benefits instead of just being technology-driven. This not only concerns the project as a whole but also holds true for the individual services developed in the project. The more obvious the benefit of these services, the easier it will be to prove the SOA's ROI.

It is also a good idea to carefully evaluate the business department that will be responsible for the realization of the pilot project. Ideally, it should be enthusiastic

---

[1] Obviously, more than one project might be chosen to pilot the SOA. For ease of presentation, our discussion will focus on a single pilot project.

toward the SOA idea, but at the very least, it should be open and positively biased. Otherwise, you risk too much friction during the delivery of the pilot scheme, which might subsequently jeopardize the entire SOA endeavor.

12.3.3 SOA TEAM

The third pillar is *setting up a special SOA team*. Such a team should focus exclusively on how to best support and establish the SOA in the enterprise. Naturally, this includes first and foremost the design and specification of overall architecture principles, standards, and processes as well as the careful monitoring of the actual application of the SOA.

The SOA team will therefore have to contain evangelists whose task it is to explain the benefits of the SOA to the different departments of the enterprise. This includes education on the fundamental standards and processes making up the SOA, as well as support in the actual implementation of these principles. The SOA team will also play an important role in setting up organizational structures within the enterprise to monitor the "correct" application of the SOA.

12.3.4 BACKERS

Finally, the fourth pillar consists of *having backers and buddies*. This is important at all levels, beginning with active *support by top management*. It is crucial to acquire budget approval and sufficient enterprise-wide awareness to get the SOA off the ground. This support will also come in handy should there be substantial opposition to the SOA as a whole or to some of the various processes and standards necessary to establish it. It is therefore important for top management to explicitly include the SOA in the strategy planning, covering a three- to five-year perspective.

Equally important is the backing of the *key business departments*. After all, business-driven projects will implement and use service functionality. If the departments providing and consuming the business functionality are not supportive of the SOA, it will be next to impossible to successfully establish it. Although an SOA is not primarily a technical issue, it is infeasible to implement it without assistance from *key IT management and staff.*

You should always keep in mind that backers have their own interests and that they have to sell the SOA to others. In order to successfully introduce an SOA, it is therefore crucial to have arguments for various target groups, for example in the form of fact sheets or elevator pitches (see Chapter 11, "Motivation and Benefits"). On one hand, these pitches should be used to convince relevant actors in the enterprise to become supporters. On the other hand, they should be made available to supporters to facilitate their own selling of the SOA to others. The easier it is for backers to sell the SOA, the more likely it is that they will support it.

Thus, before approaching potential supporters, the following questions should be carefully answered:

- Who are the target groups and key actors?
- What are the three main arguments for and against an SOA (per target group/key actor)?
- Whose support will be likely?
- Who is to be convinced or overruled?

12.4 An Ideal World

In the previous section, we discussed four pillars for ensuring the successful introduction of an enterprise's SOA. In this section, we will describe in more detail those structures and processes that should be established to achieve success. In doing so, we will draw the rosy picture of an ideal world. Subsequent sections will deal with the intricacies you will encounter in real-world scenarios.

12.4.1 STRUCTURES AND PROCESSES

A number of building blocks are useful for the successful introduction of any new enterprise-wide technology or methodology, namely:

- Whitepapers
- SOA board
- Multi-project management
- Standard processes
- Support of all actors

The following paragraphs will describe these generic building blocks in more detail. We will then address issues that are specific to the introduction of an SOA.

Whitepapers are a good medium for describing basic principles and should be used to manage the "why" and "how" issues. Ideally, there should be several whitepapers, each dealing with a particular aspect of the SOA (see Figure 12-5). A *strategy whitepaper* should explain the overall goal of the enterprise's SOA and its perspective over the next three to five years. Aspects to be addressed include, for example, integration with the existing infrastructure, the main business drivers behind the architecture, and the potential for integration across enterprise boundaries, such as with suppliers, partners, and customers.

A *business whitepaper* should focus on the business benefits expected from the introduction of an SOA. Ideally, it should contain a business case including predictions concerning the ROI. It should at least demonstrate the benefits of an increased reuse of implemented business functionality and the potential for the efficient development of new services for customers, employees, and partners. It could also highlight those aspects of business functionality that are ideally suited to reusability.

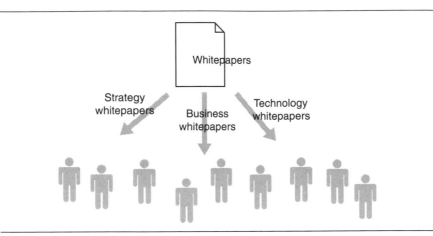

FIGURE 12-5   Whitepapers must address various target groups.

Finally, a *technology whitepaper* should address the technological issues involved in implementing the SOA. On one hand, it should explain in detail how integration of the SOA with the existing technological infrastructure is envisaged, in particular concerning issues such as asynchronous messaging or transactional behavior. On the other hand, it should describe details of the technological realization of the SOA itself. In many cases, a special platform will be used or developed to realize the technical infrastructure of the SOA—the service bus—and a technical whitepaper is a good place to specify the scope of such a platform and a roadmap for its implementation.

The repository is one of the key ingredients of an SOA, and it will be highly visible when services are available. The technical whitepaper should describe the repository structure in addition to processes for using and enhancing it.

Whitepapers are a good starting point for disseminating information about a new technology or methodology in an enterprise. However, as they are merely papers, their power is rather limited. What is definitely needed is an organizational entity responsible for making a technological vision work in everyday life. One way of achieving this is to establish a dedicated *SOA board,* which is responsible for the promotion of the SOA idea and the monitoring of its application in actual projects (see Figure 12-6).

Multi-project management is required to coordinate the development of the general SOA as a generic IT strategy, in its potential as a specific technology platform, and the individual projects implementing SOA-based business functionality.

Because reuse is one of the fundamental characteristics and benefits of an SOA, the scope of a pilot project will usually have impact on other pilot projects, too. When changing project plans, such as by postponing the implementation of a service, you must therefore examine how your choice affects other projects that might rely on the timely provisioning of the service in question.

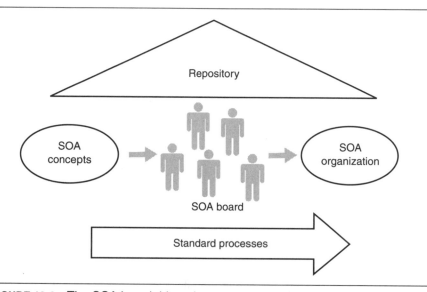

FIGURE 12-6   The SOA board drives the processes and establishes the overall standards of the SOA in the enterprise's organization.

Figure 12-7 shows an example of how individual projects and the development of the SOA's infrastructure can be dependent. In this example, we assume that there is a single ongoing effort to create the initial SOA infrastructure and develop the amendments that are required by the business projects that run in parallel. We assume that the project "Pilot 1" is rolled out in two steps. Each of these steps requires certain functionality of the SOA infrastructure. Step 1 might comprise the integration of synchronously coupled frontends, while step 2 might require asynchronous backend integration. The ongoing development of the necessary infrastructure must therefore deliver the appropriate functionality in a timely manner in order to enable the rollout schedule of this project. In addition, other concurrent business projects might also require amendments to the SOA infrastructure. In our example, there is a project "Pilot 2," which is also rolled out in several steps. The last step might require asynchronous back-end integration similar to the second rollout step of "Pilot 1." Consequently, the projects "Pilot 1" and "Pilot 2" and the infrastructure development of the SOA cannot be considered separately. Instead, multi-project management is required. Due to these dependencies, budgets must be steered not only individually but also in the context of a multi-project program.

The detailed specification of *standard processes* and procedures can help to significantly reduce the amount of work for the SOA board. Such processes should define how new application projects should proceed to make sure that the enterprise's SOA principles are adhered to. In particular, it is useful to define a process for the development and design of new services that also contains specific points at which the SOA board should be involved.

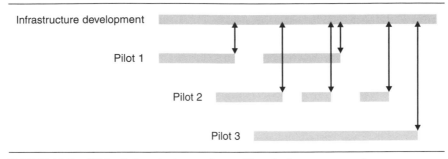

FIGURE 12-7   SOA pilot projects require multi-project management.

The process specification can be based on generic frameworks for the standardization of processes, such as 6 Sigma or ISO 9000. This is very reasonable if these frameworks are already in use within the enterprise. However, more lightweight approaches can also yield the desired effects. The important factor is to ensure that the day-to-day activities applied in designing and developing new applications or in executing projects in general comply with the principles of the enterprise's SOA.

Finally, it is vital to *include all relevant actors* in the establishment and implementation of the SOA. This includes management, the IT department(s), business departments, and administrators. Ideally, all actors should actively and enthusiastically support the SOA, but at least you should make sure that no actors oppose the SOA, either openly or covertly through sabotage or lack of activity.

Representing all relevant actors in the SOA board and the standard processes is a good starting point for ensuring their support, as is the constant communication with these actors and continuous monitoring of their contribution to the SOA. It is also important to appoint as board members only employees who are already well established in the enterprise. You should avoid the temptation to choose "new people for a new technology."

12.4.2 SOA SPECIFICS

In the previous subsection, we presented rather generic building blocks that are useful for introducing new methodologies and processes within an enterprise. This subsection addresses more specific aspects relevant for the successful establishment of an enterprise-wide SOA.

The most obvious starting point for standardization is the *service contract* used to describe and specify services. Service contracts should be made available through a *central repository*. In addition to the interface description, such as CORBA IDL (Interface Definition Language), WSDL (Web Services Description Language), or a tailor-made XML format, the service contracts should contain all information relevant for using the service in applications. This usually includes preconditions for service usage, special cases, potential errors, versioning information, and access rights.

It is important to make sure that the repository is broadly used and is the *sole* source of information regarding services. Whenever new applications are designed and developed, it should be sufficient to consult the service contracts in the repository to decide whether and how existing services can be used to build the desired functionality. If it is necessary to access additional information to make this decision, such as by interviewing service developers, this additional information should be included in the repository.

Everyone on the team must perceive the repository as a useful tool, including non-technical people. In addition to technical information, it should therefore contain detailed descriptions of the services from the business perspective. Business experts need such semantically rich descriptions to decide whether a service can be reused—that is, whether it does what a new application requires.

Finally, you need an appropriate tool to implement the repository. As we have already briefly discussed in Chapter 4, various options for implementing a repository exist. However, the particular technical solution is often not pivotal for the successful adoption of the repository. Often, it is more important to carefully design and monitor the day-to-day processes concerning the repository.

This brings us to the issue of *policies*. It is vital to establish a process to ensure firstly that all service-worthy business logic is actually implemented as a service and secondly that service reuse is maximized. In order to achieve this, policies must be set up to ensure that the implementation of a service is not only tailored toward immediate requirements but that it also takes into account potential future applications. A simple means of achieving this is through a board that reviews all proposed service interfaces and contracts.

This board should not only review the service contracts but also manage the repository, which helps to ensure that which helps to ensure that this key element of the SOA finds support across departments and business units.

Moreover, there should be a well-defined process for the design and specification of new applications. In particular, reuse of existing service functionality should be favored over implementation of new service functionality, even if such a reuse requires a modification of the original implementation. Again, such a process is best realized by involving a dedicated board.

Finally, a *bonus system* rewarding successful SOA projects and people can provide additional incentives to adhere to the enterprise's SOA principles and to apply them in day-to-day routines. As with any bonus system, the main challenge is to define the criteria used to evaluate success. The reuse factor of a service, that is, the number of consumers it actually has, is a good candidate. In addition, the usage (number of times a service is invoked) should be included in the equation.

Because money is ultimately one of the key factors both for people and the project, financial bonuses for successful projects are one of the best incentives.

This usually requires clear target agreements with all key actors. In order to reward reusability, business departments could, for example, receive retrospective funding for their development projects after the developed services have actually been reused.

It should be clear that the setup of all these techniques and tools amounts to more or less the establishment of an SOA *organization* within the enterprise. This chapter will conclude with a real-world perspective on politics and strategies.

12.5   The Real World—Organization-Wide Standards

This section presents some examples from the real world. We begin with an example of the failed introduction of a platform project, and afterwards, we summarize the positive aspects of two of the use cases presented in detail in Part III of this book. We conclude with a summary of the lessons learned from these real-word examples and a brief sketch as to how to deal with standards spanning several enterprises.

12.5.1   AN EXAMPLE OF FAILURE

The example in this subsection is based on real-world experiences in a platform development project of a large corporation. We will use the arbitrary acronym COLOSS in the following to refer to this project and the platform itself.[2] COLOSS is realistic example of a failed introduction of a new technology and offers instructive insights into the challenges and pitfalls of such an undertaking.

We would like to point out that although the following description is based on a single project, it is in no way unique. Many of the problems described here are typical for large-scale projects introducing or applying new innovative technology.[3]

The main purpose of the COLOSS platform was to provide host functionality in a standardized way, such that arbitrary frontend and mid-tier applications could easily use this functionality. The following is a brief description of the results:

> **Launch postponed.** Initially, the project was supposed to deliver a first version of the platform after three years. This is already a considerable time-frame, even for a strategic development project. However, when the platform was not "finished" after the initial three-year period, its launch was postponed several times, until after five years it became apparent that the whole endeavor was seriously flawed.

---

[2] There is definitely no connection to the EU project in the 5th framework bearing the same name, or any other projects named COLOSS that we are not aware of.

[3] In fact, we expect many readers to immediately notice parallels between COLOSS and their own experiences with similar projects.

Scope creep. During the project, more and more functionality was assigned to or claimed by the platform. This particularly included functionality for session management, security, and transactional behavior.

Obsolete technology. Due to the long project duration and the additional delay, the technology used in the project became more and more obsolete.

As a consequence, support for the COLOSS platform crumbled. Whereas in the beginning, the platform was envisaged as a significant step forward that would considerably facilitate development of new applications, it was seen as more and more of a bottleneck threatening all development projects in the enterprise.

For example, projects began to devise workarounds that would access host functionality the "traditional" way because it was unclear whether COLOSS could provide the corresponding functionality on time. Similarly, projects developed their own solution for platform functionality such as transactions, security, session management, etc.

Instead of standardizing and facilitating the enterprise-wide development process and fostering reuse, the failure of the COLOSS project caused an even more heterogeneous infrastructure with many redundancies.

In hindsight, several lessons can be learned from this failure. You should bear in mind the following key recommendations when introducing a platform based on new technology:

Avoid Technology Focus. Perhaps the most critical mistake of the COLOSS project was that it was conceived as a technical platform development project that was not immediately tied to any business project. Though this made sense from a conceptual viewpoint, the IT focus caused a lack of synchronization between IT and business projects and was also ultimately responsible for scope creep and the delayed launch.

Start Small. Instead of aiming at a fully developed platform providing a high degree of functionality, it would have been more reasonable to start with a small prototype offering limited functionality. First, such a prototype would have been finished after a smaller time span. Second, it would have been possible to combine this prototype with a specific business project, allowing for immediate evaluation.

The next section will present some positive examples from the real world, which contrast pleasantly with the failings described in this section.

12.5.2 TWO SUCCESS STORIES—SOAS AT CREDIT SUISSE AND WINTERTHUR

In this section, we briefly cover the SOA introductions at Credit Suisse and Winterthur, which will be described in detail in the respective case studies in Part III. Credit Suisse Group is a leading global financial services company headquartered in Zurich. Founded in 1856, the company operates in over 50 countries with around 64,000 staff members. Winterthur Group is a leading Swiss insurance company providing a broad range of property and liability insurance products. Winterthur Group has approximately 23,000 employees worldwide.

For the moment, we will concentrate on the main characteristics that helped to make the SOA introductions a success. Interestingly, the purpose and intended functionality of these SOA introductions are quite similar to the COLOSS project. The main focus is on making existing host functionality available in a standardized way so that it can be efficiently used by newly developed business applications.

Probably the most striking difference from the COLOSS project is that both Credit Suisse and Winterthur adopted a type of bottom-up approach. Instead of first developing a complete platform, which would then be utilized in concrete business applications, platform development was accompanied and even driven by small pilot projects.

This approach helped prevent isolation of the platform development and kept the focus balanced between business needs and technological features. It also facilitated the quick gathering of experience and the adoption of the SOA strategy accordingly.

Moreover, this approach was emphasized by the fact that both Credit Suisse and Winterthur focused on SOA as a general philosophy so that the platform used to implement it was only seen as one of several ingredients, albeit an important one. From the beginning, great care was taken to establish structures and processes supporting the SOA introduction. In particular, dedicated teams were set up whose members acted as evangelists, educating business departments and development teams of application projects using the SOA.

Both groups also allocated a sufficient budget to the pilot projects and to the SOA teams. This enabled the SOA teams, for example, to compensate the business departments for the overhead caused by aligning the pilot projects with the SOA philosophy, such as adopting reusability considerations.

Finally, special boards monitored compliance with the enterprise-wide SOA standards and "enforced" reusability of the developed services. These boards include representatives from different business departments together with those of the IT department. This yielded several positive effects. First and foremost, it guaranteed a basic level of transparency and visibility from the very beginning. Business departments that were not yet developing or using the new services were already involved in the design process to ensure reusability. As a side effect, these departments obtained information about the progress and benefits of the SOA.

This process also helped to avoid the creeping emergence of diffuse fears. Staff and departments not involved in the development of a new silver bullet that is supposed to change the whole enterprise inevitably start to worry about their own place in the enterprise's future. If this development takes place not behind closed doors but openly instead, risks of sabotage and hidden or open opposition should hopefully diminish drastically.

Due to careful planning and execution, the SOA introductions at Winterthur and Credit Suisse received widespread recognition across the enterprise. The respective SOAs are seen as a success, and departments contribute actively and apply the SOA principles in their day-to-day routines. They do so not only because these principles are mandatory but also because they can see the associated benefits for their own activities in addition to the enterprise as a whole.

12.6   Recommendations for the SOA Protagonist

This section contains major recommendations for the SOA protagonist regarding politics and tactics of SOA introduction.

Solid foundation. We identified four main pillars for success, namely securing a budget, selecting adequate pilot projects, building a team, and finding backers and buddies.

Establish processes, structures, and standards. In order to make sure that the SOA is not just a nice concept written on paper, processes, structures, and standards must be established. It is well known that there is a major difference between theory and practice. Even if employees or departments are fully supportive of the SOA idea, they might disregard its principles in their day-to-day routines for several reasons, such as a lack of resources to cope with the overhead caused by the SOA, a lack of support for the project, or simply the reluctance to familiarize oneself with the details. It is vital to make sure that the SOA principles are not just laid down on paper but are actually applied in daily practice.

Enforce substantial change. In some cases, new methodologies and technologies are introduced in an enterprise without any real change happening. Everything remains the same, except that new labels are used to describe what is done—"Yes, of course, all the functionality developed in our application projects is now service-oriented." For an SOA to become effective and more than a void bubble, it must contain substance. Only if it has an impact on existing structures and processes, such as by transforming or extending them, will it yield benefits.

Ensure business involvement. Although SOAs are not primarily about technology, technology issues can become too dominant in the SOA introduction, especially if a dedicated platform is to be developed as a basis for the SOA. Ensuring business involvement is therefore crucial from the very beginning. Projects should be driven by business needs and should yield measurable business benefits.

Focus. It is important to have a clear focus when introducing an SOA and to concentrate on feasible achievement and reasonable time frames. This ensures early visibility of benefits and minimizes the risks of individual projects failing and thereby endangering the overall SOA introduction.

Evangelize. The SOA introductions should be permanently accompanied by evangelistic activities, such as coaching, training, education programs, and whitepapers.

Cope with open or concealed opposition. Inevitably, not everyone in the enterprise will be thrilled by the prospect of an SOA. Single employees or whole departments might openly or secretly oppose the introduction of an SOA. Reasons for such opposition can be manifold. They could be rooted in a general dread of change regardless of its concrete nature, or they could be related to a specific fear of losing influence and/or control. It is important to constantly watch for signs of open or concealed opposition and deal with it adequately. In this context, it is extremely important to precisely understand the motivation of the other stakeholders and provide offerings that are actually perceived positively. If the fear of coping with change is the greatest concern, coaching or training can mitigate the opposition. If the key problem is about losing influence, it could also be helpful to integrate people into the SOA processes and give them appropriate responsibility to contribute to the SOA success.

Compensate overhead. A particular aspect that is easily overlooked is the fact that applying an SOA will create an initial overhead. This overhead must be taken into account in the budget.

Ensure visibility. In order to firmly entrench the SOA in the enterprise, high visibility should be ensured, such as by involving all relevant actors in the processes and by implementing widely used functionality as services in the pilot projects.

12.7 Conclusion

In this chapter, we examined the political and strategic aspects of an SOA introduction. We pointed out that introducing an SOA is a complex endeavor that can only succeed if it is handled professionally and with adequate focus. It usually takes several years before an SOA is really established within an enterprise.

The real-world examples have illustrated the most common challenges encountered when introducing an SOA and some suitable methods to successfully deal with them. However, SOAs address the concurrent trend towards aligning IT with overall business goals. The service-enabled enterprise facilitates more efficient SLAs between IT and the business organization, and thus IT is increasingly "being brought into the fold."

URLs

http://www.isixsigma.com

http://www.iso.ch

13

SOA-Driven Project Management

Modern project management methodologies have an interesting and eventful history. One of the earliest projects that adopted rigorous project management processes was the Manhattan Project in the 1940s, in which the United States developed the first nuclear weapon, a massive research and engineering undertaking [Gro83]. In the 1970s, practitioners in industries such as defense and construction started to adopt project management methodologies. The 1990s saw a migration toward project management methodologies, starting with TQM in the mid-80s, process reengineering in the early '90s, risk management and project offices in the late '90s, and the currently ongoing wave of mergers, acquisitions, and global projects of the new century.

Some of the generic project management practices and tools are directly applicable to software development. Gantt charts and network diagrams are frequently used not only in construction industry projects but also in software projects. Generic project management standards such as PRINCE 2 address organization, plans, controls, stages, risk management, and quality, configuration, and change control, all of which also apply to any software project. Today, a wide variety of project management methodologies address the specifics of software development projects, ranging from the simple and widely used waterfall model to sophisticated, iterative models such as Rational Unified Process or Catalysis.

As in the remainder of this book, this chapter is based on the assumption that the projects we are looking at are related to enterprise architectures, including packaged applications and bespoke software, with complex dependencies and integration requirements.

In this chapter, we limit the discussion of generic software development project management methodologies to a brief introduction. Our focus is on understanding how aspects of SOA can be used in the context of some of these established project management methodologies in a complementary manner. We introduce the concept of SOA-driven project management, configuration management, and testing from the perspective of the project manager.

13.1   Established Project Management Methodologies

Like any engineering, manufacturing, or product development project, a software project must cope with the conflicting requirements of time, resources, and functionality. However, software projects are often somewhat special in that they exhibit a number of problems not normally found in other industries. In particular, enterprise software is tightly coupled with the internal organization, processes, and business model of the enterprise, as we discussed in Chapter 1. Naturally, this means that the interfaces between enterprise software and human users have a much higher complexity than interfaces between human users and other types of complex technologies.

Take, for example, a sports car with an extremely sophisticated engine, anti-sliding system, and exhaust reduction system—at the end of the day, the interfaces exposed to the user are relatively simple: the user controls the technology through the use of the steering wheel and brakes and is typically not aware of the highly complex technology hidden under the hood.

Compare this, for example, to a software system such as a CRM system or an ERP package. Such a system requires much more complex user interfaces, and interaction with such a software package is much more direct and frequent in the day-to-day business of the end user. Thus, enterprise software projects usually require much tighter interaction with customers during the development phase—after all, it is the customer's business that we are modeling one-to-one, with all the corresponding details, day-to-day operational processes, and special cases.

Unfortunately, enterprise software projects very often suffer from the *I can't tell you what I want, but I will recognize it when I see it* phenomenon. Early project management methodologies that were developed specifically for software development projects where not able to cope with this issue. Most notably, the popular waterfall development model implicitly assumes that customer requirements are fixed at the beginning of the projects and that changes to these requirements are the exception, not the norm. The phases of the waterfall model include requirements specification, high-level and detailed design, coding, module and integration testing, and acceptance testing. The waterfall model is based on full documentation at the completion of each phase, which must be formally approved before the next phase is entered. The final delivery is one monolithic result.

Because of the limitations of this approach—in particular the inability of the waterfall model to cope with unstable requirements—a number of more evolutionary approaches for software project management have emerged over the past 20 years. These more incremental or iterative models are built on a philosophy of interaction and change, which is much better suited for coping with unstable functional requirements. These models are typically based on frequent releases, which are used as the basis for getting early and continuous customer feedback. Instead of delivering the first work result after months or even years (as in the waterfall model), the iterations of these evolutionary approaches typically last only a few weeks (or even days).

An early representative of these development processes was James Martin's *Rapid Application Development* (RAD), which is based on incremental stages. Each increment represents a short-duration waterfall. Barry Boehm developed one of the first fully evolutionary models, widely known as the *Spiral Model*, which is based on a set of full development cycles that continually refine the knowledge about the final product and help control project risks.

A number of very complex and sophisticated development process models have been commercialized in the past decade. Most of these models are based on an iterative approach in combination with some form of object-orientation, such as using UML as a formal modeling language. Probably the most prominent representative of this class of development processes is the *Rational Unified Process* (RUP), which is now owned by IBM. RUP is iterative, depends heavily on visualization through UML, and uses component-based architectures. In the same arena of relatively heavyweight iterative development processes, we would also find *Dynamic Systems Development Method* (DSDM), *Microsoft Solution Framework* (MSF), and *Catalysis*.

In the wake of the fast-moving Internet revolution of the late 1990s, a number of approaches emerged that took a much more lightweight approach to iterative software development, often referred to as *agile* development. In 2001, several representatives of this school of thought issued the *Manifesto for Agile Software Development*.[1] A prominent representative of these new lightweight methodologies is *Extreme Programming* (XP), which heavily relies on *peer programming* (i.e., two developers jointly working on a piece of code based on user stories, one focusing on the coding, the other on the design and testing of what is being developed) and *write-test-cases-before-writing-the-actual-code*. With XP, all new code is immediately integrated, and comprehensive test runs are executed every couple of hours.

Robert Martin's dX method aims at covering the middle ground between heavyweight methodologies such as RUP and lightweight methodologies such as XP. dX is a minimal implementation of RUP, based on index cards, an amalgamation of use cases and CRC cards (Class-Responsibility-Collaboration). Figure 13-1 provides an overview of some of the existing methodologies and how they relate to each other.

---

[1] www.agilemanifesto.org

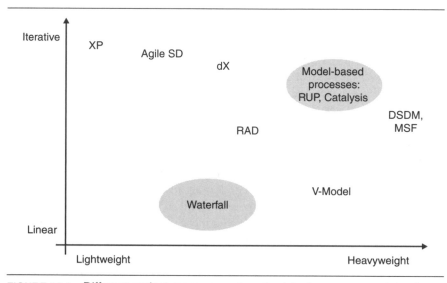

FIGURE 13-1   Different project management methodologies cover a variety of different requirements. They range from lightweight to heavyweight approaches and from linear to iterative models.

Add Service Orientation to Your Favorite Project Management Methodology

Different project management methodologies have their strengths and weaknesses, and their suitability heavily depends on the project context—including scope, complexity, and duration of the project, quality requirements, strategic importance, resources available, stakeholders involved, and so forth. This makes it difficult, if not impossible, to give generic recommendations for the right approach. Your methodology choice will depend on your own experience and established best practices. However, given the complex nature and frequently changing business requirements that we find in the context of enterprise SOA projects, we assume that the chosen approach will support iterative development, which is essential for coping with complexity and unstable requirements. Given the strategic importance of enterprise SOA projects, we expect the chosen methodology will tend a little bit more toward the side of the heavyweight processes.

Nevertheless, it is important to realize that *SOA-driven project management does not require a new methodology.* The proposals for incorporating aspects of service orientation into your project management are based on the assumption that you are choosing an established methodology, which will then be enhanced to make use of service orientation on the project management level.

13.2 SOA-Driven Project Management

As we said in the introduction, this chapter focuses on how service orientation can support project management without inventing an entirely new project management methodology. Naturally, the level to which SOA elements should be included in project management depends strongly on the expansion stage of the SOA—an organization that is already further down the road in terms of rolling out the SOA will in some cases be able to benefit more from these concepts. However, even in the early stages, an organization can benefit greatly from the concepts outlined in this chapter.

When looking at SOA-driven project management, it is important to recall that an SOA introduction happens on many different levels within an enterprise:

Business projects versus IT projects. First of all, any SOA-driven project management will have to be closely aligned with concurrently ongoing business projects, which are the source for any functional requirements. A general theme throughout this book has been the close relationship of the services developed for our SOA with concrete business functions. As outlined in Chapter 1 and consecutive chapters, the services in an SOA are often a one-to-one mapping of a business entity such as a process or a transaction. Thus, services are an ideal tool for coordinating business projects and IT projects, giving project managers from both sides a perfect means for communicating and aligning business requirements and technical implementation. Often, we find that multiple business projects will have an impact on an SOA project and vice versa.

IT program versus IT project management. Next, on the IT level, we need to differentiate between the management of individual IT projects and the management of multiple IT projects (program management). In Section 12.4.1, we introduced the concept of an *SOA board* as a key tool for coordinating multiple projects in a program. Section 12.2 provided an *organizational roadmap* and discussed how the different stakeholders and influencers must be included on the program management level. Section 12.2.1 describes how SOA artifacts can be used to control individual projects and sub-projects within them, as well as to coordinate multiple projects on the program management level.

Business services versus SOA infrastructure. Finally, it is important to remember that an SOA introduction has two architectural levels: the actual business services themselves and the required service bus infrastructure, which enables different services and service consumers to interact with each other in a controlled, secure, and reliable way. Chapter 6 outlined the different expansion stages of an SOA, including fundamental, networked, and process-enabled SOA—the level to which an SOA can be leveraged for project management purposes will depend on the expansion stage that the SOA has reached in the enterprise. If you are in the early stages of SOA development, recall our suggestions in Section 12.5.1: Start small and avoid a technical focus. In particular, if you are in the early stages of putting your SOA infrastructure in place, avoid putting too much functionality into the initial platform. In addition, don't develop the platform on its own but instead make sure that it is developed within the context of a concrete project, which ideally adds significant business value. Chapter 9 introduced the concept of a "meta service bus," which can cater for adoption of different technologies in an evolutionary way. Chapter 14 discusses a concrete case study from Credit Suisse, outlining how the company introduced a synchronous information bus, an asynchronous event bus, and a file transfer-based integration infrastructure driven by the demand from different projects, which in turn were driven by concrete business demands.

As we will see, an SOA can help cut projects into more manageable pieces, which helps program and project managers to coordinate concurrently ongoing business projects, IT application projects, and IT infrastructure projects. Figure 13-2 again highlights the different levels of dependencies that an SOA can help to coordinate.

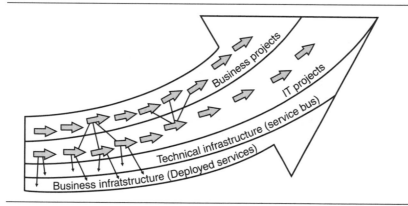

FIGURE 13-2 SOA-driven program and project management contributes to the coordination of business and IT projects. It also enables a stepwise extension of the business infrastructure (deployed services) and the technical infrastructure (service bus).

13.2.1 USE SOA ARTIFACTS AS PROJECT CONTROL ELEMENTS

A key issue in software project management has always been the mapping of project control elements (such as tasks, work breakdown structures, etc.) and software artifacts (program code, data models, specifications, and the complex relationships between all of these).

Individual lines of code are clearly too fine-grained to serve as meaningful project control elements. Modules and object-oriented classes might be more suitable as control elements within individual tasks of a project.

However, the challenge of SOA-driven project management is usually not the management of individual tasks, but rather the coordination of multiple concurrently executed projects and sub-projects. When looking at the entire enterprise IT landscape, we are usually looking at the program management level, where a program includes multiple projects. In some cases, this could even mean an application portfolio-based management approach. On this level, modules and classes are not suitable as project control elements, due to their fine level of granularity, as well as their technical orientation. Even within individual projects, we usually find that modules and classes are not suitable as project control elements on the highest level for similar reasons.

Services in an SOA, on the other hand, represent an ideal tool for decomposing complex systems into manageable sub-systems. They are a powerful tool for controlling the state, integration, quality, and business readiness of individual components and sub-systems. The reason for this is twofold: First of all, a well-designed service provides the ideal level of granularity to be used as a project control element. Recall our discussion on service granularity in Chapter 4, which stated that the granularity of a service should be on the level of a meaningful business entity. Second, well-designed services in an SOA tend to be relatively business-oriented (taking infrastructure services out of the equation for now). This makes services an ideal communication tool not only between technical people but also between the non-technical people involved in the project management. Even if we sometimes find modules or classes with a level of granularity similar to that of services in an SOA, these APIs would usually still be fairly technology-oriented, thus lacking the business orientation that is required on this level of project management.

Figure 13-3 provides an overview of the level of granularity of different types of software artifacts and how they relate to different levels of project management.

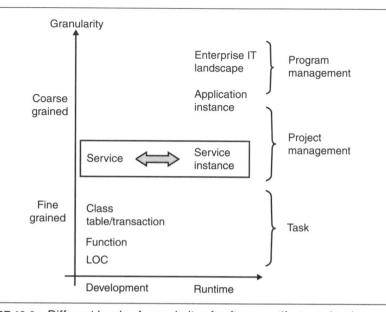

FIGURE 13-3 Different levels of granularity of software artifacts at development time and runtime.

Another factor plays an important role in enterprise-level software project management: Enterprise-level applications almost always have to be synchronized not only during development time, but also during their lifetime in a production environment. Introducing a new release of a sub-system into a production environment must not have a negative impact on the other sub-systems. This means that we not only have to ensure that the technical interfaces (service contracts) between the different components in the production system are in synch, but also that data and expected behavior are compatible. For example, the restructuring of a naming service will not change and interface definitions but will require changing the configuration of those clients that have been configured to use the old structure. Coordinating the runtime compatibility of different sub-systems is a hugely complex task.

Again, services are ideally suited for managing runtime synchronization of sub-systems. As depicted in the Figure 13-3, development time services match to service instances at runtime. As we can also see in this figure, services present something like the top-level abstraction layer for development time artifacts, as well as the bottom-level abstraction layer for runtime artifacts. This makes services ideally suited for managing the difficult region between development time and runtime synchronization.

Figure 13-4 shows how service contracts (managed in a shared, centralized service repository) can support an SOA board (see Chapter 12) by providing the backbone for coordinating multiple projects on the program level (or, alternatively, coordinating multiple sub-projects on the project level).

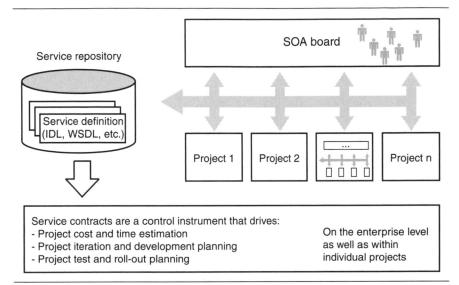

FIGURE 13-4   The SOA board utilizes service contracts in order to coordinate multiple projects.

Make Your Service Contracts Drive the Projects

Services have the ideal level of granularity and business orientation to serve as the basis for driving many important aspects of your project, including:

- Project cost and time estimation
- Project iteration and development planning
- Project synchronization
- Project test and rollout planning

In order to successfully leverage the potential that services provide as a key driving force of your projects, you must ensure that you have the right level of political support. Ideally, you should install an SOA board or a similar kind of institution that can control and push the use of services as a project management tool. It will also be responsible for the synchronization of services that are shared by different projects or sub-projects.

13.2.2 INCLUDE SERVICE DESIGNS IN THE PROJECT DEFINITION

Because services are a fundamental tool for structuring not only your architecture but also your project plan, it is only logical to demand that each project definition contain a high-level service design.

We often underestimate the importance of the project definition phase, making too many implicit assumptions, including the answers to key questions such as "What is the scope of the project" or "What are the priorities?" The project definition phase enables us to ask these basic yet important questions, define a project vision, identify the major objectives and constraints, and so forth. In particular, the project definition should enable the different stakeholders—from both the business and technology side—to develop and articulate a shared vision. As we saw earlier, services are sufficiently coarse-grained and business-oriented to serve as a perfect communication tool in this critical phase of the project.

The project definition should also contain an initial project plan, which defines the most important iterations and increments. Again, services are a very good tool for defining these and also for discussing implicit and explicit dependencies at this level.

In an SOA-driven project, the project definition should therefore always contain a first draft of the architecture, including the most critical services that have to be developed or included. In a sense, these early service definitions and architecture blueprints serve as a common denominator between the different stakeholders and help in preventing unpleasant surprises during or after the project execution.

Include a First Service Design in the Project Definition

SOA project management must assure that a first draft of the architecture becomes a key delivery of the project definition phase. You must already have identified the application frontends, the external services, and the most important basic services. With regard to the basic services, you must distinguish the following:

- New services built from scratch
- New services based on existing applications
- Extensions and modifications of existing services

The design of intermediary and process-centric services can be done later.

13.2.3   LEVERAGE SOA TO DECOMPOSE COMPLEX SYSTEMS

As with any large project or program, a key problem we must face in the early phase is the complexity of the undertaking, which requires that we find good ways of decomposing systems into manageable parts.

The loosely coupled nature of an SOA is extremely well suited for this purpose. The following takes a closer look at how to leverage the SOA approach for project and system decomposition and how to manage the decomposed parts from a project management perspective.

13.2.3.1 Vertical Versus Horizontal Slicing. Most enterprise applications can be decomposed using two different approaches, based on either vertical or horizontal slicing. A horizontal slice of a system usually presents a particular technical tier, such as the user interface, presentation layer, business logic, middleware, data management, and so forth. Vertical slices, on the other hand, represent specific business use cases, such as *open account* in a banking Web portal.

Sometimes, large projects are structured in a way where different teams are responsible for specific horizontal slices of the system—for example, one team does all the Web forms and graphics, one team does the complete database schema, one team does the business logic, etc. (see Figure 13-5). This can often lead to large integration overheads because each team is focusing only on its own specific layer, and there is a general lack of people with a good overview of the relationship between the different horizontal slices. Problems during development are potentially discovered only very late in the development cycle, usually the moment when large pieces of work that have been executed in isolation within each horizontal layer need to be integrated.

When using horizontal slicing, developers with very different skills work hand-in-hand to deliver complete end-to-end slices, from application frontend to business logic to the middleware and data layer. This approach minimizes the integration overhead between components from the different horizontal layers of a complex system. In the following section, we discuss the "thin thread" approach, which is based on vertical slicing.

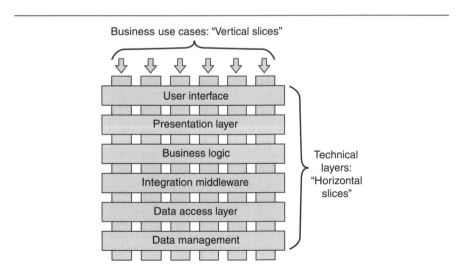

FIGURE 13-5 Whereas horizontal layers are technology driven, vertical slices are driven by use cases—that is, business functionality.

13.2.3.2 Thin Thread Model. The "thin thread" development and project management model is essentially an application of the Iterative Application Development (IAD) approach, as described, for example, in the rational unified process. The "thin thread" approach is specifically suited for IAD in the context of Service-Oriented Architectures.

A thread represents a vertical slice through the system, including an end-to-end implementation of a particular piece of application logic, going from application frontend all the way down to the database.

The basic idea of the "thin thread" approach is to start with a very thin slice (or thread), which might, for example, only comprise the functionality of capturing a single string value in the application frontend, processing this information in the middle-tier, and writing it into the database. In the next phase, the thread might be "thickened" by adding end-to-end functionality for retrieving the string value from the database and displaying it in the application frontend. In a further iteration, a more complex data structure (e.g., a customer record) might be handled in a similar way, and so on. As the project continues, additional threads can be launched (see Figure 13-6).

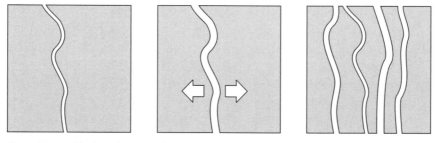

Start with one thin thread   Thicken thread   Add new threads

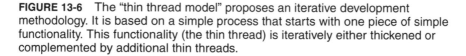

FIGURE 13-6 The "thin thread model" proposes an iterative development methodology. It is based on a simple process that starts with one piece of simple functionality. This functionality (the thin thread) is iteratively either thickened or complemented by additional thin threads.

Very often, the initial version of a thread might match an individual operation of a more complex service, and the final iteration of the thread represents the full-blown service.

Most likely, the first iteration of a thread (especially if it is the first one in a new project) will be slow. Problems will arise in the initial setup of the system (including session management, transaction handling, middleware, data access, etc.) and in the development process, deployment, testing, performance, etc. The next iteration will be considerably faster, though, because all end-to-end problems will have been addressed in the first iteration. After the first couple of threads have been tried and tested, a more aggressive rollout of threads can start, as depicted in Figure 13-7.

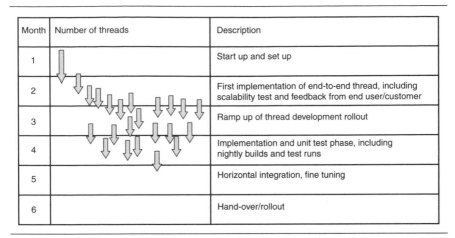

Month	Number of threads	Description
1		Start up and set up
2		First implementation of end-to-end thread, including scalability test and feedback from end user/customer
3		Ramp up of thread development rollout
4		Implementation and unit test phase, including nightly builds and test runs
5		Horizontal integration, fine tuning
6		Hand-over/rollout

FIGURE 13-7   The number of concurrently active threads varies over time.

Much of what is contained in this "thin thread" approach is obvious and common sense—effectively, it is a combination of widely established iterative application development concepts with a consequent vertical slicing approach on the architecture level. However, many projects struggle because they choose a horizontal instead of vertical decomposition approach. In addition, experience has shown that giving this approach a name (a "thread" denotes the basic work breakdown structure) and making it explicit in the project management plan simplifies planning and prevents miscommunication.

Apply the Thin Thread Approach

A thin thread represents a fully functional part of the whole system spanning all layers of the system from the frontend to the backend. The service contracts of the services involved in a thin thread define the scope and drive the development and testing.

You should implement thin threads in order to enable (and enforce) a project to approach many risks in a very early phase.

13.2.4 LEVERAGE SOA TO DRIVE DEVELOPMENT ITERATIONS

Service orientation is particularly well suited for supporting iterative application development, especially when combined with what we described in the previous section as the "thin thread" approach, which is effectively an iterative development approach based on vertical slices.

Because SOA is particularly aimed at enterprise-level development projects, we often find situations where many projects (or sub-projects) are running in parallel often over long time periods. A key problem for such long-running parallel projects is the stabilization of the development process, which is required to decouple projects from each other, shielding each project from the dynamics of the other projects.

Traditionally, the elements that can stabilize a project are the user interface and data model. However, in a distributed architecture with many layers between user interface and database, achieving stability in the top and bottom layers is often not sufficient for achieving overall stability.

Service contracts are the ideal tool for stabilizing the development process in distributed architectures. They are conceptually located between the user interface and the data model, and if we carefully control the evolution of these contracts, we can greatly enhance the stability of the overall development process. Effectively, projects and sub-projects should evolve in parallel to the service contracts they share.

We already discussed the loosely coupled nature of an SOA, referring largely to technical coupling. However, an SOA provides benefits beyond this technical loose coupling—an SOA also enables loose coupling of tasks in a project. This reduction of dependencies between different tasks is directly related to the technical independence of different services, and it greatly enhances the flexibility of project managers with respect to the scheduling and coordination of different tasks. Effectively, although SOA does not eliminate dependencies between different projects, it documents them and helps to address them in an organized way.

Use Service Contract Iterations as the "Heartbeat" of the Project

In a truly SOA-driven project, service contracts should be a key driver of the project. Consequently, the iterations that these service contracts go through should represent the "heartbeat" of the project.

The role of the SOA board is to control this "heartbeat." Effectively, this board becomes similar to a conductor in a large orchestra, who is responsible for ensuring that each of the individual orchestra members is properly synchronized with the rest of the orchestra.

13.2.4.1 Use SOA as the Basis for Divide & Conquer Strategies. In addition to the "vertical slicing" of the thin thread approach, you often need to further decompose tasks, especially in phases where the initially "thin" threads start to "thicken"—that is, a richer set of functionality is associated with the individual threads under development.

In this case, it can often make sense to further decompose development tasks (i.e., threads) into "horizontal" slices. However, notice that this should always be the second step—after the initial "vertical" slicing. As depicted in Figure 13-8, service contracts can help with the synchronization of this horizontal subdivision. We discussed earlier that the biggest problem with a horizontal slicing approach is the integration of the individual horizontal slices. In order to address this issue, service contracts should be leveraged as the key sync point between the individual slices, such as the application frontend and backend services. Service definitions are a result of the joint analysis and planning activities, which involve both sides of the service contract. The jointly agreed upon service contract should be approved by the *SOA board* and captured in the central, shared service repository. Based on the initial service contract (or its next iteration), both sides can now independently start development and testing of their respective parts (frontend or backend). Automatically generated test frontends and backends are an essential support tool for facilitating this divide-and-conquer approach. Only after the different sides of the service contract have reached a reasonable level of stability should they be deployed in a shared test environment, in which they can be integrated and tested further.

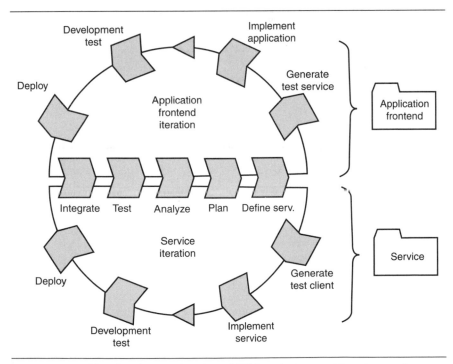

FIGURE 13-8 The development cycles of SOA projects are driven by service contracts, which are the major outcome of the activity "define service."

Of course, a lot of these divide-and-conquer principles have been successfully used in the past. However, especially in distributed system development, where we often have complex infrastructures and project team members with very different skill sets (e.g., Java GUI programmers and COBOL mainframe developers), it would be helpful if these principles were adopted more often and if the appropriate support tools—such as automated frontend and backend test tools—were provided.

13.2.4.2 Use SOA to Manage Parallel Iterations.   After service contracts have been established as the "heartbeat" that drives the overall project, it makes sense to look at them as a tool for enabling parallel development as well.

As depicted in Figure 13-9, service contracts can serve as the basis for multiple service implementations that are developed in parallel (application frontends #1–#N and backend services #1–#M in this example). As a prerequisite, the underlying application scenarios #1–#N will have to be analyzed, an iteration plan developed, and the service contract defined. After this, the individual frontend and backend services can be developed independently before they are eventually integrated.

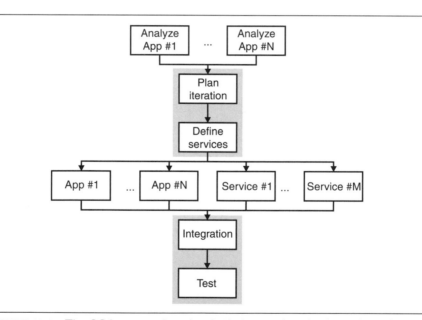

FIGURE 13-9 The SOA approach makes both the synchronization points of independent tasks and concurrent development efforts explicit.

Figure 13-10 shows how service contracts can serve as sync points, which help in coordinating the development and integration of multiple application frontends and services.

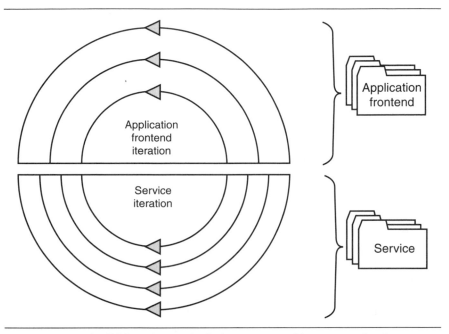

FIGURE 13-10   An SOA project typically has to cope with many application frontends and services developed in parallel.

Their granularity and business-orientation make services ideal candidates for the breakdown and parallel execution of complex development tasks in distributed enterprise environments. This is an extremely powerful feature of any SOA-driven project, especially if time to market is critical and large development teams need to be synchronized.

13.2.5   TAKE A STEP-BY-STEP APPROACH TOWARD PROCESS INTEGRITY

To finish our discussion on SOA and iterative application development, we now look at transactionality and process integrity. In Chapter 8, we introduced the concepts of process integrity and how they relate to data integrity, transactions, and long-lived processes. A key discussion of that chapter was the tradeoff between process integrity on one hand and related costs on the other. Achieving 100% process integrity is almost impossible in most cases, unless we are prepared to spend the money usually required to build super-reliable systems, such as redundant electronics in an airplane or a nuclear power plant control system. "Normal" systems (such as an online banking portal, a stock trading system, or a telecom billing system) with "normal" budgets will have to accept the fact that certain rare failure situations will lead to process inconsistencies, which usually require human intervention to fix (e.g., through an DBMS administrator who is uses an SQL console to go directly into the system and fix problems reported by end users).

However, in the real world this rarely presents a problem. Of course, it would be ideal if complex IT systems were completely self-sufficient and no system administrators were required to fix data or process inconsistencies caused by system failures. However, if the cost of building 100% reliable systems by far outweighs the cost of employing system administrators, the latter solution seems acceptable.

The following describes a set of guidelines for introducing high levels of process consistency through an evolutionary approach, which helps in minimizing the cost and complexity of the development:

- Avoid making the entire system transactional, e.g., through the use of distributed transaction properties in every single service interface. Instead, build the system based on lightweight tracing and recovery mechanisms.
- As a general rule of thumb, as long as we can trace a problem (or the history of a partially executed process), we can always manually fix it. Chapter 9 provides more details on infrastructures for distributed logging and tracing.
- Throughout the initial testing period and in the early launch phase, you will find out which services and processes are particularly vulnerable to failures—either because failures occur frequently, or because fixing process inconsistencies caused by them becomes very difficult. In the case of frequently occurring failures, attempt to fix the problem at its root cause (i.e., analyze the problem and fix the bug). In the case of particularly critical complex processes, analyze common or likely failure situations (such as a disk crash) based on your experience with the evolving system and provide recovery mechanisms that are specifically suited to fit the needs of these critical processes and failure situations.
- You will quickly learn that the number of services or processes that require specific transaction or recovery mechanisms will be extremely low—in almost all mission-critical systems, 85–95% of system functionality does not require advanced transaction or recovery functionality. This is because usually only 5–15% of system functionality deals with modifications of mission-critical data (such as a money transfer), while the rest of the functionality has read-only or purely administrative characteristics.
- In the early phases of deploying the system and gaining experience with the system's as well as the end user's behavior, you will most likely require relatively high tracing levels in order to ensure that you are not missing any critical information that might be required in order to step in after a potential failure. As the user load increases, tracing overhead becomes a more limiting factor, but because at the same time the system also matures and you gain experience with its runtime behavior, you will be able to limit tracing to those parts of the system that you have identified as mission-critical.

This approach will enable you to identify the few really critical parts of your system in an evolutionary msanner and focus on them specifically from a process integrity point of view (e.g., by migrating them onto a more reliable transaction model). This approach should be accompanied by a risk analysis of your services and processes, based on your formal service definitions. Table 13-1 shows an example of how this analysis should look (see also Figure 8-4).

Table 13-1   Technical Risk Analysis

	Is update operation	Is idem- potent	Is part of complex transaction	Compensating operation	Risk level
Customer					
get_profile()		X			
update_profile()	X	X			
create_itinerary()	X				MEDIUM (non-idempotent update)
get_itineraries()		X			
Itinerary					
add_reservation()	X				MEDIUM (non-idempotent update)
get_reservation()		X			
update_reservation()	X	X			
update_itinerary()	X	X			
confirm itinerary()	X	X	finalize_booking()	cancel_itinerary()	HIGH (no guarantee that cancellation will work without incurring cancellation fees)
cancel_itinerary()	X	X			HIGH (attempt to cancel might still incur cancellation fees)
Billing					
create_invoice()	X				HIGH (invoices can only be cancelled if itinerary was cancelled without incurring cancellation fees)
cancel_invoice()	X	X			
get_invoice()		X			
update_invoice()	X	X			
Incident manager					
create_incident()	X				MEDIUM (non-idempotent update)
get_incident()		X			
update_incident()	X	X			

Reduce Risk by Applying Best Practices of SOA

SOA project management enables you to significantly reduce project risk by applying a set of best practices that do not replace a proven methodology introduced at your enterprise but add to it:

- Divide et impera: decompose your system.
- Create the first service design in the project definition phase.
- Decouple development teams by service contracts.
- Apply a thin threads approach.
- Leverage reuse wherever technically and economically feasible.
- Renovate and simplify your architecture step by step.
- Involve the business department.
- Utilize improved documentation provided by service contracts.
- Create a regression test environment for services.

13.3 Configuration Management

Configuration management in an SOA project requires an approach that is somewhat different from usual practice. Traditionally, each project creates a single repository in configuration management systems such as CVS, Rational Clear Case, or Telelogic's Continuus. Such an approach is not practical in an SOA for the following reasons:

- Services often do not belong to a single project.
- Service infrastructure is used across all participants of the SOA.
- The SOA should enable the independent deployment of individual services.
- The access to the source code of individual services must be controlled independently.

We discuss these issues in great detail in the next section along with some proposed solutions.

13.3.1 CHALLENGES FOR AN SOA CONFIGURATION MANAGEMENT

In an SOA, not all artifacts generated by a project will ultimately be owned by this project. Instead, the services that are intended to be reused in other projects will be owned by the organization. This is necessary due to the mode of reuse that one strives for with SOA.

Traditionally, reuse has been achieved by either reusing source code or sharing libraries between different applications. This will lead either to transfer of ownership of the copied code fragments to the new project or to tying the project to a certain version of a library that has been used. SOA, on the other hand, focuses on the reuse of software components at runtime, effectively reusing existing business systems including the life data they own. This creates a set of dependencies completely different from those of the reuse of code or libraries. Reuse of existing services will raise the need to amend these services or to fix errors within these services that are only discovered in subsequent reuse. At the same time, a project can be expected to come up with some services that will in turn be made available to the entire enterprise (see Figure 13-11).

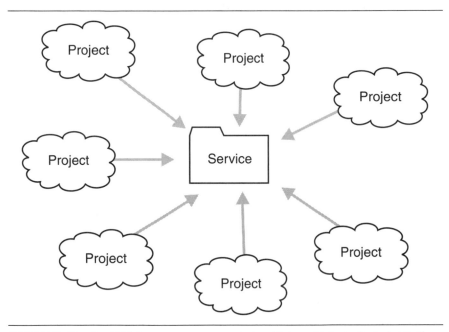

FIGURE 13-11   An SOA leverages a scenario in which multiple projects typically share common services.

Much the same holds true for certain support code that is written for a number of specific services, regardless of the eventual ownership of these services. Examples include logging components (see Chapter 9) and transaction handling (see Chapter 8).

It seems beneficial to be able to maintain, build, release, and deploy all shared services—and to some extent the supporting code—independently from each other. Otherwise, the agility that the SOA approach enables might be undermined by the requirements of the release and deployment process.

There is no apparent reason why independent services that are created during any particular project should only be deployable and maintainable together. In fact it seems largely beneficial to separate them as much as possible. Consider a service that provides customer-related information within an airline corporation. This service might have been created originally to support booking services during a booking project. As a typical cross-corporate service, it can be reused by other projects. All requested amendments apply to the customer service but not the booking application and its booking services. Ownership of the customer service itself might at some point actually move into another project, for example one that supports a customer retention program. Here, the customer service will be developed and deployed totally detached from its origin—the booking application.

13.3.2 RECOMMENDATIONS FOR THE SOA INTEGRATION TEAM

Although the creation of an appropriate structure for configuration management (CM) is a difficult problem, it is actually a benefit of an SOA in that it highlights the parts of a project that should be grouped together in their own CM containers. Traditional projects tend to squeeze everything into one container in order to cut corners when defining the build and deployment process. It is only after several iterations into the project delivery—or the application lifecycle—that the problems of this approach become painfully obvious. Interdependencies of project artifacts all too often mean that a fix cannot be delivered in time or that changes to a library send ripples—or even shockwaves—through the application fabrics.

When viewing an application from the viewpoint of an SOA, the division into different CM projects happens rather naturally from the bottom up. To start with, all basic services should be put into their own CM container. There might actually be some intermediary services that are closely related to one basic service, and they should be put into the same CM container. As long as other intermediary and process-centric services are designed for reuse, they should be stored separately. Where appropriate, the application frontend and related project-specific services can be grouped together—often by the specific functionality they offer or by the customer base they target.

After such a separation is made, common libraries will usually emerge that are reused by more than one service. These libraries themselves are, of course, prime candidates to be grouped in several independent CM containers.

In the end, any project will consist of one or more "frontend" CM containers and will use multiple CM containers that provide services of variable complexity and libraries. Ultimately, the best and most obvious driver for finding the right CM container layout and granularity is to start with a CM container for each reusable service and work upwards.

> ### Create a Standalone Project in Configuration Management for Every Reusable Service
>
> Creation of standalone projects (or subprojects) enables individual services to be developed, maintained, and deployed in an independent fashion. This enables truly agile development. Services can be maintained and upgraded without cross-dependencies to an overall multi-project schedule.

At first glance, it might seem that this implies a need for an enterprise-wide CM management system to properly manage all these different containers. Given that most organizations run multiple versions of different CM systems at the same time, this would seem quite scary. In fact, however, quite the opposite is true. A CM container exists to separate a certain code and configuration set from another one, and there is no compelling reason why these sets should be maintained within the same product (see Figure 13-12). Of course, any organization can only support a limited number of CM systems, and the systems will differ in their capability to integrate with automated build tools of various vendors. This can actually be a good thing, as certain CM environments might be better suited for creating Java-based Unix service development, while others are better suited to support C++-based Windows services or COBOL-based Mainframe development.

Throwing away an existing CM infrastructure is usually not an option. It is far better to identify a number of suitable CM systems based on the ones that are already available in the organization, but at most one to match each target platform that is available. Also, you should gradually retire CM environments that differ conceptually from the rest in a significant way. If part of an existing code base is not present in one of the target CM systems, you then could migrate it to these systems in the course of service enablement or during subsequent projects. This will eventually enable you to retire all legacy CM systems.

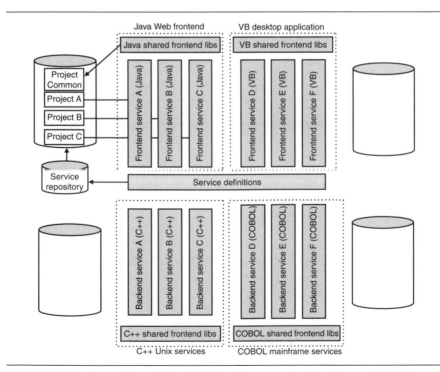

FIGURE 13-12 In practice, different CM systems are involved in one SOA. The service repository plays a key role by abstracting from the actual technologies.

Obviously, runtime reuse—as it is leveraged by SOA—requires a dedicated version of management. Although you can go to great lengths to ensure that services are maintained in a backward-compatible way, this is not always strictly possible. Sometimes, there might be changes to a system that requires new operation signatures, or a service operation might need to be removed. Because each actual software project is likely to consist of various independent services, along with project-specific and enterprise-wide support libraries, tight tracking of the dependencies of individual software artifacts is required. This includes information about which application frontends or service versions are compatible with other service's versions and the dependency on versions of libraries and runtime environments (see Figure 13-13).

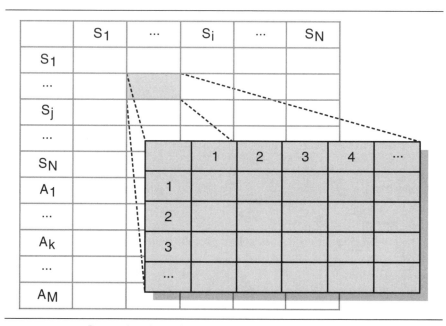

FIGURE 13-13   Dependencies exist between the various SOA artifacts—application frontends and services.

This is different from traditional monolithic software versions, where each version in configuration management was created as a single entity, with clearly defined dependency. An example is a traditional software project that depends on, say, a specific version of a byte manipulation library, whereas the multiple services in their respective current versions might very well use different versions of the same library.

At first, you might think that the SOA creates a new problem that requires the creation of such an interoperability matrix. Quite the opposite is true. The creation of a service environment forces important decisions or makes them at least explicit:

- A documentation of dependencies between runtime components is required
- This documentation belongs to a central and easily accessible place
- The information provided by such a documentation is particularly required for multi–project-management.

13.4 Testing

Testing is probably the major quality control tool in any software development. The term testing in this context refers to systematic, automated, reproducible testing, rather than the ad-hoc testing approach that is still dominant in many software development efforts. This formal approach generates objective and measurable test results that can be used to obtain a measurement of the quality of the created software artifact.

Testing is best grouped into different categories, depending on the required objective and level of granularity. First, load testing and functional testing must be distinguished.

Load testing means testing a component under a specific load for a defined time. It is crucial to judge whether the software can meet any required SLAs. Load testing normally requires that the test be conducted against an environment where all the backend systems of the component are available and perform and scale as they will in the live environment. Otherwise, the response times or stability numbers don't mean much. For example, if a test is carried out against a simulation of a message queueing system, there is no knowing if systematic failures of the actual system will keep the performance of the testing component within the required range.

Functional testing means ensuring that the operational results of a software component are consistent with expectations. Functional tests that execute a single call with a given set of parameters and that then compare the result of these calls with the expected result are referred to as unit tests. Several unit tests can be chained into a testing series, testing several related and possibly sequential actions. In addition, test robots can automate tests of an entire application frontend by simulating user actions, again comparing results with expectation. Automated test tools can execute thousands of tests in short periods of time, usually far more than can be done manually. This special form of chained unit testing is commonly known as an end-to-end functional test. When a single component—such as an individual service—is tested, functional testing might well allow for a certain part of the application to be simulated. For example, persistence using an object relational mapping library can be replaced using a simulation of the library. The upside of this approach is that database setup scripts and resources need not be available and initialized at time of testing, reducing testing time and speeding the quality assurance process. In contrast, when a component is functionally tested with all its backend components available, this is referred to integration testing for this component.

Of course, some overlap exists between the test types because load test tools often provide some mechanism for result checking and unit test tools provide some mechanism for generating increased load. Still, the test scenarios described remain different because they address different problems, often at different stages in the development lifecycle.

Systematic testing, in particular functional development time testing, has become widely popular with the advent of agile development methodologies such as extreme programming. However, it often poses a non-trivial problem—deciding which of the created artifacts justifies creation of a dedicated test. Test design is by no means easy because any functional test must be reproducible and must achieve as much coverage as possible. The danger of "testing the obvious" is real, and even large test sets have limited value if they break the first time the components are called with unexpected parameters. In addition, building tests is development work in its own right and might require building dedicated software components, for example a simulation of a backend or initialization scripts for databases. Still, tests must be as simple as possible to avoid the need to create a "test for the test."

The nature of SOAs can facilitate finding the most important functional test cases. Mission-critical enterprise applications might be rendered useless if one of the service components stops functioning properly after a new release. For this reason, the service component itself is the prime candidate for functional, integration, and load testing. This does not mean that end-to-end testing or testing of single libraries will no longer be required. It merely dedicates a large portion of the testing effort to testing services.

Consider the example in Figure 13-14, which shows a customer retention service that is composed from multiple services. Two of these services are shown in the figure: a printing service and a service that provides basic customer data. The customer retention service has multiple clients, among them a browser-based call center application that supports telephone marketing to the existing customer base and a number of batch programs that are used to create mailings to the customers. The system is based on various operating systems and programming languages.

As the new customer retention service and its client are created, testing is traditionally confined to ad-hoc testing. Call center agents would be testing the HTML frontend for the call center, while printouts from the print service would be manually checked.

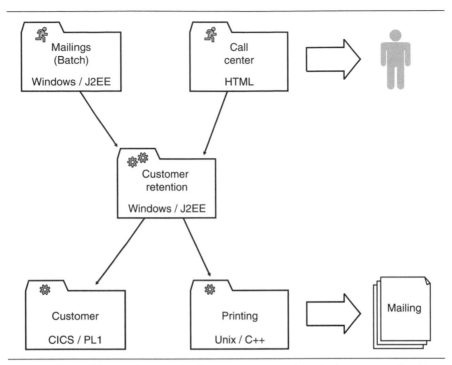

FIGURE 13-14   The customer retention program consists of a customer retention service that is written in J2EE and deployed on a Windows platform. It relies on an existing mainframe-based customer service and a printing service based on a Unix platform. Call center clients connect using a Web application, and a number of Windows-based batch programs are used to create mass mailings.

To perform testing in a more meaningful manner, the test should be automated using a test driver. This is illustrated in Figure 13-15. In this case, the backend services are not real services but are simulations that behave in the way that the real time services would. This will enable us to test and debug the newly created business logic in the customer retention service without using valuable mainframe computing time or printing hundreds of sheets of paper. The driver tests the functioning of the customer retention service by comparing results to expectations. It also checks the results that are created in the printing service simulation.

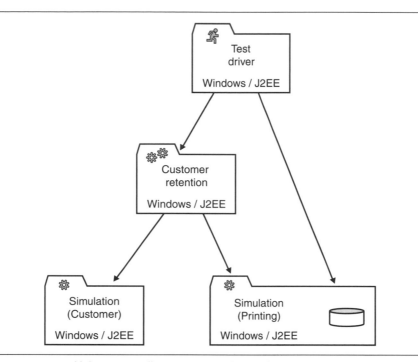

FIGURE 13-15   Using a test client to test methods of the customer retention service. In this scenario, the service relies on a simulation on its dependent services.

In a second scenario shown in Figure 13-16, the HTML user interface is tested using a test robot. To start the test, the test robot initializes a mainframe customer service. The robot then performs various actions at the user interface, checking if the result is in accordance with expectations. Finally, it checks the database of the printing service to determine if the correct number and type of printouts have been created during the simulated call center interaction. Apart from the actual printing, this example provides almost a full end-to-end test scenario, where all the components are properly integrated.

To create a satisfactory test suite, you will need many more tests than those illustrated here. In particular, test scenarios will include some load testing. Of course, the customer retention service and the print service will usually have their own tests in place. In addition, each test will include numerous calls with different parameter sets that simulate boundary conditions as well as invalid input.

The previous examples make clear that any test must be repeatable. For a functional test of a service, this means in particular that it must be repeatable with a new version of the service using the old parameter set for input and expected output. This ensures that a new software component is essentially "backward-compatible" with the older component. Such a test is referred to as regression test. Regression tests are mostly functional tests, but there might also be the need to create regression tests that are load tests—ensuring that the performance of a new software version still delivers appropriate response times and throughput.

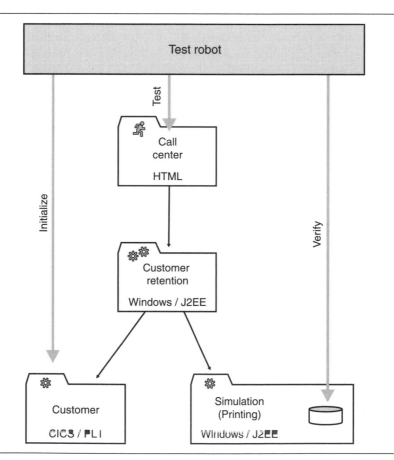

FIGURE 13-16   In this scenario, the behavior of the graphical user interface is tested against the actual mainframe-based customer service. The printing service is still simulated in this test.

When testing services, regression tests should cover all reusable services. Here, it will usually be necessary to test a number of calls in sequence to ensure proper operation. Regression tests should particularly be created on basic services so that basic services can be updated and tested on their own. Regression tests on services will often require actual backend operation—not only for load testing but also for functional testing. This is because, due to their very nature, a lot of services will be technology gateways or adapters whose main purpose—and therefore the main objective in testing them—lies in accessing various backend systems.

Tests will usually be conducted using a general test driver—an environment that is capable of running tests and reporting the test results (see Figure 13-17). Tests are usually defined using scripts or mainstream programming languages. Test drivers often also provide mechanisms to trigger initialization of resources upon which the tests rely—for example, initializing a database in a certain state or providing a specific file for input. Generic test drivers are available for both load and unit testing. Popular load testing tools include Mercury Interactive LoadRunner, the Grinder, and Jmeter. To some extent, they can also be used as end-to-end tools, particularly when testing Web applications. End-to-end testing is traditionally the domain of test robots such as Rational Robot. Functional test tools include, for example, Junit and Nunit. However, in the unlikely event that none of the available tools meets the particular needs of the tester, most tools on the market can be easily extended and customized.

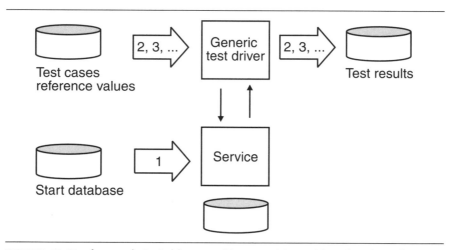

FIGURE 13-17   A generic test driver used in an end-to-end functional test for a service. The database is initialized into a defined state, and a sequence of tests is run against the service using the generic test driver. Results of the tests are logged and can later be analyzed.

Create a Regression Test Environment for Most Services

Every basic service and most other services should be complemented by a full regression test environment. Regression testing will create confidence for users and maintainers of the service.

Note that test definition should be maintained with the actual application and service source code in configuration management as it is a vital element of the final delivery. In fact, one might argue that the tests actually enable confident reuse of the service. Functional tests should be an integral part of any build process. In fact, some configuration management (e.g., Continuus) and various build tools (e.g., Jakarta Ant) provide out-of-the-box support for test generation and test result reporting.

13.5 Conclusion

In this chapter, we presented best practices for SOA projects. Most importantly, these practices do not represent or require a new project management methodology. SOA-driven project management means adopting a set of useful, SOA-specific practices that are complementary to an established methodology.

SOA project management starts in the first minute of a new project. A first draft of the high-level service design is a major deliverable from the project definition phase. At the core of SOA-driven project management, we find SOA artifacts—in particular, service contracts and services, which we leverage as project control elements. Most important, SOA-driven project management enables the efficient decomposition of complex, potentially heterogeneous distributed systems into manageable sub-systems and the disentanglement of the dependencies between them. If used properly on the project management level, *service iterations* are the right tool for managing the *heartbeat* of the project.

Furthermore, SOAs enable enterprises to put an efficient configuration management in place. Nevertheless, configuration management is regarded as a highly complex task, reflecting today's heterogeneous enterprise reality.

Finally, we described service-driven regression testing as another key factor in SOA success. The particular service design enables efficient testing of enterprise applications, that is, the encapsulation of services, their distinguished business meanings, and the clearly defined, coarse-grained interfaces.

References

Groves, Leslie R. *Now It Can Be Told: The Story of the Manhattan Project*. Da Capo Press, 1983. [Gro83]

URLs

http://www.agilemanifesto.org

PART III

REAL-WORLD EXPERIENCE

The third part of this book describes four cases of successful SOA introductions on the enterprise level, looking at them from the business and the technical perspective. The case studies include Deutsche Post, Credit Suisse, Winterthur Insurance, and Halifax Bank of Scotland.

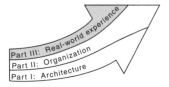

14

Deutsche Post AG
Case Study

This chapter describes the introduction of a Service-Oriented Architecture at Deutsche Post. Deutsche Post belongs to Deutsche Post World Net, a multinational group with more than 275,000 employees, comprising also the brands DHL and Postbank. The SOA described in this chapter was set up for the MAIL Corporate division at Deutsche Post, a partner to three million business customers, providing services to 39 million households through 81,000 delivery staff, 13,000 retail outlets, 3,500 delivery bases and 140,000 letterboxes. Deutsche Post is Europe's leading letter mail service provider and the number one direct marketing company in the German market. Currently, the SOA is also rolled out at DHL, which counts 50 percent of the "Forbes 500" companies that have logistics requirements among its customer base. DHL has a global presence in 150 countries, a total of 430 terminals/warehouses and a total of 45,000 employees.

Deutsche Post's decision to introduce a Service-Oriented Architecture was based on several considerations. Deutsche Post's IT landscape grew significantly for the last years. Such a huge, distributed and complex infrastructure is not easy to maintain especially concerning the core business processes. In addition, the development of new applications became difficult. Numerous applications were so-called island solutions instead of holistic, business-driven solutions. Moreover, applications did not have clear functional boundaries, which led to considerable functional redundancy between applications and made modifications complex and resource intensive.

Finally, the maintenance of the IT architecture used up a considerable amount of the overall IT budget and offered hardly any access to core information about revenues, cost, and competitor information, which is crucial in today's dynamic business environment. This information was scattered over many components of the IT landscape and had to be consolidated via complex processes. The need for a consistent and centralized data storage became apparent.

Given this situation, Deutsche Post decided to introduce a business-driven SOA.[1] The initial concept of this SOA was produced in 1999, and the actual implementation started in 2000. In addition to business services, a service infrastructure, the Service Backbone (SBB), was also realized. This backbone was launched in December 2001 and has since then been successfully used as the technical basis for Deutsche Post's SOA.

As we have indicated in Chapter 12, a great deal of an SOA's success depends on properly defined processes and comprehensive documentation. Deutsche Post therefore provided a set of three articles defining the foundation of their SOA (see [HBa04], [HBr03], [HS03]). This case study makes extensive use of this worthwhile documentation.

This chapter describes in some detail how the SOA has been implemented at Deutsche Post. In Section 14.1, the general scope of Deutsche Post's architecture is presented, both from a business and technical perspective. Section 14.2 then discusses the organizational structures and processes used to implement the SOA. The technological perspective is presented in detail in Section 14.3. Finally, Section 14.4 describes the lessons learned, the benefits achieved by Deutsche Post, and future perspectives.

14.1 Project Scope

Deutsche Post sees its SOA as a business-oriented IT strategy. The main objective is to standardize access to functionality and to ensure reusability. The SBB (Service Backbone)—the major outcome of the infrastructure development—is described in detail here.

When starting to restructure its IT landscape, Deutsche Post followed the approach summarized in Figure 14-1.

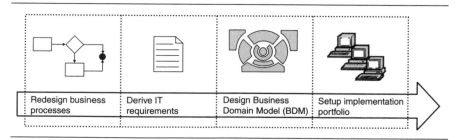

FIGURE 14-1   Deutsche Post's use of a Business Domain Model to get from business processes to IT applications.

---

[1] The SOA is called Business Domain Model (BDM) at Deutsche Post.

The first step was the creation of a business requirement evaluation, which led to the redesign of many business processes according to the analyzed input-output relations. The Business Domain Model (BDM) that was designed in further process steps is comprised of modular components. Closely related functionalities and data are bundled in domains.[2]

14.1.1 BUSINESS IMPACT

One of the most important benefits of Deutsche Post's BDM is the fact that it enables a view of IT applications from the business perspective by providing appropriate representation of business-oriented components, their interfaces, and interconnections.

Deutsche Post utilizes an insightful metaphor to promote its SOA internally (see [HBa04]). Deutsche Post compares the concept of its SOA to a map of a city. BDM's high-level components are called domains. They describe reasonably separated components, which contain the main business logic. Deutsche Post compares these domains to different districts of a city. Every district (such as airport, residential area, industry parks, etc.) has a clearly defined purpose. The urban infrastructure (such as streets, and electricity and water supply) connects the different districts to each other and is compared to Deutsche Post's Service Backbone, which provides access to the business logic encapsulated by the domains.

Figure 14-2 shows the Business Domain Model used at Deutsche Post and its use of the domain concept. As the main components of this construct, domains contain modularly defined functionality and thus enable the support of business processes and the underlying data.

According to Deutsche Post's motivation paper [HBa04], the main characteristics of domains are as follows:

- Domains encapsulate their functionality and data.
- Functionality is implemented without redundancy, and information is consistent.
- Functionality and data can be used everywhere within the domain, and they can be combined to support new business processes.
- New projects can build upon existing assets, and investments are secured.

---

[2] A brief remark regarding terminology: The domains at Deutsche Post correspond to what is called "services" in this book, they provide a cluster of functionality. The service implementations at Deutsche Post correspond to what is called "interface" in this book.

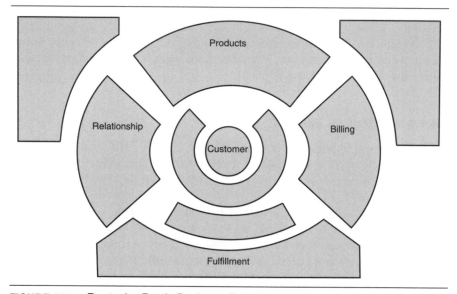

FIGURE 14-2   Deutsche Post's Business Domain Model with domains.

One of the first services to be realized was *Customer Management*,[3] that is, management of core customer data. This service was chosen because it is widely used within Deutsche Post. It offers about a dozen operations, including operations for inserting, searching for, or deleting customer data. Currently, there are around ten service consumers of the customer-management service with a resulting workload of approximately 0.5 million calls per month.

Another widely used and visible service is *Complaint Management*.[4] Although only one service consumer uses the implemented service, this service consumer is connected to more than 1,000 clients.

Altogether, the business services implemented so far are used by a double-digit number of applications, issuing approximately 2 million service calls per month. In addition to services providing business functionality, the SOA at present also contains about a dozen technical services with altogether 80 service operations.

In general, the focus of the implemented business services is on intra-corporate use. Deutsche Post's SOA was developed for Division Mail, which is very business- and IT-oriented and open for innovation. A dedicated IT business unit was set up at Division Mail that is, among other things, responsible for the implementation of both the business services and the underlying infrastructure (the Service Backbone).

---

[3] A service belonging to the domain *Customer*.
[4] A service belonging to the domain *Relationship*.

In addition to the intra-corporate usage of the SOA, there are also some pilot projects exploring the external use of the implemented services. These pilot projects reuse the services' interfaces and enhance them by adding an extra layer based on WSDL (Web Services Description Language), thereby turning them into full-fledged Web services.[5]

Moreover, based on the success of Deutsche Post's SOA at Division Mail, a rollout for DHL (another major brand of Deutsche Post) is currently in preparation. The idea is to reuse the methodology developed at Division Mail and the technical infrastructure (i.e., the Service Backbone). However, services will be developed by DHL themselves.

14.1.2 TECHNOLOGY IMPACT

Deutsche Post's SOA has a strong technical focus on Java applications. Although there is an adapter to C++ and JDBC, the support of heterogeneous environments is not in Deutsche Post's main focus.

At Deutsche Post, the integration infrastructure needed for an SOA is realized with the Service Backbone (SBB). Its main functionality is to receive service calls from service consumers and to forward them to dedicated service providers (see Figure 14-4). The key features of the SBB are (see [HBa04]):

- Easy-to-use interface to connect technically to SBB
- Comprehensive directory for all available services
- Syntax and type validation of all documents transported by Service Backbone
- Transportation mechanisms for different interaction styles, including data compression
- Exhaustive user directory used for authentication and authorization
- Transformation engines for structural document mappings between XML schemes as well as content matching

The purpose of the SBB is purely technical. The entire business logic of the SOA is placed in domains. Existing custom-built applications and off-the-shelf packages like SAP are encapsulated according to the standards of the SBB in a way that their functionality can easily be used by SBB participants. The whole philosophy of SBB is federal because the business is federal, too. Data transformation is also handled with care: To ensure that no business logic is incorporated directly into the Service Backbone, the necessary transformation is performed by using mapping tables. The SBB only provides the basic functionality for the execution of these transformations. The contents of the tables, that is, the actual mappings, are maintained on the business level, however, in the service implementation of the domain. The respective business units enter the required infor-

---

[5] It should be noted that crossing the enterprise boundary requires more than just enabling an Internet-friendly protocol (see Chapters 6 and 7).

mation into the mapping tables and check table updates into the SBB runtime environment.[6]

14.2 Implementation

As mentioned previously, the main reason for implementing the SOA at Deutsche Post was the realization that the IT landscape existing at that point in time was too expensive and complex to maintain and extend. Interestingly, this was not due to the existence of mainframes and host applications, as is often the case in large corporations.[7] No such systems were in use at Division Mail. Complexity simply stemmed from the interfaces and the high degree of intertwining between the existing point-to-point interfaces and applications.

As this complexity led to the failure of projects at Deutsche Post, it prompted a change in the infrastructure. No real alternative to an SOA was investigated in detail, as no other option seemed sufficient. At the beginning of the SOA introduction, costs for the initial business projects and for the Service Backbone development were estimated. However, no detailed business case was compiled, as it seemed obvious that changing the infrastructure into an SOA was inevitable.

Although there was no resistance on the conceptual level against the SOA approach, some problems arose as soon as implementation started. The next section describes the processes and structures used by Deutsche Post to overcome these challenges.

14.2.1 PROCESSES AND STRUCTURES

Deutsche Post differentiates two major types of components in its SOA. There are service providers, which offer services, and service consumers, which use those services. Obviously, a piece of code can act as a service consumer with respect to some services and as a service provider with respect to other services (see Chapter 5 for the discussion of basic and intermediary services).

---

[6] Classic EAI tools usually prefer a hub-and-spoke approach for integration, which requires a part of the business logic within the integration tool. This can lead again to complex dependencies between business applications and the integration infrastructure that have been avoided by Deutsche Post.

[7] This is further evidence for the fact that the quality of a software architecture is largely independent of technology. Both brand new developments comprising Java, C++, and decentralized servers and traditional environments based on COBOL, C, and centralized mainframes can equally serve as a base for an efficient architecture.

Deutsche Post defined a clear process for achieving a service design that was accepted across the borders of a single department (see [HBa04]). When implementing a new service provider, the following steps must be executed:

- Identify all potential service consumers.
- Specify business functionality of the new service according to the requirements of all potential service consumers.
- Match business requirements to Business Domain Model and implemented services.
- According to the findings, define and start an implementation project for this new service provider.
- Create a service description, service-level agreement, and an XML Schema for publishing the service to potential service consumer.
- Connect service provider to Service Backbone by deploying the SBB interface locally.
- Register service provider in SBB user directory.

In order to connect a new service consumer to the SBB, the following two steps must be processed:

- Insert service consumer information in SBB user directory for authentication and service authorization.
- Connect service consumer to SBB by deploying the SBB interface locally.

As we mentioned earlier, when this process of service development was introduced at Deutsche Post, some problems emerged that were mostly related to division of labor and sharing of responsibilities. For example, when a project initiated the development of a service, all potential consumers of the service had to be consulted. On one hand, it was not easy to get future consumers interested, and on the other, it meant that actors "not paying" for the service development gained influence. In general, business units were concerned that they would lose control over their services.

The SOA development at Deutsche Post started with a "closed user group," which helped to keep resistance limited. The business units involved in the initial projects were in principle in favor of the SOA. But even here they had to be constantly convinced that the SOA would help them to make their own development projects more efficient and less expensive. They were also offered support by the SOA team on the technical level.

However, it became clear quickly that introducing the SOA at Deutsche Post amounted to a paradigm shift within the corporation. To successfully perform this shift, a dedicated business unit was set up. This unit comprises teams that are responsible for supporting the individual business units, making sure that each business unit has a specific team available to help them with the implementation of the SOA.

Work in the unit centered around two focal points: governance and business support. Governance was concerned with the development of strategies and guidelines and was mostly internal. Business support consisted of helping the business units involved in development projects with any SOA-related challenges they encountered. In doing so, adherence to the internally developed strategies and guidelines was also ensured.

Half of the business unit was hired externally through head hunters, contacts within the SOA community, and word of mouth. Only a few employees from Deutsche Post were included in the business unit. This was because the number of IT experts available for internal relocation at Deutsche Post was simply not sufficient. In addition, employees of this new business unit needed special skills.

The skill profile demanded, on one hand, extensive knowledge of Service-Oriented Architectures, object-oriented programming, XML technology, and open W3C standards such as Web services. This included in particular knowledge about available state-of-the-art tools, discussion topics in forums, and current trends in these areas. On the other hand, employees had to have experience regarding project management, quality assurance, requirements analysis, and the corresponding soft skills needed in team-oriented development projects.

The business unit is directly responsible to the management board of Division Mail at Deutsche Post AG and is thus on the same level as Marketing, Sales, or Production.

Another concern with the introduction of the SOA consisted of the overhead it caused during the initial development of services. Deutsche Post used two means to make sure that reusability was taken into account during the design process. First, potential service consumers were involved in the design process. Second, the IT strategy unit reviewed the service designs and insisted on a level of abstraction that would make sure that the services would be reusable.

Interestingly, the experience gained regarding the SOA overhead was that the *additional costs were rather limited*. In particular, they were mostly caused by increased communication requirements and not related to technological issues. Nevertheless, it is important to take into account the communication overhead when planning project budgets. One way that Deutsche Post dealt with it was allowing the central business unit responsible for the SOA introduction to subsidize the overhead resulting at the business units. Of course, to make this possible, a suitable budget has to be foreseen for these subsidies.

14.2.2 SERVICE REGISTRY

Deutsche Post uses a registry to store information about available services. It basically contains:

- Syntax of the service interface
- Meta information concerning security, binding, and authorization
- Versioning information

Versioning turned out to be a particularly important aspect of service development at Deutsche Post. Because services were developed incrementally, it often happened that new versions had to be released to address new requirements. Because it was not feasible to migrate all service consumers immediately to new service versions, different service versions were provided in parallel. However, obsolete versions were only supported for a transitional period to avoid uncontrolled growth of service variants.

14.2.3   PROJECT MANAGEMENT

For Deutsche Post, the SOA's main benefit from the project management point of view consists of the reduction of interface complexity and the decentralization of software development. Because individual service implementation projects can be carried out flexibly and in a decentralized fashion, the risks inherent in large projects are substantially reduced. Moreover, the application landscape can be developed step by step, while the strategic flexibility is maintained in the long term.

Although its general approach to project management did not change drastically, Deutsche Post did have to make some adjustments and extensions. The most obvious innovations concerned the establishment of a dedicated IT strategy unit (see Figure 14-3) and the process for service design as depicted in Section 12.1.1. As a consequence, development became slightly more complex, and new roles and activities had to be included because of the reusability aspect. However, it should be noted that the effort for developing the functionality itself was not affected. An overall service coordination had to be established, which had two main purposes. First, guidelines had to be developed including standards for service interface design. Second, adherence to these guidelines had to be checked constantly during the development process.

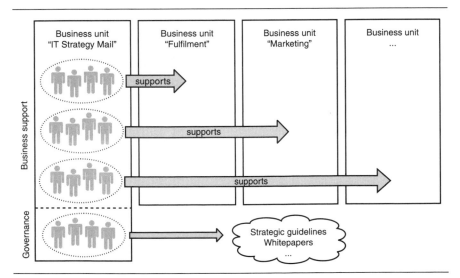

FIGURE 14-3   The business unit "IT Strategy Mail" provides distinct teams supporting the individual business units.

14.3 Technology

The service concept of Deutsche Post's SBB is similar to the Web service concept. Web technologies such as SOAP and HTTP are combined with reliable messaging through an underlying MOM-based on JMS (Java Messaging Service). Furthermore, the SBB supports important features such as version management, safety, and dynamic binding and thus offers enriched functionality compared to standard Web services. For the future, Deutsche Post plans to publish SBB services as Web services based on WS-I Basic Profile 1.0.[8]

14.3.1 ARCHITECTURE

The SBB is built of three key components, which we will describe in detail (see [HS03]):

- Local SBB interface
- Central infrastructure components
- Technical service participants

Local SBB interfaces enabling the connection are implemented in each service participant. There are two kinds of local SBB interfaces: Service providers use a Service Programming Interface (SPI), whereas service consumers are connected by an Application Programming Interface (API). When a consumer calls a service, it uses the API, sending a message that contains the input parameters. This message (XML) is sent to the provider's SPI by SBB, and the requested operation is started.

For the processing of a service call, two central infrastructure components are involved—the Service Registry (currently based on LDAP, UDDI in development) and the message queue (based on JMS). To ensure high availability, Deutsche Post replicates and clusters these infrastructure components. Figure 14-4 shows a service call using SBB functionality.

This call information mainly consists of an XML document containing attributes of the business objects that are to be created, manipulated, or modified. Additional parameters can be used to control synchronous or asynchronous behavior or other aspects, such as the number of results to be returned when calling a search service.

The Service Registry is the central source for all information needed for the communication between service participants. It should be noted that all interfaces always access the Service Backbone, regardless of their interaction style, which can be synchronous, asynchronous, publish/subscribe, or request/reply. Which

---

[8] WS-I Basic Profile 1.0 is a profile developed by WS-I (Web Services Interoperability) to ensure interoperability between Web services platforms from different vendors (see http://www.wsi.org).

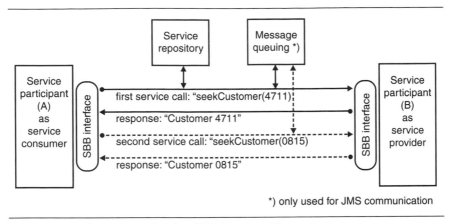

*) only used for JMS communication

FIGURE 14-4 A service call using SBB functionality.

interaction type is used depends on the business requirements. When calling the interface, the interaction type is passed through a parameter.

The call to the Service Backbone is realized as a Java call, where the main argument containing the business object information is represented as an XML document. The structure of the XML documents is described through service-specific XML Schemas. Internally, SOAP is used on top of Java, and there are also wrappers and adapters for C++ and non-XML arguments.[9] Actually, before the Service Backbone initiative started, the IT Strategy of Deutsche Post was based on C++. The need to easily integrate the associated software assets using the aforementioned wrappers and adapters is a major requirement of the new SOA.

The Service Backbone itself is built in a loosely coupled fashion, relies on standards, and avoids proprietary features. Although for example MQ Series is used for message handling, no proprietary features are used. Instead, connection to MQ Series is realized by using the JMS interface. A similar approach is used with other components in order to ensure that products can be easily interchanged and no vendor-dependency is created by using non-standard features.

Deutsche Post currently uses various *technical service participants*— including *Transformation, Service Registry Administration, Data Integration,* and *Single Sign On. Privilege Management* and *Service Registry* are candidates planned for further releases.

14.3.2 REPOSITORY, SERVICE INTERFACES, AND CONTRACTS

In order to maximize reusability, Deutsche Post designed their service operations in a rather coarse-grained fashion. When retrieving customer data, for example, almost 100 attributes are returned by the service, which then can be filtered on

---

[9] For the Java wrappers of C++-Code the product Junc++ion from codemesh is used, which supports various C++ dialects, including GNU and .NET.

the client side. The alternative would have been to perform filtering within the service, which would have restricted reusability.

Exceptions to this general approach are only made in the context of critical performance requirements. Although it is important to insist on generic and reusable interfaces, it is also necessary to remain flexible and sometimes acknowledge the need for a custom-built interface. However, these exceptions have been minimized as far as possible and were only authorized if there were very convincing arguments for them.

The registry contains information about all services currently available at Deutsche Post's Division Mail. For each service, an XML Schema describing the XML document it expects as an argument is specified in the registry. In addition, information regarding binding and IP addresses is specified, as well as some meta information, concerning service-level agreements for example.

Currently, the registry implementation is based on LDAP. Deutsche Post is planning to use UDDI as the basis for its registry in the future. This is mainly motivated by the desire to keep up with development in Web services.

14.3.3 CHOREOGRAPHY, SECURITY, AND MANAGEMENT

There is currently no support for distributed transactions or workflow management within Deutsche Post's Service Backbone. These topics are seen as important challenges both from the business and technical perspectives. However, currently the process logic is implicitly contained in the service implementation and is not explicitly modeled in a declarative process format. The Service Backbone is thus only responsible for the transport of data between the service consumer and the service provider.

Although the Service Backbone is logically a centralized component, its physical realization is highly distributed. This is to ensure loose coupling and to avoid bottlenecks and single points of failure created by centralized solutions. Approximately 90% of its functionality runs locally based on libraries, which are installed throughout the network. As we have already mentioned previously, there are only two centralized components, the directory and the queue.

As a consequence, there is no central control of all the interaction between service consumers and providers on all machines in the network. Monitoring is thus currently restricted to local monitoring. In the future, this will have to be enhanced in order to provide unified information about the overall system behavior. However, it is not yet clear how to achieve this without violating the principle of loose coupling.

Finally, security is realized through modeling access rights based on users, groups, and roles. Access rights are checked on the general service and operation level. Because use is so far restricted to intra-corporate applications within the demilitarized zone, no encryption is performed. This would be necessary for supporting external usage.

14.4   Lessons Learned, Benefits, and Perspectives

After more than two years of successfully running its SOA and the associated service infrastructure SBB, Deutsche Post has gained much useful experience, which is summarized in the following practical advices [HBa04]:

- If you want to reduce IT complexity through integration, start with the business (logical) view and use an architectural approach.
- Focus on services (multiple use of data and functionality), not on data interchange (point-to-point communication).
- Don't neglect the integration infrastructure layer—this is much more than just "data transport."
- The technical integration infrastructure is characterized by long-term stability, so stay vendor-independent and stick to open standards.
- The success of a whole integration project mainly depends on the acceptance of all business-driven service participants. So, don't let the IT professionals drive the effort alone!

Deutsche Post managed to reduce time to market significantly. The realization of new services only takes a few days due to the integrated infrastructure. Using the SBB helps keep implementation projects manageable and lean. These projects can focus on service implementations and do not have to worry about data connectivity. Moreover, the SBB can be maintained and updated without having to modify the services themselves.

As we mentioned, there were also some challenges to overcome when introducing the SOA. In particular, the effort initially needed to convince service providers to take reusability into account in their development process was higher than expected. A mixture of persuasion, subsidies, and coercion was necessary to achieve the desired compliance with the SOA standards.

A particularly visible success story was the adoption of the service "*Customer Management*" in the call center application, which today provides additional functionality such as registered mail. Before this adoption, all call center contacts were manually recorded by the agents, which led to typos and data duplication. Now call center agents have direct access to customer data by simply typing in the customer identification number.

The SOA and the Service Backbone have proved to be successful at Deutsche Post and are constantly extended by involving current and potential users in the overall process.

According to [HBr03], the following extensions are planned for the next major release (SBB Release 3.0) of the Service Backbone:

- Instrumentation and service management
- Service call routing with intermediaries
- "Users and Rights" as a service participant
- Pluggable core architecture

▪ Support of "Process Integration" (phase 1) as a service participant

After the successful introduction of the SOA at Division Mail, a rollout at DHL is now under way. In doing so, Deutsche Post will reuse the basic methodology and the Service Backbone developed already. A special team will be set up at DHL that will be responsible for integration and consolidation. This team will be supported by the IT strategy team at Division Mail. The decision to extend the SOA to DHL is also a sign of the positive perception of the SOA at the level of Deutsche Post's top management.

References

Herr, Michael and Uwe Bath. *SBB Motivation Paper: The business-oriented background of Service Backbone*. http://www.servicebackbone.org/, January 2004. [HBa04]

Herr, Michael and Stefan Brombach. *SBB Management Paper: Benefits and application range*. http://www.servicebackbone.org/. September 2003. [HBr03]

Herr, Michael and Ursula Sannemann. *SBB Technical Paper: The Architecture of Service Backbone*. http://www.servicebackbone.org/. October 2003. [HS03]

Schulze, Jan. *Geschäftsprozesse bestimmen die Architektur: EAI senkt IT-Risiko der Post*, Computerwoche No. 28 of July 12, 2002, http://www.computerwoche.de. [Sc02]

Links

http://www.computerwoche.de

http://www.servicebackbone.org

http://www.wsi.org

15

Winterthur Case Study

In this chapter, we will describe the Service-Oriented Architecture implemented by the Winterthur Group, a leading Swiss insurance company with its head office in Winterthur. As an international company, the Group provides a broad range of property and liability insurance products in addition to insurance solutions in life and pensions that are tailored to the individual needs of private and corporate clients. The Winterthur Group has approximately 20,000 employees worldwide, achieved a premium volume of 33.5 billion Swiss francs in 2003, and reported assets under management of 138.7 billion Swiss francs as of December 31, 2003.

In 1998, Winterthur's Market Unit Switzerland developed a concept for an Application Service Platform. Since then, this application and integration platform called "e-Platform" has been implemented and used as the technological basis for the realization of a Service-Oriented Architecture. Its main purpose is to provide a common set of standards, guidelines, processes, frameworks, and integrated products in the form of a single package suite to access functionality available on the mainframe through standardized service interfaces. This functionality is then used to provide customer data access, claims notifications, financial reports, life insurance quotations, analysis and management of company risks, and information systems for insurance brokers.

The main focus of Winterthur's SOA is to provide reusable coarse-grained and technology-independent services for the application frontends in order to enable the access of backend functionality on the mainframe. This matches the purpose of an SOA, which is to decouple the existing system components by applying the principles of modularity and encapsulation.

The main business driver for the SOA introduction was Winterthur's plan to offer their customers, partners, and employees new channels, in particular access using the Internet/Intranet, which required a tighter integration of existing functionality. The monolithic mainframe system provided a major obstacle to those plans, and therefore they decided to use an SOA to start it. They hoped that the SOA, which was technologically based on CORBA, would significantly reduce the overall complexity of the system and help to lower soaring maintenance costs. It was the desire to reuse as much of the implemented services as possible.

In the meantime, the platform has become a suite of integrated software infrastructure technologies, consisting of an integration framework, a portal framework, a security framework, and enterprise application servers. Today, it is not only used in Switzerland but also abroad in other Market Units of Winterthur.

The case study presented in this chapter will show in some detail how the SOA has been implemented at Winterthur, both at the organizational and technical levels. Section 15.1 describes the general scope of Winterthur's architecture. Section 15.2 discusses the organizational structures and processes used to implement the SOA. A more technological perspective is presented in Section 15.3, and finally, Section 15.4 describes the lessons learned, benefits achieved, and future enhancements for the company.

15.1 Project Scope

The scope of Winterthur's SOA introduction is mainly defined by the requirements of innovative business-driven projects and the need to reuse existing mainframe applications.

15.1.1 BUSINESS IMPACT

The first pilot project to be implemented within the SOA was wincoLink, an interactive customer service of Winterthur Leben, the life insurance branch of Winterthur. It provided corporate customers with online access to all contracts and contained direct information about, for example, vested benefits. It also supported changes of contract information, such as the inclusion of new employees in a corporate contract or a change to address data.

wincoLink was chosen as the pilot project because it not only was restricted to the passive browsing of static content but also involved user interaction. This provided Winterthur with the prestigious benefit of offering the first interactive life insurance Internet application. In addition, wincoLink promised significant cost-saving potential because it reduced Winterthur's customer support by enabling customers to access and change contract information directly, avoiding the need to go through Winterthur staff. In addition, wincoLink increased customer satisfaction because the online content available for inspection was always up-to-date.

Finally, wincoLink offered the advantage of a restricted user group, namely corporate customers, which could be enlarged step by step. It was thus possible to increase the support organization and the necessary processes incrementally, while extending the user group in a parallel manner. In fact, the wincoLink project turned out to be ideal for collecting experiences associated with the SOA without any major risks.

15.1.2 TECHNOLOGY IMPACT

The focus of Winterthur's SOA is on the integration of existing host applications. One of the major incentives for the new architectural approach was the soaring cost for maintaining monolithic applications on the mainframe computer. In addition, Winterthur wanted to add new "sales" management channels to their IT infrastructure, in particular through the Internet and Intranet in order to make their applications and solutions widely available.

In Winterthur's SOA, a service is defined as a set of operations granting access to a simplified business context or to enterprise information in the form of core business entities. Winterthur distinguishes three types of services (the terminology used for this distinction is Winterthur's):

Domain-specific business services.[1] These services belong to a defined domain, using the domain-specific model to manage enterprise information. The focus is on reusing functionality related to core business entities. These services are implemented within the domain service layer that in return provides core business functions grouped by domains such as partner, product, contract, or claims. This function is subsequently reused across several applications, protecting the enterprise data by ensuring that business rules are correctly applied.

Services implementing business processes.[2] These services orchestrate domain specific processes from different domains in order to provide functionalities and composite information for a single business activity. Business activities are the defined atomic steps within a business process. The focus is on providing a functional, simplified business process. Reuse, however, is not the main issue at this layer. Instead, these services are implemented within the application layer and are responsible for providing the business-process context to the domain service layer. In other words, this layer acts as a facade to combine and extend services to implement the business functionality described by use cases. This layer is accessed by the presentation layer that enables the user to interact with the system.

Technical services. Technical services provide functionalities related to security or system management, including configuration, user administration, printing, and code services. These are based at different technical layers and are not described further in this case study.

In addition to these services, there are also application frontends, which, according to Winterthur's terminology, belong to the presentation layer:

Presentation layer. This layer contains GUI application, which are mostly HTML based (i.e., accessible using standard web browsers).

---

[1] According to the terminology used in this book, these would be basic services.
[2] According to the terminology used in this book, these would be intermediary services, mostly facades.

Figure 15-1 shows the 3-tier architecture used by Winterthur (a more detailed architecture will be presented later in Section 15.3). This logical layering of the architecture, which is more or less standard for current Enterprise Systems, distinguishes between a presentation layer, an application layer, and the domain and data layers and is not to be confused with physical deployment. These layers are distributed according to non-functional requirements using one of the patterns illustrated in Figure 15-2.

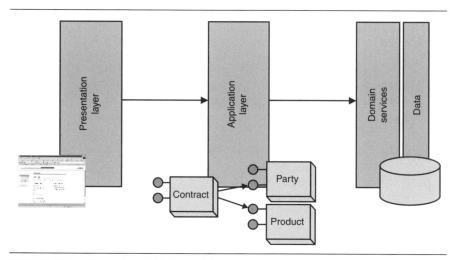

FIGURE 15-1   Winterthur's N-tier architecture.

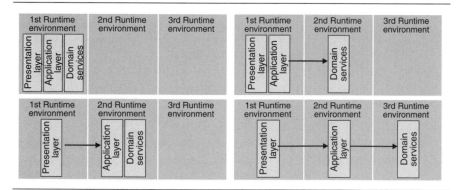

FIGURE 15-2   Example patterns for layer distribution.

The initial implementation of the SOA and e-Platform focused mainly on offering reusable domain services on the mainframe computer. Its main purpose was to allow the applications to be implemented in the application layer and to use standardized interfaces to access data and functionality on the host.

As we explain in more detail later on, CORBA was used to implement the domain services. Extensions of the e-Platform that include the necessary standards, processes, tools, and guidelines toward EJB, asynchronous messages and Web services are currently being defined.

Figure 15-3 shows the services landscape of Winterthur with six top-level domains and their respective sub-domains. Winterthur uses these domains to structure their services and define degrees of decoupling. Whereas services within a sub-domain are not necessarily completely decoupled, there are no dependencies between services from different domains—that is, decoupling is complete across domain boundaries.

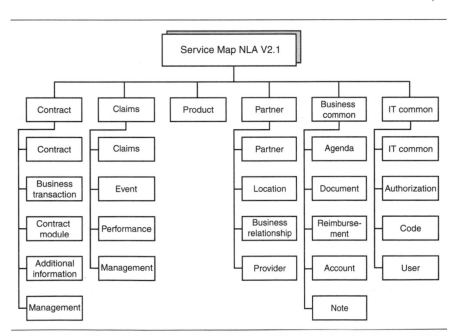

FIGURE 15-3   Winterthur's Non Life Applications (NLA) services landscape 2003.

One reason for this "mixed" approach is that decoupling is both costly and risky at times. It is therefore reasonable to place an initial limit on the degree of decoupling and choose a rather coarse-grained structure, as illustrated by the top-level domains in Figure 15-3. These top-level domains constitute the main application groups offered by Winterthur and provide a clear intermediate structure for which service contracts and application frontends can be designed.

According to the SOA philosophy underlying Winterthur's e-Platform, services provide given functionality as coarse-grained operations. To capture this functionality, technology-independent service contracts are established. These contracts are published in a repository and contain interface definitions and descriptions of data elements used. From the SOA's point of view, services are completely defined by these contracts—that is, a service constitutes a black box with respect to all internal aspects of the service implementation and is not visible in the contract.

This black box approach allows a rather effective decoupling of clients and servers in addition to the transparent location of service implementations.

Currently, 66 services are in production, another 21 are under development, 26 are in the test phase, and 3 additional services are planned for the near future. Every service contains one to three operations.

15.2   Implementation

This section deals with the processes and structures that Winterthur established to guarantee the success of the SOA, the repositories constructed to make information on services available, and the project management techniques employed.

Selling SOA within the Winterthur was difficult, especially explaining its benefits and its cost. It took also a relatively long time to make its specific concepts understood and to develop an understanding of the systems' implications and the necessary process adjustments.

Two reasons led to the initial support for the SOA. First, the problems resulting from the monolithic structure of the mainframe applications were blatantly obvious, in particular regarding maintenance costs and lack of flexibility. Second, architects, and analysts advertised for the SOA at all major IT events.

In particular, the local CIO strongly supported the SOA. Building on the previously available e-Platform infrastructure, a project team accomplished the necessary standards, guidelines, training modules, processes, and organization to define and implement the SOA. The project team was staffed with a resort architect, an e-Platform architect, e-Platform engineers, members of the software development support group and data management, host application developers, and an external consultant.

15.2.1   PROCESSES AND STRUCTURES

Figure 15-4 shows the development process based on the Rational Unified Process proposed by the e-Platform. It distinguishes between a business view and a technological view on one hand and the three standard development disciplines (Requirements, Analysis & Design, and Implementation) on the other.

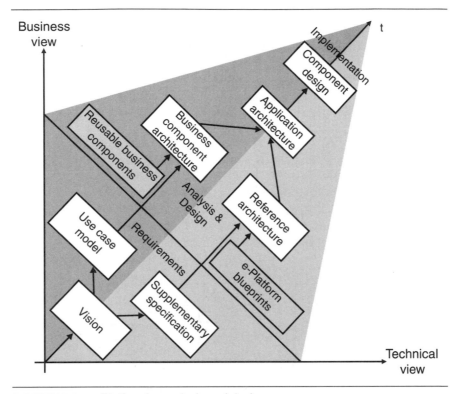

FIGURE 15-4   e-Platform's analysis and design process.

The business view focuses on functional requirements and develops use case models and a component landscape. In doing so, it explicitly aims at designing *reusable* business components that provide their functions through services. The technological view deals with the non-functional requirements and concentrates on the reference architecture based on e-Platform blueprints. The application architecture is formed by the integration of the business view and the technological view.

Figure 15-5 shows the key aspects of Winterthur's design process in more detail. In order to capture the requirements, use case models, user interfaces, and conceptual business models are developed. These roughly corresponded to the three tiers of the architecture—the presentation layer, the application layer, and the domain service layer. The models are used as a basis for the realization of the use case and the service design, and they consider both static and dynamic aspects of the system. Whereas the static service design focuses on the service interfaces and data elements, the dynamic service design addressed workflow issues, that is, how service operations are to be combined in order to obtain the business activity-oriented services identified in the design of the use-case realization.

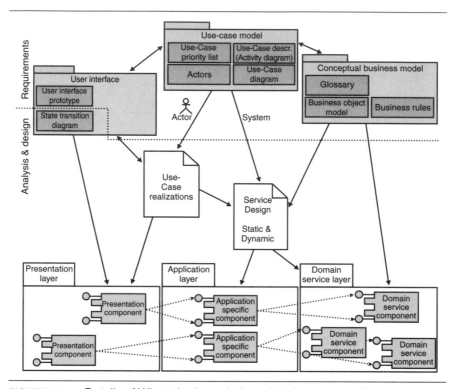

FIGURE 15-5   Details of Winterthur's analysis and design process (focused on the business view).

In order to ensure that the general design process is actually applied to specific services, a dedicated team called Application Services was established within the Winterthur Market Unit Switzerland. One of its tasks is to advise the application project teams on how to leverage the Service-Oriented Architecture in the best possible way. To do so, members of the group support the business developers when new services were designed. The group also offers training and instruction courses on its Service-Oriented Architecture, service-oriented design principles, and repository use. It is also responsible for QA on service definition.

15.2.2   SERVICE REPOSITORY

As shown in Figure 15-6, the repository contains information about available services. Note that this information is provided at the contract level—it forms an abstraction of technical details concerning implementation. The repository acts as a link between the more conceptual levels of the business context and the more technological levels covering the actual implementation.

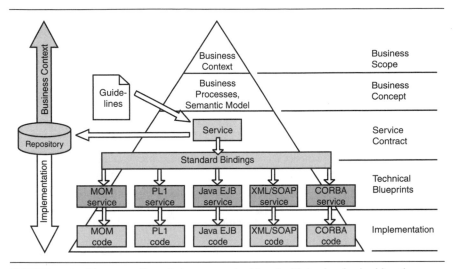

FIGURE 15-6   The repository links conceptual level with technological levels.

The main purpose of this abstraction and layering is to guarantee independence from a particular technological solution, which in turn significantly increases flexibility. Because a service contract does not depend on whether the service is implemented using MOM, PL/1, EJB, SOAP, or CORBA, it is possible to exchange service implementations with minor modifications for client applications using the services. Such an exchange is concerned only with the implementation and deployment on a different blueprint, whereas at the contract layer there is no visible change. The major change concerns the corresponding technology binding—that is, the code that maps the service interface specified in the contract to a particular technology.

The repository also contains metadata describing the implemented services, which are useful for application designers and developers. This includes information such as service ID, service name, service status, domain, owner, and short descriptions. The service contract, also stored in the repository, additionally describes special cases, errors, quality of service, versioning, etc. We provide a more detailed description of Winterthur's service contracts and the implementation of the service repository in Section 15.3.

15.2.3 PROJECT MANAGEMENT

The Application Service Team, described beforehand, is responsible to make sure that SOA is applied correctly. The team keeps the focus on reusability and captures and categorizes, together with the data management team and the service owner, the data used in the different applications.

Specific requirements with respect to project management arise from the fact that services have to be designed so that they are as reusable as possible. In particular, the analysis phase in which the basic business requirements are compiled becomes more complex. Instead of simply involving the business experts for the new application, experts from potential future applications have to be included in the design process. The Application Service Team and the service owners therefore have to make sure that future requirements are taken into consideration during the analysis phase in order to guarantee reusability of the developed services.

The Application Services and the Data Management Team responsible for the analysis and design of new services consist of seven employees. Their main task is to establish the service contract, which serves as a basis for the IDL specification of the service interface, and to implement the IDL and the interface module. Members of application development teams then build the actual implementation of the services.

In general, a mixture of a top-down and bottom-up approach is used in Winterthur's projects. On one hand, services are implemented when they are needed by applications. On the other hand, services are implemented with reuse in mind, and technological considerations are taken into account from the beginning. In particular, granularity of services is designed with performance issues in mind; too finely grained services are generally avoided because they pose performance risks due to the many time-consuming remote calls that would be needed to perform a single business activity.

Change management is realized by using a versioning system. The repository contains detailed information about the various service versions available, including expiry dates for obsolete versions.

15.3 Technology

This section provides more detail about the technologies used to implement Winterthur's SOA and the e-Platform. Winterthur's host applications had been mostly developed in PL/1 and COBOL, and most program maintenance still requires PL/1 and COBOL (IMS and CICS on z/OS).

15.3.1 ARCHITECTURE

Figure 15-7 shows the different architectural issues to be dealt with in the technical part of an application specification.

Figure 15-8 provides a detailed overview of the e-Platform's internal structure. It consists of HTML, Web services, Java clients in both Internet and intranet, secure proxies screening high-level communication protocols at the entry of the Intranet, Web and application servers, and enterprise information systems.

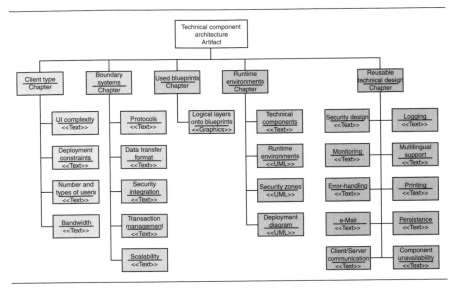

FIGURE 15-7   Technical part of application specification.

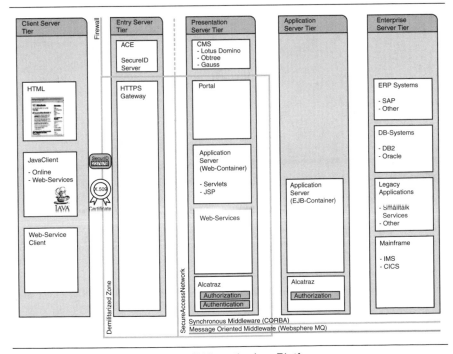

FIGURE 15-8   Internal structure of Winterthur's e-Platform.

A key concept underlying Winterthur's SOA and its e-Platform are *blueprints*. These blueprints are reusable reference architectures that propose standards concerning how business components can be distributed and integrated. They specify technical aspects of platform-specific environments, components, and protocols for various distribution patterns.

Figure 15-9 contains two sample blueprints, one employing a remote communication between an EJB and a CORBA service, and the other using a local communication between an EJB and a domain service implemented in Java.

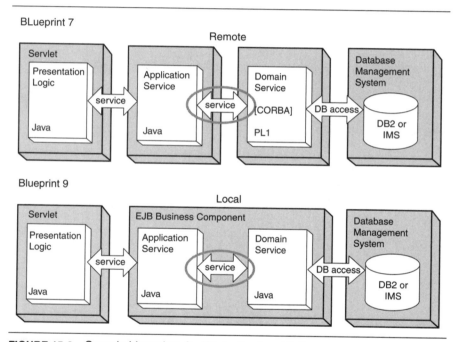

FIGURE 15-9   Sample blueprints for Winterthur's e-Platform.

The e-Platform contains blueprints for Java Clients, Servlets, EJBs, CORBA, Message-oriented middleware, Database connectivity and File transfer.

15.3.2   REPOSITORY, SERVICE INTERFACES, AND CONTRACTS

The repository contains two main types of information: the descriptions of the enterprise data elements at the level of attributes and the specification of services (see Figure 15-10). The data element descriptions are reused for the database definition and for the definition of the parameters within a service. All data elements must be approved by a central unit—the data management team.

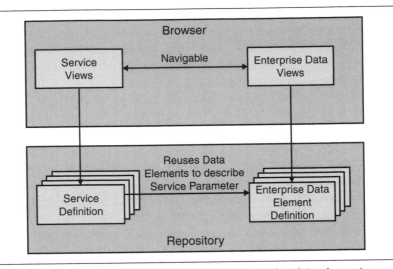

FIGURE 15-10   Service definitions are based on enterprise data element definitions.

The application service team uses these data elements to define, in close cooperation with the respective service owners, the detailed service specifications. Data elements and service information are accessible for all developers using browsers within the Intranet.

So far, the focus of Winterthur's SOA development has been on synchronous services offering a request-reply function. These services provide IDL interfaces and have been implemented as CORBA services. It should be noted, however, that the contracts are modeled independently of CORBA and are thus platform-independent. Currently, a second type of service is under development that will offer message-type functionality.

The idea is to use WSDL for a protocol-independent service definition and implementation. The following list contains some of the information that is included in the service contracts and available through the repository:

Service description. Provides a high-level and a detailed description of the service and its individual operations, including versioning.

Timetable. Provides information regarding the availability of the service in both test and production systems.

Operation properties. Provides information concerning its granularity and specific properties for each operation, e.g., concurrency, multiple calls.

Contract conditions. Provides information concerning pre- and post-conditions for each operation.

Special cases. Provides explanations of special cases for each operation.

Service operations and signatures. Provides lists of input and output parameters with detailed explanations concerning admissible values and their respective meanings for each operation.

Errors. Provides a list of possible errors that can occur after operations are invoked for each operation.

Service level. Provides quantitative information concerning the intended service level, i.e., average load/peak load per hour/day/month and response times.

15.3.3 CHOREOGRAPHY, SECURITY, AND MANAGEMENT

The SOA implemented at Winterthur is mainly concerned with providing basic services using widely existing host functionality through service interfaces. Most services are data-centric and thus leverage fundamental SOA functionality. At this point, however, the SOA has not integrated the more advanced functionalities such as service composition.

Thus, there is currently no common modeling approach for the workflow used in the applications accessing host service operations. Instead, the workflow is captured "only" at the conceptual level—in the dynamic models of the use case realizations. Thus, the workflow can be said to be the sum of all use cases. However, the workflow is coming more and more into focus and is to be expected to play a major role in future enhancements of Winterthur's SOA.

At this point, there is also no support for defining distributed transactions in Winterthur's current SOA. One way to ensure transaction-like behavior is to develop a coarse-grained (CORBA) service, spanning all PL/1 objects involved in the transaction. The latest release of the e-Platform enhances the CORBA blueprint with distributed transactions. However, because there are risks when relinquishing control of host transactions to "untrustworthy" client systems (e.g., locking of critical system resources in cases where transactions are not closed), different boards must decide how to best exploit new technical possibilities in Winterthur's environment.

Winterthur's SOA is used by internal and external applications, and security is therefore a major issue. The underlying framework will set credentials so that they will not appear in the operations' signature (otherwise credentials and user ID could be modified programmatically to obtain more privileges). These credentials are used to determine whether a client is authorized to access the functionality provided by a service operation.

Finally, monitoring functions are provided by special platform services and tools that allow an end-to-end monitoring of service execution. A small framework has been developed that periodically calls test programs that check the status of host transactions and CORBA adapters and transmit error reports should a host service be unavailable. These error reports and the monitoring framework are accessible using an HTML-based browser interface.

15.4   Lessons Learned, Benefits, and Perspectives

The introduction of the SOA has already delivered substantial benefits. The development of new applications has been significantly simplified due to the flexible nature of the implemented services and the resulting reusability.

What is particularly noteworthy is the fact that Winterthur has achieved these benefits by using very simple and basic SOA concepts: service orientation, explicit contracts, reused policies, and a descriptive but concise repository. Winterthur did not employ any advanced SOA concepts, such as service composition or distributed transactions.

One of the major success factors was the efficient process established at Winterthur to ensure reusability of developed services and e-Platform blueprints. However, it also became clear that designing services with focus on reusability generates a considerable overhead. It transpired that only one in three or four services was actually used by more than one application. Additional new application frontends, however, are enhancing the reuse rate. A further lesson was learned: design focused solely on reuse can lead to overly fine-grained services (e.g., to have an overview of a customer or a contract, you might have to call many fine-grained services to get all information related to an overview). Performance will be less than optimal if the service is accessed remotely, which leads to performance-optimized remote services that internally called fine-grained services accessed by local interfaces. The same fine-grained services can be easily encapsulated by a CORBA interface and called by a remote client. Further optimization was found in the so-called "multiple" services. Rather than retrieve a single contract or person through a single key, a whole list of business entities can be obtained with a single remote call using a list of keys.

Also due to performance issues related to remote communication, both domain layer services using CORBA and in some cases application layer services[3] were implemented on the host.

One way of minimizing the overhead caused by reusability is to explicitly distinguish between public and private services. Only the former are designed with reusability considerations in mind, whereas the latter are to be used solely by the application for which they were originally developed.

Apart from these qualifications, however, the reuse of implemented services was rather successful. All applications using host data are migrating to use them through the newly developed services. The SOA has therefore become the cornerstone of Winterthur's IT integration.

Another major benefit is the widespread use of the repository. The information available in the repository turned out to be an excellent documentation of the already implemented functionality. In contrast to traditional documentation that quickly becomes complex and voluminous, the information contained in the

---

[3] Process-centric services according to the terminology of this book.

repository is very concise. This is mainly due to the fact that the information to be published in the repository is restricted to essential facts required to adequately use the service in applications. On the other hand, the simple fact that the repository imposes a standardized format also contributes to its usability and offers an advantage over traditional documentation, which is usually crudely structured.

The development of Winterthur's SOA and its underlying e-Platform still continues. The main direction of enhancements concerns the removal of platform limitations, in particular regarding the SOA support of message-type communication, EJBs, and Web services.

Whereas emphasis has been on host applications in the beginning, focus now shifts to the application layer and non-host applications. Because the application layer is largely based on EJBs, the main task is to extend the SOA standards, guidelines, and processes that are currently based on synchronous CORBA to encompass EJBs, asynchronous messages, and Web services.

Another area of extension concerns workflows. To date, workflows are not explicitly modeled and supported in the e-Platform. They are only contained in the dynamic models of use case realizations developed in the design phase. The integration of workflows to support specification, automatic execution, monitoring, and optimization of workflows is currently under investigation.

These extensions will be defined by different long-term Winterthur IT substrategies such as the Swiss Insurance IT Platform definition, Integration strategy, Solution Delivery Process, and the Technical Platform.

16

Credit Suisse Case Study

In this chapter, we will describe the introduction of a Service-Oriented Architecture at Credit Suisse. The Credit Suisse Group (CSG) is a leading global financial services company headquartered in Zurich. The business unit Credit Suisse Financial Services provides private clients and small- and medium-sized companies with private banking and financial advisory services, banking products, and pension and insurance solutions from Winterthur. The business unit Credit Suisse First Boston, an investment bank, serves global institutional, corporate, government, and individual clients in its role as a financial intermediary. Credit Suisse Group's registered shares (CSGN) are listed in Switzerland and in the form of American Depositary Shares (CSR) in New York. The Group employs around 60,000 staff worldwide. As of March 31, 2004, it reported assets under management of CHF 1,241.3 billion.

Given the magnitude of operations, why did CSG decide to introduce an SOA? At the end of the 1990s, the complexity of the Credit Suisse IT infrastructure reached a critical level. The CIO made the decision to introduce an integration architecture based on a Service-Oriented Architecture. After the successful introduction of an information bus providing synchronous communication, Credit Suisse added an event bus for asynchronous communication. Whereas the information bus connects host applications with application frontends, the event bus is used for backend to backend integration. Currently, a third type of integration bus operates using file transfer for communication.[1]

In general terms, the authors of this book are critical of the integration bus concept. Firstly, the requirements for such an integration bus are usually too diverse to be covered by a single, homogeneous framework. Secondly, innovation cycles for products and standards in this area tend to be very short.

---

[1] Essentially, this creates an environment very similar to the one outlined in Chapter 9, Figure 9-2. The notable difference is that rather than one software bus, three different busses are used. However, unlike in Figure 9-3, only one software bus technology per communication model is used.

The approach taken by CSG, however, turned out to be very clever. They defined and implemented an integration bus according to their most pressing needs and obtained immediate benefits. They subsequently implemented a second bus that was based on similar principles but that satisfied slightly different technical requirements and therefore provided complementary benefits.

It is also noteworthy that this case study is very well complemented by various articles that provide in many respects an even more detailed discussion of the technology and the architecture (see [Ha03], [FMP99], [KM99]).

The case study presented in this chapter will show in detail how the SOA was implemented at Credit Suisse, both at organizational and technical levels. Section 16.1 describes the general scope of the Credit Suisse architecture, Section 16.2 discusses the organizational structures and processes used to implement the SOA, Section 16.3 presents a more technological perspective, and finally, Section 16.4 describes the lessons learned, the benefits achieved by Credit Suisse, and future perspectives.

16.1 Project Scope

The central book entry system of Credit Suisse comprises approximately 5 million accounts with roughly 218 million account movements per year. The service architecture described in this chapter covers the banking business. Winterthur,[2] who also belong to the Credit Suisse Group, have their own IT infrastructure.

The Credit Suisse IT infrastructure is typical of a large financial corporation and comprises around 600 applications, approximately 12 million lines of code (counting only core systems), and an application landscape based on heterogeneous platforms (IBM mainframe, Unix, Windows) grown over several decades. The roots of its IT systems reach back to the 1970s and terminal-based applications. At the end of the 1980s and the in the early 1990s, client/server applications were added, based on the then-innovative 4GL generators and object-oriented technologies using Smalltalk. With the rise of the Internet and intranets, multi-tier architectures were favored, and today, new applications are mostly built using Java. However, mainframe applications are still supported and updated, and the mainframe continues to be the preferred platform for transaction-oriented applications.

16.1.1 BUSINESS IMPACT

The main driver for the SOA introduction at CSG was the fact that the former IT infrastructure could no longer support the required business functionality. Ad hoc

---

[2] See Chapter 15 for the Winterthur case study.

solutions for integrating IT systems, such as after mergers and acquisitions, were not successful.

Credit Suisse was dissatisfied with point-to-point integrations.[3] This had made development of new applications extremely complex and sometimes unfeasible. Although no business plan was compiled prior to introducing the SOA, the decision for the SOA was made directly by the CIO in connection with two other major projects at Credit Suisse: the reconstruction of the data centers, which was necessary due to a number of mergers and acquisitions, and the clearing up of the data warehouse.

The SOA introduction started with small pilot projects in 1997, but it was the intention from the very beginning to use it as a basis for the overall IT infrastructure of Credit Suisse, in particular for providing host access functionality.

From the business point of view, the SOA infrastructure should become the basis for

- Multi-channel banking
- Online trading
- Consolidation of the core-business application portfolio

As the foundation of its SOA Credit Suisse designed a business-critical infrastructure that was meant to provide

- Centralized administration and management
- 24-7 operations
- Support for several thousands concurrent users
- High throughput
- Sub-second response time

The applications built on top of the new infrastructure were supposed to provide access to customers over the Internet and to employees over the intranet. This included all types of clients. Finally, extra gateways were built to realize B2B integration with partners over the Internet.

16.1.2 TECHNOLOGY IMPACT

According to [Ha03], CSG had five main goals when introducing its SOA-based integration architecture:

Technical integration. The management of dependencies between technical platforms.

Logical integration. The management of dependencies between applications and components at the level of business semantics.

---

[3] In fact, Credit Suisse suffered from the classical middleware overload created by too many products and point-to-point connections. Scenarios like that ultimately create the famous "integration spaghetti."

Process and desktop integration. The integration of heterogeneous applications according to business processes and end user workflows.

Integration of purchased software. The introduction of methods and tools to integrate external software as efficiently as possible.

B2B integration. The integration with partners, suppliers, and customers.

CSG addressed these five goals with three different types of complementary integration infrastructures, accompanied by a workflow infrastructure for process integration. The Credit Suisse Information Bus supports synchronous communication, the Event Bus Infrastructure supports asynchronous communication, and the Bulk Integration Infrastructure uses file transfer as the basis for communication. Together, the three infrastructures form the foundation of the Credit Suisse IT landscape, whose goal is to connect business applications based on clearly defined contracts.

Figure 16-1 illustrates the domain-based integration approach underlying the Information Bus. Communication across different domains, such as securities, sales support, logistics, or data analysis, is achieved using the Information Bus and ensures a loose coupling between domains. As you can see from these examples, some domains correspond to products offered by Credit Suisse, whereas others are more horizontal and product-independent.

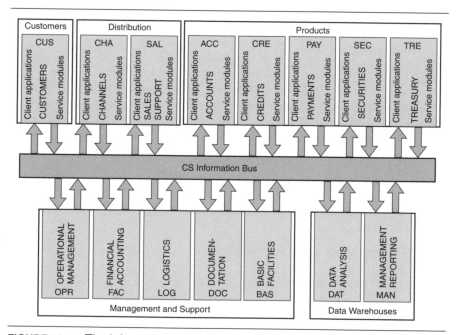

FIGURE 16-1 The Information Bus integrates different domains.

With respect to asynchronous communication, the main technical requirement was guaranteed once-and-only-once delivery of messages. The main architectural requirements for message-based interaction were

- Asynchronous connectivity and message transformation
- Real-time dissemination of critical data
- Static and content-based routing
- Topic-based publish-and-subscribe
- Point-to-point messaging
- Increased data consistency across multiple applications
- Integration of standard software

The backend core applications for integration were mainly running under IMS (80%) and CICS (20%) on large S/390 mainframes. Applications were also hosted on Unix and Windows servers. The application frontends, which were partly in use and partly under development, were based on technologies such as J2EE, C++, Smalltalk, HTML, COM, and Visual Basic.

When the Information Bus went live in 1999, five application frontends were in place, providing 35 business services to about 800 users. One year later, available applications had already risen to 21, with 173 business services and 9,000 users. These figures increased rapidly to 500 business services in 2000, used by more than 50 application frontends and over 100,000 users (this includes both Internet banking customers and internal staff).

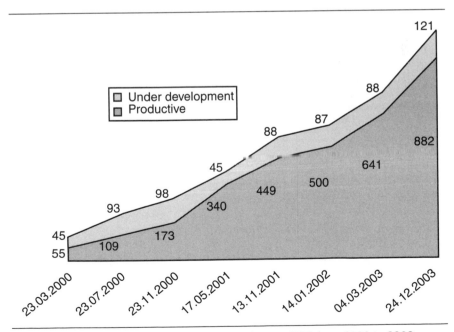

FIGURE 16-2   Development of available services at CSG from 2000 to 2003.

Currently, the information bus offers more than 700 services and handles between 1.5 and 2 million requests per day, with a total of 10 million requests per week or 50 million requests per month. The Event Bus, which serves about 20 applications, processes another 500,000 messages per day.

Figure 16-2 shows the development of available services at CSG from 2000 to 2003. Figure 16-3 shows the corresponding development of service calls. The stagnation during 2001 and 2002 was due to the difficult business environment.

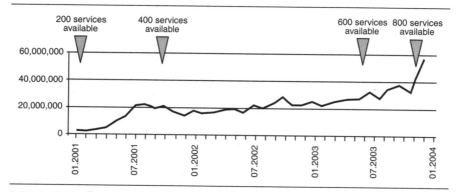

FIGURE 16-3   Development of service calls at CSG from 2000 to 2003.

16.2 Implementation

Although the CIO backed the SOA, uncertainty remained, mainly regarding technical issues. The main problem was its complexity and the overheads it created. Specifically, ensuring reusability was considered by many as a major factor in the increase of the design process cost. In addition, technical objections to the use of CORBA, which is the base of CSG's service bus, arose. Host developers believed it to be too resource-intensive, and Java developers argued that a pure J2EE approach would be more slender and thus preferable.

From the outset, Credit Suisse took this opposition seriously. The architecture was given a strong, central position within the IT department, and it was made clear that exceptions and deviations from the chosen approach would not be tolerated. Reuse was demanded, documented, and aggressively marketed, as was decoupling of systems.

A strict pursuit of the aims of the SOA and the application of rigorous processes helped to make the Credits Suisse SOA a success, and most opponents were eventually convinced by the benefits obtained by the SOA.

16.2.1 PROCESSES AND STRUCTURES

Credit Suisse established two infrastructure teams dedicated to the establishment of the SOA-based integration architecture—one responsible for engineering the required middleware, and the other supporting developers using the technology. These teams were responsible for several different though related tasks and were supported by integration architects from the central architecture department (see Figure 16-4).

First, the teams had to set up processes and structures accompanying the SOA introduction. In particular, this concerned stipulations for the service contracts and interfaces, in addition to the definition of a clear design and development process for services.

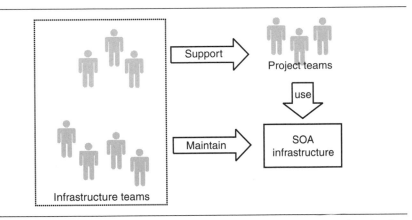

FIGURE 16-4 Different teams at Credit Suisse support the projects and maintain the SOA infrastructure.

Second, the team had to educate and support developers from the different business units with respect to these concepts. The central challenge was to sell the concept of reusability, which at first glance, generated nothing but overheads from the perspective of developers and individual projects.

Finally, the teams were responsible for reviewing service definitions and thus acting as a kind of quality assurance. Again, reusability was the key concept here and was also the distinguishing factor compared to "traditional" project management. The team had to ensure that service development followed the established processes and fulfilled the requirements imposed by the integration architecture. In particular, it had to ensure that business units did not succeed in circumventing the SOA and get permission from management to make "exceptions."

One of the most important aspects of the SOA introduction was the establishment of a clearly defined process for service development. This process started with a communication between service consumers and service providers and resulted in a coarse-grained specification.

Based on these specifications, a decision was taken to either develop a new service or to use an already available service, which potentially had to be modified or extended to fit the new application. The architecture board reviewed this decision before the design and implementation of the service could commence.

The architecture board is composed of experienced service designers from the central architecture group and from development support.

Service development proceeded in a strict bottom-up manner—no prior planning of the service landscape took place. Instead, a service would be defined and implemented whenever a specific client application required the respective functionality (see Figure 16-5). This enabled the construction of the service architecture to take place in an efficient and incremental fashion.

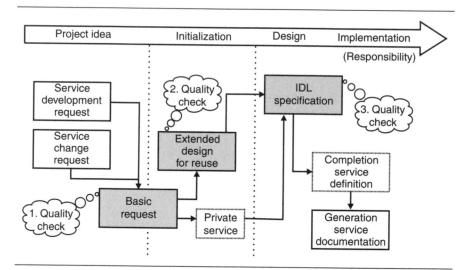

FIGURE 16-5 The SOA-based design process at CSG: Requests are generated bottom-up, and quality assurance is ensured top-down.

16.2.2 SERVICE REPOSITORY

Credit Suisse uses a central repository to publish all relevant information about a service. The main building blocks are the business-level description of the service and the technical interface specification based on IDL (CORBA's Interface Definition Language).

Usually, different user groups require both descriptions types, but in some cases, developers access the business-level description to first produce the coarse-grained specification and then the IDL description during the actual implementation phase.

The repository also contains information about service updates, which is of particular importance for enhancing Credit Suisse services.

16.2.3 PROJECT MANAGEMENT

As explained previously, the complexity of the CSG IT infrastructure reached a critical level at the end of the 1990s. Because a complete reimplementation of the existing functionality was economically and technologically infeasible, the *Managed Evolution* [Ha03] approach was adopted, whereby the system is transformed step-by-step into a new state. Each project in this step-by-step process is expected to contribute to the structural optimization of the IT system.

Figure 16-6 illustrates this principle, which comprises two basic dimensions of an IT infrastructure: IT efficiency on one hand and business value on the other. Whereas IT efficiency captures how quickly and inexpensively the system can be changed, business value regards the benefit of the infrastructure for its users, that is, the business units in the enterprise. Each project should ideally contribute positively on both dimensions (see Chapter 1, "An Enterprise IT Renovation Roadmap").

In order to guarantee this level of contribution to the overall architecture, clear guidelines, processes, and structures must be established to help distinguish "good changes from bad ones." Credit Suisse has a special architecture team responsible for defining such guidelines and monitoring their application with the chief architect reporting directly to the CIO.

The Credit Suisse methodology for the management of concrete business projects is mainly based on the waterfall model. However, the critical success factor of business projects at Credit Suisse is its control over deliveries such as interface specifications and coordination with the appropriate infrastructure teams.

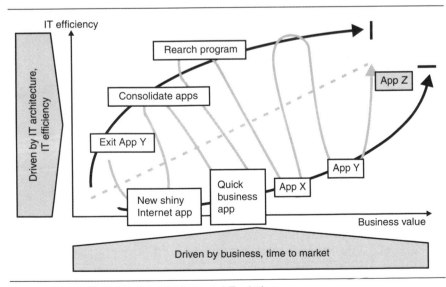

FIGURE 16-6 The principle of Managed Evolution.

16.3   Technology

This section describes in more detail the technology used to construct the SOA at Credit Suisse. It comprises a sketch of the architecture used to implement the information and event buses, an overview of the repository structure, the contracts and the service interfaces, and a summary of how security, workflows, and management are handled.

16.3.1   ARCHITECTURE

As we mentioned earlier, the integration architecture deployed at Credit Suisse combines three different integration paradigms.

Whereas the Credit Suisse Service Infrastructure provides synchronous communication and is used for providing frontend access to host applications, the Event Bus Infrastructure (EBI) uses asynchronous communication to integrate new non-host applications. Finally, the Bulk Integration Infrastructure uses file transfer for communication.

16.3.1.1   Synchronous Integration with the CSIB.   When introducing the Information Bus, CSG began with an initial structuring of the existing applications, which was achieved by partitioning the applications into approximately 20 domains (refer to Figure 16-1) where an application domain combines all data and applications belonging to a certain business area. Figure 16-7 shows how applications are encapsulated inside domains. Whereas coupling is tight within a domain, it is loose across domains where coupling uses the information bus.[4]

---

[4] The concept of a domain at CSG is largely similar to the notion of service in this book. The approach taken by CSG is somewhat similar to the approach laid out in Section 10.2.1, "Service Enablement," and depicted in Figure 10-4. However, CSG decided not to make an effort to refactor any logic within the domain or between domains, where communication was not through one of the service buses. Thus, the actual applications remain in fact tightly coupled, even if the service interfaces might not expose the coupling to the client. Over time, replacement and upgrades of the underlying application and changes in the inter-domain communication models might facilitate an adoption of decoupled infrastructure without any significant impact on the already existing service clients.

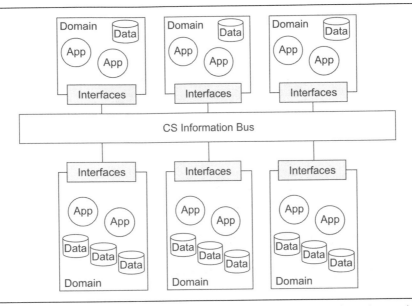

FIGURE 16-7   Partitioning of applications into domains, which are loosely coupled.

The CSIB was first implemented using CORBA technology. Figure 16-8 provides a detailed overview of the initial architecture (which did not include the Event Bus) and the respective technologies used for the different layers.

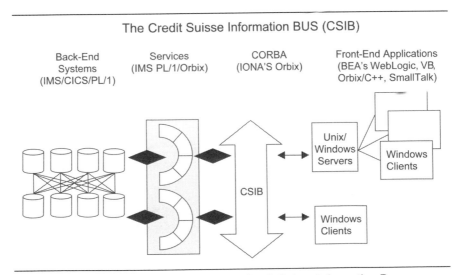

FIGURE 16-8   Initial implementation of the Credit Suisse Information Bus.

As an alternative to CORBA, DCE and DCOM were evaluated but discarded. The integration of CORBA and EJBs used to implement the application frontends was built by Credit Suisse. Due to strict abstraction from the underlying technology, CORBA could in principle be replaced by another technology, such as Web services. So far, experiences with CORBA have been mainly positive, and it is still used in implementing new services.

16.3.1.2 Asynchronous Integration with the EBI. In 2000, when the Information Bus had been successfully introduced and had proven to be robust and scaleable, Credit Suisse decided to add a second integration platform. The basic idea was to address backend-to-backend application integration (within one domain or across different domains) with the same basic concepts that had proven successful when introducing the SOA and the Information Bus.

Credit Suisse calls its approach of adding an event bus to the Information Bus a generalization of the SOA toward a component-based architecture. They reserve the term "service" for the synchronous communication used in the Information Bus. However, the approach to SOA advocated in this book is much more generic and also comprises asynchronous communication as used in the Credit Suisse event bus.

As we already stressed, it is not so much the technology that characterizes a SOA as the general methodology associated with it. This is nicely illustrated by the fact that Credit Suisse "reused" all concepts developed in conjunction with the introduction of the information bus for the introduction of the event bus. Furthermore, CSIB and the EBI share the same service implementations, which facilitates the reuse of business logic and live data sharing beyond the scope of a single infrastructure, demonstrating that the CSG SOA is truly technology-independent.

The Event Bus Infrastructure is currently a message-based integration solution supporting topic-based routing and transformations. At the moment, it is not process-based—that is, there are no workbaskets and no specific process layer. However, extensions in this direction are envisaged for the mid-term future (see Figure 16-9).

Technically, the EBI is based on message queues. The current implementation relies on products of IBM's WebSphere suite. WebSphere MQ (MQ Series) provides the reliable base for the transportation and storage of messages, while WebSphere Business Integration Message Broker provides facilities for message transformation and publish-and-subscribe.

Credit Suisse particularly stressed the fundamental importance of managed interfaces and contracts. These two key prerequisites for successfully decoupling applications are used rigorously by Credit Suisse for both the information and event buses.

In fact, the boards and processes for the event bus are identical to those established for the Information Bus. This is not limited to the abstract nature of the design and development process but also covers technical details. Thus, the service interfaces for the event bus messages are specified using IDL. Moreover,

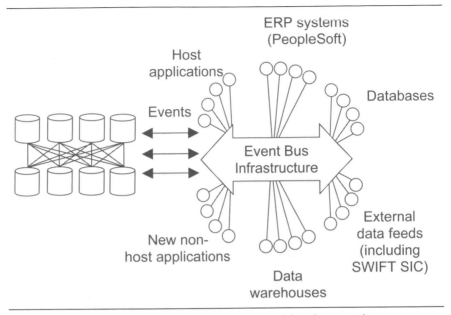

FIGURE 16-9   CSG's integration architecture comprising the event bus.

events and messages using the same type of information as an existing information bus service reuse the data structures already modeled for the service.

16.3.1.3 Bulk Integration Infrastructure.   The Bulk Integration Infrastructure is the third type of software bus to be developed at CSG.

Figure 16-10 illustrates the interplay between the various CSG software buses. It already contains the third infrastructure component, which is currently under construction: a bulk integration infrastructure, which will be responsible for a consistent management of file-based data exchange.

Again, this third infrastructure component will reuse the same methodology as both the information and event buses. It is currently under development and uses conventional point-to-point file transfer. The goal is to establish a file broker to support a centralized control of the various transfers. This extension is currently in the evaluation phase.

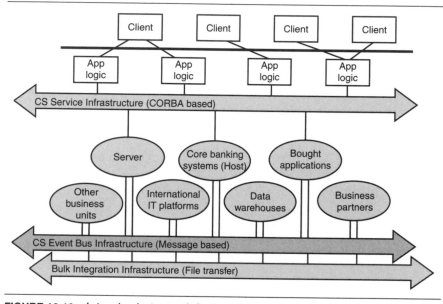

FIGURE 16-10   Interplay between Information Bus and event bus.

16.3.2 REPOSITORY, SERVICE INTERFACES, AND CONTRACTS

The repository has been developed by CSG and contains information regarding design and management of services and events. For each service, the following information is available:

Service interface. The IDL interface specification of the service.

Properties. Specific properties of the service, such as effect on data (e.g., read, write), availability (e.g., public, private), and current status (e.g., test, production).

Planning. Information regarding dates on which tests have occurred or are planned and the date on which the service went into production.

Contact information. Relevant contact persons, such as developers, owner, designer, and/or client/user.

Implementation details. Information concerning the service implementation, such as modules and databases used.

Service conditions. A textual description of preconditions and corresponding post conditions guaranteed by the service.

Exceptions. A list of exception codes with brief explanations.

Service level. Information regarding the target response times (round trips) and expected requests per hour, day, and month (average and maximum).

Parameter descriptions. A detailed description of the in and out arguments of the service.

16.3.3 CHOREOGRAPHY, SECURITY, AND MANAGEMENT

The SOA implemented at Credit Suisse does not incorporate complex SOA solutions for choreography, security, or management.

Workflow components are only used for workflows involving human users. At the service level, however, there is no explicit process modeling in which service operations are orchestrated into complex workflows. CSG's SOA can be classified as networked with respect to its expansion stage (see Chapter 6, "The Architectural Roadmap"). Credit Suisse closely monitors the growing functionality provided by application servers in this area and is considering the integration of service composition and workflow modeling for future enhancements of its SOA.

CSG uses the mechanisms based on optimistic logging that are depicted in Chapter 8, "Process Integrity," to implement distributed transactions. If an operation of a logical transaction fails, logged information is used to trigger compensating actions. These compensations reverse the effects of already executed operations of the same logical transaction. There are no ACID transactions across the boundary of a domain.

The *security solution* employed at Credit Suisse is based on PKI (Public Key Infrastructure). The PKI solution is used for internal integration only at the moment. External integration currently operates using dedicated connections. However, a PKI solution for external integration is under construction, although this type of security is more suited to current enterprise application landscapes (see Chapter 9, "Infrastructure of a Service Bus").

To manage the distributed services and the underlying infrastructure, a wide variety of tools are used. Special CORBA tools support general system management. In addition, Credit Suisse developed tools that access and process data stored in a central logging component. This logging component contains detailed information regarding executed services, including information on data input and output during service execution.

16.4 Lessons Learned, Benefits, and Perspectives

The SOA implemented at Credit Suisse is now firmly established within the enterprise and is considered to be a major success. The main benefits experienced can be summarized as follows:

Reuse of services. The business services are used across applications. Although the average reuse factor is only 1.6 when taking into account all services, some business services are used by up to 12 applications. The low average factor is mainly due to the fact that many services are currently used by a single application. Because services are built as soon as there is a single user, it can take some time before a second user materializes. Reuse is driven by the centralized repository containing the service interfaces and detailed documentations.

More efficient application development. Due mainly to the reuse of services, application development has been accelerated considerably. Usually, when a new application is under development, 75 to 80 percent of the required services are already available in the repository. This improves time-to-market of new solutions dramatically and also offers significant cost savings for the development process.

Increase of collaboration. Another benefit consists of the increased collaboration between the business unit developers and the programmers implementing the core business applications. It was also observed that experienced PL/1 programmers, who had become demotivated over the years, participated actively in the development process.

However, these benefits were not achieved without hard work. For one thing, there was continuous uncertainty regarding the approach taken with the integration architecture. This included, for example, complaints that CORBA was too resource-intensive, too complex, and too slow. This objection was not broad-based, however, and the consistent support from top management overcame it.

There was also a critical stage when the Information Bus threatened to fall victim to its own success. As more users accessed the applications built on top of the CSIB, performance, reliability, and availability became indispensable. Again, having management backing and sufficient budget helped to overcome problems during this critical phase.

It also transpired that the decoupling, which had been achieved for internal integration, did not necessarily suffice for external integration, which posed even more demanding requirements on the degree of decoupling.

Finally, the strict bottom-up approach applied throughout the development of the SOA will probably be complemented by top-down considerations in the future. This included more systematic decisions concerning reuse and more specific targets for service developers. One idea is to reduce the overhead for the development of services that might never be reused. Another aspect is the identification of "missing" services, even if they are not immediately needed by an application.

Credit Suisse stresses four main SOA aspects that were crucial to its success:

- Interfaces
- Processes
- Management commitment
- Solid technology

Evidence for the success of the Credit Suisse SOA-based integration architecture is based on the fact that the concepts and methodologies initially developed for the synchronous information bus could be reused one-to-one when introducing the asynchronous event bus. Furthermore, the implementation of the Bulk Integration Infrastructure is also based on the same foundation. This demonstrates that both the concepts and the methodology actually produced the desired results and that they are independent from the underlying technology.

References

Hagen, C. *Integrationsarchitektur der Credit Suisse. Enterprise Application Integration - Flexibilisierung komplexer Unternehmensarchitekturen.* GITO-Verlag, Berlin, 2003. [Ha03]

Froidevaux, W. S. Murer and M. Prater. *The Mainframe as a High-Available, Highly scalable CORBA Platform.* International Workshop on Reliable Middleware Systems, October 1999. [FMP99]

Koch, T. and S. Murer. *Service Architecture Integrates Mainframes in a CORBA Environment,* 3rd IEEE conf. on Enterprise Distributed Object Computing, September 1999. [KM99]

17

Halifax Bank Of Scotland: IF.com

Halifax Bank of Scotland (HBoS) is a UK Financial Services provider with divisions in Retail Banking, Insurance & Investment, Business Banking, Corporate Banking, and Treasury. HBoS is the UK's largest mortgage and savings provider with a customer base of about 22 million. The annual results of 2003 reported £3.8 billion profit before tax and £408 billion assets under management. HBoS group was formed through the merger of Halifax and Bank of Scotland.

Intelligent Finance was launched as a division of Halifax plc with the aim of attracting new customers from outside Halifax and specifically to target the UK clearing banks. Intelligent Finance was launched as Project Greenfield in 2000, starting an entire new banking operation from scratch. Three years later, by the end of 2003, Intelligent Finance had 820,000 customer accounts, representing assets of £15.5 billion. In March 2004, Intelligent Finance announced that it had broken even in 2003—the project had been a huge success.

In order to prevail in a highly competitive market, a unique product concept had to be devised, enabling customers to link a range of personal banking products—mortgages, credit cards, personal loans, savings, and current accounts—in any chosen combination with interest charged only on the difference between their debit and credit balances.

In order to enable Intelligent Finance to provide cost-effective products, it was decided to use only direct channels—that is, not to rely on expensive branch offices. Because market research at the time showed that customers would prefer to do business with a bank that combined Internet banking with phone banking, it was decided to offer a solution that combined telephone and Web access.

At the heart of the Intelligent Finance system is a generic banking engine, which offers access to products and services for the different customer access channels. The Intelligent Finance system was probably one of the largest and most advanced SOA deployments in the Financial Services industry in Europe at the time. Because of time pressure under which the project was delivered—it took almost a year for the complete implementation of the bank—it was decided early on in the project to take a full-blown SOA approach for its transactional aspects. The banking engine provides a suite of XML Web services, processing over 1,000,000 SOAP transactions a day.[1] This chapter will take a closer look at the history of the project, the impact that the SOA approach had on the overall architecture, and the lessons learned in the project.

17.1 Project Scope

Before delving deeper into the technical details of the Intelligent Finance project, we will look at the scope of the project from both a business and technology point of view.

17.1.1 BUSINESS IMPACT

In 1999, Halifax was one of the most respected banks in the UK but was also overshadowed by the "big four"—Barclays, Royal Bank of Scotland, Lloyds TSB, and HSBC (Halifax ranked fifth at the time). These four banks together controlled over 80% of the UK banking market in 1999. In order to attack the market share of the "big four," Halifax needed a distinct offering, which would differentiate Halifax in the market, as shown in Figure 17-1.

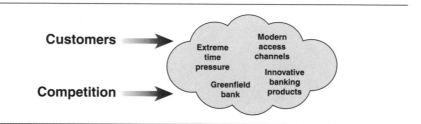

FIGURE 17-1   Competition and customer demand were the main drivers for Halifax to move toward new innovative banking products and modern access channels.

At the same time, the UK banking market had seen something of an e-banking gold rush in 1999, with the Co-operative Bank's Smile, followed by Prudential's

---

[1] Intelligent Finance adopted SOAP in the very early stages of the specification process. The SOAP version in use was upgraded several times throughout the project, in order to stay in line with the development of the SOAP specification. Service interfaces where initially defined in a proprietary, XML-based IDL, which was later updated to the emerging WSDL standard.

Egg, HSBC First Direct's 'Little Fella,' and Abbey National's Cahoot launched in quick succession.

As a result, Halifax was under huge pressure to deliver their new bank in an extremely tight timeframe. Halifax management at the time estimated that they would have about one year to execute their plan and create a product that was good enough to succeed in this highly competitive market.

17.1.1.1 Greenfield Project. In order to meet these challenging timelines, Halifax decided to invest GPB 120 million to build the new bank. In October 1999, Halifax hired Jim Spowart, the former chief executive of Standard Life Bank, to head the new company, which was initially called *Greenfield*. Three months later, the new bank identity was rolled out with the brand *Intelligent Finance.*

The benefit of being given a blank sheet of paper to create what was internally dubbed the *bank of the future* was that there were no legacies—the IF management team was free to reinvent the ways the bank should look and how it should interact with its customers.

But there were also some obvious challenges and disadvantages in the Greenfield approach: There were literally no existing structures or processes; everything had to be invented from scratch.

17.1.1.2 Offsetting. In order to differentiate itself in the market, Intelligent Finance adopted a new concept, called *offsetting*. CEO Jim Spowart and his team developed the concept of inter-linked accounts, which they called *jars*. These jars would allow customers to see how the money in their debit and credit balances measured up. They envisaged an offsetting function across all products. As a result, customers are only charged interest on the money they actually owe the bank. For example, if a customer had borrowings of £150,000 and £50,000 in savings and/or a current account with Intelligent Finance, interest would only be charged on the £100,000 outstanding loan, in return for no interest being charged on the savings or current account. Because no interest is earned on credit balances, the customer is not required to pay tax. Over the term of the loan, this can save thousands in interest charges and enable the customer to pay off the loan early.

17.1.1.3 The IF.com Success Story. As we mentioned earlier, since it fully launched in November 2000, Intelligent Finance has been a huge success. In November 2001, Intelligent Finance announced that it had a total of £8.9 billion in balances in hand and forecast to complete. Savings and current account balances amounted to £2 billion.

About one year later—in February 2003—Intelligent Finance announced that savings and current account balances increased by 50 percent to £3.3 billion, and customer accounts doubled to 600,000. In March 2004, Intelligent Finance announced that break-even was achieved the previous year. By the end of 2003, the bank had assets of £15.5 billions, with customer accounts reaching 820,000. Figure 17-2 provides an overview of Intelligent Finance's development from a business point of view.

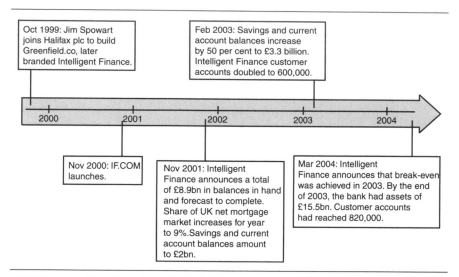

FIGURE 17-2   Timeline of Halifax Intelligent Finance project.

17.1.2   TECHNOLOGY IMPACT

The decision to build the new bank on a green field also had a huge impact on the technical architecture. On one hand, it is often easier to develop new systems without worrying about existing systems that require an integration effort. On the other hand, starting from scratch involves a lot of decisions that do not have to be made when you have existing systems. Given the extreme time pressures of this project, many decisions were made very rapidly. This included hiring and training over 1,000 new staff members, finding office space, putting management infrastructure into place, and designing the actual software architecture.

17.1.2.1   IF's Service Architecture.   At the heart of the architecture is the IF Banking Engine (initially referred to as *OnePlan Engine*). This engine comprises three major parts: Open Account, Fulfillment, and Service Request. In addition, it provides abstractions for business entities such as Customer, Financial Consolidation, and Underwriting Modeling and infrastructure services such as Process (Workflow), Alerts, and Messaging.

The IF architecture had to integrate a large number of heterogeneous subsystems, including back-office and front-office systems. The back-office systems include customer account management systems, credit scoring, links to other banks and external credit-card providers, scanning and imaging, document management, printing, and workflow management. The user access channels include call center and IVR (Interactive Voice Recognition), Web channel, and email. Figure 17-3 provides an overview of the Service-Oriented Architecture as implemented by Intelligent Finance.

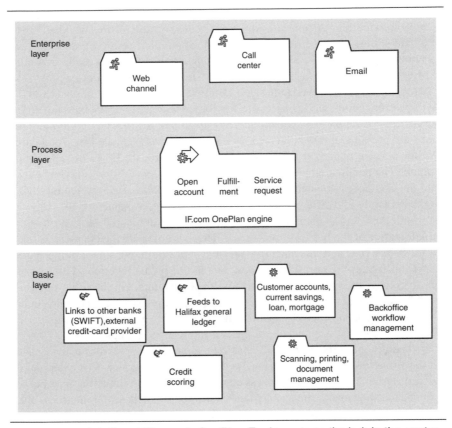

FIGURE 17-3   Intelligent Finance's OnePlan Engine acts as the hub in the center of its banking application landscape.

17.1.2.2   Basic, Intermediary, and Process-Oriented Services.   Referring to our service classification as defined in Chapter 5, "Services as Building Blocks," the Intelligent Finance service architecture can be divided into two service layers: a large number of basic services in the backend and one very large service in the middle, which is a mixture between a process-centric and an intermediary service.

There are different kinds of basic services in the backend. A good example is the Halifax-owned current account system, which provides XML-based services for accessing customer accounts that reside on the mainframe. Intelligent Finance decided to leverage this existing system from Halifax and to combine it with an off-the-shelf banking package that added mortgage, savings, and personal loan accounts to the existing account functionality on the Halifax systems.

The second service layer in the system is occupied by one very large service, which represents the Intelligent Finance banking engine, covering the functionality required to provide the seamless integration of the different accounts.

Technically, the banking engine represents a mixture between a *process-centric service* and an *intermediary service*. For example, the banking engine provides access to the different customer accounts that reside on different subsystems. This part of the banking engine functionality does not really add much business functionality; it has the characteristics of a *service access layer* (see Chapters 5 and 6) designed to provide a unified interface to a set of *basic services* with heterogeneous service access technology. Other parts of the banking engine service provide *process-centric* logic. For example, all the *service request* features are provided through the banking engine, such as "replace lost credit card." All the *service request* features of the banking engine are based on a workflow engine. The banking engine provides the interface between the workflow engine and the user access channels through a set of *process-oriented* service interfaces. Approximately 250 different service request types are implemented this way.

Another set of banking engine interfaces is dedicated to the *offsetting* functionality of the bank. Again, these interfaces combine the characteristics of *process-oriented* and *intermediary services*. On one hand, the banking engine service provides the necessary *process functionality* that is required for customers to control the balances on their individual accounts. On the other hand, the banking engine acts as an *intermediary service* to the extremely complex calculations in the basic services, which take place, for example, if mortgage and credit-card interest is being set off against interest on savings.

The design of the *centralized banking engine service* provides many benefits to the frontends (user access channels) that access the service. For example, the current design enables all user access channels to share the same functionality and provide end customers with a consistent view throughout the different access channels. In addition, the design enabled very efficient integration between the different access channel technologies. For example, the call center application provides agents with co-browsing capability (see Chapter 10), effectively enabling them to get exactly the same view that the end user would get on his own data through the Internet. In addition, call center agents have a so-called *super screen,* which provides additional information, such as the customer's contact history.

On the other hand, the centralized design of the banking engine service also has some disadvantages, which we will discuss later. The most important problem related to the design of the service is the lack of modularity and the cross-dependencies between the different interfaces provided by the service, which in particular make development and maintenance of the service difficult. Given the tough schedule the Intelligent Finance team was under when designing the first version of the system, this issue simply was less important; the team is currently in the process of addressing it successfully.

17.1.2.3 Project Schedule.
Fueled by the fierce competition in the UK banking market and the boom in Internet-based e-banks, the schedule of the Intelligent Finance project was extremely tight. Figure 17-4 provides an overview of the most important events that led to the successful launch of the bank at the end of the year 2000.

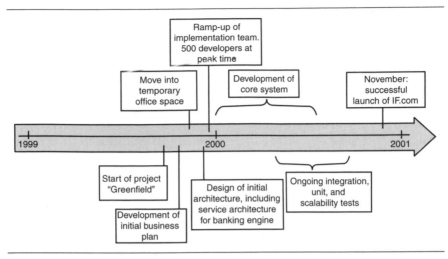

FIGURE 17-4   Development schedule of IF.COM.

After the decision was made in the middle of 1999 to go ahead with the project, Halifax started to recruit the core team to find key suppliers of technology and IT services and to undertake all the associated activities necessary to set up the bank.

By the end of 1999, the initial architecture of the system was finalized, including the service design for the core banking engine. The actual development of the system mainly happened in the first half of 2000, with ongoing integration tests, unit test, and scalability tests happening in the middle of 2000. During the peak time of the project, 500 consultants, project managers, and developers were involved.

Given the scale and timeframe of the undertaking, it must be credited to the skills and commitment of the project team that the actual launch of the system went smoothly and without any major glitches. While other organizations experienced serious problems during the launch of their Internet identities in 1999, the Intelligent Finance was a huge success from the very beginning.

17.2   Implementation

In this section, we describe the key implementation details of the Intelligent Finance project, including the service implementation concept, service repository, and project management.

17.2.1   XML SERVICES

Because of the extremely tight schedule and the high integration requirements of the multi-channel architecture, it was decided early on in the project that existing

EAI blueprints and middleware technology would not be suitable for this project, due to their long and complex implementation cycles.

XML had just emerged as a new and flexible toolkit that enabled high productivity and provided very good ad-hoc integration features. It was therefore decided to use XML as the *lingua franca* within the technical architecture. However, although the great flexibility of XML provided a huge benefit over more stringent integration technologies such as CORBA, this flexibility also represented a problem in many respects. Especially in an environment where requirements are changing on a daily basis, it is often tricky to strike a good balance between flexibility and strictness.

Approximately 250 different service request types exist in this system. A way was needed to leverage the XML technology to model the behavior of the Intelligent Finance banking engine, which was at the heart of the system architecture. WSDL and SOAP were new standards at the time, but the architecture team decided to adopt them to specify the interfaces of the banking engine anyway. The often-problematic experience with distributed object systems that the architecture team had made in many previous projects naturally led to the adoption of a Service-Oriented Architecture. Even if the term was not defined at the time, the underlying concepts were applied in the design of the bank.

17.2.2 SERVICE REPOSITORY

Intelligent Finance uses the CCC Harvest source control system as the central service repository for all service definitions used by the project. All services are defined as XML Schema definitions and WSDL definitions.

The service repository and the service definitions in it are managed by a technical architect who holds the role of *XML Tsar* (this role is described in more detail in the following project management section). The XML Tsar works with the different development streams as well as the business side to develop and maintain the service definitions.

The content of the service repository is used by the IF.com build manager to generate type-safe APIs and stubs for a variety of different programming languages, including Java, C++, and VB (see Figure 17-5). These stubs enable client- and server-side programmers to write service components and access them in a transparent way. These stubs are managed in separate repositories together with the actual source code of the application. One can debate whether it makes sense to actually manage the generated code in a repository because one should be able to regenerate the stubs at a later point in time. However, there is a danger that the exact version of the compiler used for the particular build in question might not be available any more, and therefore there is a danger that one would not be able to reconstruct an older version of a build. For this reason, it was decided to include the generated code in the source code repository.

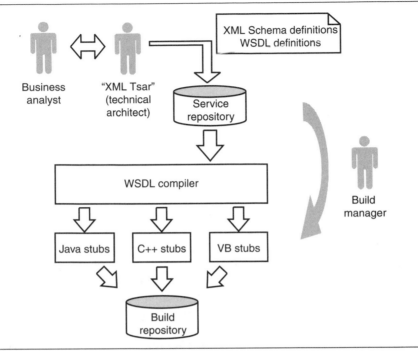

FIGURE 17-5   IF.com service repository.

17.2.3   PROJECT MANAGEMENT

The huge scale and extremely ambitious schedule of this project put significant pressure on project managers. Starting from scratch, the Intelligent Finance management team had to build the entire Intelligent Finance organization, including HR, sales, marketing, legal, IT development and operations staff, call center staff and management, and the banking back-office. In parallel, every piece of infrastructure had to be put in place from scratch, including offices for the development team, plus the acquisition of two new buildings for the call center and banking operations. In addition, communications infrastructure had to be put in place, including telephony and IP networks.

17.2.3.1   Design in Action.   The IT implementation project was probably the most critical and most complex piece of the puzzle. The basis for the IT implementation project was the *Design in Action* plan (DIA). The DIA was created in about eight weeks, providing a detailed outline for addressing the key challenges of the project. The DIA included the blueprint for the multi-channel architecture of the bank, the banking engine with the balance netting features, and the backend integration. The DIA also provided a delivery program, including mobilization plans, training plans, and an outline of the required systems infrastructure.

The implementation of the mobilization plan took about three months, at the end of which 500 technical staff were brought on-site to the new development center, plus a large number of on-site technicians from IT systems suppliers.

17.2.3.2 Work Streams and IT Steering Committee.

A cornerstone of the project management strategy was the division of the project into 23 different work streams, including banking engine, architecture, service design, DB design, workflow, mainframe integration, Web design, call center, and so forth. This structure helped to reduce some of the hugely complex dependencies between the different tasks that had to be executed in parallel.

An IT steering committee was responsible for coordinating the work of the different work streams. The steering committee consisted of the managers from the different work streams plus members from the business side and the architecture team.

17.2.3.3 Architecture Board.

The architecture board consisted of six senior IT architects who were responsible for the overall design of the new bank. This included the system hardware and software infrastructure, the design of the XML service middleware, the service contracts themselves, the database design, the integration with the backend systems, control, and event flow, and so on.

17.2.3.4 The XML Tsar and His XML Tsardom.

While the IT steering committee was a great management tool for coordinating the work of the 23 work steams on the project level, an essential piece was missing from the beginning. As it turned out, the people in each work stream initially had only vague ideas about how they would integrate their own functionality with the functionality provided or required by the other work streams on the technical level. Although XML was set as the default way for describing interactions and data exchange between the components from the different work streams, there was a clear lack of communication and coordination of the interfaces between the different sub-systems.

As we mentioned before, in order to address this problem, the architecture board decided to create the role of *XML Tsar.* This person was given the responsibility of coordinating the development of the technical interfaces between the components implemented by the different work streams.

The XML Tsar assembled technical representatives from each work stream in his *XML Tsardom,* including representatives from open account, service request, workflow, call center, IVR, FundsTransfer, and document management.

The XML Tsar and his team met on a weekly basis to discuss and define the evolution of the XML-based service definitions, that is, the XML Schemas and WSDL definitions. The most important goal was to stabilize the development process and to reduce friction losses due to unstable interface specifications.

Each work stream actually sent two members to the weekly meetings, an XML designer and a build engineer. The XML designer was responsible for the coordination of the XML specifications. The XML build engineer was responsible for taking the newly released XML specifications and using the WSDL compiler to generate corresponding stubs, which would be used in his team. Given the huge diversity of technical staff—ranging from Web designers and junior programmers to senior EJB and mainframe developers—it was essential to include the role of XML build engineer in the concept of XML Tsardom to ensure consistency amongst the different programmers. In fact, the majority of developers in the project was never aware of the underlying XML-based service infrastructure—they stayed in their particular programming language environment, using the stubs to provide service components to other work streams or to call into components provided by other work streams.

As would be expected, the impact of changes to the XML service definitions on the internal release cycle of the project was quite significant—especially in the late phases of the development, even small changes could have severe effects on the unit integration and test schedule. The XML Tsar therefore also closely cooperated with the IT steering committee and the project's release managers.

An interesting aspect of the structure of the XML Tsardom was that it enabled communication between key technical people from different work streams for the first time. The managers of the different work streams who met in the IT steering committee meetings tended to discuss topics related to the overall status of the project. On the other hand, the technical people who met in the XML Tsardom meetings had a very different perspective, which focused more on the technical details of the interfaces, and for most of them, the XML Tsardom quickly became the most important platform for communicating with members from the other work streams on the technical level. This helped significantly to reduce friction losses due to inconsistencies between the service interfaces of the different sub-systems.

17.3 Technology

Having discussed the implementation aspects of the project, we now want to take a closer look at the actual technology employed. This discussion will cover the technical architecture, XML service definitions, and technical infrastructure.

17.3.1 ARCHITECTURE

The technical architecture of the IF.com system required the integration of a wide range of heterogeneous technologies. The banking engine in the Mid-Tier is implemented based on Java and BEA WebLogic. The Web Channel (Web server to render HTML pages) is based entirely on Microsoft. This is due to the fact that IF already had a security approval for this Microsoft-based architecture based on their first-generation online bank. Call center and IVR (Interactive

Voice Recognition) are based on the Genesys CTI suite, using customized C and C++ on Unix. In the backend, a variety of mainframe, Unix, and NT systems had to be integrated. Figure 17-6 provides a high-level overview of the technical architecture of the system.

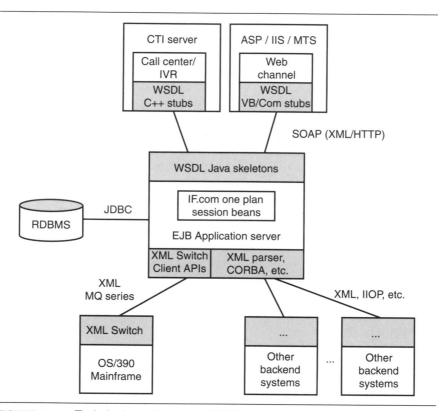

FIGURE 17-6   Technical architecture of IF.COM.

17.3.2   SERVICE REPOSITORY, SERVICE INTERFACES, AND CONTRACTS

As we discussed previously, the IF.com service architecture is divided into two main layers: a number of basic services in the backend, and a central service in the middle, which is a mixture of an intermediary and a process-centric service. All services are "hard-wired" through configuration files—that is, there is no explicit service registry. Given the nature of the project (all services are controlled by the same project), this approach makes sense. The following describes the service operations and contracts of the banking engine service and the basic services in the backend.

17.3.2.1 Basic Services. The basic services implemented by the Intelligent Finance system are based on a number of very different technologies, ranging from CORBA to DCOM to XML and MQ Series.

Interestingly, Halifax itself started to develop a Service-Oriented Architecture for its mainframe-based core banking system, which was also used in the Intelligent Finance project. The so-called *message switch* for the Halifax mainframe is based on XML and MQ Series. A technique similar to the one described in Chapter 3 is used to simulate synchronous service operations by using message correlation to group matching requests and responses together.

17.3.2.2 Banking Engine Services. The IF.com banking engine is based on approximately 1,300 XML Schema definitions, 120 WSDL Web service interfaces, and 600 Web service operations. Halifax is now processing over 1,000,000 XML SOAP transactions a day. This makes Halifax Intelligent Finance one of the biggest and most successful Web services projects today.

The banking engine service is divided into a number of different namespaces, including `Common`, `ContactCentre`, `Workflow`, `OpenAccount`, `PersonalAdvisors`, `QuickQuote`, and `Service Request`. The `OpenAccount` namespace, for example, includes service interfaces such as `AddressMgr`, `ApplicationMgr`, `BroadRequest`, `OfferEngine`, `CreditCardApplication`, `CurrentAccountApplication`, and so forth. The `OfferEngine` includes, for example, XML Schema definitions such as `DebtType`, `MortgageProductDetails`, and `MortgageOffer`. The `OfferEngine` service interface provides operations such as `renegotiate-MortgageOffer()`, `getMortgageOfferAcceptance()`, and so on.

In general, the granularity of service operations is closely tied to the granularity of screens used by the Web channel and call center channel.

The banking engine service runs on a standard J2EE application server, using session beans to implement service interfaces. To support the SOAP runtime protocol, a WSDL compiler and code generator was used. For example, it is able to generate Java skeletons that accept incoming SOAP messages and dispatch them to the Java session beans (refer to Figure 17-6). The same tool was used to generate VB client code (for the IIS-based Web servers) and C++ client code (for the CTI product that provided computer telephony integration for the call center). Obviously, today this functionality would be available out-of-the-box for most programming platforms, but in 1999/2000, XML Web services technology was just emerging, and therefore proprietary compilers were developed to support early version of the WSDL and SOAP specifications.

17.3.2.3 Service Versus Service Interfaces. Recall our discussion on different service types in Chapter 5. One of the key messages was that data ownership amongst services has to be clear and that different services should not share access to the same data (see Section 5.1.3.1). However, as discussed in Chapter 4, one service might have multiple interfaces that provide shared access to the data owned by the super ordinate service. In addition, the code base of independent services should be structured in a way such that there are no cross-dependencies between the different service implementations. If we apply this definition to the Intelligent Finance situation, it becomes clear that the banking engine really represents one large service with multiple interfaces but not multiple independent services. In effect, this has created a somewhat monolithic service, with some disadvantages. In the Intelligent Finance case, the key disadvantages are dependencies of the code base behind the different service interfaces: these dependencies complicate the maintenance of individual services because work cannot easily be split into individual tasks. In addition, relatively complex test environments are required. If the different service interfaces were truly independent services, much less complex development and test setups could be used.

Intelligent Finance has recognized this challenge and has significantly invested in the breaking up of the monolithic service architecture into services that are truly independent on the code as well as the data level. The resulting more loosely coupled service design has helped tothe s significantly enhance maintenance productivity and the ability to introduce new functionality much more quickly.

17.4   Lessons Learned, Benefits, and Perspectives

Probably the most important lesson learned in the project was that putting a Service-Oriented Architecture in place requires not only a sound technical design but also a project management initiative that supports the technical architecture on the project level. The *XML Tsardom* that was established in the early phase of the project was a key management tool for coordinating the development of a large set of technical interfaces that spanned 23 different work streams. In effect, the concept of the *XML Tsardom* as deployed by Intelligent Finance adopted many of the concepts that we have outlined in our discussion on SOA as a driver for project management in Chapter 13.

Another interesting observation is related to the evolution of the design of the central banking engine service: During the development phase of the project, priorities were very different than during the following maintenance and enhancement phase. The initially relatively tightly coupled architecture made a lot of sense during the development phase, providing the different frontend developers with an easy-to-use, ubiquitous interface. However, the same design became more problematic during the maintenance phase, which required a much more loose coupling. This led to the break-up of the initial service design into multiple independent services, which helped reduce dependencies and provide the maintenance and enhancement process with much higher agility.

Finally, it is interesting to observe that about 90% of the functionality that exists today was developed in the first nine months of 2000. The focus today is on maintenance, third-party integration, and increasing system agility. The original technical and functional design provides an excellent foundation for these activities. The key architecture decision—in particular the decision for the Service-Oriented Architecture—are still valid today and have provided Intelligent Finance with one of the most advanced IT architectures in the banking world.

URLs

www.if.com

http://www.if.com/aboutus/media/keymilestones.asp

http://www.if.com/aboutus/media/press2004.asp

http://www.vision.com/clients/client_stories/if.html

http://www.actiontech.com/library/Documents/GetDocs.cfm?ID=INTELLEXEC

http://www.lynx-fs.com/cms_view/news_details_all.asp?article_ref=46

Index